GOD CARES

Vol. 1

GOD CARES

Vol. **1**

CARES

The Message of **Daniel**
For You and Your Family

C.Mervyn Maxwell, Ph.D

Pacific Press Publishing Association
Boise, Idaho
Montemorelos, Nuevo Leon, Mexico
Oshawa, Ontario, Canada

Front cover transparencies: Mother and baby, Four By Five; youth on pier, B. Kreye; man in hard hat, Max Scheler; feeding pigeons, H. Thanhauser—these three from The Image Bank

Spot drawings by James Converse

ISBN 0-8163-0390-8

86 87 88 89 • 6 5 4

Preface

God Cares

A Christian nurse stood by a hospital bed, as a small child of the inner city opened the wrappings of a Christmas present. The gift, donated through a charity, had a note attached. "With lots of love," the nurse read aloud.

The boy's mind groped for understanding. "What does 'love' mean?" he asked.

Concealing her surprise, the nurse flung her arms around the neglected child and squeezed him. Then she disengaged her arms and kissed his cheek. "That's love," she explained.

"I like love," the little boy replied.

Of course he did. We all like love. To be loved is to be treated with kindness. To be thought about and planned for. To be wept over and rejoiced with. To be talked to and listened to. To have nice things done for us.

To be loved is to have someone truly care about us.

The Bible says that "God is love." 1 John 4:8. It also says, "Cast all your anxieties on him, for *he cares about you*." 1 Peter 5:7.

This is the message of the entire Bible. And it is the message of the two books of the Bible called Daniel and Revelation. GOD CARES.

God can do far more to prove His love than to hug and kiss us. The books of Daniel and Revelation show Him ready to do stupendous things for us if we trust Him:

To preserve us from danger. Daniel 3:17.

To deliver us from the power of sin. Revelation, chapters 3 and 4.

To raise us from the dead. Daniel 12:1, 2; Revelation 1:18.

To set up and remove whole empires. Daniel, chapters 2 and 7.

To lift the veil and reveal secrets and mysteries of the past, present, and future. Daniel 2:28; Revelation 1:1.

"The Lord God does nothing," the Bible says, "without revealing his secret to his servants the prophets." Amos 3:7.

Daniel was written over 2500 years ago; Revelation, 1900 years ago. But they were written to reveal events that will take place "hereafter" (Revelation 1:19), "in the latter days" (Daniel 2:28), at "the time of the end" (Daniel 8:17). In view of what Daniel and Revelation reveal about our own immediate future, they are as up-to-the-minute as next week's news.

In addition the book of Revelation is specifically introduced as "the revelation of Jesus Christ." Symbolized as a "lamb" and as the "Son of man" and in many other ways, Jesus Christ is the most prominent feature of Daniel and Revelation. The books were written to reveal what God plans to do for His people in the end of time—in our time—*through Jesus Christ*.

The Bible adds: "The secret things belong to the Lord our God; but the things that are revealed belong to us and to our children for ever." Deuteronomy 29:29. God loves our children as much as He loves us, and it is a matter of great concern to Him that what we learn from Him we pass on to them.

Many youth today are taught in school that life is no more than a "fatal disease," that people are born over an open grave while the gravedigger holds the forceps, and other such pessimistic nihilism. The Bible says that in Christ we are born to live; to live forever; to live in order to enjoy God's blessings and to share them; to be happy and to help other people be happy. God has great plans for youth as well as for adults. Wonderful plans for wonderful happiness.

These plans are revealed throughout the Bible but especially in Daniel and Revelation. "The things that are revealed belong to us and to our children." May your whole family be blessed as you read.

A Note About the Bible Translation Used

The "Authorized" or "King James" Version (K.J.V.) of the Bible came off the press in 1611. It was an excellent piece of work and served most English-speaking Protestants as "the" Bible for over three hundred years.

The "Rheims-Douay-Challoner" version (Douay) of the Bible appeared in stages between 1582 and 1752. It also was a fine piece of work, though handicapped by having been translated from the Sixto-Clementine Latin Vulgate rather than from the original Hebrew, Aramaic, and Greek. Thus it was a translation of a translation. Nevertheless, the Douay version was unmistakably the Word of God, and it served English-speaking Catholics

well for hundreds of years.

As everyone knows, in recent decades there have appeared numerous new translations—Catholic, Protestant, and Jewish—each with some special merit that sets it apart from the others. These translations are justified because over the years scholars have learned much about the original manuscripts of the Bible and about the languages in which these manuscripts were written, and also because the English language itself has undergone remarkable changes.

This present volume is based on the Revised Standard Version as presented in *The New Oxford Annotated Bible with the Apocrypha: An Ecumenical Study Bible* (New York: Oxford University Press, 1977). This particular translation was selected for the following reasons:

1. It is the first Protestant translation to win Protestant, Orthodox, *and* official Catholic endorsement. Thus it provides a basis on which all English-speaking Christians can study the Bible together.

2. The R.S.V. is a sound and sensible translation, and *The New Oxford Annotated Bible* takes advantage of the second edition (1971) of the Revised Standard Version New Testament.

3. The R.S.V. retains much of the wording and flavor of the King James Version, an asset for everyone who loves the K.J.V.

This volume, GOD CARES, I, does *not* depend on the notes in the *Oxford Annotated Bible*.

All biblical references in this book are from the Revised Standard Version unless otherwise noted.

All emphases in biblical quotations used are supplied by the author of this book.

vi

Contents

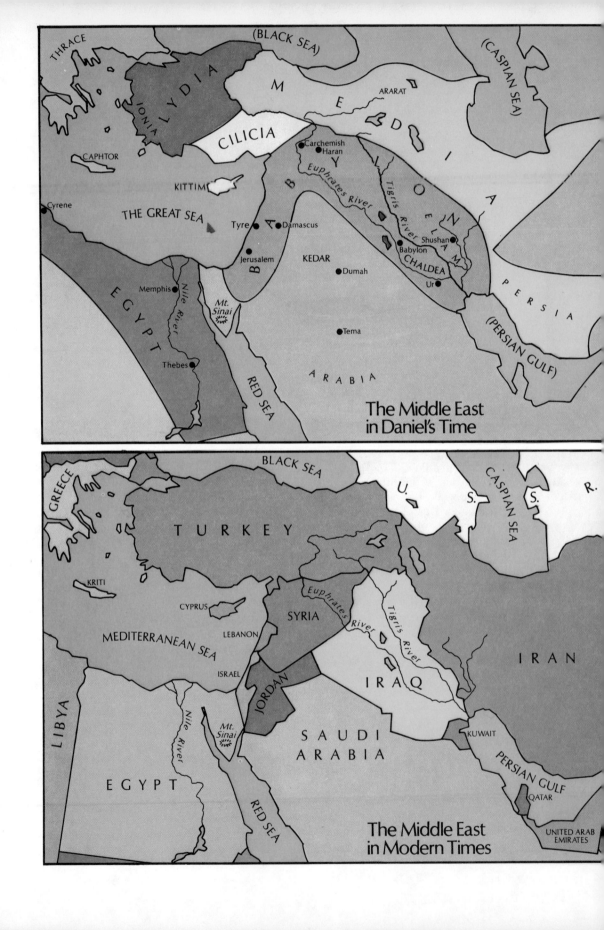

The Middle East
in Daniel's Time

The Middle East
in Modern Times

Who Was Daniel?

**A Brief Sketch About His
Life and Times**

On the Tuesday before His crucifixion, Jesus gathered His disciples together on the Mount of Olives and talked about the end of the world. During the "Olivet Discourse" which ensued, Jesus called attention to something said by Daniel almost 600 years earlier. In doing so Jesus referred to him as "the prophet Daniel." Matthew 24:15.

Daniel was indeed a prophet—a prophet of a special kind. Isaiah, Jeremiah, and Ezekiel were prophets who spent their lives teaching and preaching. They were "minister" prophets. Daniel, however, was a layman prophet. Exiled to Babylon in his late teens, he spent his adult years as a statesman and government consultant. His daily contacts with international politics gave his writings an extra quality of practicality. How God handled things so that this boy prisoner became the principal adviser to the king who captured him makes good reading!

Daniel the prophet was born into an upper-class Jewish family living in Palestine around 622 B.C. (Remember that "B.C." means "Before Christ," and that B.C. dates get smaller, not larger, as the years go by, because they represent less and less time remaining until the birth of Christ.) Daniel passed his childhood in Judea, or the kingdom of Judah, and his adulthood in Babylonia. Thus he spent his entire life in the dynamic Middle East—an area prominent in current TV news.

A glance at the map (page 10) will help. Judea was located along the east coast of the Mediterranean Sea, occupying approximately the southern half of the territory that modern Israel occupies today. Babylon was located on the River Euphrates close to the site of the modern city of Baghdad, Iraq. The twin rivers, Tigris and Euphrates, watered a flat valley edged on the east by mountains and on the west by desert. This flat valley is called "Mesopotamia, the land between the rivers."

Using the map again, trace with your eye a kind of semicircle from Judea, up the seacoast, across to the Euphrates, and down through Mesopotomia to the Persian Gulf. This semicircle has always been suitable for agriculture, in contrast to the ocean, mountains, and desert that lie beside it. Because of its shape and fruitfulness, it has long been known as the Fertile Crescent.

The Assyrian and Babylonian Empires, figuring prominently in the Bible, occupied more or less territory in and adjacent to the Fertile Crescent. Babylon, even at its height, was in fact mostly restricted to the Fertile Crescent. Yet Assyrian and Babylonian kings spoke of the territories they ruled as if they were the whole world. We can easily understand. Even today "world" is not always the same as "planet Earth." We speak of the business world, the music world, the new world, the third world, worlds apart, this world, and the next world. We realize that an illiterate person's "entire world" may be limited to his isolated village.

Daniel was born into a world that was undergoing great change. The terribly cruel Assyrian Empire, which had dominated the Fertile Crescent for about 300 years, was grinding to its close. The newest contender for "world" power was Babylon.

Strictly speaking, Babylon was a single city, or a city-state with included adjacent towns. It was also known as Akkad, and as "The Land of the Chaldeans." Nimrod the Mighty Hunter founded it (Genesis 10), and it was anciently the site of the well-known Tower of Babel (Genesis 11). It achieved prominence around 1800 B.C. under the leadership of the famous lawmaker, Hammurabi, some three and a half centuries before Moses, another famous lawmaker, led the Israelites out of Egypt. After Hammurabi's death Babylon was eclipsed by other city-states in Mesopotamia. In time it and the other states were amalgamated unhappily into the Assyrian Empire. Between 626 and 612 B.C.—the period during which Daniel was born—Nabopolassar, the king of Babylon, crushed what was left of Assyria and became the founder of the Empire of New Babylon (Neo-Babylonia). His son, Nebuchadnezzar II, brought Babylon to its golden age.

Nebuchadnezzar II is the Nebuchadnezzar (NEB-you-kud-NEZ-er) of the book of Daniel. Sometimes in the Bible his name is spelled Nebuchadrezzar (see, e.g., Jeremiah 21:2 and Ezekiel 26:7). In Babylonian his name was Nabu-kudurri-usur, a term that expressed a prayer to the god Nabu for protection.

New Babylon, even under Nebuchadnezzar, did not control all the territory that Assyria had once controlled. The Medes, for example, who had helped the Babylonians revolt against Assyria, insisted on their independence. In Daniel's day four principal nations controlled the Middle East: Egypt, Lydia, Media, *and* Babylonia. But during Nebuchadnezzar's lifetime Babylonia was clearly dominant. At Nebuchadnezzar's death Media asserted itself further; and when Media was joined to Persia, the Medo-Persian Empire annexed Babylon, Egypt, and Lydia.

In Daniel's boyhood Egypt was still a force to reckon with. The kingdom of Judah, Daniel's homeland, repeatedly sought mutual alliances with Egypt in order to gain protection from the encroaching Babylonians. When, in his empire building, Nebuchadnezzar gained control of Jerusalem for the first time, in 605 B.C., he compelled the incumbent Jewish king, Jehoiakim, to break with Egypt and sign a treaty with Babylon instead. Not long after Nebuchadnezzar departed, however, Jehoiakim renewed his special relationship with Egypt. International diplomacy was unstable in the Middle East even then.

Nebuchadnezzar made three trips to Jerusalem, inflicting a stricter punishment each time. On his first visit, the one to which we just referred, he carried off many of the precious utensils that he found in the magnificent temple which Solomon had built there. He also took hostage a number of carefully selected Jewish youth. On his second visit, in 597 B.C., he was pleased when King Jehoiachin (not to be confused with King Jehoiakim) gave up his rebellion and surrendered to him, but he confiscated a *large* quantity of temple utensils and took 10,000 captives. Later, after a serious revolt by Judah's King Zedekiah, Nebuchadnezzar returned to Jerusalem for a third visit; and, in 586 B.C., at the conclusion of an extended siege, he leveled the city to the ground, completely destroying the temple. He also took almost all the remaining residents of Judea into captivity, leaving behind only the "poorest of the land." 2 Kings 24; 25.

Ezekiel the prophet was taken captive on Nebuchadnezzar's second visit. Daniel was taken on the first.

Nebuchadnezzar also transplanted to Babylon the citizens of many of the other countries that he conquered. Jeremiah the prophet promised, on the word of the Lord, that "after seventy years" God would see to it that at least the Jewish captives would have a chance to return home. Jeremiah 29:10, K.J.V. This reminds us (Daniel 1:21) that Daniel lived in Babylon until **"the first year of King Cyrus"** (538/537 B.C.), when the seventy years were nearly completed.

King Cyrus the Great was the conqueror who ended the Babylonian Empire and established the Medo-Persian (or Persian) Empire. To many people Cyrus seemed always to do and say the right things. For centuries after his untimely death he was regarded throughout the Middle East as the Ideal Man, a kind of Abraham Lincoln perhaps. Isaiah 44:28 and 45:1 speak well of him too.

One of the first and finest things King Cyrus did after he defeated Babylon was to issue a decree allowing all exiles and their descendants to return to their homelands if they desired to do so. Not the Jews only, but also all the other people whom Nebuchadnezzar had carried away were thus given their freedom. Cyrus further offered to return all of their gods that Nebuchadnezzar had taken away. In the case of the Jews, who of course had no image of God, this meant the return of the sacred temple utensils and even a promise to rebuild the Jerusalem temple at state expense!

Thus **"the first year of King Cyrus"** was a good year to be alive—a memorable year for all the exiled peoples and their religious leaders. It was a wonderful thing to live long enough to enjoy the first year of King Cyrus. Actually, Daniel lived even longer. His last vision is dated in the third year of King Cyrus (Daniel 10:1), by which time he must have been around eighty-seven years of age.

In this final vision God promised that Daniel's writings would be well understood at **"the time of the end,"** and that thus in a special sense Daniel would fill his **"allotted place"** at **"the end of the days."** Daniel 12:4, 13.

Daniel the prophet was by now too old to take advantage of the opportunity to return to Palestine. But he had lived a good life, one that God had blessed from beginning to end. And he had the warm assurance that the book which God had inspired him to write, and which would provide immense comfort in every subsequent century, would be found particularly appropriate for the generation that would live at the end of the world.

Daniel 1
God and Daniel in Babylon

Introduction

The book of Daniel begins with a story. It tells how Daniel, a Jewish youth from Palestine, came to be an official in the government of New Babylon (Neo-Babylonia), under the blessing and guidance of God. But Daniel 1 isn't merely a story. As we shall see later, it contains a condensation of all the basic messages of the books of Daniel and Revelation.

Nebuchadnezzar visited Jerusalem for the first time in the summer of 605 B.C. He did not make a friendly visit. In 605 the kingdom of Judah was in alliance with Egypt (see page 12). About the first of June that year Nebuchadnezzar defeated an Egyptian military outpost at Carchemish near the river Euphrates, many miles to the north. With the fall of this garrison Egypt virtually lost its dominance over Syria and Palestine, leaving Nebuchadnezzar free to march south to Jerusalem. (In 601 B.C. Nebuchadnezzar would try an attack on Egypt itself—and would be repulsed, with heavy losses on both sides.)

In Jerusalem, Nebuchadnezzar compelled King Jehoiakim to renounce his treaty with Egypt and make another one with Babylon. Then, presumably to ensure the king's good behavior, he took a number of upper-class youth hostage, including Daniel. As a symbol of his god's victory over the Lord God of the Jews (or so he thought), he also removed some of the sacred gold and silver utensils that he found in the temple of God, with the purpose of placing them in a temple in Babylon.

Barely had Nebuchadnezzar accomplished these things when a runner informed him that his father, King Nabopolassar of Babylon, had died on August 15. Ten days had passed while the messenger was traveling. Intrigue might be afoot. Instantly Nebuchadnezzar left for home by the dangerously dry but relatively short trail across the desert. He took along a small body-guard and left word for the main army to return by the regular route.

The regular trade route from Jerusalem to Babylon stretched more than 1500 kilometers (about 1000 miles). Daniel was probably required to walk it, with the army. If so, he must have found it a very long distance!

Because the afternoon heat was intense, Babylonian buglers aroused the army at dawn, when cocks crowed, the air was chilled, and sandals were soaked with dew. Daniel rolled out of his blanket at the same time. As the sun arose, everyone struck camp and headed north on the mountain road to Samaria. Then along the sloping shores of Galilee. Then between the twin mountain ranges of fabled Lebanon.

Near Carchemish, the site of its June victory, the Babylonian army turned

Daniel and his three friends refuse the unhealthy diet at the kings's palace.

15

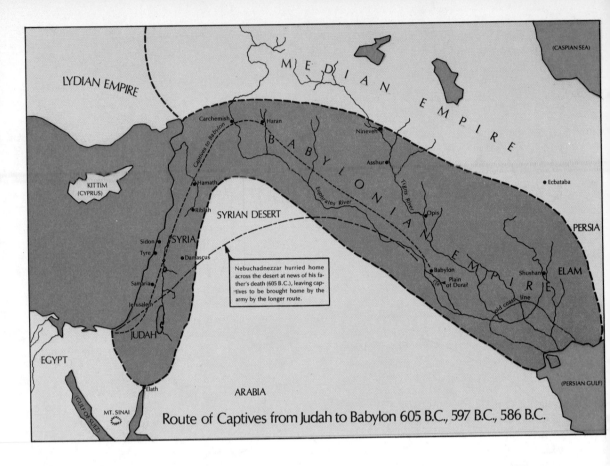

Nebuchadnezzar hurried home across the desert at news of his father's death (605 B.C.), leaving captives to be brought home by the army by the longer route.

Route of Captives from Judah to Babylon 605 B.C., 597 B.C., 586 B.C.

right and headed southeast along the Euphrates. The ground was remarkably fertile here but monotonously flat. Its surface was broken principally by numerous irrigation canals. Government officials appeared frequently, checking dikes and settling disputes over water rights. Peasants paused in the fields and villages to watch the long procession of soldiers and to speculate on the future of the hostages.

Nebuchadnezzar, traveling light, crossed the desert at the almost incredible speed of more than eighty kilometers (more than fifty miles) a day and arrived at the capital on September 7. He found faithful officials holding the throne for him. The main army likely averaged no more than twenty-five kilometers (about fifteen miles) a day. If so, it was after a seemingly endless

two months that at last Daniel caught his first glimpse of Babylon's skyline on the southern horizon—dominated by its famous ziggurat, the Tower of Etemenanki, or Tower of Babel. Another day's march and he was led through the city's massive gates and placed in custody with the other Jewish prisoners to await further developments.

What those further developments turned out to be is narrated briefly in the first chapter of the book of Daniel. Nebuchadnezzar, a vigorous and intelligent dictator, ordered his hostages to be examined for their ability to master the **"letters and language"** (verse 4) of his kingdom. He wanted the best of them trained for service in his government. Daniel and three of his friends were found to be eminently qualified and were assigned to the royal college for appropriate education. Each was also given a new name. Daniel's new name, Belteshazzar, honored the Babylonian god Bel.

Arriving at the college, the Jewish youth discovered to their dismay that their generous conqueror daily provided the school with **"rich food"** that they considered unsuitable. Nebuchadnezzar meant well, but Daniel recognized the diet to be unhealthful and contrary to the rules ordained by God in Deuteronomy 14. Much of it, no doubt, was also offered in sacrifice to the idols of Babylon. Eating it constituted a kind of communion service with false gods. See Exodus 34:15; 1 Corinthians 8:7; 10:14-22.

Most teenagers are deeply embarrassed to be different. Youthful Daniel, however, overcame any embarrassment he may have felt and **"resolved that he would not defile himself"** (Daniel 1:8) with the king's rich food and wine. His three youthful friends joined him in his dedication.

The young men did not, however, allow their convictions to make them discourteous. Very politely they requested permission from Ashpenaz himself, the king's **"chief eunuch,"** to be served a simple vegetarian diet. Ashpenaz seemed willing to help the boys, but he was afraid of the possible consequences. So the youth tactfully asked their steward to grant them a ten-day trial. We may assume that Ashpenaz knew of the proposal and gave at least tacit approval. To the joy of all concerned, at the end of the ten days the four lads looked significantly healthier than the other students and were gladly permitted to continue their special diet.

At the conclusion of their course of study, Daniel and his classmates were examined by King Nebuchadnezzar in person. Imagine the nervous anticipation among students and faculty! Daniel and his three friends passed their tests with flying colors, head and shoulders above the rest. Immediately they **"stood before the king"**; that is, they were appointed to positions of responsibility in the government.

17

1

GOD CARES   GOD AND DANIEL IN BABYLON

CHAPTER 1

1 In the third year of the reign of Jehoiakim king of Judah, Nebuchadnezzar king of Babylon came to Jerusalem and besieged it. ² And the Lord gave Jehoiakim king of Judah into his hand, with some of the vessels of the house of God; and he brought them to the land of Shinar, to the house of his god, and placed the vessels in the treasury of his god. ³ Then the king commanded Ashpenaz, his chief eunuch, to bring some of the people of Israel, both of the royal family and of the nobility, ⁴ youths without blemish, handsome and skilful in all wisdom, endowed with knowledge, understanding learning, and competent to serve in the king's palace, and to teach them the letters and language of the Chaldeans. ⁵ The king assigned them a daily portion of the rich food which the king ate, and of the wine which he drank. They were to be educated for three years, and at the end of that time they were to stand before the king. ⁶ Among these were Daniel, Hananiah, Mishael, and Azariah of the tribe of Judah. ⁷ And the chief of the eunuchs gave them names: Daniel he called Belteshazzar, Hananiah he called Shadrach, Mishael he called Meshach, and Azariah he called Abednego.

8 But Daniel resolved that he would not defile himself with the king's rich food, or with the wine which he drank; therefore he asked the chief of the eunuchs to allow him not to defile himself. ⁹ And God gave Daniel favor and compassion in the sight of the chief of eunuchs; ¹⁰ and the chief of the eunuchs said to Daniel, "I fear lest my lord the king, who appointed your food and your drink, should see that you were in poorer condition than the youths who are of your own age. So you would endanger my head with the king." ¹¹ Then Daniel said to the steward whom the chief of the eunuchs had appointed over Daniel, Hananiah, Mishael, and Azariah; ¹² "Test your servants for ten days; let us be given vegetables to eat and water to drink. ¹³ Then let our appearance and the appearance of the youths who eat the king's rich food be observed by you, and according to what you see deal with your servants." ¹⁴ So he hearkened to them in this matter, and tested them for ten days. ¹⁵ At the end of ten days it was seen that they were better in appearance and fatter in flesh than all the youths who ate the king's rich food. ¹⁶ So the steward took away their rich food and the wine they were to drink, and gave them vegetables.

17 As for these four youths, God gave them learning and skill in all letters and wisdom; and Daniel had understanding in all visions and dreams. ¹⁸ At the end of the time, when the king had commanded that they should be brought in, the chief of the eunuchs brought them in before Nebuchadnezzar. ¹⁹ And the king spoke with them, and among them all none was found like Daniel, Hananiah, Mishael, and Azariah; therefore they stood before the king. ²⁰ And in every matter of wisdom and understanding concerning which the king inquired of them, he found them ten times better than all the magicians and enchanters that were in all his kingdom. ²¹ And Daniel continued until the first year of King Cyrus.

18

The Message of Daniel 1

I. God's Concern for the Jews

Many concepts in Daniel 1 are basic and fundamental to understanding the message of Daniel and Revelation as a whole.

As we look at these concepts, it will be helpful to realize that in Bible times the word *prophet* did not mean merely a person who predicts the future. Bible prophets did predict the future, and prediction was Daniel's specialty; but the word *prophet* basically means "a person who *speaks for* somebody else." The Bible prophets *spoke for* God. They passed along *any* message that God delivered to them through the inspiration of the Holy Spirit. Thus the message of Daniel and Revelation is not always predictive—but it is always helpful.

The first concept we shall look at in Daniel 1 is God's concern for the Israelites, or Jews.

When Nebuchadnezzar claimed the kingdom of Judah for his father's empire, he undoubtedly credited his success to his own vigor and intelligence (see chapter 4). Nothing, however, could have been further from reality. The Bible says that *"the Lord gave* **Jehoiakim king of Judah into his** [Nebuchadnezzar's] **hand."** Daniel 1:2.

But how could God give an Israelite king into the power of a heathen imperialist? The answer reveals insights uniquely important to us about the character of God. It also provides a key to the understanding of Daniel and Revelation.

Deuteronomy 32:9 tells us that by the time of the Exodus from Egypt (often dated 1445 B.C.) God had selected the Israelites to be in a special sense "His people." Acts 13:47, 48 explains that God did not do this to be nice to the Israelites alone but in order to bring salvation and happiness to all people. He wanted the Israelites to be "a light for the Gentiles." He wanted them to witness to other nations about the goodness of God and about the wisdom of His laws.

Great favors presuppose great faithfulness. In order to witness effectively about God's goodness, the Israelites would necessarily have had to live in harmony with His laws and seek to reflect His pure and gracious character. But God does not compel obedience. He left the Israelites free to make their own choice. *"If you will obey my voice and keep my covenant,"* He said to them, "you shall be my own possession among all peoples; . . . and you shall be to me a kingdom of priests and a holy nation." Exodus 19:5, 6.

Sad to say, through the years most of the Israelites chose not to love and obey God. Like many Christians today, they often refused even to get along with one another. Around 931 B.C., after the reign of King Solomon, they divided into two separate and quarreling nations—the kingdom of Judah in the south and in the north, the kingdom of Israel, sometimes called "Ephraim."

Incredible as it may seem, Israel, the northern kingdom, officially adopted a kind of paganism. 1 Kings 12:25-33. Even so, God did not immediately or willingly

19

"give up" Israel. He sent prophet after prophet—Elijah, Amos, Hosea, and others—over a period of two centuries to plead with the nation and to offer complete pardon if the people would repent.

Meanwhile the empire of Assyria arose on the horizon, conquering every nation it attacked. If the inhabitants of Israel would repent and choose to reflect the pure and gracious character of God, God would work a miracle to protect them from the Assyrians. Such a miracle would also encourage other people everywhere to choose to emulate the character of God. But "God shows no partiality." Acts 10:34. If Israel insisted on going her own way, God would have no choice but to let her suffer the natural consequences just as other nations had to. How the thought of doing so pained Him!

> How can I give you up, O Ephraim!
>   How can I hand you over, O Israel! . . .
> My heart recoils within me,
>   My compassion grows warm and tender. Hosea 11:8.

In 722 B.C. God finally "gave up" Israel to the Assyrians, but He did so with much regret.

As time continued, Judah's apostasy became even more serious than Israel's. There were exceptions, however. For example, when the Assyrians laid siege to Jerusalem, King Hezekiah turned to God for help rather than to idols. He sought God's mercy earnestly, and God worked a miracle for him. An angel slew a vast number of Assyrian soldiers. 2 Kings 18; 19. God was just as willing to protect King Jehoiakim when the Babylonians arrived. But by this time the people of Judah were tragically engrossed in their sins.

And what were the terrible sins that the prophets complained about? Dishonesty, injustice to the poor, murder, breaking the Sabbath, persecuting true prophets, favoring preachers who promised prosperity without condemning vice, and worshiping Baal (see Jeremiah 9:14; 17:19-27; 22:1-5; 28). The worship of Baal involved a variety of "sexual preferences"—premarital, extramarital, homosexual, and bestial. Sabbath breaking dishonored God and deprived people of a day of rest and a time for public worship. Injustice to anybody gave the lie to God's impartial generosity.

Sins like these must have seemed very ordinary to most people at the time, but evidently they were not "ordinary" to God. They undermined the truth about His pure and gracious character, and they also debased the characters and homes and society of the people who practiced them.

"Cry aloud . . . declare to my people their transgression," God urged in Isaiah 58:1. "Turn back, turn back from your evil ways; for why will you die, O house of Israel?" He pleaded in Ezekiel 33:11.

Prophet after prophet appealed to the southern kingdom of Judah as other prophets had appealed to the northern kingdom of Israel. Micah, Isaiah, Habak-

20

kuk, Zephaniah, Jeremiah, and others offered pardon in exchange for repentance; but they preached to the wind.

"The Lord, the God of their fathers, sent persistently to them by his messengers," the Bible says, "because he had compassion on his people and on his dwelling place; but they kept mocking the messengers of God, despising his words, and scoffing at his prophets, till the wrath of the Lord rose against his people, till there was no remedy. Therefore he brought up against them the king [Nebuchadnezzar] of the Chaldeans." 2 Chronicles 36:15-17.

The translation of this passage by Monsignor Knox heightens the emphasis on God's concern: "He, the God of their fathers, sent messengers to warn them; never a day dawned but he was already pleading with them, so well he loved his people and his dwelling-place. And they? They mocked the Lord's own messengers, made light of his warnings, derided his prophets, until at last the Lord's anger was roused against his people, past all assuaging. Then it was that he embroiled them with the king of Babylon."

We will have more to say about the special meaning of God's "wrath" and "anger" in the comments on Revelation 12 and 19. For now it is enough to remember that when Jesus came to reveal to us in person what God is like, He treated even His tormentors with tenderness. As the soldiers were crucifying Him, He groaned in prayer, "Father, forgive them." Luke 23:34.

When God "gave" Jehoiakim and the kingdom of Judah into the hands of their enemy, He did so only after first trying very hard to save them. He really cared!

Because He had compassion on His people, God sent prophets repeatedly to persuade them to change their ways.

II. God's Concern for "Atonement"

When God "gives up" a person or a nation, obviously a serious separation is involved. God is separated from His people. This separation grieves God.

As we have just seen, God does not separate Himself from us; we separate ourselves from Him. Isaiah 59:2 says:

> Behold, the Lord's hand is not shortened, that it cannot save,
>   or his ear dull, that it cannot hear;
> but your iniquities have made a separation
>   between you and your God,
> and your sins have hid his face from you
>   so that he does not hear.

(If perhaps your prayers are not being answered just now, it may be that a sin against God or against some of your neighbors separates you from Him.)

Even after God "gave up" the Jews to their enemies, He still offered them another chance. He promised that after seventy years of exile in Babylon, He would see to it that they received permission to return home. Jeremiah 25:11, 12; 29:1. Far more, He promised that He would change their hearts—if they would let Him—so that they would enjoy doing right and being united to Him again: "I . . . will bring you into your own land. . . . And I will put my spirit within you, and cause you to walk in my statutes and be careful to observe my ordinances. . . . And you shall be my people, and I will be your God." Ezekiel 36:24-28. See comments on pages 170, 171.

Sinners are at odds with God and with one another. They are separated by selfishness and other sins. God through the prophets and in a unique sense through Jesus Christ has set in motion a wonderful process to bring us into reconciliation with each other and with Himself. This wonderful process of "at-one-ment" is called "the atonement" (a-TONE-ment).

We shall have much to say about the atonement as we discuss the message of Daniel and the Revelation. It is the greatest theme of the two books. It is the supreme evidence that "God cares."

III. God's Concern for His Temple

The sacred buildings—temples, sanctuaries, shrines, churches, or mosques— which worshipers dedicate to their deity are often considered special symbols of their deity's presumed presence and effectiveness. When Nebuchadnezzar removed sacred utensils from the **"house of God"** in Jerusalem and placed them (presumably) in the Esagila—the main temple of his god Marduk in Babylon—he naturally supposed that his god had triumphed over the God of the Jews.

But, of course, just as God "gave" His kingdom of Judah into the hands of Nebuchadnezzar, so the Bible says He **"gave"** him the vessels of His temple, and for the same reasons (see Daniel 1:2).

22

Keep your eyes on the sanctuary and its furnishings as we study the books of Daniel and Revelation! As for the utensils, Nebuchadnezzar made two further trips to Jerusalem until he had acquired a collection of 5469 of them. But their possession did the Babylonians no good (see chapter 5 and Ezra 1:9-11). When we study Revelation, the vessels of the sanctuary will appear again, with very great significance.

The temple itself is treated as a symbol in Daniel and Revelation. In one of the truly great verses in the Bible we are informed that at the end of time **"the sanctuary shall be restored to its rightful state."** Daniel 8:14. In Revelation 11:19 John says that at the end of the world "God's temple in heaven" will be "opened" and "the ark of his covenant" will be seen. These are pregnant phrases for the twentieth century.

God is very concerned about His temple, and He wants us also to take a keen interest in it.

IV. God's Concern for Young People

At the very beginning of his exile Daniel was found to be **"skilful in all wisdom, endowed with knowledge, understanding learning."** Daniel 1:4. Evidently he had already received considerable education as a Jewish student in the kingdom of Judah. In ancient times the sons of wealthy and noble families were usually educated in various disciplines. At their best the Jews were notably devoted to education.

But most people in the kingdom of Judah were so corrupt that God finally had no choice but to "give them up." How was it possible then for Daniel to come through his education and still be so fine and good?

"How can a young man keep his way pure?" asks the Bible.

"By guarding it *according to thy word,*" says Psalm 119:9.

Apparently Daniel guarded his life by studying the Word of God, the Bible. Daniel did not have access to as much of the Bible as we have now. None of the New Testament and not all of the Old had been written yet. But he did have most of the Old Testament. From studying what he did have he knew how to distinguish between the true God of Israel and the false gods of Babylon. He could separate suitable foods from unsuitable foods in harmony with Deuteronomy 14. He saw the danger in drinking wine. Leviticus 10:1-11. He knew the importance of being faithful and honest in all his dealings. Daniel 6:4. And he knew how to pray effectively. Daniel 2:17-23.

When God chose the Israelites to be His special witnesses, He asked Israelite parents to teach His Word diligently to their children. He told them to talk about it "when you sit in your house, and when you walk by the way, and when you lie down, and when you rise"—that is, in the early morning, at mealtimes, at bedtime, and when traveling. Deuteronomy 6:4-7. Later Moses explained: "The things that are revealed belong to us *and to our children* for ever, that we may do all the words of this law." Deuteronomy 29:29. God wanted children to receive an education that was spiritual and God-centered, so that they would reflect to others the character of their wonderful God.

We are curious to know who it was who first directed little Daniel to the Word of God. Was it his father and mother, as it should have been? A godly home is suggested by his name. "Daniel" means "God is my Judge" or "God is my Vindicator."

Jeremiah was prophesying in Jerusalem when Daniel was a boy. Perhaps he too led Daniel to the Lord and to the Word.

If Jeremiah did teach Daniel, it is quite possible, incidentally, that he showed him a prediction that Isaiah the prophet had made to King Hezekiah nearly one hundred years earlier (about 700 B.C.): "Behold, the days are coming, when all that is in your house . . . shall be carried to Babylon; . . . and some of your own sons . . . shall be taken away." Isaiah 39:6, 7.

When Daniel entered his teens, did he like other youth rebel against God for a while? If so, was it during that long, long walk to Babylon—possibly under a date palm one humid night by the river Euphrates—that he fully and finally decided to pattern his life by the Word of God?

We do not know. But this we do know, "The things that are revealed" belong not only to "us" who are adults but also "to our children"—so that they, too, can learn to keep their ways pure and to be persuasive witnesses for God. God wants it this way. It is an evidence of His concern for young people.

Jeremiah prophesied in Jerusalem when Daniel was a boy and may well have helped young Daniel discover God's love.

V. God's Concern for Individuals

Even though God "gave up" the kingdom of Judah as a whole, He stood beside Daniel as an individual. And he did so even though Daniel was a citizen of a conquered race, a member of an ethnic minority, and only a teenager. It's reassuring to know this in these days of population explosions and rush hours and crowded urban ghettos.

"God gave **Daniel favor and compassion in the sight of the chief of the eunuchs."** Daniel 1:9. *"God gave"* to Daniel and his friends **"learning and skill in all letters and wisdom."** Verse 17. God was with them. Indeed God responded so very helpfully to their dedication that, in spite of the collapse of their own kingdom, they ended up helping to rule a much greater kingdom!

This of course illustrates another great message of the book of Daniel. When all ordinary kingdoms that ever will exist on planet Earth have come and gone, then **"the God of heaven will set up a kingdom which shall never be destroyed."** Daniel 2:44. *And* **"the kingdom and the dominion and the greatness of the kingdom under the whole heaven** *shall be given to the people of the saints of the Most High."* Daniel 7:27.

Daniel 1 is a short chapter; but in its few paragraphs it reveals God's concern for nations and individuals, for young people, for His temple, and for the ultimate reunification of every willing soul with Himself and with one another. These concerns are themes of the entire book of Daniel and of Revelation too.

Daniel 1 shows God at work. God **"gives up"** the Jews to enable them to see the consequences of their rebel ways and to be led back to a higher way of life. He **"gives"** Daniel just the help he needs to transform a young exile into a competent government administrator and counselor. God does these things, it appears, not only for Daniel's sake but for ours too; He wants us to *know* that He can keep His promise to make us all heirs with Christ of the kingdom to come.

Daniel 1 provides practical, down-to-earth proof that God is both concerned and capable. What He promises, He is "able to do." Romans 4:21. He not only cares; He can!

1

GOD CARES

Your Questions Answered

1. What subjects did Daniel study in school? The Babylonians enjoyed a civilization notably advanced in many ways. Mathematics was their speciality. For a thousand years prior to Daniel's arrival they had solved problems using quadratic equations, and they used tables of reciprocals, squares and square roots, cubes and cube roots. They employed both the base-10 (decimal) system and the base-60 (sexagesimal) system. They divided the hour into sixty minutes and the circle into 360 degrees, units we still recognize. According to *The Exact Sciences in Antiquity* by Otto Neugebauer,[1] their greatest contribution in mathematics was their development of a form of the "place value" system so important to mathematics today, in which, for example, "57" is not $5 + 7 = 12$ but $(5 \times 10) + (7 \times 1) = 57$.[2]

Although their most brilliant period in astronomy was a few centuries yet in the future, in Daniel's time the Babylonians had long (since 747 B.C.) been recording eclipses—and sometimes predicting them—so accurately that their records are of great value to astronomers and archaeologists today.

Their architects employed the brick arch, invaluable for the construction of public buildings, mansions, and bridges in a land that abounded in clay but offered no readily available stone or steel. Their surveyors laid out irrigation canals and right-angle street patterns. Their businessmen were adept at bills, receipts, promissory notes, letters of credit, a kind of check-writing system,

1.

2.

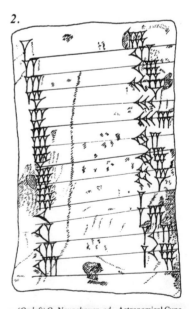

(On left) O. Neugebauer, ed., Astronomical Cuneiform Texts, 3 vols. (Princeton, N.J.: Institute for Advanced Study, c. 1955), 3:238; cf. 1:226-240. (Mathematical tablet above) H. V. Hilprecht, ed., The Babylonian Expedition of the University of Pennsylvania, Series A: Cuneiform Texts, vol. 20, part 1, by H. V. Hilprecht (Philadelphia: Dept. of Archaeology, University of Pennsylvania, 1906), plate I.

and (thanks to their knowledge of mathematics) compound interest.

On the darker side, the Babylonians studied divination, magic, a form of astrology, and pagan mythology.

In view of Daniel's elevation to high government leadership, we may assume that he became more or less acquainted with all of these techniques and subjects. The Bible specifically mentions that he became proficient in the **"letters and language of the Chaldeans."** The "language" included (1) Akkadian, the national language of Babylon, (2) Sumerian, the language of traditional religion, and (3) Aramaic, the language of international commerce and diplomacy.

The reference to "letters" reminds us of the way these languages were written. As a child in Judah, Daniel had already learned to write Aramaic and also Hebrew, which was related to it. Both languages employed an alphabet and could be written with a pen or brush. The two languages to which he was introduced in Babylon, however, employed around 625 cuneiform (cyu-NEE-uh-form) characters and were usually written on clay tablets.

Cuneiform characters could represent either single sounds or full syllables. "Cuneiform" means "wedge-shaped." Cuneiform writing was produced by holding a conveniently shaped piece of moist clay in one hand and, with the other hand, pressing the tip of a square reed into it. The reed was held at an angle so that it made wedge-shaped impressions somewhat deeper at one end than at the other. When the message was finished, the tablet was baked for preservation.

1. Cuneiform tablet (from Nippur in Babylonia) contains complex instructions for calculating intervals between sunrise and moonset immediately before and after full moon. British Museum: B.M. 35399.

2. Cuneiform multiplication table for "six times." Numbers 1 to 13 can easily be read in the left column and numbers six times as large in the right column. University of Pennsylvania: C.B.M. 3335.

3. Mesopotamian clay provided tablets for writing and also bricks for large buildings, some with arches, like the Ishtar Gate, built by Nebuchadnezzar.

DANIEL R. GUILD

27

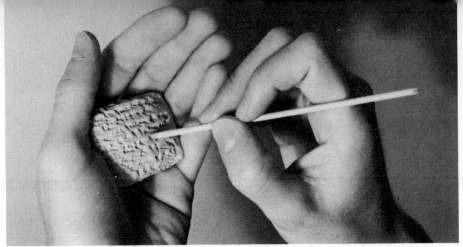

Modern hands illustrate correct technique for writing ancient cuneiform.

Here is "Daniel" spelled in Hebrew characters, with Roman letters supplied underneath. Not all the vowels are shown. In Daniel's time, written Hebrew omitted most vowels. The characters are to be read from right to left.

דניאל

l'ind

Here is Nebuchadnezzar spelled in cuneiform letters.

god na bi um ku du úr r ú su úr

2. Was Daniel's "vegetable" diet adequate? Most commentators point out that what Daniel requested was a diet of food from "things sown," "*zeroim*" in the Hebrew language. In other words Daniel requested a vegetarian diet that included vegetables, cereals, legumes, and also berries and dates.

In Deuteronomy 14 God distinguished between "clean" foods, such as mutton, and "unclean" foods, such as pork. When Daniel was out of school and more easily able to control the choice and source of his food, he may have broadened his diet somewhat. Research has shown that a strict plant-food diet may be deficient in essential vitamin B_{12}. However, research has also shown that a vegetarian diet that excludes all meat but includes small quantities of milk and eggs (that is, a lacto-ovo-vegetarian diet) is actually superior in many ways to a diet that depends heavily on meat. *The Science of Nutrition*, a typical textbook on nutrition, speaks favorably of the lacto-ovo-vegetarian diet:

> A number of dietary studies have demonstrated the nutritional adequacy of the lacto-ovo and the pure vegetarian diets in adults as well as in adolescents and pregnant women. . . .
>
> There is less obesity among vegetarians and some statistics indicate there is less heart disease. Incidence of heart disease among Seventh-day Adventist men who are lacto-ovo vegetarians is only 60 percent as high as among average California men, and the age of incidence is a full decade later. This may be related to lower intakes of total fat, saturated fat, and cholesterol, and perhaps of refined sugars.
>
> The high fiber content of the vegetarian diet appears to lower blood cholesterol levels, possibly by interfering with absorption of cholesterol from the digestive

tract. Fiber has been tentatively associated with decreased incidence of large bowel abnormalities such as polyps, appendicitis, and hemorrhoids, and perhaps colon cancer.[3]

3. Was Nebuchadnezzar ever mentioned in ancient writing outside the Bible? The name of Nebuchadnezzar is stamped on so many thousands of bricks used to construct buildings during his lifetime that no one has attempted to count them all. His name also appears on many business documents as part of the date. In addition other records have survived that speak of him more fully.

Berosus (c. 300-c. 250 B.C.), a priest of the Bel temple in Babylon, wrote books on astronomy and astrology and also on the history of Babylon. In the first century A.D. the famous Jewish historian, Josephus, quoted from Berosus's history. Here are a few sentences. They tell the story about Nebuchadnezzar's victory at Carchemish and his later dash across the desert.

> His father Nabopolassar, hearing of the defection of the satrap in charge of Egypt, Coele-Syria, and Phoenicia, and being himself unequal to the fatigues of a campaign, committed part of his army to his son Nabuchodonosor, still in the prime of life, and sent him against the rebel. Nabuchodonosor engaged and defeated the latter in a pitched battle [at Carchemish] and replaced the district under Babylonian rule. Meanwhile, as it happened, his father Nabopolassar sickened and died in the city of Babylon. . . . Being informed ere long of his father's death, Nabuchodonosor settled the affairs of Egypt and the other countries. The prisoners—Jews, Phoenicians, Syrians, and those of Egyptian nationality—were consigned to some of his friends with orders to conduct them to Babylonia, along with the heavy troops and the rest of the spoils; while he himself, with a small escort, pushed across the desert to Babylon.[4]

A few lines from a cuneiform tablet, a Babylonian chronicle kept in the British Museum (B.M. 21946), record the same events.

> Nebuchadrezzar, . . . the crown prince, mustered (the Babylonian army) and . . . marched to Carchemish which is on the bank of the Euphrates, and crossed the river (to go) against the Egyptian army which lay in Carchemish. . . . He accomplished their defeat. . . . At that time Nebuchadrezzar conquered the whole area of the Hatti-country [Syria-Palestine]. For twenty-one years Nabopolassar had been king of Babylon. On the 8th of the month of Ab [August 15, 605 B.C.] . . . he died; in the month of Elul Nebuchadrezzar returned to Babylon and on the first day of the month of Elul [September 7] he sat on the royal throne in Babylon.[5]

References

1. O. Neugebauer, *The Exact Sciences in Antiquity*, 2d ed. (New York: Dover Publications, Inc., 1969).

2. *Ibid.*, pp. 5, 18-22.

3. Marian Arlin, *The Science of Nutrition*, 2d ed. (New York: Macmillan Publishing Co., 1977), p. 96.

4. Josephus, *Against Apion*, 1:134-137. Text and trans. by H. St. J. Thackeray. Ralph Marcus, and Louis H. Feldman, *Josephus: With an English Translation*, 9 vols., Loeb Classical Library (London: William Heinemann, 1956-1965), 1:216, 217.

5. D. J. Wiseman, *Chronicles of Chaldean Kings (625-556 B.C.)* in the British Museum (London: The Trustees of the British Museum, 1956), pp. 67-69.

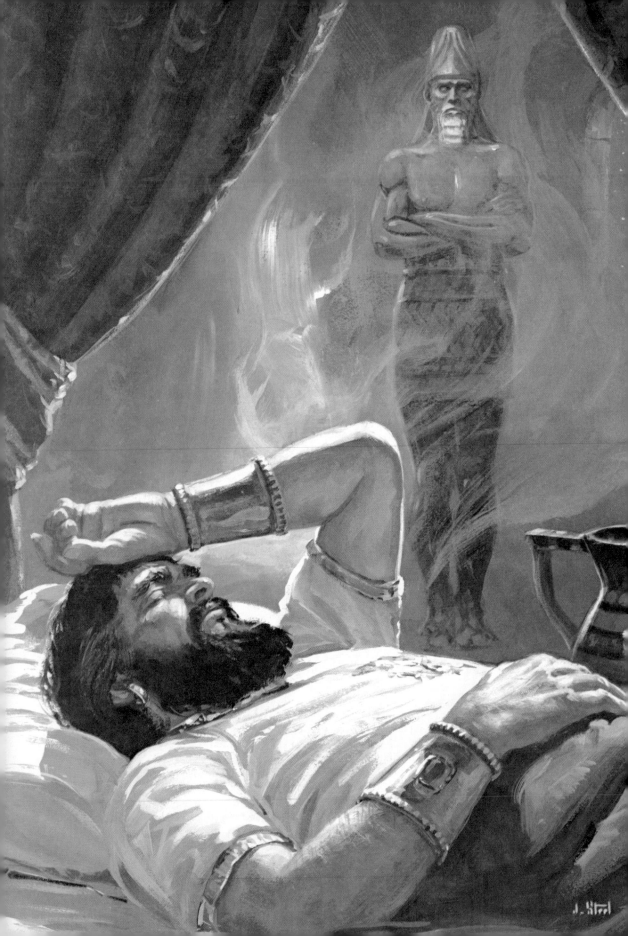

Daniel 2
God and the World's Future

Introduction

An ingenious archaeologist, after analyzing ancient clay tablets, has concluded that the first greeting a person received each morning in Babylon came in the form of a kiss.[1] We don't know whether Nebuchadnezzar favored such a custom at his palace; but if he did, he was in no mood for kisses on a certain morning during the second year of his reign (spring 603 to spring 602, B.C.). He had just had an impressive dream. He was sure that it meant something extremely important.

And he could scarcely remember any of it.

As soon as Nebuchadnezzar was dressed and ready to be seen, he sent for a large group of his **"wise men."** Trained at state expense, the wise men claimed to be in close contact with the gods. They had stock interpretations ready for thousands of dreams and other omens. In response to Nebuchadnezzar's summons, they stepped reverentially into the king's hushed chambers and bowed deeply.

But when the wise men asked the king to tell them his dream so that they could know which interpretation to apply, they touched a sensitive nerve. Nebuchadnezzar exploded. If they couldn't tell him his dream, he reckoned, they couldn't give him a true interpretation of it. He offered them one more chance. When they insisted

that only **"the gods, whose dwelling is not with flesh"** could do what the king requested, he angrily turned them over to Arioch, his executioner, with orders to eliminate them. Other despots of the day would have done the same.

Daniel was one of the wise men, but he was not present at the meeting. When he learned of the danger threatening him, he went directly to the king and asked him for a delay. Nebuchadnezzar really did want to know what his dream meant. Touched by the young man's courage, he granted his request. Daniel hurried home, gathered his friends together, and prayed earnestly during the rest of the day.

That night God gave Daniel the same dream He had given the king. He also supplied the interpretation. Daniel enthusiastically sang God's praises at morning worship, dashed over to Arioch to have him grant a stay of execution, and then, accompanied by Arioch, hurried to the palace.

In the king's presence Arioch claimed full credit for discovering Daniel. Daniel claimed no credit for himself. **"There is a God in heaven who reveals mysteries,"** he said modestly, **"and he has made known to King Nebuchadnezzar what will be in the latter days."** Daniel 2:28.

Daniel told Nebuchadnezzar exactly what he had seen in his dream and proceeded confidently to tell him what it

Nebuchadnezzar is troubled by an impressive dream.   31

meant. In the process Daniel outlined a sweep of history-in-advance uniquely classic in its simplicity. Nebuchadnezzar had dreamed no ordinary dream. God—the true God, the God of heaven **"whose dwelling is not with flesh"**— had sent him prophetic information of immense benefit to himself and to us as well.

Nebuchadnezzar was delighted. He was also deeply impressed with the power of the God whom Daniel worshiped. **"Truly,"** he said to Daniel, **"your God is God of gods and Lord of kings, and a revealer of mysteries, for you have been able to reveal this mystery."** Daniel 2:47. In his reverent but still half-pagan excitement, the king

ordered sacrifice and incense to be offered to Daniel as a living representative of the God of heaven. He promoted Daniel to be ruler of the province of Babylon and also to be prefect over the wise men. And when Daniel asked that his three companions-in-prayer be promoted also, the king was only too happy to oblige.

The second chapter of Daniel is fundamental to an understanding of the rest of the book and of the book of Revelation. In the kindness of God it is remarkably pleasant to read and easy to understand. Like the first chapter, its profound message is delivered to us as a story. It is best read in one sitting. We'll have comments following.

Trusting the "God in heaven who reveals secrets," Daniel confidently explained Nebuchadnezzar's dream about a future that extended to our day.

CHAPTER 2

1 In the second year of the reign of Nebuchadnezzar, Nebuchadnezzar had dreams; and his spirit was troubled, and his sleep left him. 2 Then the king commanded that the magicians, the enchanters, the sorcerers, and the Chaldeans be summoned, to tell the king his dreams. So they came in and stood before the king. 3 And the king said to them, "I had a dream, and my spirit is troubled to know the dream." 4 Then the Chaldeans said to the king, "O king, live for ever! Tell your servants the dream, and we will show the interpretation." 5 The king answered the Chaldeans, "The word from me is sure: if you do not make known to me the dream and its interpretation, you shall be torn limb from limb, and your houses shall be laid in ruins. 6 But if you show the dream and its interpretation, you shall receive from me gifts and rewards and great honor. Therefore show me the dream and its interpretation." 7 They answered a second time, "Let the king tell his servants the dream, and we will show its interpretation." 8 The king answered, "I know with certainty that you are trying to gain time, because you see that the word from me is sure 9 that if you do not make the dream known to me, there is but one sentence for you. You have agreed to speak lying and corrupt words before me till the times change. Therefore tell me the dream, and I shall know that you can show me its interpretation." 10 The Chaldeans answered the king, "There is not a man on earth who can meet the king's demand; for no great and powerful king has asked such a thing of any magician or enchanter or Chaldean. 11 The thing that the king asks is difficult, and none can show it to the king except the gods, whose dwelling is not with flesh."

12 Because of this the king was angry and very furious, and commanded that all the wise men of Babylon be destroyed. 13 So the decree went forth that the wise men were to be slain, and they sought Daniel and his companions, to slay them. 14 Then Daniel replied with prudence and discretion to Arioch, the captain of the king's guard, who had gone out to slay the wise men of Babylon; 15 he said to Arioch, the king's captain, "Why is the decree of the king so severe?" Then Arioch made the matter known to Daniel. 16 And Daniel went in and besought the king to appoint him a time, that he might show to the king the interpretation.

17 Then Daniel went to his house and made the matter known to Hananiah, Mishael, and Azariah, his companions, 18 and told them to seek mercy of the God of heaven concerning this mystery, so that Daniel and his companions might not perish with the rest of the wise men of Babylon. 19 Then the mystery was revealed to Daniel in a vision of the night. Then Daniel blessed the God of heaven.
20 Daniel said:
"Blessed be the name of God for ever
        and ever,
    to whom belong wisdom and might.
21 He changes times and seasons;
    he removes kings and sets up kings;
  he gives wisdom to the wise
    and knowledge to those who have
        understanding;
22 he reveals deep and mysterious
        things;
    he knows what is in the darkness,
    and the light dwells with him.
23 To thee, O God of my fathers,
    I give thanks and praise,
  for thou hast given me wisdom and
        strength,
    and hast now made known to me what
        we asked of thee,
    for thou hast made known to us the
        king's matter."

24 Therefore Daniel went in to Arioch, whom the king had appointed to destroy the wise men of Babylon; he went and said thus to him, "Do not destroy the wise men of Babylon; bring me in before the king, and I will show the king the interpretation."

25 Then Arioch brought in Daniel before the king in haste, and said thus to him: "I have found among the exiles from Judah a

33

man who can make known to the king the interpretation." [26] The king said to Daniel, whose name was Belteshazzar, "Are you able to make known to me the dream that I have seen and its interpretation?" [27] Daniel answered the king, "No wise men, enchanters, magicians, or astrologers can show to the king the mystery which the king has asked, [28] but there is a God in heaven who reveals mysteries, and he has made known to King Nebuchadnezzar what will be in the latter days. Your dream and the visions of your head as you lay in bed are these: [29] To you, O king, as you lay in bed came thoughts of what would be hereafter, and he who reveals mysteries made known to you what is to be. [30] But as for me, not because of any wisdom that I have more than all the living has this mystery been revealed to me, but in order that the interpretation may be made known to the king, and that you may know the thoughts of your mind.

31 "You saw, O king, and behold, a great image. This image, mighty and of exceeding brightness, stood before you, and its appearance was frightening. [32] The head of this image was of fine gold, its breast and arms of silver, its belly and thighs of bronze, [33] its legs of iron, its feet partly of iron and partly of clay. [34] As you looked, a stone was cut out by no human hand, and it smote the image on its feet of iron and clay, and broke them in pieces; [35] then the iron, the clay, the bronze, the silver, and the gold, all together were broken in pieces, and became like the chaff of the summer threshing floors; and the wind carried them away, so that not a trace of them could be found. But the stone that struck the image became a great mountain and filled the whole earth.

36 "This was the dream; now we will tell the king its interpretation. [37] You, O king, the king of kings, to whom the God of heaven has given the kingdom, the power, and the might, and the glory, [38] and into whose hand he has given, wherever they dwell, the sons of men, the beasts of the field, and the birds of the air, making you rule over them all—you are the head of gold. [39] After you shall arise another kingdom inferior to you, and yet a third kingdom of bronze, which shall rule over all the earth. [40] And there shall be a fourth kingdom, strong as iron, because iron breaks to pieces and shatters all things; and like iron which crushes, it shall break and crush all these. [41] And as you saw the feet and toes partly of potter's clay and partly of iron, it shall be a divided kingdom; but some of the firmness of iron shall be in it, just as you saw iron mixed with the miry clay. [42] And as the toes of the feet were partly iron and partly clay, so the kingdom shall be partly strong and partly brittle. [43] As you saw the iron mixed with miry clay, so they will mix with one another in marriage, but they will not hold together, just as iron does not mix with clay. [44] And in the days of those kings the God of heaven will set up a kingdom which shall never be destroyed, nor shall its sovereignty be left to another people. It shall break in pieces all these kingdoms and bring them to an end, and it shall stand for ever; [45] just as you saw that a stone was cut from a mountain by no human hand, and that it broke in pieces the iron, the bronze, the clay, the silver, and the gold. A great God has made known to the king what shall be hereafter. The dream is certain, and its interpretation sure."

46 Then King Nebuchadnezzar fell upon his face, and did homage to Daniel, and commanded that an offering and incense be offered up to him. [47] The king said to Daniel, "Truly, your God is God of gods and Lord of kings, and a revealer of mysteries, for you have been able to reveal this mystery." [48] Then the king gave Daniel high honors and many great gifts, and made him ruler over the whole province of Babylon, and chief prefect over all the wise men of Babylon. [49] Daniel made request of the king, and he appointed Shadrach, Meshach, and Abednego over the affairs of the province of Babylon; but Daniel remained at the king's court.

The Message of Daniel 2

I. God Knows and Reveals the Future

On a recent Sunday morning the National Weather Service forecast only a 20 percent chance of rain for the area in which I live. That same morning, to everyone's surprise, no less than four inches (ten centimeters) of rain fell within 45 minutes, causing extensive damage. The weather people are often very helpful. When they make mistakes in spite of their sophisticated equipment and scientific education, they remind us of how inept we all are at predicting the future.

None of us knows even what will happen to us between now and bedtime! Accidents, unexpected company, good news and bad news, all may change our plans in an instant. But the central message of Daniel 2 is that God knows all about the future and that He reveals to us those portions of it good for us to know. Happily, the forecast that He made to Nebuchadnezzar extends to our time.

"There is a God in heaven who reveals mysteries, and he has made known to King Nebuchadnezzar what will be in the latter days." Daniel 2:28.

In ancient times people performed public worship at the feet of the images of their gods. Some of these images were very large. Perhaps for these two reasons God chose to reveal coming events to the heathen monarch by means of an immense and dazzling statue.

This particular statue was unique in that it was composed of four sections (head, breast and arms, belly and thighs, legs) made respectively out of four different metals (gold, silver, brass, iron) and a fifth section (feet and toes) made of a strange mixture of iron and clay.

Suddenly a supernatural stone, **"cut out by no human hand,"** landed at the statue's feet—where a pagan might have stood to worship it—and ground the entire colossus into infinitesimal fragments. Then the stone expanded until it covered the earth, and it lasted forever.

The interpretation that God gave to Daniel was that the four metal divisions represented four *successive kingdoms,* or empires, of vast eminence in world history (see pages 106, 110). The gold head stood for Nebuchadnezzar himself. **"You are the head of gold."** Daniel 2:38. Daniel proceeded to say that after **"you"** there would arise **"another kingdom"**; so we know that the gold head stood not only for Nebuchadnezzar but also for his kingdom of Babylon. Nebuchadnezzar was the genius behind the success of his empire. After he died in 562 B.C. the Babylonian Empire ran rapidly downhill. Media and Persia, powers inferior to Babylon during Nebuchadnezzar's lifetime, were united together and linked to Lydia by Cyrus, king of Persia. They conquered Babylon in 539 B.C.

The Medo-Persian Empire continued for a while to expand in wealth, power, and size (adding Egypt); but like Babylon it too went into decline. In 331 B.C. it was vanquished by Alexander the Great, founder of the Macedonian Greek Empire. After Alexander's death his dominion was divided into a number of Hel-

35

lenistic Greek kingdoms. Meanwhile Rome was evolving in the west and, in due course, began to influence the Hellenistic kingdoms. By 168 B.C. Rome dominated the Mediterranean as the fourth empire of the statue prophecy.

Babylonian, Medo-Persian, Greek, Roman—the list of empires is simple and can be memorized in a moment. Any good history book will confirm the sequence. I have in front of me Stewart C. Easton's college textbook, *The Heritage of the Ancient World.*[2] The table of contents lists "The Chaldeans and New Babylonia," "The Great Persian Empire," "The Greek Civilization," and "The Foundation of the Roman Empire."

There are four empires in the statue series, not five or six. The Roman Empire did not capitulate to a fifth monolithic empire. It deteriorated over a very long

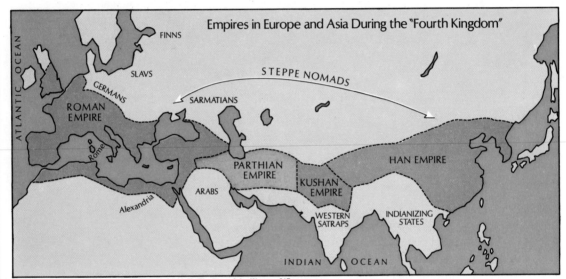

Adapted from Béla Petheö, artist, in William H. McNeill, *The Rise of the West*, p. 317.

Rome covered the area where most of the people lived who, in the first century, read the Bible and believed in God. Manifestly, it would have done little good for God to have given a major prophecy about the Kushan or Han Empires, where none of His people lived.

Similarly, when Babylon, Persia, and Greece were at their peak, they were not the only empires in the world, but they *were* the ones where a sizable number of God's followers lived.

Thus we arrive at a principle: Bible prophecies about nations tend to deal with those parts of the world where the people live who, through their knowledge of the Bible and their faith in God, can benefit from the prophecies the most.

36

period and was appropriated piecemeal by whatever tribal coalition was ambitious enough to grab a portion. France, Italy, Great Britain, the two Germanies, and other nations of Europe are contemporary results of this piecemeal and long-continued process.

"**As the toes of the feet were partly iron and partly clay, so** [1] the kingdom shall be partly strong and partly brittle. **As you saw the iron mixed with miry clay,** so [2] they will mix with one another in marriage, but [3] **they will not hold together, just as iron does not mix with clay.**" Daniel 2:42, 43.

The prophecy is specific. It has to be understood on its own terms. It is not talking about the entire habitable globe up to this point but about Babylon and its successors. It does not say that no group of nations till the end of time will be able to unite for any common action. It says that **"they,"** that is, the divided nations that replaced the Roman Empire, will never be politically united into a single empire. The British Empire at its peak united a complex group of widely scattered nations, but that is not the concern of this prophecy. Individual citizens from the nations of Europe have linked hands with astonishing friendliness in the United States of America, but this amalgam of nationalities is also not the focus of this prophecy. The feet and toes represent the nations of modern Europe—some strong, some weak—that dwell in the territory of the western Roman Empire. These are the nations that will never be politically united.

In spite of this prophecy many attempts—some quite honest and wise—have been made to unite the nations of the Old World. Daniel said, for example, that they would **"mix with one another in marriage."** For many years the royalty of Europe attempted conscientiously to assure permanent peace by means of inter-marriage. At the outbreak of the first world war almost all the ruling houses of Europe were interrelated. At the outbreak of the first world war! The words **"They will not hold together"** proved only too true.

The church did its part. For centuries it upheld the ideal of Europe as a "Holy Roman Empire," politically united under one king, religiously united under one pope. But the nations quarreled, and clerical pressures bred their own problems. God had predicted, **"They will not hold together."**

Many ambitious and talented men have tried to unite Europe. Charlemagne tried to do so in the eighth century, Charles V in the sixteenth, Napoleon in the nineteenth, the Kaiser Wilhelm II and Adolf Hitler in the twentieth. Millions still living remember Hitler's piercing voice as in seemingly endless harangues he portrayed the Nazi goal, "Germany over all [Deutschland über alles]." But the five simple words **"They will not hold together"** held true in his case also.

The next empire portrayed by Daniel's prophecy will be the worldwide king-dom of God, introduced by Jesus Christ Himself at His glorious second coming. **"In the days of those kings the God of heaven will set up a kingdom which shall never be destroyed, nor shall its sovereignty be left to another people. It shall break in pieces all these kingdoms and bring them to an end, and it shall stand for ever."** Daniel 2:44.

WILL ONE POWER RULE THE WORLD?

TOPICAL PRESS

At the height of Hitler's power, the Signs of the Times, *relying on Bible prophecy, fearlessly predicted the dictator's downfall.*

"The things that are revealed belong to us and to our children." Deuteronomy 29:29. I was fourteen when Hitler violated Poland's Danzig Corridor. I can still see my family hovering around our radio listening to Britain's declaration of war, as the shortwave came in successively loud and soft, clear and garbled. The future was dark, but I had been brought up on Daniel 2, and I knew that sooner or later Hitler would be defeated either by the Allies or by the second coming of Christ.

After Dunkirk and the fall of France, some students of prophecy cautioned my father, Arthur S. Maxwell, editor of *Signs of the Times,* not to continue writing editorials on Hitler's future defeat. "How do we know that the prophecy of Daniel 2 will apply in this case?" they asked. My father replied by dedicating his issue for July 2, 1940, to the interpretation of Daniel 2 and inviting his readers to preserve their copies!

"This prophecy is the only one in the Bible," he wrote buoyantly, "to which the words 'certain' and 'sure' are both attached [Daniel 2:45]. If for no other reason, with these two seals upon it we can surely trust it with complete confidence. It cannot fail."

My father used to tell me that when *he* was fourteen, in England, it was an evangelist's sermon on Daniel 2 that first attracted his widowed mother to the

38

study of the Bible. However it did not at first attract *him* to study the Bible. More than once he locked himself in the upstairs bathroom to escape the evangelist's house calls, then climbed to freedom down the outside English plumbing.

He gave his heart to Christ when he was sixteen, about two years before the outset of the first world war. During that terrible conflict he watched Kaiser Wilhelm II match his might for four years against the image of Daniel 2. My father's confidence in the impregnability of the prophecy was confirmed.

His faith was ready when Adolf Hitler took his turn.

This prophecy of Daniel is an introductory lesson. It prepares us for the even more stupendous predictions that come later. As we observe its fulfillment in international affairs over the centuries, our minds are opened to understand other outstanding prophecies in Daniel and Revelation that deal with vital developments in the Christian church; and we are prepared for still other, reassuring predictions about the wonderful things Jesus is doing for us right now. Arranging the prophecies in order, from simple to complex and from public to personal, is another evidence of how much God cares for us.

Even better, the presence of these prophecies and their remarkable fulfillment is precious proof that **"there *is* a God in heaven"** (Daniel 2:28) who knows the mysteries and troubles of our lives and is prepared to help us deal with them.

II. God's Love for Astrologers

It is heartwarming to learn that the first thing Daniel did after his early-morning praise service was to find Arioch the executioner and secure the safety of the wise men. As a "Christian" student in a "state college," he had presumably suffered his share of ill-humored jibes, but we find not a hint of bitterness in the account, no evidence of any self-flattering verdict that "God gives sinners the punishment they deserve." Daniel was amiable as well as earnest. People said there was **"an excellent spirit"** in him. Daniel 6:3.

But Daniel would have been helpless if God hadn't given him the vision. By telling Daniel what Nebuchadnezzar wanted to know, God saved not only Daniel's life but the lives of all the wise men too. I like to think that God loved the wise men. When He miraculously released the apostle Paul from prison one midnight, He generously released all the other prisoners as well. Acts 16:25, 26. When He saved Paul in a shipwreck, He saved all the sailors. Acts 27:21-25. God loves sinners as well as saints!

But in His love for the wise men, God showed them that they were *dead wrong*. Their embarrassment in Nebuchadnezzar's palace revealed the bankruptcy of their profession.

One reason this information is important to us is that astrology[3] is experiencing a remarkable resurgence in western nations today. Horoscopes and other astrological instruction are offered in popular magazines and hundreds of newspapers, and at newsstands everywhere. It was estimated in the late 1970s that 10,000 astrologers were at work full time and 175,000 part time in the United States alone—far more than the 40,000 ordained Southern Baptist ministers who serve America's largest Protestant denomination. If an American Nebuchadnezzar were to summon all his wise men today, he would fill his palace for sure.

In His love for them God showed the astrologers and other **"wise men"** in Nebuchadnezzar's day how wrong they were. In order to get the full impact of what God did, we must not sell these people short. Highly trained and apparently well motivated, they were charged with discovering the will of the gods, something that surely seemed important. The **"enchanters"** (Daniel 2:2) were trained to keep the gods happy. The **"magicians"** and **"sorcerers"** (Daniel 2:2) attempted to protect the people by warding off demons. The **"astrologers"** (Daniel 2:27) interpreted omens and predicted the future.[4] The **"Chaldeans"** (Daniel 2:2) offered a variety of services and together constituted the ruling ethnic group in Babylon.[5] (Babylon was sometimes spoken of as the land of the Chaldeans. See Jeremiah 25:12.)

The whole body of wise men saw themselves as scholars and scientists. They believed that the events of people's lives, even the trivial events, were controlled moment by moment by natural forces. If nature could be properly understood, they said, people should be able to explain past failures, heal present illnesses, and secure future successes. These are honorable goals.

In order to understand nature, the wise men made thousands of observations. They studied things like the livers of sheep, the behavior of birds in flight, the spread of an oil drop over water in a vessel, the shape of clouds at sunset, and the color of the dawn. They valued dreams as direct communications from the gods. They regarded the heavenly bodies as very special objects of investigation. Their thousands of observations were painstakingly recorded on hundreds of clay tablets, whose comprehension entailed years of specialized study and constant, continuing research.

We may take it for granted that the wise men intended to be scientific. At best their astronomical observations and calculations do command our respect. But because there cannot really be any relationship between, say, the lobes of a sheep's liver and the success of a military campaign or between the flutter of fowl and the outcome of a projected business venture, their science, for all its sophistication, was often superstition.

Modern astrology is no better. It also is based on the assumption that natural events around us control our destiny. For all its seriousness and sophistication, it too is superstition. There cannot really be any effective relationship between the future happiness of a proposed marriage and the location of selected constellations at the groom's birth. Modern horoscopes give no more genuine guidance than a spreading oil drop did in ancient times.

In some ways, in fact, contemporary astrology is less scientific than the ancient type. Modern astrologers base their predictions on the location of the constellations of the zodiac, not as they appear today, but as they appeared in the days of the second-century astronomer, Claudius Ptolemaus! As a result of the "precession of the equinoxes"* since the second century, people who astrologers say are born under the sign of Libra, for example, are really born under Virgo. Modern astrology attempts to regulate our lives by the constellations according to the positions that they *would have been* in had we been born seventeen hundred years ago![6] In spite of its detailed scientific terminology, modern astrology is not based on good astronomy.

Furthermore its predictions are not supported by observable evidence. According to astrology, Aries and Scorpio are the signs under which soldiers are born, but an exhaustive test of 154,000 Marine reenlistments in the United States has shown that persons born under Aries and Scorpio are no more likely to become soldiers than so-called peace-loving Librans. Librans, according to astrology, are supposed to become musicians and painters. A study of 2000 artists has not supported this idea either.[7]

Once accepted, unfortunately, superstition of any kind is hard to shake off. The black cat or the broken mirror or the position of the planets just *may* have an effect, the person fears. So it is important for parents to start early to prevent their children from becoming superstitious.

But we should not merely tell our children that astrology is "superstition" and thus arouse their curiosity. Let us tell them the story about God and the wise men in Daniel 2.

Help your children memorize Psalm 31:14, 15: "Thou art my God. My times are in *thy* hand."

Teach them that Christians have no superstitious fears. Instead, they sing with David, "The Lord is my light and my salvation; whom shall I fear? The Lord is the stronghold of my life; of whom shall I be afraid?" Psalm 27:1.

Our lives, if we are Christians, are not pawns in the power of nature but are safe in the hands of the God who created nature. "No one," said Jesus, "shall snatch them [His children] out of my hand." John 10:28.

The wise men of Daniel's day were probably honest, and they were undoubtedly well trained, but it was foolish for anyone to trust their kind of science. Wrote Isaiah ironically:

> Let your astrologers come forward and save you—
>   those people who study the stars,
> who map out the zones of the heavens
>   and tell you from month to month
> what is going to happen to you.
>
> They [themselves] will be like bits of straw,
>   and a fire will burn them up!
> They will not even be able to save themselves. Isaiah 47:13, 14, T.E.V.

---

*The pull of the sun and moon twists the poles slightly, with the result that the sun appears to move slowly westward each year in relation to the constellations.

Babylon's astrologers were certainly unable to save themselves from Nebuchadnezzar's fiery anger. God saved them through Daniel. He did so because He loved them and wanted them to change their ways.

He did it also because He loves us. He wants us to put our confidence, not in the false predictions of astrologers, but in His own divine prophecies found in Daniel and Revelation.

III. Getting Ready for God's Kingdom

Before we leave Daniel 2, let us look once more at the vision itself. Its promise that God will one day destroy the nations and set up His own kingdom is deeply appealing. Everyone would like to belong to a kingdom of light, love, and happiness. At the same time, of course, no one wants to be part of a nation that is destroyed. The question of getting ready for God's kingdom deserves serious attention.

First, though, who or what is the **"stone"** that strikes the image, breaks it in pieces, and brings the nations **"to an end"** (Daniel 2:35, 44)?

The Bible makes plain that this stone is Jesus Christ. The Bible often refers to Christ (and to God the Father) as a rock or a stone. First Corinthians 10:4, for example, speaking of another symbolic rock in the Old Testament, says, "the Rock was Christ." Isaiah 28:16 speaks of Christ as a special kind of stone, a "precious cornerstone." Jesus of course understood these Old Testament symbols. In Luke 20:17, 18 He said about Himself, "The very stone which the builders rejected has become the head of the corner." Here he was referring to Himself as Isaiah's cornerstone. He continued: "Every one who falls on the stone will be broken to pieces [that is, converted]; but when it falls on any one it will crush him." The stone that crushes is Daniel's supernatural stone.

The Rock of Ages, then, and not the statue, is the most impressive symbol in Nebuchadnezzar's dream. It represents Jesus Christ. But *when* will Jesus smite the **"feet of iron and clay,"** crush the image, and set up His new kingdom? Some commentators say that He has already done this! They say that He set up His kingdom when He lived on earth nineteen hundred years ago. But did Jesus at that time grind the nations to powder and **"bring them to an end"**? Daniel 2:44. Not at all. The Roman Empire (the legs of iron) continued for hundreds of years after Christ's time, and the countries of Europe (the feet and toes) have continued ever since. They have not yet been brought to an end, though we believe they will be soon.

If we are to understand the vision correctly, we must remember that the supernatural stone did not hit the image on its golden head (Babylon), or on its silver chest (Persia), or on its bronze thighs (Greece), and neither did it strike its iron legs (Rome). The Bible says that it hit the *feet and toes,* and that it would be **"in the days of *those* kings"** that the God of heaven would set up a kingdom that should never be destroyed. Daniel 2:44.

The mistaken idea that Christ hit the image at His first coming is based on a misunderstanding. To avoid making this mistake, it is helpful to realize that Jesus talked about His kingdom as coming in two different phases. One of these phases is known today as the "kingdom of grace." In the kingdom of grace Christ is a gracious king who forgives repentant sinners and helps them to live happy new lives. The other kingdom is called the "kingdom of glory." In the kingdom of glory Jesus reigns as a literal king, maintaining world peace and promoting universal prosperity.

When Jesus began to preach long ago, His basic message was, "Repent, for the kingdom of heaven is at hand." (See Matthew 4:17; 10:7). His hearers eagerly assumed that the "kingdom of heaven" was the kingdom of glory. They wanted to believe that the time had come for God to defeat their enemies and make Jerusalem, not Rome, the capital of the world. After Jesus fed thousands of people with a boy's lunch, some of the Jews wanted to compel Him to be king—their military kind of king. John 6:1-15. But Jesus dismissed them quietly and went off to a private place to pray.

In spite of this rebuff, when Jesus made a ceremonial entrance into Jerusalem on a donkey one year later, many of the people made a similar mistake again. They recalled the prophecy of Zechariah 9:9, "Lo, your king comes to you . . . , humble and riding on an ass," and they welcomed him excitedly, as if He were a triumphant earthly king. Luke 19:29-40.

How they misunderstood! Jesus had tried repeatedly to explain that the kingdom He was setting up at that time was not the kingdom of glory but the kingdom of grace. "The kingdom of God is not coming with signs to be observed," He said. Or "The Kingdom does not come in such a way as to be seen." Luke 17:21, T.E.V. Instead Jesus said that the kingdom of heaven is like the yeast that a woman stirs into bread dough or like the seed that a farmer sows in his fields. Matthew 13:13; Mark 4:26-29. It grows quietly and peacefully.

When someone asked who was going to be the greatest person in the kingdom, Jesus didn't point to an armed soldier or a clever politician but to the children attentively listening to His stories. He said that everyone in the kingdom would have to be like them. Matthew 18:1-4. Not childish, but childlike in innocence and humility.

When Jesus was on earth, He talked mostly about the kingdom of grace. But He *also* talked about the *future* kingdom of glory that Daniel predicted—the kingdom that He will set up after His second coming. For example, at the Last Supper He promised, "I shall not drink again of this fruit of the vine until that day when I drink it new with you in my Father's *kingdom*." Matthew 26:29. He also discussed the kingdom of glory with His disciples when seated on a hillside a few days before His crucifixion. "When the Son of man comes in his glory," He said, "and all the angels with him, then he will sit on his *glorious throne*. Before him will be gathered all the nations, and he will separate them one from another as a shepherd separates the sheep from the goats, and he will place the sheep on his right hand, but the goats on his left. Then the King will say to those at his right

43

hand, 'Come, O blessed of my Father, inherit *the kingdom* prepared for you from the foundation of the world.' " Matthew 25:31-34.

The book of Revelation also speaks about the kingdom of glory and about the separation of good from bad which accompanies it. "Nothing unclean shall enter it, nor any one who practices abomination or falsehood, but only those who are written in the Lamb's [that is, Christ's] book of life." Revelation 21:27. "As for the cowardly [people who are afraid to do right], the faithless, the polluted, as for murderers, fornicators, sorcerers, idolaters, and all liars, their lot shall be . . . the second death." Revelation 21:8.

It is beautiful to contemplate a time when God will populate the earth entirely with honest people. When my wife goes for a walk at night or we are leaving home for a vacation, we wish we could be certain that everyone in at least our section of town was perfectly trustworthy. Imagine a whole world filled with trustworthy people!

Millions of people, unfortunately, seem to like being dishonest, self-seeking, adulterous, even violent, whenever it appears to be to their advantage. Before God can populate our planet exlusively with moral, kind, and honest people, the immoral, unkind, and dishonest people will have to disappear—either by being transformed or by being left out. How else could it be done?

This is a serious matter. The Bible says plainly that all liars, for example, will be left out. How honest are you and I? And if it is to be an ideal kingdom, all dictators will have to go. Both the big dictators and the little ones—the goose-stepping national kind and the ever-scolding family kind. The new earth will provide no pleasure to our families if we constantly irritate them. "Fathers," says Ephesians 6:4, "do not provoke your children to anger."

The purpose of the kingdom of glory is to perpetuate happiness.

The purpose of the kingdom of grace is to help sinners get ready for the happy kingdom of glory.

The purpose of the judgment which precedes the kingdom of glory is to decide who has chosen to be changed by the kingdom of grace.

When Jesus said that people who fall on the Stone will be broken, He was talking about the kingdom of grace. He meant that when we come to Him, He helps us to be sorry for our selfish ways and to apologize and confess and be forgiven and be changed into new people. Those who wait until the Stone falls on top of them at the second coming will be crushed. They will be excluded from the kingdom, because they would spoil the happiness of others.

God's kingdom predicted in Daniel 2 is the kingdom of glory that will be set up at the second coming of Christ. Everyone will be fit to enter that kingdom who has first let Christ set up His kingdom of grace in his heart.

Your Questions Answered

1. Do the metals themselves symbolize anything? Some commentators, when writing about the multi-element image of Daniel 2, observe that the gold, silver, bronze, and iron are arranged in decreasing order of monetary value and increasing order of hardness. Then they try to draw meaning out of their observation. Some commentators also conjecture that the two legs of the image represent the famous eastern and western divisions of the Roman Empire.

The Bible states that the metal sections represent a series of kingdoms. It states that the second kingdom was to be **"inferior"** to the first. It also says that the fourth kingdom was to be **"strong as iron"** and **"like iron which crushes,"** and that the iron in the feet had **"firmness"** and did **"not mix with clay."** Daniel 2:39, 40, 41, 43. The Bible says nothing further about the meaning of the metals or about their hardness or relative value. As for the legs, it makes no point of the fact that there were two.

When it comes to *our* evaluation of the metals, we need to remember that whereas gold is very valuable for ornaments, iron is obviously more valuable for armaments. And what about the *two* legs? Well, what about the two eyes? The ten fingers? The twenty-four ribs? What about the navel? Are we to treat them all as symbols and develop extensive interpretations for each of them?

Involved here is a vital principle for all prophetic interpretation. Sometimes context does compel us to attach meaning to a symbol when the meaning is not expressly supplied by Scripture. Even in such cases we must be wary. But when the Bible doesn't even mention a symbol, we must be even more wary, lest we teach things that God never intended and thus unwittingly write our own Bible.

"The secret things belong to the Lord our God; but *the things that are revealed* belong to us and to our children." Deuteronomy 29:29.

2. Is there a problem in Daniel 2:1? The first verse of Daniel 2 says that Nebuchadnezzar saw his miraculous dream in **"the second year"** of his reign. This date seems to conflict with the report in Daniel 1:5, 18, that the young men completed *three* years of study prior to the king's dream. Indeed, right after interpreting the dream Daniel was appointed prefect over the wise men. It seems unlikely that he took his final examination (Daniel 1:18) after such a promotion!

Learned critics of the Bible have challenged the dating of Daniel 2, denouncing it as a glaring error and calling into question the validity of the entire book of Daniel and, in fact, the entire Bible. They should have waited.

Research in the twentieth century has shown that Scripture chronology is astonishingly dependable.[8] In order to recognize this dependability, however, we need to understand something about how Bible writers thought. Just as they wore different clothes, used different alphabets, and talked different languages from ours, so Bible writers counted time differently. Three principles clear up all our difficulties:

1. *Spring-to-spring years and fall-to-fall years*. No ancient people prior to the Romans started the year on January 1 as we do. In the time of Daniel the kingdom of Judah commenced the civil year in the *fall*, about the time when the "early rain" greened the landscape after the summer drought. The kingdom of Babylon, however, commenced the year in the *spring*. Compared to our January-to-January years, ancient years commenced in one year and ended in another; hence they are often designated by dual numbers linked by a diagonal slash—606/605, 605/604, etc.

2. *Accession-year reckoning*. When a king died, the "first year" of his successor's reign was not counted from the day of the old king's death but from the following New Year's Day (in the spring or in the fall as the case might be). The period in between was known as the new king's "beginning-of-reign" or "accession year" and was not assigned a number.

3. *Inclusive reckoning*. Strange as it may seem to us, almost everyone in Bible times counted time *"inclusively."* We call the interval between noon on one Monday and noon on the next Monday, seven days. In ancient times people would have called it eight days, because they would have "included" all of the first Monday and all of the second Monday, even though only a portion of each was involved. Similarly, the interval between events in a king's fifth and seventh years was not two years to them, as it is to us, but three years. They included all of the fifth and all of the seventh years, even though only a portion of each was involved.

Inclusive reckoning, incidentally, explains how the Bible can speak of Christ's period in the tomb as "three days." We would call the period less than two days but not the folk in Bible times. Portions of Friday and Sunday were involved (in addition to all of Saturday); and so, in their idiom, it was "three days." If this seems strange to us, think how strange the word "weekend" would have seemed to them. A weekend, incredibly, includes not only the end of one week but also the *beginning* of the next week!

DANIEL'S THREE YEARS OF EDUCATION

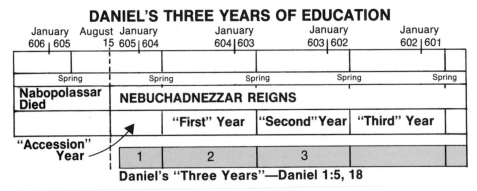

Daniel's "Three Years"—Daniel 1:5, 18

Apply these three simple principles to Daniel's dates, and all the difficulties disappear. First, though, let us remind ourselves again that B.C. means "Before Christ" and A.D. means *"Anno Domini"*—"in the year of our Lord," or simply, "After Christ." Successive dates B.C. get smaller rather than larger because they represent ever fewer years before the birth of Jesus. Using B.C. and A.D. is *our* way of dating events. In ancient times events were usually dated by the reigns of kings.

Now Nebuchadnezzar's father died on August 15, 605 B.C. Nebuchadnezzar rushed home and "acceded" to the throne on September 7. But according to the "accession year" and "spring to spring" principles, the "first year" of his reign did not commence officially until New Year's Day in the spring of 604 B.C. His **"second year"** (Daniel 2:1) thus commenced in the spring of 603, and his dream occurred somewhere between then and spring 602.

Daniel was taken hostage in the summer of 605 B.C., just before Nebuchadnezzar learned about his father's death. He arrived in Babylon in the fall of 605 and was immediately sent to school. According to the principle of inclusive reckoning his three years of training were (1) Nebuchadnezzar's accession year—the period that remained between the death of Nabopolassar in the fall of 605 and New Year's day, spring 604; (2) Nebuchadnezzar's first year—the full calendar year between spring 604 and spring 603; and (3) the first portion of Nebuchadnezzar's second year—during which Daniel completed his training. Inasmuch as Daniel's graduation could have occurred at *any time* after New Year's Day in the spring of 603, his **"three years"** of education may have been, by our modern calculations, actually less than two years!

In any case Daniel's third year is seen to have ended during Nebuchadnezzar's second year, and the problem is completely solved.

References

1. Georges Contenau, *Everyday Life in Babylon and Assyria,* trans. K. R. and A. R. Maxwell-Hyslop (London: Edward Arnold, 1954), pp. 64, 65.

2. Stewart C. Easton, *The Heritage of the Ancient World: From the Earliest Times to the Fall of Rome* (New York: Rinehart and Company, 1956, 1960).

3. For scholarly and popular discussions of ancient and modern astrology see Neugebauer, *Exact Sciences;* Michel Gauquelin, *The Cosmic Clocks: From Astrology to a Modern Science* (n.p., 1967); William J. Petersen, "Astrology: Fad, Fact, or Fraud?" *These Times,* September 1, 1978, pp. 22-25; William J. Petersen, ed., *Run Your Life by the Stars?* (Wheaton, Ill.: Victor Books, 1972).

4. Petersen, "Astrology."

5. Contenau, *Everyday Life,* pp. 281-295.

6. Gauquelin, *Cosmic Clocks,* pp. 78-80.

7. Petersen, "Astrology." Compare a study of 50,000 persons in Gauquelin, *Cosmic Clocks,* pp. 83-86.

8. Siegfried H. Horn, "The Babylonian Chronicle and the Ancient Calendar of the Kingdom of Judah," *Andrews University Seminary Studies* 5 (1967):12-27. Edwin R. Thiele, *The Mysterious Numbers of the Hebrew Kings,* rev. ed. (Grand Rapids, Mich.: Wm. B. Eerdmans Publishing Company, 1965).

Daniel 3
God and the Fiery Furnace

Introduction

The third chapter of Daniel is as up to date as any in the Bible. Even while you read it, devout Christians in certain countries of the world will be suffering in prison for their faith, and some may be facing death. Pray for them.

The situation will get worse. Revelation 13 says that at the end of time persecuting authorities will erect a *symbolic* image and require everyone to worship it or be killed. Daniel 3 tells about an attempt in Bible times to compel the worship of a *literal* image under pain of death. It also tells how God stood by those who trusted Him.

This blasphemous image of Daniel 3 was visible for some miles, its gilt surface flashing light as the sun struck it. The technology and expense of its construction must have been topics of conversation for months.

Nebuchadnezzar had been profoundly impressed by the gold-headed image he had seen in his dream. He had been deeply moved by the ability of Daniel's God to repeat the dream and to provide an intelligent interpretation of it when all the trained astrologers and other wise men were helpless. His promotion of Daniel to high position no doubt stimulated interest in the true God and His teachings throughout the empire.

But initial impressions have a way of wearing off. Nebuchadnezzar seems to have become increasingly resentful of the words, **"After you shall arise another kingdom, inferior to you."** With the active and impatient temperament of a top executive, he determined one day to write his own prophecy of future events. He would make an image entirely of gold from head to toe, symbolic of a golden Babylon that would never be replaced. And he would make the image taller than any image he had ever heard of—taller even than the towering statues of Egypt. Compatible with the customs of the day, he would gather government officials from each administrative province of his empire and have them all bow down to the image in a universal pledge of allegiance. The perpetuity of his dynasty would be guaranteed.

A clay tablet, translated and published in 1956,[1] reports that a serious mutiny erupted in Nebuchadnezzar's army in December 594 in the tenth year of his reign. Nebuchadnezzar squelched the rebellion vigorously and, the tablet says, "slew many of his own army. His own hand captured his enemy." Perhaps his decision to summon the officials to the dedication of his image was triggered by this revolt.[2]

Long before the day of our social security numbers, the wise men of Babylon assigned mystical religious numbers to their many deities. The leading god of their classical trio was

49

Nebuchadnezzar discovered that he could not burn the three men who would not bow to his image.

Anu. His assigned number was 60, the base figure in the sexagesimal system.[3] Nebuchadnezzar decided that his all-gold image, together with its massive foundation, should stand a full 60 cubits high. A Babylonian cubit (the distance from elbow to fingertip) was standardized at approximately half a meter, or 19.6 inches. Thus the image was to rise 30 meters, or nearly 100 feet, above the level plain.

Executive orders were drafted, the image was commissioned and erected, and the officials were gathered. We can imagine parades and banquets and military displays. And the climax on the Plain of Dura. The herald stills the throng. ''When the music begins,'' he shouts, ''everyone is to bow low before the image or be thrown as a traitor into a furnace.'' Dark smoke ascends from a nearby brick kiln to underscore his threat to be serious and final.

The music sounds. The crowd falls prostrate. Nebuchadnezzar is at peace. His empire is united, its future assured.

But his triumph is short-lived. As the crowd rises to its feet, some eager Chaldeans—leaders from the dominant ethnic group—interrupt him and indicate that they have imperative information. Three of the Jews whom the king had appointed to positions of responsibility have defied him. While the music played, the informants say, these Jews, like rebels, remained on their feet.

The three Jews were Shadrach, Meshach, and Abednego, Daniel's friends. What they, and the king, *and God* did next constitutes one of the most famous and inspiring narratives in the Bible.

CHAPTER 3

1 King Nebuchadnezzar made an image of gold, whose height was sixty cubits and its breadth six cubits. He set it up on the plain of Dura, in the province of Babylon. ² Then King Nebuchadnezzar sent to assemble the satraps, the prefects, and the governors, the counselors, the treasurers, the justices, the magistrates, and all the officials of the provinces to come to the dedication of the image which King Nebuchadnezzar had set up. ³ Then the satraps, the prefects, and the governors, the counselors, the treasurers, the justices, the magistrates, and all the officials of the provinces, were assembled for the dedication of the image that King Nebuchadnezzar had set up; and they stood before the image that Nebuchadnzzar had set up. ⁴ And the herald proclaimed aloud, "You are commanded, O peoples, nations, and languages, ⁵ that when you hear the sound of the horn, pipe, lyre, trigon, harp, bagpipe, and every kind of music, you are to fall down and worship the golden image that King Nebuchadnezzar has set up; ⁶ and whoever does not fall down and worship shall immediately be cast into a burning fiery furnace." ⁷ Therefore, as soon as all the peoples heard the sound of the horn, pipe, lyre, trigon, harp, bagpipe, and every kind of music, all the peoples, nations, and languages fell down and worshiped the golden image which King Nebuchadnezzar had set up.

8 Therefore at that time certain Chaldeans came forward and maliciously accused the Jews. ⁹ They said to King Nebuchadnezzar, "O king, live for ever! ¹⁰ You, O king, have made a decree, that every man who hears the sound of the horn, pipe, lyre, trigon, harp, bagpipe, and every kind of music, shall fall down and worship the golden image; ¹¹ and whoever does not fall down and worship shall be cast into a burning fiery furnace. ¹² There are certain Jews whom you have appointed over the affairs of the province of Babylon: Shadrach, Meshach, and Abednego. These men, O king, pay no heed to you; they do not serve your gods or worship the golden image which you have set up."

13 Then Nebuchadnezzar in furious rage commanded that Shadrach, Meshach, and Abednego be brought. Then they brought these men before the king. ¹⁴ Nebuchadnezzar said to them, "Is it true, O Shadrach, Meshach, and Abednego, that you do not serve my gods or worship the golden image which I have set up? ¹⁵ Now if you are ready when you hear the sound of the horn, pipe, lyre, trigon, harp, bagpipe, and every kind of music, to fall down and worship the image which I have made, well and good; but if you do not worship, you shall immediately be cast into a burning fiery furnace; and who is the god that will deliver you out of my hands?"

16 Shadrach, Meshach, and Abednego answered the king, "O Nebuchadnezzar, we have no need to answer you in this matter. ¹⁷ If it be so, our God whom we serve is able to deliver us from the burning fiery furnace; and he will deliver us out of your hand, O king. ¹⁸ But if not, be it known to you, O king, that we will not serve your gods or worship the golden image which you have set up."

19 Then Nebuchadnezzar was full of fury, and the expression of his face was changed against Shadrach, Meshach, and Abednego. He ordered the furnace heated seven times more than it was wont to be heated. ²⁰ And he ordered certain mighty men of his army to bind Shadrach, Meshach, and Abednego, and to cast them into the burning fiery furnace. ²¹ Then these men were bound in their mantles, their tunics, their hats, and their other garments, and they were cast into the burning fiery furance. ²² Because the king's order was strict and the furnace very hot, the flame of the fire slew those men who took up Shadrach, Meshach, and Abednego. ²³ And these three men, Shadrach, Meshach, and Abednego, fell bound into the burning fiery furnace.

24 Then King Nebuchadnezzar was astonished and rose up in haste. He said to his

counselors, "Did we not cast three men bound into the fire?" They answered the king, "True, O king." [25] He answered, "But I see four men loose, walking in the midst of the fire, and they are not hurt; and the appearance of the fourth is like a son of the gods."

26 Then Nebuchadnezzar came near to the door of the burning fiery furnace and said, "Shadrach, Meshach, and Abednego, servants of the Most High God, come forth, and come here!" Then Shadrach, Meshach, and Abednego came out from the fire. [27] And the satraps, the prefects, the governors, and the king's counselors gathered together and saw that the fire had not had any power over the bodies of those men; the hair of their heads was not singed, their mantles were not harmed, and no smell of fire had come upon them. [28] Nebuchadnezzar said, "Blessed be the God of Shadrach, Meshach, and Abednego, who has sent his angel and delivered his servants, who trusted in him, and set at nought the king's command, and yielded up their bodies rather than serve and worship any god except their own God. [29] Therefore I make a decree: Any people, nation, or language that speaks anything against the God of Shadrach, Meshach, and Abednego shall be torn limb from limb, and their houses laid in ruins; for there is no other god who is able to deliver in this way." [30] Then the king promoted Shadrach, Meshach, and Abednego in the province of Babylon.

The Message of Daniel 3

God Is With Us

When Nebuchadnezzar discovered that he could not burn the men who would not bow to his image, he exclaimed excitedly, **"There is no other god who is able to deliver in this way."** He was awestruck. God had delivered His faithful three from the hottest fire the king had ever known. He had even sent His angel to walk in the flames with them. Daniel 3:28-30.

If Nebuchadnezzar had known God better, he would have been far less surprised at this turn of events—although, of course, he would have been just as excited. Four centuries earlier King David, who knew God very well, had written, "God is our refuge and strength, a very present help in trouble." Psalm 46:1. "The angel of the Lord encamps around those who fear him, and delivers them." Psalm 34:7. One century before the fiery furnace experience, God had promised through Isaiah, "When you pass through the waters I will be with you: . . . and when you walk through fire you shall not be burned," and again:

> Fear not, for I am with you,
>   be not dismayed, for I am your God;
> I will strengthen you, I will help you,
>   I will uphold you with my victorious right hand. Isaiah 43:2; 41:10.

Shadrach, Meshach, and Abednego knew that God had delivered the Jews from Egypt by opening up the Red Sea (see Exodus 14). More recently, God had delivered Jerusalem by sending an angel to destroy a vast number of Assyrian soldiers (see Isaiah 37).

To their everlasting honor, Shadrach, Meshach, and Abednego *also* knew that although God is always with us, He *does not always* choose to deliver us in the way we would like Him to. Only a few years prior to the event at the fiery furnace, God had *not* worked a miracle to protect the prophet Uriah, who preached against the crimes of King Jehoiachin. God allowed Jehoiachin to execute him (see Jeremiah 26:20-23).

Sometimes the Christian employee who never steals anything is miraculously kept on the job when the rest of his unit is laid off. But not always. Sometimes the Christian girl who insists on remaining a virgin is later voted high school queen. But not often. More often than not, the Christian boy who doesn't laugh at a dirty joke gets laughed at.

In Gethsemane Jesus prayed, "Father, if it be possible, let this cup pass from me; *nevertheless,* not as I will, but as thou wilt." Matthew 26:39. The answer was death on Calvary.

God can deliver us, but often He chooses to have us witness for Him in apparent defeat rather than in obvious victory.

So Shadrach, Meshach, and Abednego said to the king, **"If it be so, our God whom we serve is able to deliver us from the burning fiery furnace; and he will deliver us out of your hand, O king. *But if not,* be it known to you, O king, that we will not serve your gods or worship the golden image which you have set up."** Daniel 3:17, 18.

The phrase "but if not," like Jesus Christ's "nevertheless," epitomized their faith. They didn't want to die; even more, however, they didn't want to disappoint the wonderful, personal God who was always with them. In the Ten Commandments they knew that God had said:

> You shall have no other gods before me. You shall not make for yourself a graven image, or any likeness of anything that is in heaven above, or that is in the earth beneath, or that is in the water under the earth; you shall not bow down to them or serve them; for I the Lord your God am a jealous God, visiting the iniquity of the fathers upon the children to the third and the fourth generation of those who hate me, but showing steadfast love to thousands of those who love me and keep my commandments. Exodus 20:3, 4.

(God describes Himself here as being "jealous" because He loves everyone. It deeply grieves Him when He sees parents teach their children and grandchildren to worship or to place their own other gods and values and goals above His—decisions that can only hurt them.)

Because Revelation 13 warns us that there is to be another great contest over loyalty to God in the last days, it is appropriate for us to ask, "Is God *still* able to deliver from danger people who obey Him?" One of my favorite answers is the experience of Corporal Desmond Doss—a Seventh-day Adventist and the only noncombatant in World War II to receive the Congressional Medal of Honor, the highest military award offered by the United States.

Desmond Doss grew up in a Christian home and knew all about God and the fiery furnace. He had also memorized the Ten Commandments. When he was inducted into the U.S. Army on April 1, 1942, he applied for service in the medical corps. Respectfully he stated that his religion would not permit him to break the sixth commandment by killing anyone—or to break the fourth commandment by doing ordinary, routine work on the Sabbath. Emergency medical service, he believed, God would approve on any day.

When Desmond Doss knelt to pray at bedtime on his first night in the Army, other soldiers, undressing, hurled their boots at him. He became much more popular, however, when bullets flew on Guam, Leyte, and Okinawa.

On Saturday, May 5, 1945, the 10th U.S. Army ordered the 77th Division to launch a major assault on the Maeda Escarpment—a long fifty-foot cliff which held the key to the control of Okinawa. Unknown to the American command, the Japanese had chosen the same day for their major counterattack, to be launched from the same escarpment.

For rescuing seventy-five wounded men under heavy fire, Desmond Doss received the Congressional Medal of Honor from President Harry Truman.

The platoon of which Doss was the only surviving medic, and which had been beefed up to 200 men, was assigned to climb the cliff and neutralize the Japanese command post, hidden in a cave a few hundred feet over the brow of a hill.

The engagement was bewildering and vicious. The platoon suffered 100 casualties in a matter of minutes, and the 55 men who could still move climbed back down for cover. Doss alone remained on duty, his uniform soon caked with blood, seeking out the wounded under very heavy fire. His enthusiastic buddies and officers reported later that, almost incredibly, he helped 75 men reach safety that day, in addition to performing numerous other exploits on other occasions. They eagerly recommended him to Congress for the Medal of Honor.

Doss told me that it took him *several hours,* operating alone, to remove so many men to safety. A few moments' calculation will show that it must have been so. During most of that time he was under crossfire from rifles, machine guns, and mortars. Twice an artillery barrage opened up.

A battalion of the enemy—hundreds of men—tried for hours that Saturday in May 1945 to kill a single, earnest Christian, and they couldn't hit him. Doss attributes his miraculous deliverance to God's promise in Psalm 91 (K.J.V.): "He that dwelleth in the secret place of the most High shall abide under the shadow of the Almighty. I will say of the Lord, He is my refuge and my fortress: my God; in him will I trust." Doss also says, "During all the time I was in the Army my great

55

source of strength was the daily study of the Bible and prayer. . . . When I talked with God I seemed to lose my sense of fear. . . . To God be all the honor."[4]

On a nighttime surprise mission a few days after the Maeda Escarpment was finally won, Doss was wounded severely in both legs by a hand grenade. But he insisted on helping another soldier, and in the process he was hit in the left arm. His health suffered for years. Desmond Doss understands the meaning of **"but if not."** He also knows that God can still deliver those who trust Him.

But back to the Plain of Dura, to the story of the three courageous men who wouldn't bow to Nebuchadnezzar's image. Can you see the laborers shoveling oil-soaked chaff into the furnace in obedience to King Nebuchadnezzar's command? Can you see the heat reddening their flesh, drying the sweat as fast as it streams from their pores? Can you see immense clouds of greasy blackness belching skyward, darkening even the golden image itself? Can you see livid tongues of flame leaping angrily into the billowing smoke?

Our three heroes were ready! When they first came to Babylon, they resolved unequivocally not to compromise themselves even in the matter of healthful living. Through the years that followed, they kept before their minds God's goodness in honoring them in that college and in answering their prayer in connection with Nebuchadnezzar's dream. When word was first circulated about the proposed worship of the image, they remembered their God, His promises, and His Ten Commandments, and they made up their minds. They would trust and obey Him whether He delivered them or not.

And God did deliver them. He sent His Son to walk in the flames with them. By an almost incredible miracle He demonstrated to the Babylonian Empire that He cared. "Great peace have those who love thy law." Psalm 119:165.

"Fear not, for *I am with you.*" Isaiah 41:10.

Further Interesting Reading

In Arthur S. Maxwell, *The Bible Story,* vol. 6:
    "The Golden Idol," beginning on p. 33.
    "Thrown to the Flames," beginning on p. 38.
In Ellen G. White, *Prophets and Kings:*
    "The Fiery Furnace," beginning on p. 503.

Your Questions Answered

1. Was the furnace really heated "seven times hotter"? Some critics have professed that it would have been impossible for the Babylonians to heat the furnace seven times hotter and that therefore this story—and the rest of the Bible—cannot be trusted. But the Bible does not say that the furnace was actually heated seven times hotter. It says only that Nebuchadnezzar, in a fit of temper, demanded that it be so heated. Under the circumstances he might have said almost anything irrational! Incidentally, the phrase does not necessarily mean raising the temperature to seven times whatever degrees it was at the time on the Fahrenheit or Celsius scale. Everyone knows that only 20 or 30 degrees can change a "cold" morning into a "hot" afternoon—and that a few percentage points of humidity can change the same "hot" afternoon into one that seems to be at least "twice as hot."

2. Where was Daniel? Why isn't Daniel mentioned in the story of the fiery furnace? No one knows. He may have been ill; he may have been away on a royal assignment; he may have been excused from attending by the king, his friend, to avoid mutual embarrassment.

Daniel was found to be still absolutely faithful to God even in his very old age, in the experience of the lions' den. Daniel 6.

3. What were the musical instruments like in Daniel 3? The **"horn"** was a trumpet made from metal or the horn of an animal. The **"pipe"** was a flute, probably made from a hollow reed. The **"lyre"** was a common stringed instrument, with several strings stretched across a nearly square frame with an attached sounding board. The **"trigon"** had four strings on a triangular frame with an attached sounding board. Both the lyre and the trigon compared approximately in size with a modern guitar and produced a relatively high tone when plucked with a finger or stroked with a plectrum. The **"harp"** resembled our modern harp but had fewer strings (only eleven or twelve) and a lower tone. The **"bagpipe"** was of Greek origin and resembled the Scottish bagpipe, except that its bag was probably made from the hide of a dog. Its presence in the book of Daniel has

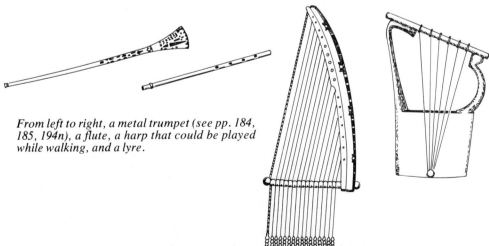

From left to right, a metal trumpet (see pp. 184, 185, 194n), a flute, a harp that could be played while walking, and a lyre.

been used by critics as clear proof that the story of the fiery furnace is not genuine. But it is now known that in the sixth century B.C. Greeks were active in Babylon as traders and were employed in the Babylonian army and on Babylonian construction projects. Evidently their strange musical instrument attracted Nebuchadnezzar's attention.[5]

References

1. See Wiseman, *Chronicles,* p. 73.

2. The exact date for the fiery furnace experience is not known. It seems likely, however, that it occurred in 594/593 B.C., the year that coincides with the fourth year of King Zedekiah of Judah. According to Jeremiah 51:59 Zedekiah made a journey to Babylon in his fourth year. It is quite possible that he made this journey in order to attend the dedication of the golden image. If so, he evidently bowed down even though he was a Jew and knew the Ten Commandments. His name occurs frequently in the book of Jeremiah. He appears as a king who occasionally wanted to do right but had a weak character.

3. Contenau, *Everyday Life,* pp. 246-248, 258.

4. Arthur Whitefield Spalding, *Origin and History of the Seventh-day Adventists,* 4 vols. (Washington, D.C.: Review and Herald Publishing Association, 1961, 1962), 4:301: see Booton Herndon, *Unlikeliest Hero* (Mountain View, Calif.: Pacific Press Publishing Association, 1967).

5. For a discussion of the Greek terms for the musical instruments in Daniel 3 see T. C. Mitchell and R. Joyce, "The Musical Instruments in Nebuchadnezzar's Orchestra," in D. J. Wiseman, et al., *Notes on Some Problems in the Book of Daniel* (London: Tyndale Press, 1965), pp. 19-27. On the presence of Greeks in the Near East in Daniel's time see E. Yamauchi, *Greece and Babylon* (Grand Rapids, Mich.: Baker Book House, 1967).

Daniel **4**

God and Nebuchadnezzar's Pride

Introduction

The fourth chapter of Daniel was written by King Nebuchadnezzar. How amazing! Even more amazing, it is an official edict containing the king's personal testimony to God's leadership in his life.

Nebuchadnezzar had dreamed another dream. Once more he had summoned the wise men, but even though this time he could remember his dream distinctly, the wise men offered no explanation. Perhaps they were afraid to. Just then the superintendent of the wise men, Daniel himself, walked in.

Nebuchadnezzar described his dream again. He said that he had seen a magnificent tree that kept growing and growing until its top seemed visible from all over the earth. Then a "watcher" appeared, who ordered it felled to the ground and its branches lopped off. But the watcher stipulated that the tree should not be destroyed entirely. Its stump should be left standing among the **"tender grass of the field,"** he said, and should be secured with a hoop of **"iron"** and **"bronze."**

With an ominous shift from **"it"** to **"him,"** the watcher continued: **"Let him be wet with the dew of heaven; let his lot be with the beasts in the grass of the earth; let his mind be changed from a man's, and let a beast's mind be given to him; and let seven times pass over him. The sentence is by the decrees of the watchers, the decision by the word of the holy ones, to the end that the living may know that the Most High rules the kingdom of men, and gives it to whom he will, and sets over it the lowliest of men."** Daniel 4:15-17.

Daniel knew at once what the dream meant. But he hesitated to tell.

The date for this dream may credibly be placed at about 569 B.C., after Nebuchadnezzar had been king for 35 years. By then Daniel and he had been friends for a long time. Daniel was a praying man. (You can read one of his more eloquent prayers in Daniel 9. See also chapters 2 and 6.) Without doubt he often prayed for Nebuchadnezzar, pleading with God for his conversion. And now God was about to answer his prayers—by depriving Nebuchadnezzar of the full use of his mind for a period and then restoring it to him, in this way leading him to confess his weakness and surrender himself to the Lord.

As Daniel hesitated, not from fear but from wonder, Nebuchadnezzar encouraged him to speak the truth. He knew he could fully trust this exceptional counselor. And so Daniel told him what God had revealed to him, namely, that if Nebuchadnezzar would not change his ways, his mind would become deranged and he would begin to act like an animal and would have to be turned out into the fields to eat grass.

The condition that Daniel described

is known by psychiatrists as lycanthropy (the wolf-man syndrome) or boanthropy (the ox-man syndrome). It was fairly common centuries ago, when even civilized people lived close to their animals. It is a mental state in which a person comes to think that he or she has turned into an animal and begins to act like the animal.

Daniel said that Nebuchadnezzar would remain in this condition until **"seven times,"** or seven years, had passed by. His uncut, uncombed hair would mat together till it looked like eagle feathers. His fingernails would grow long and coarse, like claws. But like the stump left in the ground, his right to rule would survive; and as soon as he came to his right mind and admitted God's lordship, his kingdom would be restored to him.

At the end of the interpretation Daniel pleaded with his royal friend. **"O king,"** he said, **"let my counsel be acceptable to you; break off your sins by practicing righteousness, and your iniquities by showing mercy to the oppressed, that there may perhaps be a lengthening of your tranquillity."** Daniel 4:27.

This counsel to break off his sins and practice righteousness must have added to Nebuchadnezzar's anxiety. When he had completed his great summer palace, he had erected a plaque which called attention to the building's massive security system. "The bad, unrighteous man cometh not within," it declared[1]—a reference to the palace's safety from burglars and other kinds of criminals. But now Daniel was implying that Nebuchadnezzar, the builder and principal resident of the palace, was himself a bad, unrighteous man.

Nebuchadnezzar appears to have taken Daniel's words thoughtfully. A full year passed before the judgment fell. It was an exciting and satisfying year for the king, for in it he succeeded at last in conquering Egypt. As a young man he had fought Egypt to a bitter tie; now as an old man he overpowered it at last. Without doubt his Babylon was the capital of a mighty empire.

And what a city it was! The savage Assyrians had razed it to the ground in 689 B.C., but international opinion had demanded its rebirth as a home of the gods. Nebuchadnezzar's father, Nabopolassar, had eliminated the Assyrians and assisted in the city's regrowth. Nebuchadnezzar had enlarged it to nearly three times its original size

and had made it the largest city in the world.

And the grandest! Whereas Nabopolassar had built a single palace, Nebuchadnezzar had built three palaces, each one larger and more luxurious than its predecessor. One of them was roofed with a garden of exotic trees and shrubs, the Hanging Gardens, famous among the Seven Wonders of the Ancient World. He had constructed tremendous double walls around the metropolis—in places even triple walls—for the protection of his subjects. He had also bridged the mighty Euphrates for the convenience of his people.

He had led campaigns to the Lebanon Mountains to conquer the heights where the *Cedrus libani* grows, the glorious cedar of Lebanon. He had hewed roads through solid rock to carry its sweet-smelling trunks. He had exuberantly, with his own hands, helped fell the mighty timbers. He had floated rafts of cedars down the Euphrates like so many bundles of reeds.[2]

He had demonstrated his gratitude to the gods by encouraging no fewer then 53 temples, 955 small sanctuaries, and 384 street altars! Babylon was truly a religious city.[3]

And how beautiful the city looked! Its outer walls were brick-yellow in color. Its principal gates were glazed in blue. Its palaces were faced with rose-colored tiles, and its myriad temples with gleaming white. Towering above all, as evidence of Babylon's traditional leadership in the worship of the gods, loomed the seven-tiered, multicolored Etemenanki. Its tallest shrine rose 100 meters, or 300 feet, above the floor of Esagila, the principal temple of Marduk—the most famous temple in the East.

"What a magnificent city it really

Etemenanki, the 100-meter temple tower in Babylon (as reconstructed), is thought by archaeologists to have resembled other known ziggurats.

is," Nebuchadnezzar mused with growing pride. "And to think that I am the one primarily responsible for it!" The fateful words gushed out: **"Is not this great Babylon, which I have built by my mighty power as a royal residence and for the glory of my majesty!"** Daniel 4:30.

Even as he boasted, a voice from heaven pronounced the judgment foretold twelve months earlier. Nebuchadnezzar lost his reason and was driven into the fields to eat grass like an ox.

But at the end of the assigned period, he tells us, when his reason returned to him, he lifted up his eyes to heaven, and **"blessed the Most High."** Daniel 4:34.

The entire chapter, Daniel 4, was evidently inscribed in cuneiform letters on official clay tablets. Someday perhaps an archaeologist will discover one of these tablets, and newspapers and magazines will print it with keen excitement. In the meantime you can read Nebuchadnezzar's words as they appear in your Bible.

4

CHAPTER 4

1 King Nebuchadnezzar to all peoples, nations, and languages, that dwell in all the earth: Peace be multiplied to you! 2 It has seemed good to me to show the signs and wonders that the Most High God has wrought toward me.

3 How great are his signs,
  how mighty his wonders!
His kindgom is an everlasting kingdom,
  and his dominion is from generation to generation.

4 I, Nebuchadnezzar, was at ease in my house and prospering in my palace. 5 I had a dream which made me afraid; as I lay in bed the fancies and the visions of my head alarmed me. 6 Therefore I made a decree that all the wise men of Babylon should be brought before me, that they might make known to me the interpretation of the dream. 7 Then the magicians, the enchanters, the Chaldeans, and the astrologers came in; and I told them the dream, but they could not make known to me its interpretation. 8 At last Daniel came in before me—he who was named Belteshazzar after the name of my god, and in whom is the spirit of the holy gods—and I told him the dream, saying, 9 "O Belteshazzar, chief of the magicians, because I know that the spirit of the holy gods is in you and that no mystery is difficult for you, here is the dream which I saw; tell me its interpretation. 10 The visions of my head as I lay in bed were these: I saw, and behold, a tree in the midst of the earth; and its height was great. 11 The tree grew and became strong, and its top reached to heaven, and it was visible to the end of the whole earth. 12 Its leaves were fair and its fruit abundant, and in it was food for all. The beasts of the field found shade under it, and the birds of the air dwelt in its branches, and all flesh was fed from it.

13 "I saw in the visions of my head as I lay in bed, and behold, a watcher, a holy one, came down from heaven. 14 He cried aloud and said thus, 'Hew down the tree and cut off its branches, strip off its leaves and scatter its fruit; let the beasts flee from under it and the birds from its branches. 15 But leave the stump of its roots in the earth, bound with a band of iron and bronze, amid the tender grass of the field. Let him be wet with the dew of heaven; let his lot be with the beasts in the grass of the earth; 16 let his mind be changed from a man's, and let a beast's mind be given to him; and let seven times pass over him. 17 The sentence is by the decree of the watchers, the decision by the word of the holy ones, to the end that the living may know that the Most High rules the kingdom of men, and gives it to whom he will, and sets over it the lowliest of men.' 18 This dream I, King Nebuchadnezzar, saw. And you, O Belteshazzar, declare the interpretation, because all the wise men of my kingdom are not able to make known to me the interpretation, but you are able, for the spirit of the holy gods is in you."

19 Then Daniel, whose name was Belteshazzar, was dismayed for a moment, and his thoughts alarmed him. The king said, "Belteshazzar, let not the dream or the interpretation alarm you." Belteshazzar answered, "My lord, may the dream be for those who hate you and its interpretation for your enemies! 20 The tree you saw, which grew and became strong, so that its top reached to heaven, and it was visible to the end of the whole earth; 21 whose leaves were fair and its fruit abundant, and in which was food for all; under which beasts of the field found shade, and in whose branches the birds of the air dwelt— 22 it is you, O king, who have grown and become strong. Your greatness has grown and reaches to heaven, and your dominion to the ends of the earth. 23 And whereas the king saw a watcher, a holy one, coming down from heaven and saying, 'Hew down the tree and destroy it, but leave the stump of its roots in the earth, bound with a band of iron and bronze, in the tender grass of the field; and let him be wet with the dew of heaven; and let his lot be with the beasts of the field, till seven times pass over him'; 24 this is the interpretation, O king: It is a

Nebuchadnezzar glows with pride over the magnificent city of Babylon.

decree of the Most High, which has come upon my lord the king, ²⁵ that you shall be driven from among men, and your dwelling shall be with the beasts of the field; you shall be made to eat grass like an ox, and you shall be wet with the dew of heaven, and seven times shall pass over you, till you know that the Most High rules the kingdom of men, and gives it to whom he will. ²⁶ And as it was commanded to leave the stump of the roots of the tree, your kingdom shall be sure for you from the time that you know that Heaven rules. ²⁷ Therefore, O king, let my counsel be acceptable to you; break off your sins by practicing righteousness, and your iniquities by showing mercy to the oppressed, that there may perhaps be a lengthening of your tranquillity."

28 All this came upon King Nebuchadnezzar. ²⁹ At the end of twelve months he was walking on the roof of the royal palace of Babylon, ³⁰ and the king said, "Is not this great Babylon, which I have built by my mighty power as a royal residence and for the glory of my majesty?" ³¹ While the words were still in the king's mouth, there fell a voice from heaven, "O King Nebuchadnezzar, to you it is spoken: The kingdom has departed from you, ³² and you shall be driven from among men, and your dwelling shall be with the beasts of the field; and you shall be made to eat grass like an ox; and seven times shall pass over you, until you have learned that the Most High

rules the kingdom of men and gives it to whom he will." ³³ Immediately the word was fulfilled upon Nebuchadnezzar. He was driven from among men, and ate grass like an ox, and his body was wet with the dew of heaven till his hair grew as long as eagles' feathers, and his nails were like birds' claws.

34 At the end of the days I, Nebuchadnezzar, lifted my eyes to heaven, and my reason returned to me, and I blessed the Most High, and praised and honored him who lives for ever;

for his dominion is an everlasting dominion,
and his kingdom endures from generation to generation;
³⁵ all the inhabitants of the earth are accounted as nothing;
and he does according to his will in the host of heaven
and among the inhabitants of the earth;
and none can stay his hand
or say to him, "What doest thou?"

³⁶ At the same time my reason returned to me; and for the glory of my kindgom, my majesty and splendor returned to me. My counselors and my lords sought me, and I was established in my kingdom, and still more greatness was added to me. ³⁷ Now I, Nebuchadnezzar, praise and extol and honor the King of heaven; for all his works are right and his ways are just; and those who walk in pride he is able to abase.

The Message of Daniel 4

I. God and Our Pride

Many parents take pride in their children. Craftsmen take pride in their work. So what was wrong with Nebuchadnezzar's pride?

Some words have several definitions. To a pet lover, "cat" is a furry little animal. To a construction worker, "cat" is a Caterpillar tractor.

Dictionaries say that "pride" in one's work or family can be a "wholesome delight," a "reasonable self-respect," a "justifiable sense of satisfaction." But there is another kind of "pride" defined as "inordinate self-esteem." This is the pride that Nebuchadnezzar cherished.

The Bible reminds us that pride and haughtiness lead to disaster (Proverbs 16:18) and tells us that God hates pride (Proverbs 8:13). One reason that God hates this kind of pride is that when we think too highly of ourselves, we tend to think less highly of other people and to treat them unkindly. Daniel said to proud Nebuchadnezzar, **"Break off your sins by . . . showing *mercy*."** Daniel 4:27. The Bible also says:

> He has showed you, O man, what is good;
>   and what does the Lord require of you
> but to do *justice,* and to love *kindness,*
>   and to walk *humbly* with your God? Micah 6:8.

If pride gives us wrong feelings about other people, it also separates us from God. God feels bad about both situations and does all that He can to persuade us to be more humble.

When God set about helping Nebuchadnezzar to love Him more so that he would be more merciful to his citizens, He did not *make* Nebuchadnezzar go insane. God is the Creator and Source of all life. "In him we live and move and have our being." Acts 17:28. He surrounds every individual with an indispensable life-support system. All that God needed to do in Nebuchadnezzar's case was to *cease providing* some portion of that very life support which Nebuchadnezzar was trying to ignore. Pride always leads us to forget our dependence on God.

While walking down the street, a minister met a wayward member of his congregation. They passed a vacant lot which, by dint of much labor, the church member had turned into a flourishing vegetable garden.

"God has surely blessed your garden," commented the clergyman, hoping to persuade his parishioner to acknowledge his obligation to the Lord.

But the gardener replied, "You should have seen the place when God had it to Himself."

Both men had a point. Without hard work and planning, weeds do take over. But without God to provide sunshine and the genetic structure of food plants,

65

where would gardeners be? It is realistic to recognize our dependence on our heavenly Father.

When husbands and wives both hold jobs, pride often leads the spouse who earns the larger amount to look down on his or her partner. As we open our paychecks, God speaks to the Nebuchadnezzar inside every one of us: "Beware lest you say in your heart, 'My power and the might of my hand have gotten me this wealth.' You shall remember the Lord your God, for it is he who gives you power to get wealth." Deuteronomy 8:18. Humility is an essential ingredient of happy homes as well as of happy palaces.

II. God's Respect for Leadership

In Daniel 4:17 the heavenly **"watchers"** tell us that God wants the **"living"**— that is, everybody—to learn (1) that God **"rules the kingdom of men"** and (2) that He **"gives it to whom he will."**

Almost everybody criticizes leaders these days. Is it really possible that *God* is the One who puts our leaders into public office?

Well, it is not quite as simple as that! In our study of Daniel 1 we saw how *very reluctantly* God "gave up" the stubborn kingdom of Judah to the leadership of King Nebuchadnezzar. His first choice for Judah was a far happier one. It was the sinfulness of the people that led to God's decision. As the maxim says, "People get the leaders they deserve."

In this account of "God and Nebuchadnezzar's Pride," we see God as the ultimate ruler of every nation, reserving the right to give authority to this or that person and to take it away. It is comforting to realize that God can remove leaders whenever He deems it best. Nebuchadnezzar was king of the greatest nation on earth in his day, but in an instant God removed even him from public office and turned him into the fields like an ox.

But God treated Nebuchadnezzar this way in order to help him. He wanted him to repent so He could forgive him and grant him eternal life. God loves the whole world (John 3:16); and God loved that boastful, impulsive, generous, cruel person, Nebuchadnezzar.

In the New Testament, Paul says, "First of all, then, I urge that supplications, prayers, intercessions, and thanksgivings be made for all men, for kings and all who are in high positions." 1 Timothy 2:1, 2.

Prayers, intercessions, thanksgivings! How long has it been since you thanked God for your leaders? Even bad governments provide some public service. Most people agree that even tyranny is better than anarchy and that bad laws are better than no laws. We can thank God, then, for the good things in whatever government we may have.

Disagreement is one thing; disrespect is another. Suppose that everyone, all Christians anyway, never spoke disrespectfully about their leaders! Suppose that Christian families discussed government leaders openly but understandingly and prayed earnestly for God to guide them—and to forgive them!

Jesus showed this kind of respect for leaders when He lived on earth. For example, one day a group of leaders heartlessly led a certain woman to Him to be publicly condemned. Jesus knew at a glance that although her sins were bad enough, their sins were worse. He could have embarrassed them easily enough. Instead He knelt and wrote their sins with His finger on the dusty ground. When the leaders noticed what He was doing, they quietly stepped away. When they were all gone, the first sandals to pass over the spot obliterated the record (see John 8:1-11).

Jesus respected those sinful leaders because He loved them and wanted to save them. "The Son of man," He said once, speaking of Himself, "came to seek and to save the lost." Luke 19:10.

It is true that on another occasion (Matthew 23) Jesus preached a sermon in which He listed the leaders' sins publicly. But this was in an effort to save those very leaders—three days before He died on the cross. Christ's voice as He listed their sins was that of a brokenhearted lover.

The message that **"God rules the kingdoms of men"** is repeated in Romans 13, where Paul says: "You must all obey the governing authorities. Since all government comes from God, the civil authorities were appointed by God, and so anyone who resists authority is rebelling against God's decision, and such an act is bound to be punished. . . . The authorities are there to serve God: they carry out God's revenge by punishing wrongdoers. You must obey, therefore, not only because you are afraid of being punished, but also for conscience' sake." Romans 13:1-5, Jerusalem.

Earnest Christians sometimes find themselves in a situation where they feel that obedience to a particular state regulation would be a "violation of conscience." In the trials that are to characterize the last days, such situations will increase. And Acts 5:29 says, "We must obey God rather than men."

But it is important to remember that part of our obedience to God is obedience to the state. "The authorities are there to serve God." Romans 13:4, Jerusalem. If a person's conscience leads him to think he should disobey the state, he should remember that the Bible says, "You must obey, . . . for conscience' sake." Romans 13:5, Jerusalem.

There *are* times when we must disobey the state, but in such cases our consciences may not be safe guides! One person's conscience says, "Join the army and kill the enemy." Another person's conscience says, "Stay out of the army and be a pacifist." A third person's conscience says, "Join the army if the state requires it, but use the opportunity to heal people rather than to kill them *because the Bible says,* 'You shall not kill.' Exodus 20:13." (This last was Desmond Doss's position. See pages 54-56.)

Since conscience alone cannot be a safe guide, the only safe guide is the Bible.

As a worshiper of the true God, young Daniel had probably felt very awkward about enrolling in the Babylonian "state college" of his day. He knew it was corrupted with idolatrous and pseudoscientific principles. But when the king assigned him to attend, he knew of no Bible command that said he should not; so he obeyed the king. But when unhealthful food which the Bible forbids was served (Leviticus 11), he refused to eat it, at the risk of his life.

Shadrach, Meshach, and Abednego would no doubt have preferred to stay away from the Plain of Dura. They knew it was morally dangerous to stand on the site of so severe a temptation. But the king ordered them to attend; and, knowing no Bible command against doing so, they obeyed. But the Bible says plainly that we should not bow down to images (Exodus 20:4-6); so they refused to bow, even at the risk of the fiery furnace.

"The things that are revealed belong to us and to our children." Deuteronomy 29:29. I encourage my students to believe that if a policeman arrests them when they have been violating traffic laws, they should remember that "the civil authorities were appointed by God" and "are there to serve God: they carry out God's revenge by punishing wrongdoers." Romans 13:1, 4, Jerusalem. One day one of my students reported that he had remembered my counsel. After the policeman completed his ticket, the young man asked if he could read him a passage from the Bible, and proceeded to read the first few verses of Romans 13.

When I mention this incident to my friends, they ask, "Did the policeman tear up the ticket?" And when I say No, they seem disappointed. But what actually happened was more impressive. The policeman went away with renewed determination to be faithful, and the student drove on determined to drive carefully—and with a happy spirit instead of bitterness.

God respects leadership, and He wants us to as well.

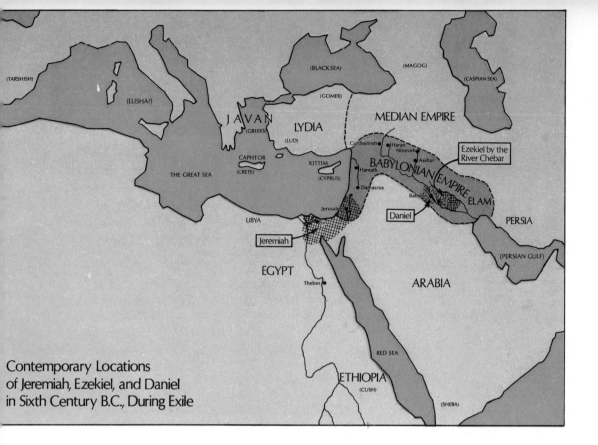

Contemporary Locations
of Jeremiah, Ezekiel, and Daniel
in Sixth Century B.C., During Exile

III. God Is Generous in Appointing Prophets

When we come to the study of Revelation 12, it will be helpful if we can remember that God is generous in appointing prophets.

We have an example from the time of Daniel. When Daniel served in Babylon as God's ambassador to the royal palace, God had two other prophets in service also. Jeremiah, who was older than Daniel, worked in Palestine and later in Egypt (see Jeremiah 29:1; 43:4-8). Ezekiel worked in Babylon. Ezekiel was apparently about the same age as Daniel; and he lived in a Jewish settlement near Nippur on the important irrigation canal, Nar Kabari, known in the Bible as the River Chebar (KEE-bar) (see Ezekiel 1:1; 43:3).

The sixteen Bible prophets from Isaiah to Malachi are well known. Less well known are numerous other prophets in the Bible, such as Gad the seer (1 Chronicles 29:29) and Huldah the woman prophet (2 Chronicles 34:22). Often, as in Daniel's day, God supplied more than one prophet at a time. Micah served at the same time as Isaiah, for example. Compare Micah 1:1 with Isaiah 1:1. In the New Testament the four daughters of Philip all served as prophets at the same time (Acts 21:8, 9), as did Agabus, Judas, Silas, and others (see Acts 15:22; 21:10). Once, in the Old Testament, God put His Spirit into seventy prophets on the same day. Numbers 11:24, 25.

69

In the twentieth century, we look expectantly for the final fulfillment of Joel 2:28, "It shall come to pass afterward, that I will pour out my spirit on all flesh; and your sons and your daughters shall prophesy."

God is generous in raising up prophets. He wants to communicate with us because He cares about us.

But to return to Daniel and his times. During the great crisis of the exile God used not only Daniel in Babylon but Ezekiel also. In addition He inspired Jeremiah with prophetic messages first in Judea and later in Egypt, when certain nonexiled Jews migrated there. In His generosity God moved Daniel, Ezekiel, and Jeremiah to write over 100 chapters of prophetic material just when it was most sorely needed.

Now, we know that Daniel was acquainted with Jeremiah. Compare Daniel 9:1, 2 with Jeremiah 29:10. Probably he was also acquainted with his other contemporary prophet, Ezekiel. The town of Nippur, where Ezekiel seems to have lived, was only 80 kilometers (50 miles) southeast from the city of Babylon.

In 587 B.C., some nineteen years before Nebuchadnezzar had his dream about the tall tree, Ezekiel was inspired to tell the pharaoh of Egypt that God likened *him* to a tall tree. Ezekiel 31. Ezekiel warned the pharaoh that in order to punish his pride, God was planning to send Nebuchadnezzar to cut him down (see Ezekiel 29:19; 30:10). Ezekiel also sounded a general warning that no other tree—that is, no other king or kingdom—should aspire to grow too tall (see Ezekiel 31:14).

In view of Daniel's special status with Nebuchadnezzar and his desire to see him converted, it seems likely that Daniel showed Nebuchadnezzar this parallel message from Ezekiel to the pharaoh.

Further Interesting Reading

In *Bible Readings for the Home:*
    The chapter entitled "Meekness and Humility."
In Arthur S. Maxwell, *The Bible Story,* vol. 6:
    "The King Goes Mad," beginning on p. 44.
In Ellen G. White, *Prophets and Kings:*
    "True Greatness," beginning on p. 514.

Your Questions Answered

1. How large was the city of Babylon? After all that has been said about the magnificence of Nebuchadnezzar's Babylon, it comes as a surprise to discover that its massive walls measured only 16 kilometers (10 miles) in length and that they enclosed an area of less than 5 square kilometers (less than 2 square miles)! By contrast Los Angeles claims an area of more than 450 square miles, and São Paulo, Brazil, more than 700.

The size of Babylon becomes impressive, however, when we compare it with that of other ancient cities of renown. Nineveh, the capital of the great empire that preceded New Babylon, was only 6.6 square kilometers (2.55 square miles) in area. Jerusalem, one of the best-known cities in all the ancient world, covered slightly more than one third square kilometer (slightly more than one-tenth square mile)!

Ancient cities seem small. They were small; but it helps to remember that, for defense, they had to be surrounded by walls. Walls were costly to build and maintain. In times of siege they had to be manned by the inhabitants twenty-four hours a day. In order to keep the walls as short as possible, cities were built in compact fashion, with most of the streets narrow and few of the homes graced with gardens. The number of people said to have crowded into these cities is remarkable. Nineveh, with its 2.55 square miles, is credited with a population of 120,000. A suburban residential area the size of Nineveh may today house only one third as many.

2. Does the iron-and-bronze band stand for anything? In his dream of the tree that was prematurely cut down, Nebuchadnezzar saw that the stump of the tree was **"bound with a band of iron and bronze."** It has been suggested by some commentators that this bimetal band must be related to the iron of Rome and the bronze of Greece in Daniel 2, and so must represent the continuance of evil Babylonian principles of government throughout human history.

It is an interesting theory, but it must be rejected for several reasons. (1) The silver of the Medo-Persian Empire and the clay of modern nations are left out! (2) The order **"iron and bronze"** is opposite from the bronze-to-iron sequence in Daniel 2. (3) The only interpretation which the Bible gives for the continuance of the stump is that **"your kingdom shall be sure for you from the time that you know that Heaven rules."** Thus the Bible says that the stump represents the preservation of the kingdom for a humbled and contrite Nebuchadnezzar. It says nothing about the continuance of an evil stump-kingdom for hundreds or thousands of years. (4) The Bible does not say specifically what the band refers to, and any dogmatic interpretation is speculation.

The Aramaic word *'esur,* here translated **"band,"** is related to the verb *'asar,* which refers in 2 Kings 7:10 to the binding or tying up of animals and in Psalm

149:8 to the binding of high-class captives with iron chains. The presence of the band in Nebuchadnezzar's dream probably meant nothing more than this: when Nebuchadnezzar was driven out of the palace, he was to be bound with an iron-and-bronze chain so that he could neither come back into the palace nor wander too far away.

See the warning against speculative interpretations on page 45.

3. Who are the "watchers"? The watchers of Daniel 4:13, 17 are probably the same extraterrestrial beings that elsewhere are called "angels" (see, for example, Daniel 6:22).

First Corinthians 4:9 says that "we" have become "a spectacle [that is, something to watch] to the world, *to angels* and to men." Italics supplied.

Angels are mentioned approximately seventy times in the book of Revelation, and they are frequently referred to elsewhere in the Bible. For example, Jacob saw angels ascending and descending between earth and heaven. Genesis 28:12. An angel destroyed an Assyrian army in order to protect Jerusalem. 2 Kings 19:35. Angels sang with joy at the birth of Jesus. Luke 2:13.

Hebrews 1:14 says that angels are "sent forth to serve, for the sake of those who are to obtain salvation." Angels use their superior strength and intelligence to help us in our daily trials and temptations. We should teach our children to thank God for these unseen friends who "watch" us and "watch out" for us.

4. Do the clay tablets support chapter 4? Is there any evidence in cuneiform inscriptions made during Nebuchadnezzar's lifetime that he was in fact a boastful builder, a poet, and a mad man? Yes, there is. Here are examples:

Nebuchadnezzar was a boastful builder. In one of his edicts he boasted:

> I have made Babylon, the holy city, the glory of the great gods, more prominent than before, and have promoted its rebuilding. I have caused the sanctuaries of gods and goddesses to lighten up like the day. No king among all kings has ever created, no earlier king has ever built, what I have magnificently built for Marduk. I have furthered to the utmost the equipment of *Esagila* [the great temple of Marduk], and the renovation of Babylon more than had ever been done before. All my valuable works, the beautification of the sanctuaries of the great gods, which I undertook more than my royal ancestors, I wrote in a document and put it down for coming generations.[4]

Nebuchadnezzar was a poet. Some of Nebuchadnezzar's personal edicts took the form of poetic parallelism, another contrast with Assyrian practice but strikingly in harmony with the structure of Daniel 4. The poetic parallelism of the day involved the line-by-line repetition of thought or the line-by-line alternation of contrasting or resultative thoughts (see pages 210-213).

Here are a few lines from Nebuchadnezzar's edict in Daniel 4 (verse 4):

I, Nebuchadnezzar, was at ease in my house
  and prospering in my palace.

I had a dream which made me afraid;
  As I lay in bed the fancies and the visions
  of my head alarmed me.

Compare these poetic lines written by Nebuchadnezzar in the Bible with these other poetic lines from Nebuchadnezzar's so-called India House inscription:

When I was born,
  when I was created, even I,
  the sanctuaries of the god I regarded,
  the way of the god I walked in. . . .[5]

Nebuchadnezzar went mad. In 1975 a clay tablet was translated which may refer to Nebuchadnezzar's madness.[6] This tablet, which is in the British Museum (B.M. 34113, sp. 213), is so damaged that certain words on each line

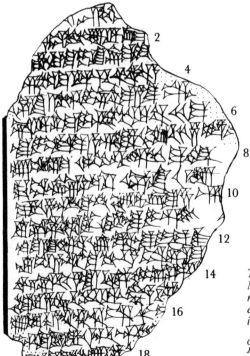

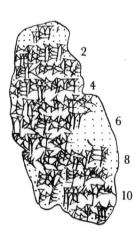

The small, badly damaged side of British Museum tablet 34114 records Nebuchadnezzar's troubles when suffering a mental disorder that resembles his illness in Daniel 4.

Credit: A. K. Grayson, Babylonian Historical-Literary Texts, J. W. Wevers and D. B. Redford, eds., Toronto Semitic Texts and Studies (Toronto: University of Toronto Press, 1975), p. 92.

are illegible and some lines cannot be read at all. But the lines that can be read carry such phrases as "Nebuchadnezzar considered. . . ." "his life appeared of no value to. . . ." "he does not show love to son and daughter. . . ." "family and clan do not exist. . . ." "his attention was not directed towards promoting the welfare of Esagila. . . ." "he weeps bitterly to Marduk. . . ." [7]

References

1. India House Inscription 9.22-44, in Charles Boutflower, *In and Around the Book of Daniel* (London: Society for Promoting Christian Knowledge, 1923), p. 74.

2. Wadi [Wadi-Brisa] Inscription, in Boutflower, *The Book of Daniel*, chap., "The Royal Woodcutter."

3. Contenau, *Everyday Life*, p. 279.

4. *The Seventh-day Adventist Bible Commentary*, ed. Francis D. Nichol, 7 vols. (Washington, D.C.: Review and Herald Publishing Association, 1953-1957), 4:799.

5. Boutflower, *The Book of Daniel*, p. 101.

6. See A. K. Grayson, *Babylonian Historical Literary Texts*, Toronto Semitic Texts and Studies, no. 3 (Toronto: University of Toronto Press, 1975), pp. 87-92.

7. See Siegfried H. Horn, "New Light on Nebuchadnezzar's Madness," *Ministry*, April 1978, pp. 39, 40.

Daniel 5
God Writes on a Wall

Introduction

On October 12, 539 B.C., Belshazzar, king of Babylon, staged a banquet to which he invited a thousand civic leaders with their wives and mistresses.[1] Wine flowed, spirits rose, and realities became blurred.

The realities were grim.

In the twenty-three years since the death of Nebuchadnezzar, Babylon had fallen a long way from its golden age.

Nebuchadnezzar had been succeeded by a series of incompetent rulers. His son, Evil-Merodach (see Jeremiah 52:31), hadn't amounted to much and had been assassinated by his brother-in-law after only two years on the throne. The brother-in-law had died four years later, leaving a minor son. Conspirators had then assassinated the boy king and appointed one of themselves, Nabonidus (Nab-uh-NYE-dus), as his successor.

Six years later, King Nabonidus had transferred his headquarters from Babylon to the distant oasis of Tema in Arabia. He had "entrusted the kingship to his son," Belshazzar,[2] and devoted himself avidly to the worship of the moon god, Sin, instead of to the Babylonian patron god, Marduk.

(In choosing to worship Sin, Nabonidus had been influenced by his mother, or grandmother, a high priestess of that deity. This amazing woman lived to the exceptional age of 107! At 104 she is reported to have said, in a cuneiform inscription, "My eyesight *was keen, my hearing excellent, . . . food and drink agreed with me.*"[3])

For ten years Nabonidus had failed—by reason of his absence—to celebrate the popular New Year's Festival in Babylon. Further, during his reign he had required even high-class Babylonians to work for the state in labor gangs. At the same time financial recession had led to a general state of disrepair at the capital. Nabonidus had become highly unpopular.

Meanwhile, Cyrus the Great, the Persian king, had begun his astonishing rise. He had taken over the kingdom of Media and added Lydia in the far west. Nabonidus, evidently alarmed at the buildup of Persian power, had returned from Tema to Babylon in 540. In a bid for popularity at the capital, he had celebrated the New Year's Festival in fine style and collected gods and goddesses from several outlying cities. But he hadn't been able to refrain from arguing theology with the leading priests, and anyway it was too late to restore his popular support.

When he met the forces of Cyrus at Opis, 185 kilometers (115 miles) north of Babylon, his own people there had rebelled against him. On October 10, 539 B.C., Nabonidus had surrendered Sippar, 80 kilometers (50 miles) north

of Babylon, without a fight and fled south to Borsippa. Meantime, a military detachment led by Darius the Mede had proceeded rapidly south and arrived at the walls of Babylon.

These, then, were the grim realities attending Belshazzar's feast: the empire virtually lost, Nabonidus in hiding, the enemy at the gates.

But why worry? The walls of Babylon were tall and stout. Its storehouses bulged with food. The Euphrates flowed with water. Any enemy would give up a blockade long before the city surrendered. Babylon was undefeatable.

Just as the *Titanic* was unsinkable.

As the wine took effect, Belshazzar blasphemously ordered his butlers to bring out the sacred utensils which Nebuchadnezzar had removed from the temple in Jerusalem long years before. And while the banqueters drank toasts to their idols out of cups dedicated to the Lord, a mysterious hand began to trace flaming letters on the plaster—the famous "handwriting on the wall."

Wild with fear, shaking like a reed, Belshazzar struggled to clear his brain and focus his eyes. The message was menacing—of that he was certain—but *what* was it? His voice sounded hollow, strange even to himself, as he yelled for someone to summon the wise men.

Time dragged as the wise men were rounded up and herded in. The king made a lavish offer of promotion to **"third ruler in the kingdom"** to anyone who could give the interpretation (see page 92). But in vain. No one could even read the writing, let alone interpret it.

At that point the queen entered the hall. Since Belshazzar's wives were already present, the "queen" in this case must have been the queen mother, a person of great respect in ancient times. Her suggestion was that Belshazzar send for the prophet Daniel.

Belshazzar agreed, and time hung heavy once more as a runner sprinted to Daniel's home. Effects of the alcohol subsided, minds began to clear, and in due course the grand old prophet came striding in. Though Daniel was in his eighties, we have no trouble imagining his **"radiant appearance"** (Daniel 10:8)—the relative smoothness of his skin, the spring in his step, the ring in his voice. What a contrast he made to the debauchery that surrounded him! How thankful to God he must have been that in his youth he had resolved not to eat or drink unhealthfully!

Daniel omitted the customary salutation, "O king, live forever!" It seemed pointless in view of Belshazzar's imminent death. He was not discourteous to the wayward monarch, but he spoke to the point. In front of the assembled guests and leaders of the nation, he reminded the king of the judgment which had fallen on Nebuchadnezzar on account of *his* pride; how his mind had become like that of an animal until he confessed that the most high God rules in the kingdom of men. These sober words followed: **"And you his son, Belshazzar, have not humbled your heart,** *though you knew all this,* **but you have lifted up yourself against the Lord of heaven"** and drunk out of His sacred vessels. Daniel 5:21-23.

The "handwriting on the wall" still lingered, glowing like a neon sign. **"MENE, MENE, TEKEL, and PARSIN,"** Daniel read, easily enough. He paused before giving the interpretation.

"MENE," he read again. **"God has**

77

While Babylonian banqueters reveled, a mysterious hand wrote the message of doom on the royal wall.

numbered the days of your kingdom and brought it to an end; TEKEL, you have been weighed in the balances and found wanting; PERES, your kingdom is divided and given to the Medes and Persians." Verses 26, 27.

(In Aramaic "Mene" means "counted" or "numbered." "Tekel" means "weighed." "Parsin" is the plural for "peres," which in the singular means "divided" but in the plural is also the spelling for "Persians.")

It seems almost grotesque under the circumstances, but Belshazzar was as good as his word. He had his aides slip a purple robe over Daniel's shoulders, hang a golden ornament of office around his neck, and proclaim him the **"third ruler"** in a kingdom that had only moments left to run.

The river Euphrates normally flowed low in October. Two ancient historians, Herodotus and Xenophon, both inform us that on the night of this fatal feast the enemy lowered the water further by temporarily diverting it. Soldiers waded through the knee-high stream, discovered the river gates still open, gained access to the streets, and slew the unsuspecting guards.

"That very night Belshazzar the Chaldean king was slain." Daniel 5:30.

Two and a half weeks later, Cyrus the Great led the main body of his troops into the city in peace, while joyous crowds symbolically tossed leafy twigs in his path. (The Jews would welcome Christ the same way when He entered Jerusalem, 569 years later.) True to prophecy, the head of gold gave way to the breast and arms of silver.

You have heard all your life about "the handwriting on the wall." You have known that it warned of a sudden end to extravagant times. Now you can read the original account of it for yourself in the Bible.

CHAPTER 5

1 King Belshazzar made a great feast for a thousand of his lords, and drank wine in front of the thousand.

2 Belshazzar, when he tasted the wine, commanded that the vessels of gold and of silver which Nebuchadnezzar his father had taken out of the temple in Jerusalem be brought, that the king and his lords, his wives, and his concubines might drink from them. 3 Then they brought in the golden and silver vessels which had been taken out of the temple, the house of God in Jerusalem; and the king and his lords, his wives, and his concubines drank from them. 4 They drank wine, and praised the gods of gold and silver, bronze, iron, wood, and stone.

5 Immediately the fingers of a man's hand appeared and wrote on the plaster of the wall of the king's palace, opposite the lampstand; and the king saw the hand as it wrote. 6 Then the king's color changed, and his thoughts alarmed him; his limbs gave way, and his knees knocked together. 7 The king cried aloud to bring in the enchanters, the Chaldeans, and the astrologers. The king said to the wise men of Babylon, "Whoever reads this writing, and shows me its interpretation, shall be clothed with purple, and have a chain of gold about his neck, and shall be the third ruler in the kingdom." 8 Then all the king's wise men came in, but they could not read the writing or make known to the king the interpretation. 9 Then King Belshazzar was greatly alarmed, and his color changed; and his lords were perplexed.

10 The queen, because of the words of the king and his lords, came into the banqueting hall; and the queen said, "O king, live for ever! Let not your thoughts alarm you or your color change. 11 There is in your kingdom a man in whom is the spirit of the holy gods. In the days of your father light and understanding and wisdom, like the wisdom of the gods, were found in him, and King Nebuchadnezzar, your father, made him chief of the magicians, enchant-ers, Chaldeans, and astrologers, 12 because an excellent spirit, knowledge, and understanding to interpret dreams, explain riddles, and solve problems were found in this Daniel, whom the king named Belteshazzar. Now let Daniel be called, and he will show the interpretation."

13 Then Daniel was brought in before the king. The king said to Daniel, "You are that Daniel, one of the exiles of Judah, whom the king my father brought from Judah. 14 I have heard of you that the spirit of the holy gods is in you, and that light and understanding and excellent wisdom are found in you. 15 Now the wise men, the enchanters, have been brought in before me to read this writing and make known to me its interpretation; but they could not show the interpretation of the matter. 16 But I have heard that you can give interpretations and solve problems. Now if you can read the writing and make known to me its interpretation, you shall be clothed with purple, and have a chain of gold about your neck, and shall be the third ruler in the kingdom."

17 Then Daniel answered before the king, "Let your gifts be for yourself, and give your rewards to another; nevertheless I will read the writing to the king and make known to him the interpretation. 18 O king, the Most High God gave Nebuchadnezzar your father kingship and greatness and glory and majesty; 19 and because of the greatness that he gave him, all peoples, nations, and languages trembled and feared before him; whom he would he slew, and whom he would he kept alive; whom he would he raised up, and whom he would he put down. 20 But when his heart was lifted up and his spirit was hardened so that he dealt proudly, he was deposed from his kingly throne, and his glory was taken from him; 21 he was driven from among men, and his mind was made like that of a beast, and his dwelling was with the wild asses; he was fed grass like an ox, and his body was wet with the dew of heaven, until he knew that the Most High God rules the kingdom of men, and sets over it whom he will. 22 And you his son, Belshazzar, have not humbled

your heart, though you knew all this, ²³ but you have lifted up yourself against the Lord of heaven; and the vessels of his house have been brought in before you, and you and your lords, your wives, and your concubines have drunk wine from them; and you have praised the gods of silver and gold, of bronze, iron, wood, and stone, which do not see or hear or know, but the God in whose hand is your breath, and whose are all your ways, you have not honored.

24 "Then from his presence the hand was sent, and this writing was inscribed. ²⁵ And this is the writing that was inscribed: MENE, MENE, TEKEL, and PARSIN.

²⁶ This is the interpretation of the matter: MENE, God has numbered the days of your kingdom and brought it to an end; ²⁷ TEKEL, you have been weighed in the balances and found wanting; ²⁸ PERES, your kingdom is divided and given to the Medes and Persians."

29 Then Belshazzar commanded, and Daniel was clothed with purple, a chain of gold was put about his neck, and proclamation was made concerning him, that he should be the third ruler in the kingdom.

30 That very night Belshazzar the Chaldean king was slain. ³¹ And Darius the Mede received the kingdom, being about sixty-two years old.

The Message of Daniel 5

I. God and the Fall of Babylon

The fall of Babylon is of great importance to our understanding of the overall message of Daniel and Revelation. Two aspects in particular demand our attention: (1) The fall of *symbolic* Babylon is one of the leading themes in the book of Revelation. It is associated there with soon-to-be-fulfilled prophecies strikingly parallel to prophecies about the fall of literal Babylon. (2) The *perfect fulfillment* of the prophecies about the fall of *literal* Babylon helps confirm our confidence in the prophecies about the imminent fall of *symbolic* Babylon.

Parallels. You will certainly want to pause at this point and at least glance over Isaiah, chapters 41, 46, and 47; Jeremiah, chapters 50 and 51; and Revelation, chapters 16 to 19. We shall study these chapters more fully when we get to Revelation, but for a few moments now you will be struck by numerous parallels in the chart below:

Ancient, literal Babylon	Symbolic Babylon
"You who dwell by many waters." Jeremiah 51:13	"Seated upon many waters." Revelation 17:1
"A golden cup in the Lord's hand." Jeremiah 51:7	Holds "a golden cup." Revelation 17:4
"Babylon has fallen." Jeremiah 51:8	"Fallen, fallen is Babylon." Revelation 14:8
"I shall be mistress forever. . . . I shall not sit as a widow." Isaiah 47:7, 8	"A queen I sit, I am no widow." Revelation 18:7
"Go out of the midst of her, my people." Jeremiah 51:45	"Come out of her, my people." Revelation 18:4
At her fall "the heavens and the earth . . . shall sing for joy." Jeremiah 51:48	At her fall, "heaven, . . . saints and apostles and prophets" rejoice. Revelation 18:20
As a stone, "shall Babylon sink, and rise no more." Jeremiah 51:64	"Like a great millstone [thrown] . . . into the sea, . . . so shall Babylon . . . be thrown down." Revelation 18:21

It is noteworthy that the final fall of both Babylons makes the universe very happy. "The heavens and the earth, and all that is in them, shall sing for joy," says Jeremiah 51:48, referring to the ruin of literal Babylon. "Rejoice over her, O heaven," says Revelation 18:20, in reference to the demise of spiritual Babylon.

God, of course, has "no pleasure in the death of the wicked" as such. Ezekiel 33:11. But the God who loves everybody certainly loves His faithful followers when they are persecuted. God seeks to convert persecutors. How hard He worked to win Nebuchadnezzar! He worked for all the Babylonians. "We would have healed Babylon," Jeremiah 51:9 reports, then adds sadly, "but she was not healed." The Jewish people experienced a rebirth in Babylon. They gave up idol worship forever and for the first time established synagogues, where they taught their children and their non-Jewish visitors about the true God. But the Babylonians as a whole rejected the truth about the true God and in various ways, at times, oppressed those who believed in Him. If cruel people persist in oppressing innocent people, then when the time comes that the oppressors are removed, God rejoices—on behalf of the oppressed.

Complete Prophetic Fulfillment. We must note another striking parallel between the two Babylons. In Revelation 18:21 a mighty angel takes up a stone like a great millstone and throws it into the sea, saying, "So shall Babylon the great [spiritual] city be thrown down with violence, and shall be found no more." In Jeremiah 51:59-64, the prophet instructs Seraiah to tie a stone to a scroll, pitch it into the Euphrates, and cry out, "Thus shall [literal] Babylon sink, to rise no more."

The instruction about the scroll and the stone was given to Seraiah by Jeremiah in the fourth year of King Zedekiah's reign, 594/593 B.C. Zedekiah made a trip to Babylon that year, possibly in connection with the dedication of the golden image of Daniel 3. Seraiah accompanied him.

It is easy to imagine the scene at the riverside. Seraiah, we may suppose, had taken his stand near a river gate, where a street ended at a ferry. A cluster of Jews huddled around him. He unrolled Jeremiah's scroll and began to read the message recorded in chapters 50 and 51.

> The word which the Lord spoke concerning Babylon . . . by Jeremiah the prophet. (50:1)
>
> Behold, I am stirring up and bringing against Babylon a company of great nations, from the north country; and they shall array themselves against her. (50:9)
>
> Lo, she shall be the last of the nations,
>   a wilderness dry and desert.
> Because of the wrath of the Lord she shall not be inhabited,
>   but shall be an utter desolation;
> Every one who passes by Babylon shall be appalled,
>   and hiss because of all her wounds. . . .
> For she has sinned against the Lord. (50:12-14)

I will dry up her sea
    and make her fountain dry;
and Babylon shall become a heap of ruins, . . .
    without inhabitant. (51:36, 37)

Wild beasts shall dwell with hyenas in Babylon,
    and ostriches shall dwell in her;
she shall be peopled no more for ever,
    nor inhabited for all generations. (50:39)

Local people, hearing Seraiah's voice and noticing the crowd, joined the group while waiting for the ferry. Children pressed between their parents' legs for a better view. A guard stepped up. But the message was in Hebrew, and he could not understand it.

Seraiah completed the scroll. He tied a stone to it and with a great sweep of his arm hurled it into the air. It splashed into the Euphrates and disappeared, leaving a bubble or two.

But how could such a prophecy be fulfilled? How could Babylon become "the last of nations," "an utter desolation," "a heap of ruins"? How could anyone dare predict that the time would come when Babylon would be "peopled no more for ever, nor inhabited for all generations"? Even as the little knot of friends

moved back through the river gate into the city, all evidence seemed against such a forlorn destiny. Workers were busy everywhere with state and private construction projects. Donkeys and oxen labored with carts loaded with building supplies. In the evening the smoke from scores of brick kilns lay heavy on the air.

Babylon, as we have seen, grew more and more beautiful, its fortifications more stout and tall, its population more numerous as the years passed. A bridge resting on imported stone piers was built across the Euphrates. Palace was added to palace, wall to wall, temple to temple.

When the Medes and Persians conquered Babylon in 539 B.C., fifty-five years after Seraiah read Jeremiah's prophecy, Cyrus actually improved the city's defenses and attempted to complete some of the architectural projects that even Nebuchadnezzar had been unable to finish. Although Cyrus retained Susa as the Persian capital (see Esther 2:8), he made Babylon a secondary capital; and it continued to be prestigious, splendid, and populated.

Approximately another sixty years passed. The citizens of Babylon rebelled against the Persians—and the Persian Emperor, Xerxes, crushed their revolt ruthlessly. He demolished the palaces and the temples and the strong outer walls, reducing them to vast piles of disorganized bricks and broken rubble! Babylon began to become "heaps." But it continued to be inhabited.

Another hundred and fifty years passed, and Alexander the Great appeared, dashing from victory to victory. He conquered the Persians with consummate skill and valor, swept eastward to take in northern India, then turned west with the purpose, it is said, of continuing as far as Spain. He paused to rest at Babylon in 323 B.C. Legendary Babylon! What more appropriate site could he select for the capital of his vast east-west empire?

At once Alexander set 10,000 men to the task of removing the ruins of Etemenanki with the intention of rebuilding that 100 meter (300 foot) "tower of Babel." A cuneiform receipt for wages paid to the laborers has been unearthed. Alexander wanted to restore Babylon's brilliance as a religious center. He also planned that Babylon should be a naval base, the center for all maritime trade with India and (using a canal between the Red Sea and the Nile) for the Mediterranean basin as well. His men began to dredge a harbor at Babylon large enough for a thousand ships. Orders went to Phoenicia for ships to be constructed in sections, carried overland to the Euphrates, assembled, and floated down.

Where now was the word of the Lord through Jeremiah, prophesying dry heaps and an uninhabited wilderness?

Ah, but Alexander too was no match for the Lord of prophecy! The youthful emperor fell ill and died in Babylon in that same year, 323 B.C. He conquered the world by the time he was thirty-two, but he could not rebuild a city that God foresaw would become desolate.

Alexander's generals divided his empire. Seleucus Nicator, one of the generals, chose to rebuild Opis instead, some 185 kilometers (115 miles) to the north, and to rename it Seleucia after himself. He dragged many of the population and millions of bricks from Babylon to help build this new capital, and Babylon sank further into obscurity.

By the time of Jesus, three centuries later, Babylon was a ghost town—gaunt and forsaken—just as God through Jeremiah had said it would be.

In the Middle Ages many of the area's dams and canals were destroyed, decommissioning the irrigation system and thus literally drying up the waters of Babylon.

And Babylon has never been reinhabited. Seraiah had read: "She shall be peopled no more for ever, nor inhabited for all generations." Jeremiah 50:39.

I have visited Babylon twice. I have seen what is left of its mighty gateways, of its celebrated hanging gardens, and of its silent banquet hall—17 by 53 meters (56 by 174 feet)—where Belshazzar is believed to have feasted his thousand lords. Babylon is indeed a dreary place—dry, drab, dusty, and *dead*.

Archaeologists have laboriously unearthed from the rubble heaps a few of the ruined buildings of once-prosperous Babylon. Notice the decorations of bulls in relief alternating with dragonlike figures. These walls were once covered with glazed bricks of various colors.

It is sad that it should be so; but I can tell you this, that the sight of its uninhabited heaps of ruin can pump vigor and resolution into the blood of anyone, young or old, who believes in Bible prophecy. Every one of its millions of abandoned bricks reconfirms confidence in the messages of Daniel and Revelation.

To date, the prophecies about literal Babylon have met with marvelous fulfillment. So too, we shall find, have many of the prophecies about symbolic Babylon. We can be absolutely certain that the remaining prophecies will be completely fulfilled. Very likely we and our families will see them fulfilled within our lifetimes.

II. God and the Judgment of Belshazzar

What were you doing on the night of October 12, 539 B.C.? The question seems foolish. But it wouldn't be foolish—if it were addressed to God!

The books of Daniel and Revelation help us realize that the God who cares for us today is eternal. He is the same God who, on October 12, 539 B.C., sent an angel to write on the walls of Belshazzar's dining room.

One of the great messages of these books is that this great, kind, *ever-living* God respects us enough to treat us as responsible individuals.

God is well aware of our weakness. "He knows our frame; he remembers that we are dust." Psalm 103:14. He protects us for a time from the consequence of many of our mistakes. He provides persuasive evidence to help us choose the way

During a banquet on October 12, 539 B.C., God wrote on a wall the imminent fate of golden Babylon.

of happiness and success. But as a clear demonstration of His respect for us, He leaves us free—free to obey Him or to disobey Him as we please. And in the judgment—since we are responsible individuals—He permits us to meet the ultimate consequence of our choices, whether good or bad. It is of utmost importance that we recognize that God does not arbitrarily decide our destiny or arbitrarily impose punishment.

Centuries prior to the days of Daniel, grand old Joshua, after a lifetime in God's service as a statesman and general, expressed God's attitude about our freedom in these famous words: "And if you be unwilling to serve the Lord, choose this day whom you will serve, whether the gods your fathers served in the region beyond the River, or the gods of the Amorites in whose land you dwell; but as for me and my house, we will serve the Lord." Joshua 24:15.

King Belshazzar of Babylon made his life choices. Later God **"weighed"** these choices to see how they measured up. In the judgment of October 12, 539 B.C., Belshazzar's choices were found **"wanting"** or deficient, and God **"gave up"** Belshazzar to their natural consequences.

Belshazzar's choices were the more serious because they were made against the light of considerable truth. Daniel reminded Belshazzar that he had known all about Nebuchadnezzar's experience, but, Daniel went on, **"You his son, Belshazzar, have not humbled your heart,** *though you knew all this."* Daniel 5:22. Nebuchadnezzar had been to some extent excusable for his pride. In his formal public inscriptions he had frequently given his gods the credit for his successes, but he had not realized that God requires sincere, heartfelt humility. God took Nebuchadnezzar's ignorance into account and sent Daniel to warn him. Then He led the king through a strange mental disease to humility and repentance. Belshazzar, however, had no excuse. He knew all about Nebuchadnezzar's illness. He knew perfectly well that pride is wicked and boasting is blasphemous. Even so he chose to sin.

God treated Belshazzar as a responsible individual in several ways. First, He allowed him to make his own choices. Second, He allowed him at last to suffer the consequence of his free choice by removing His special protection from him. Reluctantly God "gave him up" to the power of his enemies. God would much rather, we can be sure, have protected Belshazzar from the Medes and Persians just as a few months later He would protect Daniel, when the Medes and Persians lowered him into a lions' den. But Belshazzar didn't want God in his life, and God respected his decision by stepping aside.

A third way God treated Belshazzar as a responsible individual was by "giving him up" during his later years to the deepening addiction of his own bad habits. In Romans 1:18-32 the apostle Paul reveals God's attitude to everyone who chooses to live as Belshazzar did:

> The wrath of God is revealed from heaven against all ungodliness and wickedness of men who by their wickedness *suppress the truth.* . . .
> *They are without excuse;* for *although they knew God* they did not honor

him as God or give thanks to him, but they became futile in their thinking and their senseless minds were darkened. Claiming to be wise, they became fools, and exchanged the glory of the immortal God for images resembling mortal man or birds or animals or reptiles.

Therefore God *gave them up* in the lusts of their hearts to impurity, to the dishonoring of their bodies among themselves, because they exchanged the truth about God for a lie and worshiped and served the creature rather than the Creator, who is blessed forever! Amen.

For this reason God *gave them up* to dishonorable passions. . . .

And since they did not see fit to acknowledge God, God *gave them up* to a base mind and to improper conduct. . . . Full of envy, murder, strife, deceit, malignity, they are gossips, slanderers, haters of God, insolent, haughty, boastful, inventors of evil, disobedient to parents. . . . *Though they know God's decree* that those who do such things deserve to die, they not only do them but approve those who practice them.

Daniel, clear of mind and eye, reprimanded the alcohol-addled king of Babylon for desecrating the sacred vessels which Nebuchadnezzar had carried away from the temple in Jerusalem. In desecrating these vessels in the way he did, by drinking alcoholic beverages from them, Belshazzar became guilty of profaning not only the Jerusalem temple but also his own "body temple."

First Corinthians 6:19, 20 says: "Do you not know that your body is a temple of the Holy Spirit within you, which you have from God? You are not your own; you were bought with a price. So glorify God in your body." A somewhat parallel passage, 1 Corinthians 3:16, 17, reads: "Do you not know that you are God's temple, and that God's Spirit dwells in you? If any one destroys God's temple, God will destroy him. For God's temple is holy, and that temple are you."

God was not living inside Belshazzar on October 12, 539 B.C. Belshazzar's body was a violated, desecrated, blasphemed, empty temple of God. It was so, because Belshazzar chose to ignore God as much as he could and to use his living temple for gluttony and intemperance instead of for holy purposes as directed by the Holy Spirit. And God, reluctantly, "gave him up" to his "dishonorable passions."

How sad it is to read that in the United States beer drinking has to race to keep ahead of the rapid increase in wine drinking; and that respectable, thrifty mothers manufacture wine at home so that their families—including their own little Belshazzars—can have more to drink at less expense.

On October 12, 539 B.C., God in an act of judgment decreed that King Belshazzar should be permitted to meet the final consequences of his free choices. Who knows what date it will be when you read these lines? Whatever it is, *you* can still claim the words of 2 Corinthians 6:2, "Behold, now is the acceptable time; behold now is the day of salvation."

If you are tired of turning your back on truth that could change your life for the better; if you know you are desecrating your body temple by some unhealthful habit; if you are setting a wrong example before your family; if you are worshiping idols of silver coins and greenbacks; if you are hurting yourself and others by holding grudges or by being inconsiderate and selfish; if you have weighed yourself in the balances and found yourself deficient; and if you regret all these things and want to be different—then remember that God loves and respects you! He sent His Son to die for you. He will do everything in reason and love to help you. He is more than eager to forgive if you repent. "Behold, now is the day of salvation."

Thank God that we are still living in the kingdom of grace! The kingdom of glory is just ahead.

If you would like to, why not bow your head where you are sitting and offer to God this prayer:

"Dear God, I know I have done wrong. Please forgive me.

"You know I want to be a better, kinder, stronger person. Please help me.

"I believe You love me.

"I believe You accept me as Your child, now and for ever.

"Thank You, God!

"Amen."

Further Interesting Reading

In Arthur S. Maxwell, *The Bible Story,* vol. 6:
     "Writing on the Wall," beginning on p. 49.
In Arthur S. Maxwell, *Your Bible and You:*
     "The God Your Bible Reveals," beginning on p. 77.
In Ellen G. White, *Prophets and Kings:*
     "The Unseen Watcher," beginning on p. 522.

5

GOD CARES

Your Questions Answered

1. Was Nebuchadnezzar really Belshazzar's "father"? The introduction to this chapter on Daniel 5 states that Nabonidus was Belshazzar's father; yet Daniel 5:11 and 18 refer to Nebuchadnezzar as his father and 5:22 calls Belshazzar the son of Nebuchadnezzar rather than the son of Nabonidus. How can this be?

Several simple explanations can be offered.

a. In Bible times the words "father" and "son" were often used to denote *character* relationship even where no genealogical relationship existed. For example, Paul referred to Abraham as "the *father*" of everyone who believes in Jesus. Romans 4:16. Jesus said to men who were filled with a devilish spirit, "You are of your *father* the devil." John 8:44. Conversely, troublemakers were often called *"sons of Belial,"* a phrase in which "Belial" was a personification of wickedness. The idiom was common. First Samuel 2:12, K.J.V., for instance, says that "the sons of Eli [their actual father] were sons of Belial [their character father]." It is possible that Belshazzar was called a "son" of Nebuchadnezzar because both men were characterized by extraordinary pride.

b. Bible writers often used "father" and "son" for persons who, though genealogically related, were separated by more than a single generation. Jesus was called the "Son of David" even though He was separated from King David by twenty-eight generations (see Matthew 9:27; 1:17)!

Some evidence suggests that Belshazzar's long-lived grandmother served at some time as an honored wife in Nebuchadnezzar's harem, thereby making Belshazzar at least a step-grandson of Nebuchadnezzar's. In that case Belshazzar would easily have been known as Nebuchadnezzar's son.

c. There is a third possible explanation. "Son" in ancient times could mean "successor on the throne." An Assyrian inscription refers to the Israelite King Jehu as the "son of Omri," even though he and King Omri, his predecessor on the throne more than thirty years earlier, were entirely unrelated. Belshazzar was a sometime successor to Nebuchadnezzar.

2. Was Belshazzar really king of Babylon? Critics used to emphasize that the name of Belshazzar was unknown outside the Bible. They concluded with some triumph that King Belshazzar was only a fictional character and that the entire book of Daniel was unreliable.

To the chagrin of such critics, W. H. F. Talbot in 1861 published the translation of a cuneiform prayer offered by Nabonidus in which the king asked his god to bless his son *Belshazzar!*[4]

Reluctantly, the critics conceded that there must have been a Belshazzar after all; but in their hesitance to accept the book of Daniel as authentic history, some of them have continued to insist that outside the Bible Belshazzar is nowhere called "king."

However, additional cuneiform records found over the years since Talbot's time do link Belshazzar's name with that of Nabonidus, or use his name alone, in formulas where only a king's name usually occurs. These records include prayers, oaths, astrological reports, and a receipt for royal tribute.[5]

Of greatest interest is the so-called Verse Account of Nabonidus (British Museum tablet 38,299), first translated and published by Sidney Smith in 1924.[6] This official historical document attests that as Nabonidus left Babylon to go to Tema,

> He entrusted the "Camp" to his oldest (son), the first-born,
> The troops everywhere in the country he ordered under his (command).
> He let (everything) go, entrusted the kingship to him
> And, himself, he started out for a long journey.

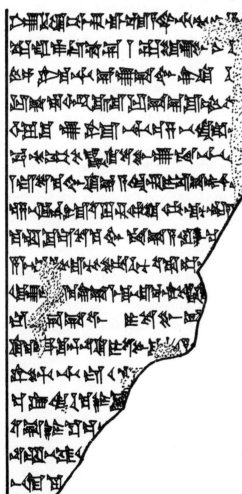

Lines 18-21 of the second column of the Verse Account of Nabonidus, preserved on British Museum Tablet 38,299, indicate that Belshazzar did serve as king of Babylon, in harmony with Daniel 5.

Credit: Sidney Smith, *Babylonian Historical Texts Relating to the Capture and Downfall of Babylon* (London: Methuen & Co., Ltd, 1924), plate VII.

It is the key phrase "entrusted the kingship to him" that deserves special attention. A modern critic like Norman W. Porteous now admits that Belshazzar at least served "as regent of Babylon." [7] A "regent" of course has much of the authority of a king. And in the Bible there are numerous accounts of kings who ruled together as coregents.[8]

When Belshazzar offered to make Daniel "third" in the kingdom, he evidently intended that Daniel would be third in command after Nabonidus, who was the principal king, and after himself (Belshazzar), the coregent who had been "entrusted" with "the kingship" when Nabonidus had left the capital for Tema.

There is further fascinating confirmation of Belshazzar's kingship. Both Herodotus, in *The Persian Wars* 1.191, and Xenophon, in his *Cyropaedia* 7.5.15, say (as Daniel does) that a banquet was in progress on the night when Babylon fell. Xenophon adds that at that feast the *king* of Babylon was killed. Now the cuneiform "Nabonidus Chronicle"[9] makes it plain that King Nabonidus was not then in Babylon; he was hiding at Borsippa and was arrested later when he returned to Babylon and submitted to the Medes and Persians. So if there was a king in Babylon on the night when it fell, and if the king was not Nabonidus, then who was he? King Belshazzar, of course!

William H. Shea, in a recent analysis,[10] suggests that Belshazzar may actually have been fully king for only a few days or even only a few hours prior to his death. Shea reminds us that it was a custom sometimes observed in ancient times for a king who was leaving with his army for a doubtful battle to appoint his son king in order to provide a clear successor in the event of his death. Herodotus says that Cyrus the Great did this for his son Cambyses. It is possible, therefore, that Nabonidus did it for Belshazzar before going north to fight Cyrus. Or again Belshazzar may have declared himself king. When an earlier king of Babylon, Hammurabi, fell ill, his son Samsuiluna proclaimed himself king so as to maintain order.[11]

So when Belshazzar learned that his father had been defeated and was in flight, he may have decided that to maintain order in the capital, it would be best if he declared himself fully king. In this light the banquet of October 12, 539 B.C., may be viewed as a celebration of his new royal status. Regardless of how he came to the throne, Belshazzar is called "king" seventeen times in Daniel 5!

References

1. The precise date of the entry of Darius into Babylon is given in the *Nabonidus Chronicle* as "the 16th day," that is, of the month Tishri. See James B. Pritchard ed., *Ancient Near Eastern Texts Relating to the Old Testament*, 2d ed. (Princeton: Princeton University Press, 1955), p. 306. That this date, within a maximum error of one day, is the equivalent of October 12, 539 B.C., is shown in Richard A. Parker and Waldo H. Dubberstein, *Babylonian Chronology, 626 B.C.-A.D. 75* (Providence, R.I.: Brown University Press, 1956), p. 29. The dates in Parker and Dubberstein commence at midnight, in

harmony with modern usage, but in Babylon in Bible times the day was conceived as commencing at sunset. If Darius entered the city before midnight on the 16th of Tishri, he entered on what we would today call October 11.

2. The Verse Account of Nabonidus (British Museum tablet 38,299) as trans. in Pritchard, *Texts,* p. 313.

3. The Stele of Nabonidus, erected in memory of his (grand?)mother, in Pritchard, *Texts,* p. 312.

4. H. Fox Talbot, "Translation of Some Assyrian Inscriptions," *Journal of the Royal Asiatic Society* 18 (1861):195.

5. See esp. the famous work by Raymond Dougherty, *Nabonidus and Belshazzar* (New Haven: Yale University Press, 1929).

6. Pritchard, *Texts,* p. 313.

7. Norman W. Porteous, *Daniel: A Commentary,* ed. G. Ernest Wright, et al., The Old Testament Library (Philadelphia: The Westminster Press, 1965), p. 76.

8. The evidence that pairs of kings ruled together as coregents escapes the ordinary reader but can be ascertained by careful study of chronological statements. Thus, for example, Asa and Jehoshaphat are seen to have been coregents for a time by studying 1 Kings 22:41, 42 and 2 Kings 8:16. Jehoshaphat was also coregent with Jehoram for a while (see 2 Kings 1:17; 3:1).

9. Pritchard, *Texts,* p. 306.

10. William H. Shea, "Daniel in Babylon" (research paper, Andrews University, 1978).

11. See A. L. Oppenheim, *Ancient Mesopotamia: Portrait of a Dead Civilization* (Chicago: University of Chicago Press, 1964), p. 157.

Daniel 6
God and the Lions' Den

Introduction

Daniel in the lions' den is one of the best-known stories in the Bible. Here we call it "*God* and the Lions' Den" to remind ourselves that the God who delivered Daniel from the lions still lives to rescue us in life's perplexities.

The proclamation issued by King Darius at the end of the story encapsulates the message of Daniel as a whole:

> **He is the living God, enduring for ever;**
> **his kingdom shall never be destroyed,**
> **and his dominion shall be to the end.**
> **He delivers and rescues,**
> **he works signs and wonders in heaven and on earth,**
> **who has saved Daniel from the power of the lions.**
> **Daniel 6:26, 27.**

The relevance of the story to our needs today is focused in Peter's warning: "Your adversary the devil prowls around like a roaring lion, seeking some one to devour." 1 Peter 5:8. The person who fixes his faith on God can be as safe from Satan's temptations as Daniel was from the lions, because the same God still lives. Our God is **"the living God, enduring for ever."**

You are eager to read the story! A few observations in advance, however, may aid your understanding.

Daniel 6 indicates that Darius, the new king of Babylon, appointed a staff of 120 satraps (governors) and three presidents, of whom Daniel was the chairman, to administer the affairs of the province. The story seems to imply that all of the 120 satraps and the two other presidents spied on Daniel while he prayed, and that all 122 of them were later thrown into the lions' den, along with all of their wives and all of their children. Some people have trouble visualizing so many people involved at each stage. But the Bible does not actually state that all 122 satraps and presidents were directly involved. The conspirators among them *claimed* that all the others were involved (see Daniel 6:7). In the final analysis it was only **"those men who had accused Daniel"** (Daniel 6:24) and not the entire 122 who, with their families, were thrown into the den.

The conspirators earned their punishment. We have seen that Belshazzar was rightly condemned because he sinned *even though* he knew about Nebuchadnezzar's experience (see Daniel 5:22). The men who tried to kill Daniel did so *even though* they were well acquainted with his innocence and with his excellent record for nearly seventy years. Like Belshazzar—and like many people who live in our day too—they "refused to love the truth" (see 2 Thessalonians 2:10).

95

Aged Daniel was saved from hungry lions by a caring God.

We deeply regret the fate of their families; nonetheless, it is likely that they did not deserve to live either. When the men talked about Daniel in their homes, their wives and children probably echoed their hostilities and reinforced them. Thus each family member contributed to the father's crime. So it was that Zeresh, Haman's wife, encouraged Haman in his plot to kill Mordecai (see Esther 5:14). So it is that many families today encourage one another to engage in gossip and character cannibalism.

The New Testament calls the tongue of a gossipy person "a restless evil, full of deadly poison." James 3:8. We may think that merely talking about people is a harmless indoor sport, but Jesus said, "I tell you, on the day of judgment men will render account for every careless word they utter; for by your words you will be justified, and by your words you will be condemned." Matthew 12:36, 37.

It seems strange to us that a king would issue a decree requiring everyone to pray only to the king himself for thirty days, but in ancient times kings were frequently treated like gods. This particular decree probably seemed reasonable enough to many people, who interpreted it as a loyalty test designed to unite everyone under the new leader. We recall the dedication of Nebuchadnezzar's golden image in Daniel 3. We need not suppose, however, that Darius's decree was made official in all parts of the Medo-Persian Empire. Darius was king only of Babylon, and Babylon— **"all the earth"** to Darius (Daniel 6:25)—was now only a subkingdom. Cyrus the Great, King of Lands, was ruler of the vast Medo-Persian Empire.

Collections of wild animals were as enjoyable long ago as nowadays. Lions were abundant in Mesopotamia. One Assyrian king claimed to have killed 970 on a single hunt.[1] Lions are mentioned more than a hundred times in the Bible (see especially Judges 14 and 1 Kings 13). Techniques were known for taking animals alive. Modern tranquilizers were not used, of course, but dull arrows were shot at the animals, weakening them or knocking them senseless long enough for brave men to tie them up.[2] Other animals were trapped in deep pits. And, as is well known, lions breed readily in captivity. There is no trouble in visualizing a group of hungry, captive lions.

But how do you visualize the lions' den? Iron was scarce in Babylon, and iron for bars on the lions' cages was unlikely. But a pit deep enough to keep the big animals from jumping out would have made sense—like today's Bear Pit in Berne, Switzerland.

As yet no such lions' den has been excavated in Babylon. The water level in Mesopotamia has risen so much over the centuries that any such deep pit would have been filled in long ago. But in Morocco a den like the one we are talking about was observed by a traveler in the nineteenth century.[3] The hole in the ground was large and square, with a low protective wall around its rim. A partition, with a door in it, divided the pit into two sections. The lions were kept on one side of the partition until that side needed to be cleaned. The keeper then tossed food into the other side, opened the gate from above, waited till the lions moved over to eat the food, closed the gate, and lowered himself into the pit to do his work.

Such an arrangement fits perfectly with the details of Daniel 6, the historical account of "God and the Lions' Den."

CHAPTER 6

1 It pleased Darius to set over the kingdom a hundred and twenty satraps, to be throughout the whole kingdom; ² and over them three presidents, of whom Daniel was one, to whom these satraps should give account, so that the king might suffer no loss. ³ Then this Daniel became distinguished above all the other presidents and satraps, because an excellent spirit was in him; and the king planned to set him over the whole kingdom. ⁴ Then the presidents and the satraps sought to find a ground for complaint against Daniel with regard to the kingdom; but they could find no ground for complaint or any fault, because he was faithful, and no error or fault was found in him. ⁵ Then these men said, "We shall not find any ground for complaint against this Daniel unless we find it in connection with the law of his God."

6 Then these presidents and satraps came by agreement to the king and said to him, "O King Darius, live for ever! ⁷ All the presidents of the kingdom, the prefects and the satraps, the counselors and the governors are agreed that the king should establish an ordinance and enforce an interdict, that whoever makes petition to any god or man for thirty days, except to you, O king, shall be cast into the den of lions. ⁸ Now, O king, establish the interdict and sign the document, so that it cannot be changed, according to the law of the Medes and the Persians, which cannot be revoked." ⁹ Therefore King Darius signed the document and interdict.

10 When Daniel knew that the document had been signed, he went to his house where he had windows in his upper chamber open toward Jerusalem; and he got down upon his knees three times a day and prayed and gave thanks before his God, as he had done previously. ¹¹ Then these men came by agreement and found Daniel making petition and supplication before his God. ¹² Then they came near and said before the king, concerning the interdict, "O king! Did you not sign an interdict, that any man who makes petition to any god or man within thirty days except to you, O king, shall be cast into the den of lions?" The king answered, "The thing stands fast, according to the law of the Medes and Persians, which cannot be revoked." ¹³ Then they answered before the king, "That Daniel, who is one of the exiles from Judah, pays no heed to you, O king, or the interdict you have signed, but makes his petition three times a day."

14 Then the king, when he heard these words, was much distressed, and set his mind to deliver Daniel; and he labored till the sun went down to rescue him. ¹⁵ Then these men came by agreement to the king, and said to the king, "Know, O king, that it is a law of the Medes and Persians that no interdict or ordinance which the king establishes can be changed."

16 Then the king commanded, and Daniel was brought and cast in the den of lions. The king said to Daniel, "May your God, whom you serve continually, deliver you!" ¹⁷ And a stone was brought and laid upon the mouth of the den, and the king sealed it with his own signet and with the signet of his lords, that nothing might be changed concerning Daniel. ¹⁸ Then the king went to his palace, and spent the night fasting; no diversions were brought to him and sleep fled from him.

19 Then, at break of day, the king arose and went in haste to the den of lions. ²⁰ When he came near to the den where Daniel was, he cried out in a tone of anguish and said to Daniel, "O Daniel, servant of the living God, has your God, whom you serve continually, been able to deliver you from the lions?" ²¹ Then Daniel said to the king, "O king, live for ever! ²² My God sent his angel and shut the lions' mouths, and they have not hurt me, because I was found blameless before him; and also before you, O king, I have done no wrong." ²³ Then the king was exceedingly glad, and commanded that Daniel be taken up out of the den. So Daniel was taken up out of the den, and no kind of hurt was found upon him, because he had trusted in his God. ²⁴ And

97

7—G.C.-1

the king commanded, and those men who had accused Daniel were brought and cast into the den of lions—they, their children, and their wives; and before they reached the bottom of the den the lions overpowered them and broke all their bones in pieces.

25 Then King Darius wrote to all the peoples, nations, and languages that dwell in all the earth: "Peace be multiplied to you. 26 I make a decree, that in all my royal dominion men tremble and fear before the God of Daniel,

for he is the living God,
    enduring for ever;
his kingdom shall never be destroyed,
    and his dominion shall be to the end.
27 He delivers and rescues,
    he works signs and wonders
    in heaven and on earth,
he who has saved Daniel
    from the power of the lions."

28 So this Daniel prospered during the reign of Darius and the reign of Cyrus the Persian.

The Message of Daniel 6

I. God Loves the Elderly

Daniel was around eighty-four years old when God delivered him from the hungry lions. God was just as interested in him in his old age as He had been in his youth. We would lose something if we didn't pause to contemplate this fact for a few moments. God loves elderly people.

On this very point, the prophet Isaiah once made a telling comparison between God and the idols of Babylon. Each spring, as a climax to the popular New Year's celebration, Bel and Nebo were conveyed by animal back along Procession Street to the great temple of Esagila. The helpless idols had to be tied onto the animals, and they tottered and bowed as the animals swayed:

> Bel bows down, Nebo stoops,
>> their idols are on beasts and cattle; . . .
>> they stoop, they bow down together.

How different, Isaiah pointed out, is the true God, who, far from being carried on the back of an animal, actually *carries us* all our lives long.

> Hearken to me, O house of Jacob,
>> all the remnant of the house of Israel,
> Who have been borne by me from your birth,
>> carried from the womb;
> Even to your old age I am he,
>> and to gray hairs I will carry you.
> I have made, and I will bear;
>> I will carry and will save. Isaiah 46:1-4.

Time and again as he watched the annual celebration, Daniel must have reflected on these words of Isaiah's. As he advanced in years, the promise must have grown the richer: "Even to your old age I am he, and to gray hairs I will carry you." During the ten years when King Nabonidus lived in Tema, the New Year's celebration was not observed in Babylon. Bel and Nebo, totally helpless, were unable to make the parade even on the backs of animals! But God carries all who believe in Him every year of their lives, from childhood to gray hairs.

It is wonderful that He does so; for all of us, no matter how young we may be, are growing old inexorably. Popular articles report research into causes and cures of the aging process. We read about neuroendocrine mechanisms, dysfunction of the immune system, cross-linkage and free-radical theories, and protein/calorie ratios. And we are compelled to be interested; for all that the thymosin, L-Dopa, tryptophan, synthetic RNA, and proteolytic soil enzymes currently being tested as cures for aging can hope to do is merely to postpone old age. Only the second coming of Christ can eliminate it.

God has not promised eternal health in this life! But He has promised to stand beside us in our old age and give us confidence, a sense of purpose, poise, faith, courage, even "joy unspeakable," whatever comes.

Daniel proved all this and more by his experience in the lions' den.

When we come to the study of Revelation, we shall find that the apostle John was an elderly exile, somewhat like Daniel, when he received his visions. But though John seemed to be alone on the isolated island of Patmos, God was most certainly with him too (see Revelation 1).

"The things that are revealed belong to us and to our children." Deuteronomy 29:29.

If God honors the elderly, it follows that He probably wants everyone else to honor them also, including youth. And so it is. In Leviticus 19:32 He teaches us, "You shall rise up before the hoary head, and honor the face of an old man, and you shall fear your God: I am the Lord."

A "hoary head" is a white or gray head; the term refers to a person with white or gray hair. In the Bible gray hair is called the "beauty," not the disgrace, of old age. Proverbs 20:29. Jesus portrays Himself as having white hair in Revelation 1.

The New English Bible translates Leviticus 19:32 this way: "You shall rise in the presence of grey hairs, give honour to the aged, and fear your God. I am the Lord." Moffatt, in his characteristic style, renders it: "You shall rise up before a man with white hair, and honour the person of an old man, standing in awe of your God: I am the Eternal."

The instruction is emphatic. God signs it by appending to it the phrase, "I am the Lord," "I am the Eternal." It is His way of calling attention to something unusually important.

The fifth commandment says, "Honor your father and your mother." Exodus 20:12. This requirement lays a serious responsibility on all parents and teachers. If children are to honor adults, then adults must teach their children to honor them. This doesn't mean shouting at them to force them to obey. Children constantly shouted at and slapped may seem to obey but inside they do not honor their parents; they hate them. Teaching children to honor their parents involves treating them in such a way that the children will love and respect them and will want to obey them as Christians themselves.

The fifth commandment contains no age limitation. It doesn't say, "Children, honor your parents until you are sixteen, or twenty, or thirty-five." It says, "Honor your father and your mother." The obligation and privilege last throughout life. According to the Bible sons and daughters are to honor their parents even in middle life and in their own old age.

Nor does the commandment say, "Honor your parents if they are nice to you or if they have a lot of money." It bids us simply to honor them. Apparently children of all ages are to live so as to bring honor to their parents at all times.

Jesus, dying in terrible pain on the cross, remembered to arrange with His disciple John to look after His mother the rest of her life. John 19:26, 27.

God wants us to honor *all* old people, not only our parents. "Do not rebuke an older man" says 1 Timothy 5:1. "Give honor to the aged," we read a moment ago; that is, be courteous to all elderly people.

Happy the parents who show their children by example how to honor the aged! As they grow old, such parents will find their children treating them with similar respect. "Train up a child in the way he should go, and when he is old he will not depart from it." Proverbs 22:6.

One of the messages of the book of Daniel is that God loves the elderly. Evidently He wants everyone else to love them and to teach their families to also.

II. Daniel Gave Thanks to God

When Daniel heard about the decree forbidding him to pray to the true God, he did a remarkable thing. He **"got down upon his knees three times a day and prayed and gave thanks before his God, as he had done previously."** Daniel 6:10.

The fact that Daniel prayed under such circumstances is noteworthy, but what impresses us most is that three times a day, as he had done before, he **"gave thanks."**

Confronted by a lions' den, anticipating open jaws and grinding teeth, Daniel gave thanks. Think of it!

Even when threatened with a lions' den, Daniel prayed–and "gave thanks"–as consistently as always.

What do you suppose he gave thanks for?

One can think of many things. Daniel knew many of God's promises. "God is our refuge and strength, a very present help in trouble." Psalm 46:1. "The angel of the Lord encamps around those who fear him, and delivers them." Psalm 34:7.

In addition Daniel could recall a lifetime of experiences and answered prayers. He could thank God for being with him all his eighty-plus years. He could thank Him for helping him, as a youth, to stand true to principle and at the same time to reach the top of his class. He could thank God for giving him the vision of the future that the king forgot, thus saving his own life and the lives of the wise men. He could thank God for delivering his friends from the fiery furnace. Best of all, perhaps, he could thank God for using him as an instrument to lead the mighty Nebuchadnezzar to humble himself before the Lord.

I expect that Daniel's keenest prayer at this moment was that, come what may, God would help him to represent Him so faithfully before Darius that in his old age he would again be an instrument in leading yet another king to accept the Lord.

Incidentally, Daniel 7:1 indicates that Daniel saw the vision of Daniel 7 several years before he faced the lions' den. From that vision he knew for certain that God could vanquish "beasts" so cruel and fearsome that by comparison lions seemed like kittens. Daniel also had full confidence in the day of resurrection. See Daniel 12:1, 2. If the lions ate him, no matter; he would live again.

When we pray, we should do as Daniel did and give thanks. It is best that we not tell God about our problems first. When we do this, our problems grow larger and our faith almost vanishes away. Instead we should begin by quoting some of God's promises, adding, "Lord, I believe You!" Then we should recall some previous answers to prayer and say, "Lord, I thank You!" After we have talked like this for a while, it is safe for us to present our problems, because by then our faith has become stronger and our problems seem more manageable; we are able to pray in faith instead of in doubt. God hears the prayer of faith and answers gloriously.

If you would like to read a magnificent Old Testament prayer like this, followed by a magnificent answer, read 2 Chronicles 20.

So Daniel gave thanks. This was one of his secrets. He gave thanks **"as he had done previously."** It was a habit with him, one of the grandest habits of his whole grand life.

People wonder how the apostle Paul was able to accomplish so much and keep going when everything seemed against him. God delivered Paul from many trials just as he delivered Daniel, but He allowed him to suffer a great many trials as well. Paul could say, "Five times I have received . . . the forty lashes less one. Three times I have been beaten with rods, once I was stoned. Three times I have been shipwrecked; a night and a day I have been adrift at sea," and so on and on. 2 Corinthians 11:24-26.

The secret of Paul's buoyancy was the same as Daniel's. Imprisoned in a dank Roman dungeon he could write to his fellow believers, "Rejoice in the Lord always; again I will say, Rejoice. . . . The Lord is at hand. Have no anxiety about anything, but in everything by prayer and supplication with thanksgiving let your requests be made known to God. And the peace of God, which passes all understanding, will keep your hearts and your minds in Christ Jesus." Philippians 4:4-7.

For years I emphasized a parallel sentence of Paul's: "*In* everything give thanks." 1 Thessalonians 5:18, K.J.V. I could understand that no situation was so bad but what we could find something in it to thank God for. Then I discovered Ephesians 5:20, where Paul says, "*For* everything give thanks"! In order to pray like that, a person must firmly believe that God will make everything, absolutely everything, work out to our good and to His glory. And this is exactly what He promises to do in Romans 8:28.

The Christian religion is a happy one. God pictures Himself as singing over the people who love Him as a bridegroom sings over his bride. Isaiah 62:5. He promises that the redeemed will come to Zion (the heavenly Jerusalem) with singing and that "everlasting joy will be upon their heads." Isaiah 51:11. He is happy if we start being joyful in the time and place where we live now.

Jesus too taught that we should not be anxious, that we shouldn't worry unduly about things. Instead, He said, we should first seek the kingdom and righteousness of God and then trust fully that everything we need will be taken care of (see Matthew 6:25-34).

Further Interesting Reading

In Arthur S. Maxwell, *The Bible Story,* vol. 6:
  "Night with the Lions," beginning on p. 55.
In Ellen G. White, *Prophets and Kings:*
  "In the Lions' Den," beginning on p. 539.
In *Bible Readings for the Home:*
  The chapter entitled "Praise and Thanksgiving."

Your Questions Answered

1. Who was Darius the Mede? Bible critics have pointed out that Darius the Mede (Daniel 5:30) is unknown outside the Bible. They have concluded that Darius the Mede therefore did not exist. In the same way, you remember, the critics concluded quite wrongly years ago that Belshazzar didn't exist because *his* name had not yet been found outside the Bible.

Inasmuch as the critics have been proved wrong about Belshazzar, it seems reasonable to believe them wrong about Darius also. In recent years considerable information has come to light which encourages us to believe fully what the Bible says about Darius the Mede.

a. The clay tablet known as the Nabonidus Chronicle[4] says that the military commander who attacked Babylon on October 12, 539 B.C., was called Gubaru. (His attack occurred about two and a half weeks before Cyrus made his triumphal entry, which took place on October 29.) The ancient novelist-historian Xenophon tells about the special help which a person called Gobryas gave to Cyrus in the conquest of Babylon.[5] Gobryas is the Greek-language equivalent of Gubaru.

b. In the Nabonidus Chronicle, Gubaru (Gobryas) is identified as the governor of Gutium. Xenophon also says that he was a governor.[6] Gutium was a province of Media. Thus Gubaru, like Darius in the Bible, may appropriately be referred to as a Mede.

c. The Nabonidus Chronicle indicates that Gubaru "installed governors in Babylon." This information harmonizes with the appointment of satraps and presidents by Darius. Daniel 6:1.

d. Gubaru governed Babylon for a full year. The Nabonidus Chronicle says that Gubaru conquered Babylon for Cyrus in the month Tashritu (roughly our October) and that he died in the month Arahshamnu (roughly our November). From reading this, many writers have assumed that Gubaru died in the month which immediately followed his defeat of Babylon.

William H. Shea,[7] however, has shown convincingly that this is a mistake. Babylonian historical records were virtually always arranged in strict chronological sequence. In the present instance, the Chronicle first gives the date for the conquest of Babylon and then says that Gubaru returned to their respective cities the gods which Nabonidus had brought to Babylon, and it says that he did this "from the month of Kislimu to the month of Addaru" (roughly from December to March). Only *after* providing this information does the Chronicle add that "in the month of Arahshammu . . . Gubaru [here spelled Ugbaru] died." It is thus clear that the autumn in which Gubaru died was at least one full year later than the autumn in which he conquered Babylon.

c. Gubaru served as king of Babylon. The title "King of Babylon" was employed by royal rulers both when Babylon was the head of its own empire and also when it was a subordinate kingdom of the earlier Assyrian Empire and, for a while, of the later Medo-Persian Empire. For example, when Babylon was a part of the Assyrian Empire, Tiglath-pileser III (745-727) chose to be known not only as the emperor of Assyria but also as "King of Babylon." In the autumn of 538 B.C., a full year after the fall of Babylon, Cyrus, the Medo-Persian emperor, added the title "King of Babylon" to his imperial title "King of Lands." He thus became Cyrus, King of Babylon, King of Lands.

As Professor Shea has shown, the fact that Cyrus took the title King of Babylon in the late fall of 538 coincides with the death of Gubaru in November of that year. Cyrus did not assume the title King of Babylon until Gubaru was dead. This evidence implies that Gubaru was King of Babylon. Further evidence that Gubaru was a king includes the fact that his death is recorded. Shea has found that the official Babylonian chroniclers almost never recorded the death of anyone except the members of royal families. The Nabonidus Chronicle not only records Gubaru's death but also mentions that a few days later "the wife of the king" passed away. A process of elimination indicates that this wife was almost certainly the wife of Gubaru. The only other king whom the scribe could reasonably have had in mind was King Cyrus; but there is no mention that Cyrus came to the funeral, as there would be if the wife had been his.

f. When Assyrian kings called themselves King of Babylon, they sometimes assumed "throne names" different from their real names. Tiglath-pileser, the Assyrian emperor we referred to a moment ago, called himself Pul as King of Babylon. Shalmaneser V (727-722 B.C.), another emperor of Assyria, called himself Ululai as King of Babylon.

We are familiar with a modern analogy. When cardinals become popes, they assume papal names. Angelo Giuseppe Roncalli became Pope John XXIII.

Conclusion. The evidence before us makes it highly reasonable to conclude that Darius the Mede was the same person as Gubaru the Gutian and that he governed Babylon, within the Medo-Persian Empire, as its local king (Daniel 6:6) from the autumn of 539 B.C. to the autumn of 538 B.C.

References

1. Robert Dick Wilson, *Studies in the Book of Daniel: A Discussion of the Historical Questions* (New York: G. P. Putnam's Sons, The Knickerbocker Press, 1917) pp. 316, 317.

2. Contenau, *Everyday Life*, p. 62.

3. See C. F. Keil and F. Delitzsch, *Biblical Commentary on the Old Testament*, 27 vols. (Grand Rapids, Mich.: Wm. B. Eerdmans Publishing Co., 1959), C. F. Keil, *Biblical Commentary on the Book of Daniel*, trans. M. G. Easton, 25:216.

4. Pritchard, *Texts*, p. 306. In the Chronicle the name "Gubaru" is twice spelled "Ugbaru," as the result, apparently, of a transposition of the first two letters.

5. Xenophon, *Cyropaedia*, 7.5.

6. *Ibid.*, 4.6.2.

7. William H. Shea, "An Unrecognized Vassal King of Babylon in the Early Achaemenid Period," 4 parts, *Andrews University Seminary Studies* 9, 10 (January 1971 to July 1972). See also William H. Shea, "Darius the Mede and Daniel His Governor" (research paper, Andrews University, 1978).

Daniel 7
God, Our Friend in Court

Introduction

If you have been eager to plunge again into the predictive chapters of Daniel, your opportunity has arrived.

But be prepared. The river of Daniel 7 flows wide and deep. The vision of Daniel 7 is even more essential for understanding Daniel and Revelation than is the vision of Daniel 2.

The *basic* message of Daniel 7 is that God is our Friend and that in the judgment every man, woman, boy, and girl who puts his or her trust in Jesus Christ will find salvation full and free. But there are, besides, many other matters of great importance to be learned from it.

The chapter begins (verse 1) by providing a date for the vision: **"The first year of Belshazzar."** God must have considered the timing significant. As we learned on pages 90-92, Nabonidus **"entrusted the kingship"** to Belshazzar in 553 B.C. So 553 B.C. must be the **"first year of Belshazzar"** and the date of this vision. Nebuchadnezzar had been dead nine years. His successors on the throne had not amounted to much, and Belshazzar did not look promising. It was a time of political uncertainty for everyone, including all the Jews who lived in Babylon.

Daniel himself was no longer a young man on the rise. He was about seventy now, though evidently not yet retired (see Daniel 8:27). The fall of Babylon (chapter 5) and his experience in the lions' den (chapter 6) were still in the future, for the chapters of the book of Daniel are not all arranged chronologically. Nonetheless, *fifty years* had passed since the vision of Daniel 2! During Nebuchadnezzar's reign, which had occupied more than forty of these fifty years, Daniel had seen Babylon amply fulfill its symbolism as the head of gold. Now its golden age was passing, and time seemed nearly ripe for the breast and arms of silver to take its place.

It was night. Daniel was dreaming—perhaps after an earnest day of prayer and the study of Scripture and of the image prophecy. Water filled his view—water in motion, agitated and stirred to turmoil by winds from every direction. Suddenly, as his eyes roamed the restless waves, his gaze was gripped by the miraculous emergence of a massive lion, one unlike any he had seen before. It was winged! And as Daniel watched, the wings were **"plucked off,"** and **"the mind of a man was given to it,"** and it stood upright **"like a man"** on its hind legs. Daniel 7:4.

The lion didn't leave the scene, but Daniel's attention was riveted next by the appearance of a bear, one which seemed strangely taller on one side than on the other. **"It was raised up on one side,"** he observed; and it had

The beasts Daniel saw (Daniel 7) parallel the same world empires depicted in Nebuchadnezzar's image (Daniel 2).

107

three ribs in its mouth. Verse 5.

The lopsided bear was soon joined by a four-headed, four-winged leopard (verse 6) and then by a ghastly monster which defied zoological classification. Daniel had never seen anything to resemble it. He described it as **"terrible and dreadful and exceedingly strong,"** **"different from all the beasts that were before it."** And, he added, **"it had ten horns."** This ugly animal, standing evidently on a spit of land, appeared in the vision to strike out murderously with its bronze claws and iron teeth. **"It devoured and broke in pieces, and stamped the residue with its feet."** Verses 7, 19.

Staring amazed at this strange and savage brute, Daniel was startled to discern an eleventh horn, a **"little one,"** working its way upward among the animal's ten horns, while three of the horns came loose and fell off, making room for it. **"And behold, in this horn were eyes like the eyes of a man, and a mouth speaking great things."** Verse 8.

At this point Daniel's attention was drawn mercifully heavenward from the grisly scene ahead to a grand and glorious scene above. There he saw the Ancient of Days in judgment near the end of time. He saw the fourth beast slain and the **"dominion and glory and kingdom"** given to **"one like a son of man."** Verses 9-14.

He should have felt greatly relieved. No doubt he did. But he also continued to be deeply concerned about that fourth beast with its ten horns and especially about its **"little horn."** Sensing a helpful presence, he was delighted to discover a heavenly personage, whom we may assume was an angel, standing nearby. He asked the angel to tell him **"the truth concerning all this."** Verse 16.

The angel replied simply, **"These four great beasts are four kings who shall arise out of the earth."** At once he directed Daniel's attention to the vision's happy ending: **"The saints of the Most High shall receive the kingdom, and possess the kingdom for ever, for ever and ever."** Verses 17, 18.

Daniel was not satisfied with a summary! He begged the angel (verses 19-22) to fill in the details about the fourth beast and its horns. And graciously the angel complied (verses 23-27).

We are glad that he did comply, for we, like Daniel, want to know as much as we can about these important matters. In the Gospels (Matthew 7:7) Jesus promises, "Ask, and it will be given you; seek, and you will find; knock, and it will be opened to you."

As the angel resumed his explanation, he said to Daniel, and through him to all of us, **"As for the fourth beast, there shall be a fourth kingdom on earth."** Verse 23.

So the fourth beast is the fourth *kingdom.* Earlier (verse 17) the angel had said that the four beasts were four *kings.* Dictatorships are often indistinguishable from their dictators. Napoleon boasted, "I am the State," and nearly everyone knows that Louis XIV is alleged to have said the same: "L'état c'est moi."

Knowing that the fourth beast is the fourth *kingdom,* we recognize at once that we are dealing with the same series of world powers that we met first in Nebuchadnezzar's image in Daniel 2: Babylonian, Medo-Persian, Greek, and Roman empires, followed in due time by the kingdom of God.

Babylon, represented in the towering image by the head of gold, is fitly represented here by a tawny lion, king of beasts. Visitors to Babylon can still see the lion-shaped bas-reliefs on Babylon's baked-brick walls and the large stone lion that after 2400 years still crouches over a fallen stone woman.

The Medo-Persian Empire, symbolized in the image by the breast and arms of silver, is easily discerned in the lopsided bear of Daniel 7. Our identification will be further confirmed when we come to Daniel 8, which explicitly identifies the two unequally high horns of a ram as **the kings of Media and Persia.**

The belly and thighs of the image stood for Greece. So does the leopard in our present sequence. In Daniel 8 the goat which attacks the Medo-Persian ram will be identified specifically as the **"king [or kingdom] of Greece."**

And the legs of iron which represented Rome in Daniel 2 are replaced here by the terrible beast that defies classification.

There can be no doubt about the identification of the four beasts, and the *waters* too are readily identified in the Bible. Revelation 17:15 explains that symbolic waters are "peoples and multitudes and nations and tongues." You may compare also Isaiah 17:12, 13 and Jeremiah 46:8; 47:1, 2. Even in common speech we refer to a large crowd of people as a "sea of humanity."

The *man's heart* symbolizes Babylon's change of character after Nebuchadnezzar's death. In the *three ribs* in the bear's mouth we may see Babylonia, Lydia, and Egypt, the three main entities conquered by the Medo-Persian Empire. *Wings* aptly connote speed. Habakkuk 1:8 describes the Babylonian cavalry as launching its attacks as swiftly as eagles, and the celerity displayed by Alexander in his leadership of the Greeks has aroused the admiration of the world. Beginning almost from scratch Alexander united contentious Greece and conquered mighty Persia in twelve lightning years. He conquered Persia and *died* by the time he was only thirty-two!

The *four heads* of the leopard will be identified in Daniel 8:22 as the **"four kingdoms"** that would divide up Alexander's Hellenistic Greek Empire after his death. Alexander died of a raging fever. As his strength ebbed, his military leaders filed past his bed in melancholy tribute. In response Alexander could only nod his head. He could not speak. He appointed no successor.

Even before they buried him, his generals began to quarrel. Twenty-two bloody years later, after the landmark Battle of Ipsus in 301 B.C., four of the generals remained in control of four

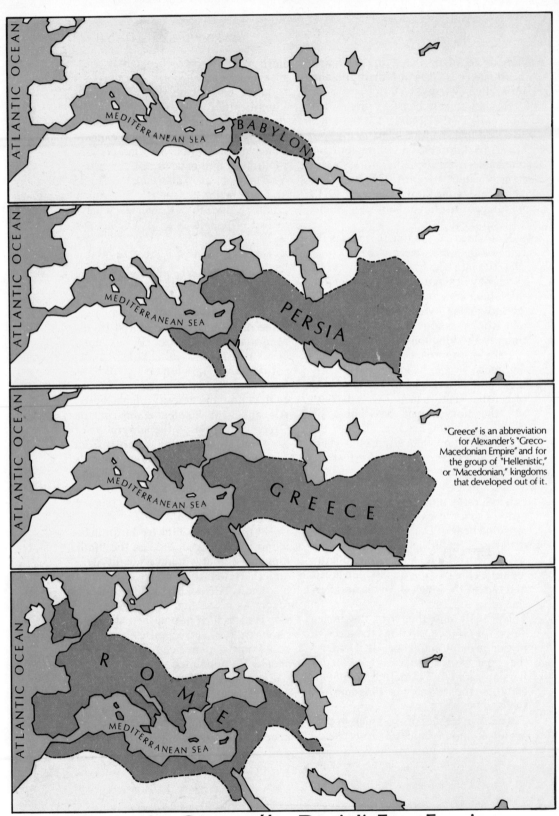

"Greece" is an abbreviation for Alexander's "Greco-Macedonian Empire" and for the group of "Hellenistic," or "Macedonian," kingdoms that developed out of it.

Territories Covered by Daniel's Four Empires

Hellenistic Greek kingdoms:* "[1] Cassander got Macedonia and Greece; [2] Lysimachus took Thrace and much of Asia Minor; [3] Ptolemy retained Egypt, Cyrenaica, and Palestine; and [4] the rest of Asia [that is, Syria and the lands Alexander had won in the east] went to Seleucus."[1]

*The Battle of Ipsus was decisive. It marked the end of the vigorous attempt by Antigonus to form a single, reunited empire. The four-way division lasted until the death of Lysimachus in 281 B.C., after which there were for a while three main Hellenistic Greek kingdoms—Syria, Egypt, and Macedonia—along with a few minor ones.

All of this is background, of course, a mere introduction, to the major themes of Daniel 7. The career of the "little horn" and the course of the heavenly judgment attracted Daniel's attention principally, and so they do ours. After you have read the chapter for yourself, we will examine what the Bible says about God and Christ in the judgment and about the horn that made war with the saints.

CHAPTER 7

1 In the first year of Belshazzar king of Babylon, Daniel had a dream and visions of his head as he lay in his bed. Then he wrote down the dream, and told the sum of the matter. ² Daniel said, "I saw in my vision by night, and behold, the four winds of heaven were stirring up the great sea. ³ And four great beasts came up out of the sea, different from one another. ⁴ The first was like a lion and had eagles' wings. Then as I looked its wings were plucked off, and it was lifted up from the ground and made to stand upon two feet like a man; and the mind of a man was given to it. ⁵ And behold, another beast, a second one, like a bear. It was raised up on one side; it had three ribs in its mouth between its teeth; and it was told, 'Arise, devour much flesh.' ⁶ After this I looked, and lo, another, like a leopard, with four wings of a bird on its back; and the beast had four heads; and dominion was given to it. ⁷ After this I saw in the night visions, and behold, a fourth beast, terrible and dreadful and exceedingly strong; and it had great iron teeth; it devoured and broke in pieces, and stamped the residue with its feet. It was different from all the beasts that were before it; and it had ten horns. ⁸ I considered the horns, and behold, there came up among them another horn, a little one, before which three of the first horns were plucked up by the roots; and behold, in this horn were eyes like the eyes of a man, and a mouth speaking great things. ⁹ As I looked,

    thrones were placed
      and one that was ancient of days took
        his seat;
    his raiment was white as snow,
      and the hair of his head like pure wool;
    his throne was fiery flames,
      its wheels were burning fire.
¹⁰ A stream of fire issued
    and came forth from before him;
  a thousand thousands served him,
    and ten thousand times ten thousand
      stood before him;
  the court sat in judgment,

and the books were opened.
¹¹ I looked then because of the sound of the great words which the horn was speaking. And as I looked, the beast was slain, and its body destroyed and given over to be burned with fire. ¹² As for the rest of the beasts, their dominion was taken away, but their lives were prolonged for a season and a time.
¹³ I saw in the night visions,
    and behold, with the clouds of heaven
      there came one like a son of man,
    and he came to the Ancient of Days
      and was presented before him.
¹⁴ And to him was given dominion
    and glory and kingdom,
  that all peoples, nations, and languages
    should serve him;
  his dominion is an everlasting dominion,
    which shall not pass away,
  and his kingdom one
    that shall not be destroyed.
15 "As for me, Daniel, my spirit within me was anxious and the visions of my head alarmed me. ¹⁶ I approached one of those who stood there and asked him the truth concerning all this. So he told me, and made known to me the interpretation of the things. ¹⁷ 'These four great beasts are four kings who shall arise out of the earth. ¹⁸ But the saints of the Most High shall recieve the kingdom, and possess the kingdom for ever, for ever and ever.'
19 "Then I desired to know the truth concerning the fourth beast, which was different from all the rest, exceedingly terrible, with its teeth of iron and claws of bronze; and which devoured and broke in pieces, and stamped the residue with its feet; ²⁰ and concerning the ten horns that were on its head, and the other horn which came up and before which three of them fell, the horn which had eyes and a mouth that spoke great things, and which seemed greater than its fellows. ²¹ As I looked, this horn made war with the saints, and prevailed over them, ²² until the Ancient of Days came, and judgment was given for the saints of the Most High, and the time came when the saints received the kingdom.

23 "Thus he said: 'As for the fourth
beast,
there shall be a fourth kingdom on earth,
which shall be different from all the
kingdoms,
and it shall devour the whole earth,
and trample it down, and break it to
pieces.
²⁴ As for the ten horns,
out of this kingdom
ten kings shall arise
and another shall arise after them;
he shall be different from the former
ones,
and shall put down three kings.
²⁵ He shall speak words against the Most
High,
and shall wear out the saints of
the Most High,
and shall think to change the times and
the law;
and they shall be given into his hand
for a time, two times, and half a time.
²⁶ But the court shall sit in judgment,
and his dominion shall be taken away,
to be consumed and destroyed to the
end.
²⁷ And the kingdom and the dominion
and the greatness of the kingdoms
under the whole heaven
shall be given to the people of the
saints of the Most High;
their kingdom shall be an everlasting
kingdom,
and all dominions shall serve and obey
them.'
28 "Here is the end of the matter. As for
me, Daniel, my thoughts greatly alarmed
me, and my color changed; but I kept the
matter in my mind."

The Message of Daniel 7

I. God and Christ in the Judgment

Do your children ever think of God as being some sort of cross old man? Do *you* think of Him that way sometimes?

You are well aware, of course, that "God is love"; but how do you actually feel about Him when, let us say, you are all alone, wondering why the phone never rings and people don't write you any letters? Or when your department committee turns down all your ideas? Or when management gives someone else the job you were preening for?

It comes almost as a surprise—and as a very happy one—that in the middle of a chapter about monstrous beasts and horns God reminds us that He cares, that He really cares, about all His people and about the way other people treat them. Not once but four times in this chapter we are taught that one day God will remove all wrong and reward all good.

In Daniel 7:9-14, in Daniel 7:18, in Daniel 7:22, and in Daniel 7:26, 27 the same message is repeated in different words: the court will sit in judgment, the beast will be slain, and the kingdom will be given to the saints.

"God is love"; there can be no doubt about that. 1 John 4:8. He *is* described in the Bible as **"the Ancient of Days"** (Daniel 7:13), but He is not a "cross old man." He is a very loving heavenly Father. John 3:16 says that God loved the world so much He gave His only Son. Ephesians 2:4 calls Him "rich in mercy." Thirty times the Old Testament in the King James Version talks about His "lovingkindness." (The R.S.V. uses "steadfast love.") Psalm 63:3 says that His lovingkindness is "better than life." Psalm 103:4 says that God "crowns us" with lovingkindness. And in Jeremiah 31:3 God Himself tells us, "I have loved thee with an everlasting love: therefore with lovingkindness have I drawn thee." K.J.V.

God's judgment throne. God is an *energetic* lover! Astronomers tell us that He has created billions of galaxies. Psalm 18:10 pictures Him symbolically as He moves around His universe:

> He rode on a cherub, and flew;
> He came swiftly upon the wings of the wind.

We are not surprised, then, that the account of the judgment scene in Daniel 7:9-14 begins with the observation that **"thrones were placed and one that was ancient of days took his seat"**; or that verse 22 says, **"The Ancient of Days *came*, and judgment was given."** When the time for the judgment arrives, God is portrayed as traveling from some other part of heaven in order to commence this particular work. This change of location will appear highly significant when we study Daniel 8:14.

Jesus, the "Son of man," is our Attorney and Judge in the judgment.

115

The Son of man. After telling us that the Ancient of Days was seated and the judgment had begun, Daniel says that the beast was slain and that **"in the night visions"** there came **"with the clouds of heaven"** **"one like a son of man,"** and that he **"came to the Ancient of Days and was presented before him."** Daniel 7:13.

Who is this "Son of man"? The answer is that more than forty times Jesus applied the term to Himself. To the disciples He said, "The Son of man is to be delivered into the hands of men, and they will kill him, and he will be raised on the third day." Matthew 17:22. To Zacchaeus, the diminutive tax collector, He said, "The Son of man came to seek and to save the lost." Luke 19:10. To Judas He said, "Would you betray the Son of man with a kiss?" Luke 22:48. And to the high priest as he sat in judgment conducting Christ's own trial, Jesus said, "Hereafter you will see the Son of man seated at the right hand of Power, and coming on the clouds of heaven." Matthew 26:64.

The "Son of man . . . on the clouds of heaven"! Commentators agree that in this salient utterance Jesus identified Himself unmistakably with the Son of man of Daniel 7.

Who is the judge? Now in Daniel 7:9-14, *after* saying that **"the court sat in judgment and the books were opened"** and *before* saying that **"there came one like a son of man"** to the Ancient of Days, Daniel mentions that he saw the beast slain and its body destroyed. It is easy to get the impression that the Son of man arrives at court only after God has completed the judgment.

But the Bible tells us in John 5:22 that "the Father judges no one, but has given all judgment to the Son"!

How can God be the judge and yet not judge anybody? Acts 17:30, 31 solves the riddle easily: "God . . . has fixed a day on which *he will judge* the world in righteousness *by a man* whom he has appointed, and of this he has given assurance to all men by raising him from the dead." So God is the Judge, but in His capacity as judge He has chosen to delegate the judging to His Son.

When President Jimmy Carter was asked in 1979 to commute the sentence of Patty Hearst, he announced publicly that he would follow whatever recommendation came to him from the lawyers in the United States Department of Justice. President Carter was the ultimate judge, but he chose to exercise his judicial responsibility by relying on the judgment of others.

Jesus, our Attorney and Judge. Now 1 John 2:1 says that Jesus is our lawyer. He is our "advocate with the Father." First Timothy 2:5 calls Him our "mediator." And Hebrews 7:25 says that He "always lives to make intercession" for us. Christ, then, is ever ready to plead our case before God as our Advocate and Mediator and Intercessor.

Yet—surprising as it may sound—Jesus has told us that He does not guarantee to intercede for us! "I do not say to you that I shall pray the Father for you." John 16:26.

Whatever can He mean?

Jesus explains Himself by saying, *"For the Father himself loves you,* because you have loved me and have believed that I came from the Father." John 16:27.

Evidently Jesus does not have to "intercede" for us in the way we may have imagined. He does not have to persuade God to love us; for, as He Himself makes clear, God already loves us.

A "mediator" is a person who helps other people understand one another and, if the other people are not friends, helps them to become friends. The words of Jesus that we have just quoted from John 16:27 provide a beautiful hint as to Christ's true role as mediator (1 Timothy 2:5) between God and man: "The Father himself loves you, *because you have loved me* and have believed that I come from the Father."

One of the several ways, then, in which Jesus serves as mediator between God and man is in showing us what God is like, because it is so difficult for us to love a God whom we have never seen. God gave His only Son and sent Him into the world so that we could love the Son and, in the process of loving the Son, learn to love the Father too.

There is no doubt that God is the Judge. "God will judge the world" (Acts 17:31)—but He will do it "by" the Man He raised from the dead. So we read in Romans 14:10, "We shall all stand before the judgment seat of *God*," and in 2 Corinthians 5:10, "We must all appear before the judgment seat of *Christ*."

In electing to make Christ our judge, God has done a very beautiful thing. To this Son of man who "became flesh and dwelt among us" (John 1:14) and who was "made like his brethren in every respect" and "suffered" under temptation (Hebrews 2:17, 18), to this Son of man who lived on earth and knows the frailty of our humanity and how much it hurts to be disappointed and lonely and to be treated harshly by other people, to this Son of man who is also the Son of God—to Him, God the Father, who is the Ancient of Days, says, "I am the judge, but My verdict will be whatever verdict You recommend."

So God is *not* a cross old man! How, indeed, could He be any more understanding?

If, then, Jesus plays a dual role in the judgment, serving both as our advocate and as our judge, it becomes evident that He must arrive on the scene of judgment before the work of judgment begins!

Thus Daniel 7:11, 12, which tells about the destruction of the beast, is seen to be parenthetical. It leaps ahead to the happy ending, as occurs so many times in this chapter as a whole. The actual order of events is as follows: (1) thrones placed, (2) Ancient of Days seated, (3) Son of man welcomed, (4) judgment held, (5) Son of man and saints rewarded, (6) beast destroyed.

Saints and fellow heirs. Although Daniel 7:14 says that **"dominion and glory and kingdom"** are given to the *Son of man*, Daniel 7:27 says that **"the kingdom and the dominion and the greatness of the kingdoms under the whole heaven shall be given to the *people of the saints* of the Most High."** So who really does receive the kingdom, Christ or the saints?

Both, of course! Hebrews 1:2 says that God has appointed Jesus to be the "*heir* of all things''; and Romans 8:15-17 says that when we call God our Father, it becomes evident that ''we are children of God, and if children, then heirs, heirs of God and *fellow heirs* with Christ.''

Christ receives the kingdom and immediately shares it with all the people who trust Him.

Fellow heirs with Christ! *You* are a fellow heir. And so is your Christian spouse. Says 1 Peter 3:7, ''Husbands, live considerately with your wives, bestowing honor on the woman . . . , since you are *joint heirs* of the grace of life.''

Christian husband! If Christ is willing to share His kingdom with your wife, can you share some of your time and thought with her? With a scarcely concealed air of superiority, some husbands crush their wives at supper with the patronizing question, ''And what did *you* do all day, my dear?'' James Dobson, author of *What Wives Wish Their Husbands Knew About Women,*[2] reminds us that ''everybody must be somebody to somebody to be anybody.'' Many wives, he says, especially those who stay home with little children and dedicate all their energies to their families, often experience deep, unexpressed depression because their husbands do not seem to appreciate them. So—how about bringing home some flowers tomorrow night; and tonight what about taking out the garbage? This is your wife you are honoring! She's a daughter of the heavenly King. A fellow heir with Christ. Your queen.

And what about your children? Have you ever called them *Brother* Mike or *Sister* Christy to remind yourself that in Jesus they are just as much fellow heirs of God's grace and of His eternal kingdom as you are? They deserve your high-quality time! They are worth the cost of family worship and regular church school!

Whatever other position she may also hold outside, Mother, as a ''joint heir with Christ,'' deserves to be treated as ''queen'' in her home.

When Father and Son sit in judgment and the beast is slain and the saints receive the kingdom, your precious spouse and children *and you* will be glad, so glad, that together you put the things of God ahead of every other consideration.

II. God's Basis for Judgment

Employees like to have company policies posted where they can read them. Children want to know the rules before being accused of breaking them. Free societies insist that even criminals have the right to have charges against them stated in writing and supported by solid evidence.

What kind of evidence and what sort of legal basis will God employ in the judgment?

God's recorded evidence. Daniel 7:10 says, **"The court sat in judgment, and the books were opened."** Revelation 20:12-15 also speaks of *"books"* that are "opened" and out of which the dead will be judged on the basis of *"what they had done."* Revelation adds that "another book was opened, which is the *book of life."* And Malachi 3:16 refers to "a *book of remembrance"* which is written about "those who feared the Lord and thought on his name."

The book of life sounds attractive! Registers of births and deaths were kept in ancient times as today. The "register of the house of Israel" is referred to in Ezekiel 13:9. In the heavenly book of life God evidently preserves a record of all who are "born again" into Jesus Christ (Revelation 21:27) and who by virtue of their faith in Jesus possess even now "eternal life." John 6:54 (see also Philippians 4:3; Luke 10:20; Daniel 12:1).

So there are three categories of books: one, containing a record of all our deeds; another, containing a selection of only the good things done by those who love God; and a third book which lists the names of all who are born again and who live in Christ.

We don't need to know what the books look like. In Daniel's day "books" were clay tablets, papyrus, or parchment. Heavenly books may be computer printouts or, very likely, something far more sophisticated.

But it is appropriate to ask why God maintains the books. He cannot possibly need them to jog His memory! He keeps them for our sakes. Of course. But our attention is drawn to the large assembly that gathers around the throne:

> **A thousand thousands serve him,**
> **and ten thousand times ten thousand**
> **stood before him;**
> **the court sat in judgment,**
> **and the books were opened.** Daniel 7:10.

In Revelation 5:11 (K.J.V.) the figure "ten thousand times ten thousand" is applied to the angels. So are the records made for the sake of angels too? Evidently yes, in part. Paul in 1 Corinthians 4:9 speaks about his being "a spectacle to the

119

world, to angels and to men." The word "spectacle" is translated from *theatron* from which our "theater" is derived. "All the world's a stage," said the playwright, more aptly perhaps than he intended. Outer space *is* peopled with intelligent beings, and they are deeply interested in the drama unfolding on planet Earth. For their sakes, then, the records are maintained. God wants them as well as us to know the evidence on which our cases are determined.

Indeed the angels are much more deeply involved in the dramatic contest between good and evil than most of us may be aware. Revelation 12 actually speaks about war in heaven! We will have more to say about this war later on.

In the meantime, how pleasant it is to contemplate the tender joy of Jesus as He opens the book of remembrance in the presence of the celestial angels. We can almost hear His voice: "Let me read the sacrificial contributions that John Smith made to some senior citizens in a city ghetto; . . . and the beautiful thing that Jane Smith said to the woman who grabbed the very item *she* wanted at a basement sale; . . . and the nice things that Jimmy Smith said and did when his mother asked him to clean up the kitchen because she had a headache."

Book of remembrance and book of life. How happy we may be for both! But what about the other books? Do you want everything you have done in your life to be paraded in detail before the universe? Praise God for 1 John 1:9: "If we confess our sins, he . . . will forgive our sins and cleanse us from all unrighteousness."

Here is the remedy that we need. Let us admit what we have suspected all along—that we *are* self-seeking sinners. Let us admit the things that we have done wrong and tell the Lord sincerely that we are sorry. And then in the light streaming from the cross let us rejoice that "the blood of Jesus his Son cleanses us from all sin." 1 John 1:7.

God's legal basis. We just talked about sin. Sin provides us a clue to the legal basis for the judgment; for in 1 John 3:4 God defines sin as "lawlessness," that is, as living or acting without due concern for law.

Without due concern for what law? God's law, of course.

Says the Bible, "Fear God, and keep *his commandments;* for this is the whole duty of man. For God will bring every deed into *judgment,* with every secret thing, whether good or evil." Ecclesiastes 12:13, 14.

When Jesus lived on earth, a lawyer asked Him which commandment He regarded as the greatest. Christ's reply has become famous: "You shall love the Lord your God with all your heart, and with all your soul, and with all your mind. This is the great and first commandment. And a second is like it, You shall love your neighbor as yourself." Then Jesus added, "On these two commandments depend all the law and the prophets." Matthew 22:35-40.

Jesus did not say, If you have these two commandments (of love for God and love for man) you can throw away all the others! He said that all the other laws and all the messages of the Old Testament prophets depend upon—are built upon—these two basic principles.

In other words, Don't throw away your Old Testament! Don't discard the Ten

120

Commandments! Instead look at them through the eyes of love. Realize that they were given by God to explain, confirm, and illustrate what true love consists of.

Most of us think that we know what love is, but without the Bible it is surprisingly easy to interpret love wrongly. A great many people these days think that love is making out with anybody they happen to like at the moment, married or not. And what heartache often results. How good it is to have God's law to remind us of the faithfulness of true love in the words, "You shall not commit adultery"!

Some people actually think it is a kind of love to get presents for people by shoplifting. Obviously this doesn't show much love for storekeepers! Most of us would agree that the Ten Commandments reveal love better by saying, "You shall not steal."

Many men think that love for their families requires them to work seven days a week so they can pay for all the pleasures and facilities of the twentieth century. But in explaining love for families, the fourth commandment says, "Remember the sabbath day, to keep it holy. Six days you shall labor, and do all your work; but the seventh day is a sabbath to the Lord your God; in it you shall not do any work, *you, or your son, or your daughter,* your manservant, or your maidservant." Exodus 20:8-10.

The Sabbath commandment reveals love for families because it involves the whole family together in its observance of rest and worship. And it *also* reveals love for God when we keep holy the very day *He* has chosen.

Now, about twenty years after the cross Paul complained that "the mystery of lawlessness" was "already at work." 2 Thessalonians 2:7. He had in mind an attitude developing among some Christians who felt that because Jesus had died for them they didn't need to keep the law anymore. How tragic that anyone should suppose that Jesus came to make us lawbreakers!

Even during His lifetime on earth some of Christ's listeners got the idea that He was undermining the Ten Commandments. He did His best to set them straight!

In His famous Sermon on the Mount, Jesus insisted that He had not come to change the law.

"Think not," he said, "that I have come to abolish the law and the prophets; I have come not to abolish them but to fulfil them. For truly, I say to you, till heaven and earth pass away, not an iota, not a dot, will pass from the law until all is accomplished." Matthew 5:17, 18.

As you read these words, let me ask you something. Is the earth still solid under your chair? Is the sky still overhead? Then in Christ's own words "not an iota, not a dot" has passed from the law!

The book of Revelation describes an "angel" as flying symbolically in the sky just before judgment day and shouting, "Fear God and give him glory, for the hour of his judgment has come." Shortly after this angel, another angel appears with the announcement, "Here is a call for the endurance of the *saints*, those who keep the *commandments of God* and the *faith of Jesus*." Revelation 14: 7, 12.

These two angels in Revelation tie together the things we have been studying here about the judgment scene in Daniel 7 and about the importance of the Ten Commandments. The saints of the Most High who receive the kingdom in Daniel's vision are shown in Revelation to be the people who through faith in Jesus keep the commandments of God. Such faith-filled, born-again Christians have their names inscribed in the book of life and need have no fear of the judgment.

III. The Horn That Made War With the Saints

The feature in Daniel 7 that interested the angel most was the judgment scene, but what fascinated Daniel most was the fourth beast and the "little horn" that grew out of its head and made war with the saints.

In view of the importance of the little horn, more space will be devoted to this present section than to most, and it will be divided into two subsections: (a) "Four Principles" and (b) "Eight Identifying Marks."

Four Principles

1. *There is more than one antichrist.* Although the little horn has the eyes and mouth of a man, it contrasts strongly with the Son of man seen in the same vision. The Son of man shares His kingdom with the saints, but the little horn devastates the saints. The Son of man comes close to God, but the little horn opposes Him and tries to change His law. No wonder then that many people have perceived the little horn as the antichrist.

Now some Christians today (called "preterists") say that the antichrist appeared long, long ago. Others (the "futurists") say that he hasn't appeared yet. And still others (the "historicists") say that the antichrist has operated throughout church history, revealing himself most especially, thus far, in the medieval Christian church.

In some sense or other they may all be right!

The word "antichrist" appears in the Bible only in the epistles of John. There we are told that antichrist "denies the Father and the Son" (1 John 2:22) and "will not acknowledge the coming of Jesus Christ in the flesh (2 John 7), and also that the

122

spirit of antichrist *is*—around A.D. 90—"in the world already" (1 John 4:3). We are also told (1 John 2:18) that "*many* antichrists have come" and that they "went out from us."

From these Bible verses it appears that "antichrist" is a term that applies technically only to apostate Christians who "went out from us" during the first century A.D. and who denied truths about Jesus and God. Most scholars see these first-century antichrists in certain Christian Gnostics. Here are antichrists of the long ago.

But in common usage the word "antichrist" has been applied for centuries to other enemies of God in addition to the antichrists of the first century. For example, a great many Christian writers have seen antichrist in "the lawless one" (or "man of sin" K.J.V.) of 2 Thessalonians 2:7, 8 whom, the Bible says, the "Lord Jesus will slay . . . and destroy . . . by his appearing and his coming." Here is an antichrist of the future.

And, through the centuries, various Roman Catholic spokesmen have felt that the pope—either the current one or a future one, or the papacy as a whole (the entire line of popes)—was the antichrist. For example, during a time of deep spiritual laxness in Rome, Arnulf, the bishop of Orleans, deplored the Roman popes as "monsters of guilt" and declared in a council called by the king of France in 991 that the pontiff, clad in purple and gold, was " 'Antichrist, sitting in the temple of God, and showing himself as God.' "[3]

Eberhard II, archbishop of Salzburg (1200-1246), stated approvingly at a synod of bishops held at Regensburg in 1240 (some scholars say 1241) that the people of his day were "accustomed" to calling the pope antichrist.[4]

When the Western church was divided for about 40 years between two rival popes, one in Rome and the other in Avignon, France, each pope called the other pope antichrist—and John Wycliffe is reputed to have regarded them as both being right: "two halves of Antichrist, making up the perfect Man of Sin between them."[5]

Martin Luther, as an Augustinian monk in the University of Wittenberg, came reluctantly to believe that "the papacy is in truth . . . very Antichrist"; setting Protestants a good example, he was willing to except individual popes from the allegation. He actually dedicated his most beautiful tract, *Concerning Christian Liberty*, to Pope Leo X on the basis that Leo was worthy of being a pope in better times.[6]

Inasmuch as the Bible speaks of "many" antichrists (1 John 2:18) and inasmuch as the word "antichrist" has been used by Christians in broader ways than the Bible uses it, it is not very helpful to debate whether this or that phenomenon is *the* antichrist, as if there were only one. In any event, our purpose in this chapter will not be to identify the "antichrist" as such but to identify the little horn.

2. *Daniel's vision purposely presents a one-sided picture of Rome.* The Roman Empire was responsible for a great many good things. Its fabulous network of paved roads comes to mind, its advanced system of law and jurisprudence, and its

famous Roman peace *(pax Romana).* * Paul was proud of his Roman citizenship and took advantage of its privileges (see Acts 22:25-29). In Romans 13 he taught that Roman authorities were God's servants, authorized by Heaven to punish evil-doers (see pages 66-68). It is alongside Paul's appreciation of Rome that Revelation 12, like Daniel 7, portrays Rome as an ugly monster. In Romans 13 God honors Rome as a *civilizing* force. In Revelation 12 God criticizes Rome as a *persecuting* force.

We all know that the Romans did persecute, but it comes as a surprise to most people to learn how few Christians they killed, relatively speaking.

Nero, it is true, had a good many Christians burned as lampposts on the charge that they had set Rome on fire. Under the Emperor Domitian the apostle John was exiled to Patmos. In Carthage (now Tunis) in North Africa, around A.D. 202, Perpetua and Felicitas surrendered their babies to the care of others and walked bravely into the arena to be eaten by wild beasts.[7]

But persecution severe enough to result in martyrs was usually local and brief. The emperor Commodus (180-192) actually ordered many Christians brought back from exile. Many a Roman governor preferred to boast when he returned to Rome from his service in a province that his sword was not bloodied by anybody's life, even by a criminal's.[8] The governors were appointed to maintain the Roman

*Under the Roman Empire the people living around the Mediterranean enjoyed a greater degree of peace for two centuries than they have for any similar period since.

Perpetua and Felicitas were only two of thousands of Christians who were brutally perse-cuted under the Roman Empire.

peace; and as long as things remained peaceful, a person could believe almost anything that he wanted to. If to quell a pagan riot against the Christians, a governor thought it expedient that someone should die, a single Christian or a handful at most might be executed and the rest left alone. When Cyprian, bishop of Carthage, was martyred in 258, his church members came out to see his end— some climbing trees for a better view—and the Roman officials laid a hand on none of them.[9]

There were only two periods of serious, methodical persecution: A short one under the emperor Decius in 250 and another one associated with the emperor Diocletian that lasted approximately a decade, 303-313. During the Diocletian persecution an eyewitness in Egypt reported that so many Christians were slain that the executioners' axes grew dull and had to be replaced, and that the executioners grew tired and had to be relieved in shifts.[10]

But using evidence compiled and analyzed by Professor W. H. C. Frend of Cambridge University, we are led to conclude that the grand total of martyrdoms under pagan Rome did not exceed 5000—a figure far smaller than the millions that some people have imagined.[11]

Professor Frend's figure, which agrees with the results of my own research, does not, of course, tell the whole story. It accounts only for Christian martyrs, the believers who were actually done to death for their faith. It says nothing about the ongoing fear of persecution that hung over the church more or less for centuries. For the most part physical persecution was sporadic; it occurred now and then, here and there. But it could happen at any time, anywhere, and the Christians knew this. The fear of persecution is, in itself, a kind of persecution and can be very damaging. The Decian persecution of 250, which we mentioned a moment ago, was a kind that resulted in relatively few martyrdoms but, through fear, caused uncounted apostasies.

Frend's figure of 5000 martyrs is also limited to the period between Pentecost (A.D. 31) and the close of the Diocletian persecution (A.D. 313). It omits the unknown but apparently large number of deaths which occurred during the fourth century when the empire, now nominally Christian, persecuted Christians who were officially regarded as heretics.

The point in referring to Professor Frend's figure is that evidently Rome did not have to kill *vast concourses* of Christians in order for prophecy to portray it as **"terrible and dreadful."** Rome was, in fact, in many ways good. It was even "ordained of God." Romans 13:1, K.J.V. Despite the brutality and immorality of its society it maintained widespread peace and order, making possible the preaching of the gospel to millions of people. But in Daniel 7 God *purposely* represented Rome as indescribably ugly to teach us how much He dislikes persecutors.

Which is something for us all to remember, isn't it? Families need firm leadership; but are you a Roman emperor (or empress) in your home, bringing in a weekly check and supplying countless comforts but at the same time insisting like a dictator that everyone obey your will?

3. *The New Testament also predicted persecution.* It may be helpful to reflect on the fact that the Old Testament prophecies about a persecuting beast and a persecuting horn are reinforced by New Testament prophecies about the persecution of the church.

As an early member of the Christian church, Paul surely knew what it meant to be persecuted. He was whipped, beaten, or stoned at least *nine* times, and imprisoned many times. See 2 Corinthians 12. It is amazing that he lived long enough to be beheaded! Taking his own experience as an illustration, Paul gave his young associate Timothy a prophetic warning that concerned all the future of the Christian church. Said Paul, "All who desire to live a godly life in Christ Jesus *will be persecuted."* 2 Timothy 3:12.

Jesus implied the same in His famous sentence about taking up our crosses. "If any man would come after me," He said, "let him . . . *take up his cross* and follow me." Matthew 16:24. Thus the New Testament, like the Old, predicted tough times for true Christians.

4. *The New Testament also prophesied apostasy.* One of the plainest, and certainly one of the saddest, New Testament prophecies concerning the course of church history has to do with apostasy. Looking steadily but, I am sure, sadly into the eyes of the elders of a large New Testament church, Paul stated in the Spirit, "I know that after my departure fierce wolves will come in among you, not sparing the flock; and from among your own selves will arise men speaking perverse things, to draw away the disciples after them." Acts 20:29, 30.

As the Christian church advanced from Paul's day to its further experience under the Roman Empire, Paul's prophecy about apostasy found continuing fulfillment. Indeed, the speed with which early Christians tobogganed into apostasy almost takes one's breath away. For example, before the end of the first century, very few church members were left in Sardis whose "garments" were "not soiled." Revelation 3:4. The Christians in Thyatira were committing spiritual and probably also physical fornication. Revelation 2:20-22. False teachers were traveling widely, calling on new believers in their homes, undermining their faith and leading whole families astray. 2 Timothy 2:18; Titus 1:11.

In the second century Marcionite Gnosticism ravaged the church from east to west with its doctrine that the Old Testament God was different from the New Testament God and should not be obeyed. Other types of Gnosticism flourished also, with sects named after their various leaders: Basilides, Valentinus, Cerinthus, and so on. The Elkesaites vaunted a new baptismal formula so potent that it was good even for dogbite![12] "Catholic" Christians (as the mainstream believers came to be known) wrote urgent documents warning one another about these heresies and advising traveling Christians not to worship in just any Christian congregation in a town but to inquire for the true one.

Thus the apostasy and the persecution which marked Christianity during the centuries have provided evidence of the reliability of Bible prophecy.

With these four principles in mind—(1) that there is more than one antichrist, and we are here trying to identify not "the" antichrist but only the little horn; (2) that in Daniel 7 God purposely presented a one-sided picture of Rome as a terrible beast in order to emphasize His displeasure at persecution; (3) that the New Testament, like the Old, foretold persecution for the church; and (4) that the New Testament also foretold serious apostasy within the church—we are ready to proceed with the eight identifying marks of the little horn.

Eight Identifying Marks

Daniel 7 provides eight marks to help us identify the little horn. They may be listed as follows:

1. It rose out of the **"fourth beast."** Verses 8 and 24.

2. It appeared after **"ten"** other **"horns."** Verse 24.

3. It was **"little"** when it was first seen, but in time it became **"greater than its fellows."** Verses 8 and 20.

4. It was to **"put down three kings"** so that, as it arose, **"three of the first horns were plucked up by the roots."** Verses 8 and 24.

5. It had **"eyes like the eyes of a man, and a mouth speaking great things,"** and it spoke **"words against the Most High."** Verses 8 and 25.

6. It was to **"wear out the saints of the Most High."** Verse 25.

7. It was to **"think to change the times and the law."** Verse 25.

8. It was allotted special powers for **"a time, two times, and half a time."** Verse 25.

Only one entity really fits all eight of these identifying marks—the Christian church which rose to religiopolitical prominence as the Roman Empire declined and which enjoyed a special influence over the minds of men between the sixth and the eighteenth centuries.

To call this Christian church the "Roman Catholic" Church can be misleading if Protestants assume that the Roman Catholic Church of, say, the sixth century was one big denomination among others, as it is today. Actually the Roman Catholic Church was virtually *the* Christian church in Western Europe for about a thousand years. Because of this early universality, both Protestants and Catholics may regard it as the embodiment of "our" Christian heritage, for better or for worse.

And very often it was for the better. Of course! Catholic universities fed the torch of learning in law, medicine, and theology. Most Catholic monasteries maintained hospitals, virtually the only hospitals that existed, and provided care also for the orphaned and the aged. Catholic Latin provided a lingua franca for diplomacy and commerce, and Catholic schools provided education for diplomats and business clerks. The Cistercian monks in Britain greatly improved that land's vital wool trade. Most importantly, Roman Catholic missionaries Christianized large areas of Western Europe and provided pastoral care. Chaucer's famous words about the country parson of the fourteenth century must have been applicable to many a priest in any century:

> Broad was his parish, with houses far apart,
> Yet come it rain or thunder he would start
> Upon his rounds, in woe or sickness too,
> And reach the farthest, poor or well-to-do,
> Going on foot, his staff within his hand—
> Example that his sheep could understand—
> Namely, that first he wrought and after taught.[13]

Protestant readers need not feel delicate about calling this Christianity "*Roman* Catholic." Professor John L. McKenzie of Notre Dame University, in his work *The Roman Catholic Church*,[14] says on behalf of at least most of his coreligionists that "Roman Catholics believe that their Romanism is a reflection of the authentic Christianity of their church."[15]

Professor McKenzie recognizes that "this belief [in the importance of 'Romanism'] may involve some misunderstanding, but," he insists, "it is impossible to discuss Roman Catholicism without admitting that Catholics accept their Romanism."[16]

Professor McKenzie, a Jesuit, has provided such a revealing work that we shall have occasion to quote from it several times. In regard to the historical shortcomings of his church, he has written with such disarming candor, however, that it would be discourteous for anyone to exploit him.

The Ostrogoths compelled Pope John I to sail to Constantinople in an attempt to curtail Catholic persecution of Arian Christians.

Mainstream Christianity in the second and third centuries was known among its membership as "catholic." The term appeared for the first time as early as A.D. 115 in a letter written by Bishop Ignatius of Antioch to the members of the church in Smyrna. It meant "universal" and "orthodox" in contrast to sectarian or heretical.

Arrival of the **"ten horns."** The shift from "catholic" to "Roman Catholic" took place at the time when the Roman Empire was declining and was being invaded by a series of Germanic tribes.

Constantine, the first Christian emperor (306-337), ruled at a time when runaway inflation, high taxes, sagging morale, and insistent military pressure on the borders made it seem advisable to move the capital from Rome to Constantinople (now Istanbul). The move left the Roman bishop almost on his own in Italy and added greatly to his stature.

In 376 a large population of uncivilized Visigoths received official permission to cross the River Danube into the territory of the Roman Empire. "They poured across the stream day and night, without ceasing, embarking in troops on board ships and rafts, and in canoes made of the hollow trunks of trees." "The man who should wish to ascertain their number," wrote the contemporary historian, Ammianus Marcellinus, quoting Virgil, "might as well . . . attempt to count the waves in the African Sea, or the grains of sand tossed about by the zephyrs."[17]

Over the next century or so the Visigoths were followed by perhaps a score of other tribes, some large, some very small, the makings of the European nations of today.[18] Of these the most significant besides the Visigoths were the Ostrogoths, the Vandals, the Burgundians, the Lombards, the Anglo-Saxons, the Franks, the Alemannians, the Heruls, and the Sueves. Here are Daniel's **"ten horns."**

Three horns uprooted. Some of these tribes had been Christianized prior to their invasion of the empire, but their Christianity was not Catholic. It was a kind of Arianism. That is, unlike the Catholics, these tribes believed that although Jesus is very great, He is not "God" essentially but is a created being. Because of their difference in belief the Catholics and Arians opposed each other. When the Arian Ostrogoths under Theodoric took over Italy in the year 493, they considerably limited the power of the Roman pope. Around 523 Theodoric even bundled off the pope to Constantinople with instructions to persuade the Catholic emperor there to stop persecuting Arians in what was left of the Roman Empire. A little later he actually put the pope in jail, where he died.[19]

But the Catholic emperors of the eastern empire found ways to help the pope by eliminating three of the Arian tribes. The Catholic emperor Zeno (474-491) arranged a treaty with the Ostrogoths in 487 which resulted in the eradication of the kingdom of the Arian *Heruls* in 493. And the Catholic emperor Justinian (527-565) exterminated the Arian *Vandals* in 534 and significantly broke the power of the Arian *Ostrogoths* in 538. Thus were Daniel's three horns—the Heruls, the Vandals, and the Ostrogoths—**"plucked up by the roots."** (For more on the three horns, See pages 145-147.)

129

"A time, two times, and half a time." Remember 538, the date for the crushing of the Ostrogoths. It so happened in 1798, 1260 years later, that the French general Berthier, under the direction of the military government of France, arrested Pope Pius VI as he celebrated the anniversary of his coronation in the Sistine chapel in Rome. France arrested and exiled the pope with the express intention of destroying not just the pope himself but the Roman Catholic Church as a whole. (For more on this event see comments on Revelation 13 in *God Cares, II.*)

Daniel's prophecy said that special prerogatives would be given to the little horn for **"a time, two times, and half a time."** In Revelation 13:5 this period is spoken of as 42 months, and in Revelation 12:6, as 1260 days.

We are dealing here with symbols. The Bible says that the four beasts are symbols of four kings or kingdoms, that the horns likewise symbolize kingdoms, and that the waters are symbolic of multitudes of people. The Bible also indicates that in symbolic prophecy days represent years.

You will recall that when Daniel lived in Babylon, the prophet Ezekiel lived at Nippur, not very far away (see page 69). In the symbolic prophecy of Ezekiel, chapters 4 to 6, God said expressly to Ezekiel, "I assign you, a day for each year." Ezekiel 4:6.

The 1260 "days" or years (538-1798) of rising and then declining influence of Roman Catholicism over the minds of men exactly fulfill the **"time, two times, and half a time"** of Daniel 7 and further confirm our understanding that the Roman

Catholic Church is the fulfillment of the little horn. (For the resurgence of Catholic influence in our day see comments on Revelation 13 in *God Cares, II.*)

"Greater than its fellows" *with* **"a mouth speaking great things."** Daniel 7:8. Back again to A.D. 538, the year when the Ostrogoths collapsed. It was out of the smoking ruins of the western Roman Empire and after the overthrow of the three Arian kingdoms that the pope of Rome emerged as the most important single individual in the West, the head of a closely organized church with a carefully defined creed and with vast potential for political influence. Dozens of writers have pointed out that the real survivor of ancient Rome was the Church of Rome.[20]

Thus the Roman Empire was replaced by the Roman Church; or, as nineteenth-century writers used to put it, pagan Rome was succeeded by papal Rome.

And the pope's power—and his religious and political claims—increased for centuries. In 1076 Pope Gregory VII informed the subjects of Henry IV, emperor of Germany, that if Henry would not repent of his sins, they would not need to obey him. Henry was the most powerful monarch in Europe at the time, but he nonetheless made a pilgrimage to Canossa in the Alps, where the pope was residing, and waited three painful days, barefoot in the snow, until Pope Gregory forgave him.

Taking his cue from Gregory VII, Pope Pius V in 1570, in the bull (or decree) *Regnans in excelsis* ("He who reigns in the heavens") declared that the Protestant queen of England, Elizabeth I (1558-1603), was an accursed heretic who hereafter should have no right to rule and whose citizens were all, by papal authority, forbidden to obey her.

Professor McKenzie acknowledges in his gracious manner that "the teaching authority of the Roman Church is vested at any given moment in men, who are not all of equal virtue and competence." He continues: "[Pope] Pius V was and is respected as a holy and learned man, but his deposition of Elizabeth I of England is recognized as one of the greatest blunders in the history of the papacy."[21]

The admission that the "teaching authority of the Roman Church" is vested in men of unequal virtue and competence contrasts with a claim made as recently as the 1890s by Pope Leo XIII. In an encyclical letter, "On the Chief Duties of Christians as Citizens," dated January 10, 1890, Leo VIII asserted that "the supreme teacher in the Church is the Roman Pontiff. Union of minds, therefore, requires . . . complete submission and obedience of will to the Church and to the Roman Pontiff, *as to God Himself.*" On June 20, 1894, in "The Reunion of Christendom," Leo claimed further that "we [that is, himself, as also the other popes] hold upon this earth the place of God Almighty."

Grand as these claims may appear today, even they are not quite so exalted as the status attributed to Pope Julius II at the Fifth Lateran Council in 1512, when Christopher Marcellus told the pope—and the pope did not rebuke him for it— "Thou art the Shepherd, thou art the Physician, thou art the Governor, thou art the Husbandman, finally, thou art another God on earth." (I have the Latin on my

131

desk in front of me: *tu enim pastor, . . . tu denique alter Deus in terris.)*[22] The words seem particularly inappropriate under the circumstances, for Julius II is described in history books as "chiefly a statesman and a military leader,"[23] "a pope in arms, . . . who led his own troops in the conquest of Bologna,"[24] and as a "hard-swearing leader of papal armies."[25]

Since the great Catholic window opening *(aggiornamento)* was inaugurated by genial Pope John XXIII, many modern Catholics have learned only too well that the teaching office of their church has been vested in men who have been much less than "another God on earth." These Catholics are struggling earnestly with an identity crisis and with the very basic question of ecclesiastical authority. Catholics today need and deserve the fervent prayers of all other Christians—who, likewise, often have to face the question of authority in their own denominations.

We mention these things here only because long ago God showed Daniel that the **"little horn"** would grow **"greater than its fellows"** and would have **"a mouth speaking great things."**

"Wear out the saints." The aspect of historical Catholicism that affects the Protestants the most is probably its record as persecutor. Although, understandably, modern Catholic authorities seek to mitigate the more startling aspects of their church's religious oppression, they do not deny them. For example, the *New Catholic Encyclopedia* recognizes that, "judged by contemporary standards, the Inquisition, especially as it developed in Spain toward the close of the Middle Ages, can be classified only as one of the darker chapters in the history of the Church." It acknowledges the killing of 2000 Protestants within 50 years in the Netherlands and admits the death of perhaps 3000 to 4000 French Huguenots in the Massacre of Saint Bartholomew, which commenced on the night of August 23, 1572.[26]

The figures are modest. They overlook the vigorous crusades conducted by the Roman Church against Albigenses and Waldenses. They also omit numerous isolated acts of religious oppression, and they say nothing about the devastating Thirty Years War (1618-1648), a largely religious conflict in which it is estimated that military and civilian casualties, Protestant and Catholic, exceeded 8,000,000. Non-Catholic research compiles far higher figures than 2000 here and 3000 to 4000 somewhere else. But we remember that the Roman Empire was called "dreadful and terrible" when it killed some 5000 Christians! And the empire was pagan. How troubled God must have been to see Christians slay their fellow Christians in any number.

"Not a single sparrow falls to the ground without your father's knowledge." Matthew 10:29, Phillips.

God cares!

Whatever the statistics, numbers alone convey little about personal anguish—such as the suffering of Englishman John Brown, when they barbecued his feet before tying him to the stake; and of Helen Stark, when they sentenced her to be stuffed with her baby into a sack and drowned; and of eight-year-old Billy Fetty, when they cudgeled him to death for sympathizing with his father, who for two weeks had been suspended by an arm and a leg.[27]

Nor can statistics convey the searing pain of legal torture. Can you conceive the excrucation of having your hands tied behind your back, then having them lifted slowly outward and upward, your shoulder joints popping apart, your arms being stretched straight up, your whole body weight finally hanging from your wrists, while the inquisitor, in the name of Jesus Christ and Holy Church, demands repeatedly, ''Will you recant? Will you recant?''

We are driven to ask ourselves how Christians could have been so cruel. We are reminded that Protestants also persecuted Catholics. And we recall that even born-again evangelicals can make ''cutting'' remarks about one another and can eagerly destroy people's reputations with unfounded gossip. Heaven help us all!

We are also reminded that in medieval times life was cheap and that even the father of starving children could be hanged for stealing a loaf of bread. But it may be most helpful to learn something from the history of legal torture.

In the courts of the Roman Empire judges often assumed, in harmony with Roman law, that an accused person was most probably guilty. They therefore applied torture routinely in order to force the person to confess his crime, and they regarded such torture as an appropriate part of the punishment. Persecuted Christians often suffered more pain in Roman law courts than they did from the actual process of execution.

When the Germanic tribes took over the territory of the Roman Empire, the practice of legal torture largely ceased. When around 850 a *church* court tortured a monk called Gottschalk, who held a non-Catholic view of predestination, the people of Lyons, France, prepared a vigorous protest. They reminded their bishop[28] that in the Bible Paul says, ''Brethren, if a man is overtaken in any trespass, you who are spiritual should restore him in a spirit of gentleness. Look to yourself, lest you too be tempted.'' Galatians 6:1.

But in the twelfth century someone discovered ancient volumes containing the laws of the Roman Empire. This discovery stimulated a great revival of Roman law and with it a revival of the Roman practice of legal torture. We quote again from the *New Catholic Encyclopedia:*[29]

> Under the influence of Germanic customs and concepts, torture was little used from the 9th to the 12th centuries, but with the revival of Roman law the practice was reestablished in the 12th century. . . . In 1252 [Pope] Innocent IV sanctioned the infliction of torture by the civil authorities upon heretics, and torture came to have a recognized place in the procedure of the inquisitorial courts.

What an astonishing fulfillment of Bible prophecy! In the most brutal and non-Christian aspect of its medieval activity, the Roman Church appears as a direct and dynamic descendant of the Roman Empire. The little horn emerged unmistakably from the head of the terrible beast.

133

"Think to change the times and the law." We have thus far reviewed evidence that Paul's prophecies about apostasy and persecution were all too sadly fulfilled in the history of the Christian church. We have not attempted to prove that the medieval Catholic Church was "the" antichrist, but we have brought to bear some remarkable data that confirm its historical identity with the little horn. We have reminded ourselves that the prophecy in this case purposefully emphasized negative elements, overlooking the large positive contribution of Catholicism to Christian knowledge and to human welfare.

There is one identifying mark we have not said much about, namely, the little horn's projected attempt to **"change the times and the law."**

The release by Pope Pius V of the English people from their allegiance to Queen Elizabeth might be regarded as the fulfillment of this prophecy if it were not that a far more striking example offers itself for our consideration.

Around the year 1400 Petrus de Ancharano made the claim that "the pope *can modify divine law,* since his power is not of man, but of God, and he acts in the place of God upon earth, with the fullest power of binding and loosing his sheep."[30]

This astonishing assertion came to practical fruitage during the Reformation. Luther claimed that his conscience was captive only to Holy Scripture. *Sola Scriptura* was his slogan, "The Bible and the Bible only." No churchly tradition would be allowed to guide his life.

But one day it occurred to Johann Eck and to other Catholic churchmen to taunt Luther on his observance of Sunday in place of the Bible Sabbath. Said Eck, "Scripture teaches: 'Remember to hallow the Sabbath day; six days shall you labor and do all your work, but the seventh day is the Sabbath day of the Lord your God,' etc. Yet," insisted Eck, "the *church* has changed the Sabbath into Sunday on its own authority, on which *you* [Luther] *have no Scripture.*"[31]

At the great Council of Trent (1545-1563), convened by the pope to stanch the onrush of Protestantism, Gaspare de Fosso, the archbishop of Reggio, in an address of January 18, 1562, brought the issue up again. "The authority of the church," said he, "is illustrated most clearly by the Scriptures; for while on the one hand she [the church] recommends them, declares them to be divine, [and] offers them to us to be read, . . . on the other hand, the legal precepts in the Scriptures taught by the Lord have ceased by virtue of the same authority [the church]. The Sabbath, the most glorious day in the law, has been changed into the Lord's day. . . . These and other similar matters have not ceased by virtue of Christ's teaching (for He says He has come to fulfill the law, not to destroy it), but they have been changed by the authority of the church."[32]

This challenge to Protestantism has not been forgotten. In the 1957 printing of Peter Geiermann's *The Convert's Catechism of Catholic Doctrine,* converts to the Catholic Church are taught this series of questions and answers:

"Q. Which is the Sabbath day?

"A. Saturday is the Sabbath day.

"Q. Why do we observe Sunday instead of Saturday?

"A. We observe Sunday instead of Saturday because the Catholic Church transferred the solemnity from Saturday to Sunday."[33]

The 1958 printing of the *Catechism of the Council of Trent for Parish Priests* states that "the Church of God has thought it well to transfer the celebration and observance of the Sabbath to Sunday."[34]

In 1893 the second edition of *The Christian Sabbath* asserted, somewhat unpleasantly to be sure, that "the Catholic Church for over one thousand years before the existence of a Protestant, by virtue of her Divine mission, changed the day from Saturday to Sunday. . . . The Protestant says: How can I receive the teachings of an apostate Church? How, we ask, have you managed to receive her teaching all your life in direct opposition to your recognized teacher, the Bible, on the Sabbath question?"[35]

Few Protestants, of course, are content to take such a challenge meekly!

But the emergence of the so-called Christian Sabbath is of such vital consequence to you and your family that we will devote a separate section to it.

IV. Love for Christ and the Christian Sabbath

Driving to church next weekend, you will no doubt want to know, for your own satisfaction, whether Catholic scholars are right when they claim that their church—and not the Bible—changed the Sabbath from Saturday to Sunday.

Some surprising things that Luther said about the Ten Commandments you can read in *Your Questions Answered,* pages 144, 145. In the meantime, we'll have to rule at the outset that the Catholics have at least one foot on base. They passed some very early Sunday laws.

The emperor Constantine issued the *very* first Sunday law, on March 7, 321. But even though Constantine is known as the first Christian emperor, his first Sunday law was basically secular. It did not set up a "Christian Sabbath." Sunday had become popular among his sun-worshiping pagan subjects, and he apparently hoped that making the day a holiday would be appreciated by pagans and Christians alike and would help unite the populace in support of his administration.

His law was couched in non-Christian language. "On the venerable day of the Sun," it began, "let magistrates and people residing in cities rest, and let all workshops be closed."

Farmers, however, were excluded from Sunday rest on the ground that farm procedures have to be taken care of at "the proper moment."[36]

By contrast, the first *religious* Sunday law in Western Europe did come from the Catholics. And, for rather obvious reasons, it was considerably more severe than Constantine's; for it insisted that on "Sunday . . . agricultural labor ought to be laid aside, in order that people may not be prevented from attending church."[37]

This significant regulation is known as the 28th canon (or church law) of the Third Council of Orleans, France. This Third Council of Orleans met in 538, the same year that the power of the Ostrogoths was broken and the 1260-year

135

prophecy began. In the eighth century (two hundred years later) strange documents began to be "discovered" which claimed to be ancient and which taught that Jesus Himself had transferred the holiness of the Sabbath from the seventh day to Sunday, the first day. (One of them, known as the "Letter From Heaven," taught that Jesus Himself had warned that if a woman worked on Sunday, winged serpents would fly at her and snatch away her breasts.)[38] At this same time church laws became so strict that in some places a person could be sentenced to seven days penance for washing his hair on Sunday.[39] So when Catholics claimed in Luther's day and at the Council of Trent that they had changed the obligation from Sabbath (Saturday) to Sunday, they had a point. Catholics had, openly and honestly, attempted in this way to change the Ten Commandments, believing that God had authorized them to do so.

But the *voluntary* observance of Sunday as a day for Christian worship did not commence at the Third Council of Orleans or with Constantine's Sunday law. And so we are curious to know how and why this voluntary practice originated. The Ten Commandments say to honor the seventh day as the Sabbath, but most Christians choose to honor the first day.

The beginning of voluntary Sunday observance. Voluntary observance of Sunday as a day for Christian worship (though not as a day of rest) seems to have been widespread before the middle of the second century—and it appears to have been motivated by a sincere love for Jesus.

Around the year A.D. 160 Justin Martyr could write, "Sunday is the day on which we all hold our common assembly."[40] Justin was widely traveled and well informed. When he said, "We all," he spoke for most believers of his day.

Just as plainly, Justin, who gave this report, must have loved the Lord dearly. Around the year 165 he willingly surrendered his life for Christ's sake and was beheaded by Roman authorities. Shortly before his arrest, but when he already knew that his life was in danger, he published a tract in which he wrote, "I boast, and with all my heart strive to be found a Christian."[41] Justin was an active Christian layman. He taught Bible prophecy to pagans and Jews and appears to have won a considerable number to the church.

What specific reasons did Justin give for Christian meetings on Sunday? Three major ones: (1) on Sunday Christ rose from the dead, (2) on Sunday God made light, and (3) Sunday is the "eighth day," which follows the seventh and, in the cycle of the week, is again the first.[42]

This "eighth day" idea need not delay us. Many early Christian writers saw a parallel between the Old Testament ritual of circumcision, performed on the eighth day of a baby boy's life, and the new Christian worship, performed on the "eighth day" of every week (the day which followed the seventh day). The "eighth day" was, of course, the same as the "first day." Early Christians felt that by worshiping on the eighth day of the week they somehow became heirs to the covenant promises given to circumcised Israelites. Barnabas, another Christian writer, tells us (around A.D. 130) that Christians celebrated the eighth day "with gladness."[43] Barnabas, like Justin, also says that Christians worshiped on Sunday because "on that day Jesus rose from the dead."

Early Christians gave many Christ-centered arguments in favor of Sunday worship. Christ was the New Law; Christ introduced the New Covenant; Christ, after His second coming, would, they said, provide heavenly rest during an "eighth day" eternity that would follow the "sabbath" millennium.[44] They acknowledged that Jesus kept the Sabbath Himself, but they insisted—though they offered no Bible text to prove it—that He had abolished it for His followers. Their favorite reason for Sunday observance was, of course, that on the first day of the week Jesus rose from the dead.

The Gospels do state repeatedly that Jesus rose from the dead on the first day of the week.[45] It is understandable that early Christians tended to look on the first day as a sort of weekly anniversary.

There is something else to be considered. By the time Jesus lived on earth the Sabbath had become encrusted with a variety of man-made regulations. For example, a sheep or an ox could be pulled out of a ditch on the Sabbath, but a person could not be treated for a chronic illness on that day. Jesus defied such traditions (see, e.g., Matthew 12:1-14). Those Christians who gave up the Sabbath in favor of Sunday most probably reasoned that they were abandoning not the Sabbath of God but a legalistic sabbath of human tradition. Sunday, with its joyous resurrection memories, must have seemed a superior monument to the Saviour's love.

We just used the words, "Those Christians who gave up the Sabbath." The truth is that the early Christians did *not all* give up the seventh-day Sabbath in favor of Sunday. An indeterminate number continued to observe the seventh-day Sabbath in some way or other. In the second and third centuries we hear about these Sabbath-observing Christians all around the Roman Empire. They lived in areas known today as Egypt, Tunisia, Turkey, Palestine, Syria, Italy, France, Yugoslavia, and more.[46] By the fifth century, in the Eastern Roman Empire, services were held regularly on Sabbath as well as on Sunday in almost all churches.[47] In Armenia and Ethiopia (Aksum) the Sabbath was observed as a rest day along with Sunday. It was principally in the Western Roman Empire, where Catholic influence was strong, that Sabbath services were not conducted on a general basis (see the map and box on pages 140, 141).

We have thus far seen that early Christians adopted Sunday because of their love for the Lord. On the other hand, many writers have said that Sunday was adopted because Jesus Christ specifically asked His followers to worship on that day. But, strange as it may seem, *not one writer of the second and third centuries ever cited a single Bible verse as authority* for the observance of Sunday in the place of the Sabbath. Neither Barnabas, nor Ignatius, nor Justin, nor Irenaeus, nor Tertullian, nor Clement of Rome, nor Clement of Alexandria, nor Origen, nor Cyprian, nor Victorinus, nor any other author who lived near to the time when Jesus lived knew of any such instruction from Jesus or from any part of the Bible.

137

Christians of the second and third centuries believed that Jesus was pleased to have them hold Sunday in special regard; but even though they often cited Bible proofs for their doctrines, they never once cited a Bible commandment requiring them to observe the first day of the week.

This of course helps to explain why it was that in the eighth century and later people had to "discover" ancient documents that claimed to teach that Jesus had transferred the Sabbath of the fourth commandment from the seventh to the first day of the week.

It also helps to explain why the term "Christian Sabbath" did not come into common use for many centuries after the church was founded. Professor Peter Heylyn, after extensive research, tells us[48] that "the first [person] who ever used this title"—Christian Sabbath, *Christianorum Sabbatum*—"to denote the Lord's day (the first that I have met with in all this search) is one Petrus Alfonsus" who lived about the year 1100.*

Sabbath keepers who loved the Lord. Now what about those early Christians we mentioned a moment ago who did *not* give up the Sabbath in favor of Sunday? Is it possible that they *refused* to give up the Sabbath because of their love for the Lord?

Unfortunately none of their writings have come down to us. Perhaps they never wrote any. Happily, however, we do know quite a bit about some other Sabbath-keeping Christians who lived in the time of Martin Luther and later. There can be no reasonable doubt that *these* Christian Sabbath keepers did keep the Sabbath because they loved the Lord.

Sabbath keepers Oswald Glait, Andreas Fischer and his wife, and John James are known to have accepted martyrdom in the sixteenth and seventeenth centuries for the sake of Jesus Christ—just as Justin and other Sunday keepers did in the second and third centuries. Other Sabbath keepers, like John and Dorothy Traske and John Bampfield, accepted jail terms.

So here is a dilemma! Some Christians who loved Christ enough to die for Him have abandoned the Sabbath and adopted Sunday, and other Christians who loved Him enough to die for Him have abandoned Sunday and adopted the Sabbath.

So who have been right?

One basic difference between these later Christian Sabbath keepers and the early Christian Sunday keepers may help us to decide. The Sabbath keepers used specific Scriptures in direct support of their position.

Martin Luther, as a Catholic teaching-priest, startled Europe and started the Reformation by championing *sola Scriptura,* "The Bible and the Bible only." Many devout Catholics, deeply stirred, followed his lead and became Lutherans, even though in many cases they lost their lives as a result. Angry bishops hanged Lutherans from trees in batches.[49]

*Heylyn overlooked the use of the term, "Christian Sabbath," by Origen in the third century, in Origen's *Homily 23 on Numbers;* but Heylyn rightly emphasized the rarity of the use of the term among Christians for over a thousand years.

Sabbath-keeping Christians met in the cave temples of Ethiopia.

139

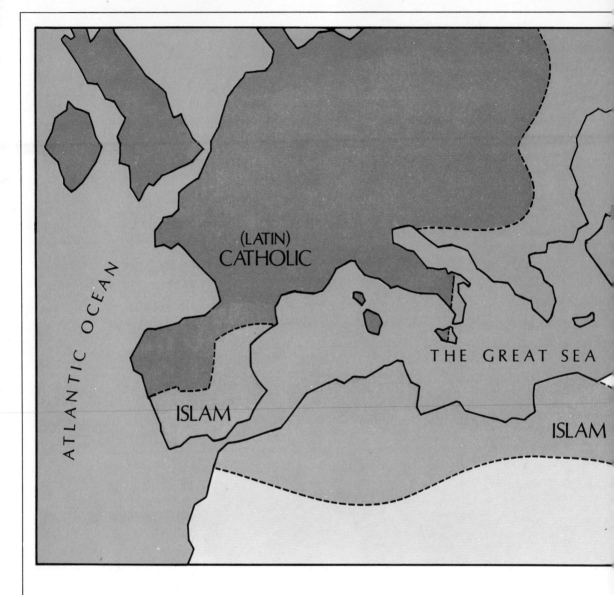

ATLANTIC OCEAN

(LATIN) CATHOLIC

THE GREAT SEA

ISLAM

ISLAM

SABBATH OBSERVANCE AS OF A.D. 1054

A.D. 1054 marks a watershed, not only in Christian history as a whole, but also in the history of Sabbath observance. In that year Orthodox Christians and Catholic Christians excommunicated each other. The Great Schism (SIZ-um), or division, which resulted lasted until 1967.

One of the principal issues which led to this tragic separation in 1054 was Rome's opposition to the Sabbath.[50] Patriarch Michael Cerularius and his associates in Constantinople insisted in 1053 and 1054 that the Roman Catholics ought to abandon their gloomy Saturday fasts. They said that the way the Catholics treated the Sabbath had no foundation in Scripture and seriously altered the intended character of the Sabbath as a day of joy.

Pope Leo IX refused to make the requested change. He insisted instead that because he was the successor of Peter his word was law for all faithful Christians to obey.

Tempers flared, and Pope Leo ordered his representative, the papal legate Cardinal Humbert, to present the patriarch of Constantinople with an official document denouncing his "Orthodox" Christians as being on a level with "the devil and his angels."[51]

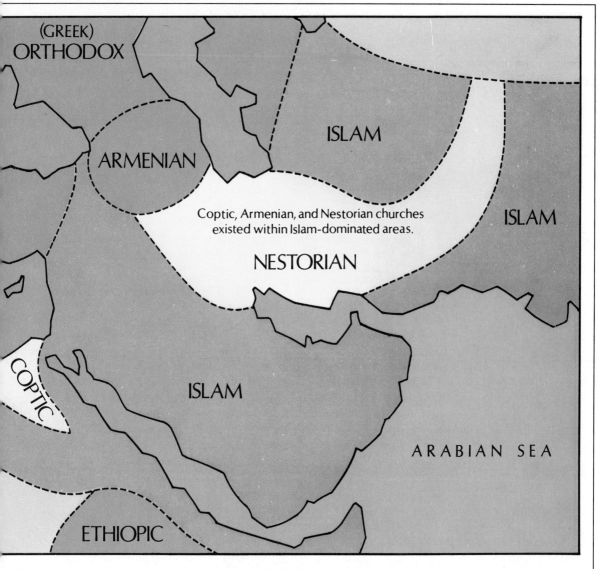

The map portrays the six major branches of Christianity as they existed in 1054: Catholic, Orthodox, Armenian, Nestorian, Egyptian (or Coptic), and Ethiopic. In the areas depicted as Orthodox, Armenian, and Ethiopic the Sabbath was honored, along with Sunday, by regular worship services. In addition to holding meetings, Armenian and Ethiopic Christians also honored the Sabbath by resting on that day as well as on Sunday.[52]

From the seventh century onward the Nestorian, Armenian, and Egyptian (Coptic) churches were outrivaled in influence by Islam as a result of the Moslem conquests. (Contrary to popular belief, the early Moslems, unlike some later ones, did not compel Christians and Jews to accept Islam or die; they stipulated instead that Christians and Jews had to pay extra taxes; then they resisted the conversion of Christians to Islam as causing an erosion of the tax base.[53] Nonetheless, Islam greatly diluted the influence of Christianity in the lands it conquered.)

Thus the Catholics emerged as *the primary Christian opponents of the seventh-day Sabbath*. This helps explain why Daniel 7 portrays the Catholic Church as "thinking to change the times and the law."

The fact that Sunday is observed by Christians in most parts of the world today to the exclusion of the Sabbath is explained by the vigorous missionary work conducted by Catholics and Protestants after the Reformation. Both Catholic and Protestant missionaries carried with them around the world the Catholic opposition to the Sabbath.

But as some of these Catholics-turned-Lutherans studied the Bible they learned to their surprise that the Christian Sunday has no clear root in Scripture. Oswald Glait and Andreas Fischer, two Lutheran ministers who had once been Catholic priests, committed themselves in 1527 to the Bible Sabbath, the "Sabbath of the Lord your God." Exodus 20:8-11.

Luther was disturbed to have his followers reach this particular conclusion. He sent some of his best theologians[54] to visit Glait and Fischer to try to change their minds. He asked the theologians to tell Glait and Fischer that the Ten Commandments as a whole were indeed binding but that the seventh-day Sabbath was a mere ceremony which Jesus Christ abolished when He died on the cross. (For a discussion of Luther's view, see *Your Questions Answered,* pages 144, 145.) Here is a summary of the dialogue between them:

1. *Isn't the Sabbath part of the ceremonial law?* asked the Lutheran theologians. No, replied Fischer and Glait. It cannot be part of the law of sacrifices and circumcision, they said, because that law was given after man sinned. It was intended to point sinners symbolically to their Saviour, Jesus. On the other hand, the Sabbath was given as soon as man was created (Genesis 2:3), *before* he had sinned. Hence the Sabbath was given, they said, before man needed any ceremonies to symbolize a Saviour.

2. *But isn't the Sabbath itself merely a ceremony?* insisted the Lutherans. No, answered Fischer and Glait. It is embodied in the heart of the Ten Commandments, and the Ten Commandments, as Luther himself admitted, was *moral* law. Observance of the seventh-day Sabbath involves a moral issue, they said.

3. *But didn't Jesus abolish the Sabbath at the cross?* No, said Fischer and Glait. To the contrary, Jesus Himself said in Matthew 5:17, 18, "Think not that I have come to abolish the law and the prophets; I have come not to abolish them but to fulfill them. For truly, I say to you, till heaven and earth pass away, not an iota, not a dot, will pass from the law until all is accomplished." Further, Jesus added, "Whoever then relaxes one of the least of these commandments and teaches men so, shall be called least in the kingdom of heaven; but he who does them and teaches them shall be called great in the kingdom of heaven." Matthew 5:19.

4. *But didn't the apostles show that the obligation of the Sabbath had been terminated?* asked the Lutherans. No, answered Fischer and Glait. Paul said in Romans 3:31 that by faith "we *uphold* the law"; we don't overthrow it. And James shows in his epistle (2:10-12) that breaking even "one point" of the Decalogue makes a person guilty of breaking it all.

5. *Then where do you think Sunday observance came from?* asked the Lutherans. To which Fischer and Glait replied by quoting Daniel 7:25. They told the Lutheran theologians that the **"little horn"** would try to change God's law—the very thing we have been studying in this chapter.

The Christian Sabbath and the love of Jesus. So which is the true "Christian Sabbath" for people who have felt the saving power of grace and who love Jesus with all their hearts?

Professor McKenzie, our helpful Jesuit professor at Notre Dame University, has no trouble at this point. He recognizes freely that the Roman Catholic Church cherishes many beliefs not found in the Bible. He defends these beliefs on the basis that they have resulted from "a kind of inner compulsion," a "surging" within, a true "religious experience" in the Catholic Church which adequately justifies them.[55]

Protestants and Catholics can agree that it was precisely such a surge of religious experience that led to the substitution of Sunday worship for Sabbath keeping.

So the question we have to ask ourselves in church school and at family worship is this: is a surge of conviction a sufficient substitute for Scripture?

With pathos Jesus asked the people of His day, "Why do you transgress the commandment of God for the sake of your tradition?" Matthew 15:3. (The "commandment of God" He was talking about was one of the Ten Commandments. See verse 4.) To His own followers Jesus said tenderly, "If you love me, you will keep my commandments." John 14:15.

Further Interesting Reading

In Arthur S. Maxwell, *The Bible Story,* vol. 6:
"Animals From the Sea," beginning on p. 60.
In Ellen G. White, *The Triumph of God's Love:*
The chapters entitled "Rejecting God's Word" and "Defending the Faith in the Mountains."
In *Bible Readings for the Home:*
The chapters entitled "The Kingdom and Work of Antichrist" and "The Change of the Sabbath."

Your Questions Answered

1. Did the early Christians believe that they were living in the time of the fourth beast? Yes, at least we know that some of them did. Hippolytus, who lived either in or near Rome from about A.D. 170 to about A.D. 236, is called by the *Oxford Dictionary of the Christian Church* "the most important 3rd cent. theologian of the Roman Church." What Hippolytus taught in the following portion of his *Commentary on Daniel* is strikingly akin to what we have been studying in our analysis of Daniel 7. The translation is taken from The Ante-Nicene Fathers, volume 5, pages 178, 179.

> The "golden head of the image" is identical with the "lioness," by which the Babylonians were represented. "The golden shoulders and the arms of silver" are the same with the "bear," by which the Persians and Medes are meant. "The belly and thighs of brass" are the "leopard," by which the Greeks who ruled from Alexander onwards are intended. The "legs of iron" are the "dreadful and terrible beast," by which the Romans who hold the empire now are meant. The "toes of clay and iron" are the "ten horns" which are to be. The "one other little horn springing up in their midst" is the "antichrist." The stone that "smites the image and breaks it in pieces," and that filled the whole earth, is Christ, who comes from heaven and brings judgment on the world.

2. What did Luther teach about the Ten Commandments? Martin Luther was a grand person, a great Christian, a thrilling writer, and a perceptive theologian. But with his enormous vigor, it was hard for him at times to be a *consistent* theologian. About the Ten Commandments and the Sabbath he said things that did not always harmonize.

When writing *Against the Heavenly Prophets* in opposition to a group of fanatics, he said, "Moses was given only to the Jewish people and does not concern us Gentiles and Christians. . . . Paul abolished the Sabbath by name and called it a bygone shadow."[56]

But when writing *Against the Sabbatarians* in opposition to Sabbath keepers like Oswalt Glaid and Andreas Fischer, Luther said surprisingly, "Lastly we want to speak also about the Ten Commandments, for the Jew perhaps too will call the Ten Commandments Moses' law because it was given on Mount Sinai, where there were then only Jews or Abraham's children, et cetera. Here you should answer: 'If the Ten Commandments are to be called Moses' law, Moses came much too late; besides, he had far too few people in front of him [when he read them]. For the Ten Commandments were not only before Moses but also before Abraham and all the patriarchs, also they have gone over the whole world. Even if no Moses had ever come, and Abraham had not been born, still in all mankind the Ten Commandments would have had to reign from the beginning, as they have done and still do.'"[57]

When writing *Against the Antinomians* in opposition to people who said

*Martin Luther on one occasion stated that "God wanted this com-
mandment about sanctifying the Sabbath to remain in force."*

that Christians do not need to keep the Ten Commandments, Luther said, "I
wonder exceedingly how it came to be imputed to me that I should reject the
law or the Ten Commandments. . . . Can anyone think that sin exists where
there is no law? Whoever abrogates the law, must of necessity abrogate sin
also."[58]

And when writing his commentary on Genesis, he said, "The seventh day
He did sanctify for Himself. This had the special purpose of making us understand that the seventh day in particular should be devoted to divine worship.
. . . Although man lost his knowledge of God, nevertheless God wanted this
commandment about sanctifying the Sabbath to remain in force."[59]

3. Can you say more about how the three tribes were uprooted? The process by
which the three tribes (or **"horns"**) were uprooted in favor of the **"little horn"**
can be read about in encyclopedias and in medieval history books available in
most local libraries.

Zeno, the Eastern Roman Emperor (474-491), grew increasingly fearful of the
Arian Ostrogoths, who were encamped in a reserve not far from Constantinople where they were becoming increasingly restless. At the same time
Zeno was deeply concerned about the Arian Heruls in Italy, whose leader,
Odovacar, in 476 had removed the last of the Western Roman Emperors and
had proclaimed himself king. (This action of Odovacar's is viewed as marking
the "fall of the [Western] Roman Empire.")

145

In 487 Zeno officially commissioned Theodoric, leader of the Ostrogoths, to march to Italy and dispose of the Heruls. Zeno reckoned that in the process he would relieve Constantinople of its ferocious neighbors. Further, whichever tribe won the contest in Italy, he would have one less Arian tribe to contend with. As things turned out, after five years of fighting, the Ostrogoths fulfilled their mission from Zeno and destroyed the Heruls, who disappeared from history. Thus the Catholic emperor Zeno accomplished the elimination of one of the Arian horns.

Theodoric died in 526. The following year Justinian became emperor in the East. Justinian was deeply committed to religious affairs, but his citizens were by no means all united with him. In fact Justinian ruled three different kinds of Christians: the Arians, principally in the West, who believed firmly that Jesus was basically human; the Monophysites, principally in the East, who believed firmly that Jesus was basically divine; and the Catholics, who believed firmly that Jesus was both human and divine. Justinian himself sided so strongly with the Catholics that in 533 he officially stated that the pope of Rome was the "head of all the holy churches"; and in harmony with this declaration he spent his long reign attempting to convert or eliminate everyone who did *not* regard the pope as head.

In the 530s Justinian launched a holy war against the Arian Vandals and the Arian Ostrogoths. He found legal pretexts for doing this, of course, but Procopius, the historian-reporter who went along on the campaign, reveals in his *History of the Wars*[60] that Justinian's real purpose was to "protect the Christians," that is, to protect the Catholics from the Arians.

Justinian commissioned his finest general, Belisarius, to sail with an army from Constantinople to North Africa and destroy the Vandals. After the crucial battle of Tricamarum the Vandals in 534 "disappeared like a mist," says the *Shorter Cambridge Medieval History*.[61]

Belisarius, obeying orders, then turned north against the Arian Ostrogoths in Italy. He took Palermo on the island of Sicily by using the masts of his ships to raise boatloads of soldiers to the top of the city walls. In December 536 he marched unopposed into Rome with a mere 5000 men. The Ostrogoths counterattacked by surrounding Rome with 150,000 men (Procopius says [62]), making Belisarius a prisoner inside the city he hoped to liberate.

The Goths then foolishly cut the fourteen aqueducts leading into Rome in the hope of driving Belisarius to surrender from lack of water. But the torrents that poured from the broken aqueducts created a quagmire that bred malarial mosquitoes and caused epidemics. The large Gothic army was so grievously reduced by disease that in March 538 Belisarius with his small force was able to defeat it handily.

Skirmishes and battles followed here and there in Italy for a number of years until the Catholic general Narses annihilated all but a couple of thousand Ostrogoths—and the Ostrogoths, like the Heruls and Vandals, disappeared

146

from history. In the process calamitous famine and pestilence drove the people to cannibalism, says Procopius, and two women alone ate seventeen men.[63] Charles Oman, in *The Dark Ages,* adds that "in the northern plain, in Picenum and Aemilia, and in the neighborhood of Rome, the whole population . . . disappeared."[64] Even for the survivors, laments the *Shorter Cambridge Medieval History,*[65] "nothing remained but to die."

And the crucial military event that lay behind this pathetic scene was the calamitous defeat of Rome in 538 when, says Thomas Hodgkin in *Italy and Her Invaders,* Catholic soldiers "dug the grave of the Gothic monarchy."[66]

Thus was the prophecy of Daniel 7 fulfilled that said, **"Three of the first horns were plucked up by the roots,"** allowing the little horn to grow greater than the rest.

References

1. Joseph Ward Swain, *The Ancient World,* 2 vols. (New York: Harper & Row, 1950), 2:40-42.

2. James Dobson, *What Wives Wish Their Husbands Knew About Women* (Wheaton, Ill.: Tyndale House Publishers, 1975). See also, James Dobson, "What Wives Wish Their Husbands Knew About Women," *These Times,* December 1978, pp. 11-15.

3. Philip Schaff, *History of the Christian Church,* 8 vols., reprint of the 3d (1910) ed. (Grand Rapids, Mich.: Wm. B. Eerdmans Publishing Co., n.d.) 4:290.

4. LeRoy Edwin Froom, *The Prophetic Faith of Our Fathers,* 4 vols. (Washington, D.C.: Review and Herald Publishing Association, 1950-1954), 1:800.

5. *Ibid.,* 2:49.

6. *Ibid.,* pp. 257, 258.

7. *The Passion of the Holy Martyrs Perpetua and Felicitas;* ANF 3:699-706.

8. Ambrose, Letter 25, in A. H. M. Jones, *The Later Roman Empire, 284-602,* 2 vols. (Norman, Okla.: University of Oklahoma Press, 1964), 2:983.

9. Pontius the Deacon, *The Life and Passion of Cyprian, Bishop and Martyr,* 18; ANF 5:274.

10. Eusebius, *Church History,* 8.9; NPNF, 2d ser., 1:330.

11. W. H. C. Frend, *Martyrdom and Persecution in the Early Church: A Study of a Conflict from the Maccabees to Donatus* (New York: New York University Press, 1967), pp. 308-394. Frend calculates that a maximum of 3500 died under the Diocletian persecution and only "hundreds" under the Decian persecution. Inasmuch as all other persecution was spotty, local, and occasional during the period under study, he is led to conclude that between Pentecost and the close of the era of persecution under pagan Rome the total number of martyrdoms did not exceed 5000.

12. Hippolytus, *The Refutation of All Heresies,* 9.10; ANF 5:132, 133.

13. Geoffrey Chaucer, *Canterbury Tales,* in modern English. Translated by Frank Ernest Hill (London: Everymans, Green & Co., 1930).

14. John L. McKenzie, S.J., *The Roman Catholic Church,* ed. E. O. James, History of Religion Series (New York: Holt, Rinehart and Winston, 1969).

15. *Ibid.,* p. xii.

16. *Ibid.*

17. Ammianus Marcellinus, *History,* trans. in James Westfall Thompson and Edgar Nathaniel Johnson, *An Introduction to Medieval Europe, 300-1500* (New York: W. W. Norton & Co., 1937), p. 89.

18. Compare the list in Thompson and Johnson, *Medieval Europe,* pp. 88, 89.

19. *The Book of the Popes (Liber Pontificalis)*, trans. Louise Ropes Loomis, eds. James T. Shotwell et al., Records of Civilization, Sources and Studies, no. 3 (New York: Columbia University Press, 1916), pp. 131-138.

20. See, e.g., McKenzie, *Catholic Church*, p. 14.

21. *Ibid.*, p. 204.

22. J. D. Mansi, ed., *Sacrorum Conciliorum . . , Collectio, 32·761.*

23. *Oxford Dictionary of the Christian Church* (1957 ed.), art. "Julius II."

24. Roland H. Bainton, *The Reformation of the Sixteenth Century* (Boston: The Beacon Press, 1952), p. 18.

25. Thompson and Johnson, *Medieval Europe*, p. 1015.

26. *New Catholic Encyclopedia*, arts. "Inquisition," "Auto-da-Fé," and "St. Bartholomew's Day, Massacre of."

27. John Foxe, *Book of Martyrs* (New York: Charles K. Moore, 1847), chaps. on persecutions in Scotland under Henry VIII and in England under Mary.

28. See George E. McCracken and Allen Cabaniss, eds., *Early Medieval Theology*, eds. John Baillie, John T. McNeill, and Henry P. Van Dusen, The Library of Christian Classics (Philadelphia: The Westminster Press, 1957), vol. 9, pp. 168, 169.

29. *New Catholic Encyclopedia*, art. "Torture."

30. See Lucius Ferraris, *Prompta Bibliotheca*, 8 vols. (Venice: Caspa Storti, 1772), art. "Papa, II."

31. John Eck, *Enchiridion of Commonplaces of John Eck Against Luther and Other Enemies of the Church*, trans. F. L. Battles, 2d ed. (Grand Rapids, Mich.: Calvin Theological Seminary, 1978), 8v, p. 13.

32. Mansi, *Sacrorum Conciliorum*, 33:529, 530.

33. Peter Geiermann, *The Convert's Catechism of Christian Doctrine* (St. Louis, Mo.: B. Herder Book Co., 1930), p. 50.

34. *Catechism of the Council of Trent for Parish Priests* (New York: Joseph W. Wagner, 1934), pp. 402, 403.

35. *The Christian Sabbath*, 2d ed. (Baltimore: The Catholic Mirror [1893]), pp. 29-31.

36. Constantine's first Sunday law can be read in many places. One place is Henry Bettenson, ed., *Documents of the Christian Church*, 2d ed. (London: Oxford University Press, 1963). In classical times it appeared in the *Corpus Juris Civilis*, 2.127.

37. Mansi, *Sacrorum Conciliorum*, 9:19. Cited as the 29th canon and trans. in part in John Nevins Andrews, *History of the Sabbath and First Day of the Week*, 2d ed. (Battle Creek, Mich.: Steam Press of the Seventh-day Adventist Publishing Association, 1873), p. 372.

38. See Robert Priebsch, *Letter From Heaven on the Observance of the Lord's Day* (Oxford: Basil Blackwell, 1936).

39. John T. McNeill and Helena M. Gamer, *Medieval Handbooks of Penance: A Translation of the Principal* Libri Poenitentiales *and Selections from Related Documents*, eds. Austin P. Evans et al., Records of Civilization, Sources and Studies, no. 29 (New York: Columbia University Press, 1938), p. 272.

40. Justin, *First Apology*, 67; ANF 1:186.

41. Justin, *Second Apology*, 13; ANF 1:192, 193.

42. Justin, *First Apology*, 67, and *Dialogue with the Jew Trypho*, 24; ANF 1:186, 206.

43. Barnabas, *Epistle*, 15; Compare the trans. here with ANF 1:147.

44. E.g., *ibid.*

45. Matthew 28:1; Mark 16:2, 9; Luke 24:1; John 20:1, 19.

46. See, e.g., for Ephesus and Rome, Justin, *Dialogue*, 47; ANF 1:218. For North Africa, Tertullian, *On Prayer*, 23; ANF 3:689. For Syria, *Didascalia Apostolorum*, trans. with intro. and notes R. Hugh Connolly (Oxford: Clarendon Press, 1929), pp. 236-244. For Pettau, in modern Yugoslavia, Victorinus, *On the Creation of the World;* ANF 7:341, 342.

47. Socrates Scholasticus, *Church History,* 5.22: NPNF, 2d ser., 2:132.

48. Peter Heylyn, *History of the Sabbath* (London, 1636), part 2, chap. 5, sec. 13.

49. Roland H. Bainton, *Here I Stand: A Life of Martin Luther* (New York: Abingdon-Cokesbury Press, 1950), p. 316. For an old woodcut, see Oscar Handlin, *A Pictorial History of Immigration* (New York: Crown Publishers, 1972), p. 49.

50. R. L. Odom, "The Sabbath in the Great Schism of A.D. 1054," *Andrews University Seminary Studies* 1 (1963): 74-80.

51. In Albert Henry Newman, *A Manual of Church History,* rev. ed., 2 vols. (Philadelphia: The American Baptist Publication Society, 1933), 1:626.

52. Kenneth A. Strand, ed., *The Sabbath in Scripture and History* (Washington, D.C.: Review and Herald Publishing Association, 1981). See esp. chaps. by Werner Vyhmeister.

53. See, e.g., William H. McNeill, *The Rise of the West: A History of the Human Community* (Chicago: University of Chicago Press, 1963), pp. 430, 508-512.

54. See Gerhard Hasel, "Sabbatarian Anabaptists of the Sixteenth Century," two parts, *Andrews University Seminary Studies* 5 (July 1967): 101-121, and 6 (January 1968):19-28.

55. McKenzie, *Catholic Church,* p. 214.

56. Martin Luther, *Sämmtliche Schriften* [Collected Works], ed. J. G. Walch, 23 vols. in 25 bks. (St. Louis, Mo.: Concordia Publishing House, 1891-1910), vol. 20, cols. 146-148.

57. *Ibid.,* col. 1952.

58. *Ibid.,* cols. 1613, 1614.

59. Comments on Genesis 2:3. Martin Luther, *Luther's Works: American Edition,* eds. Jaroslav Pelikan and Helmut T. Lehman, 55 vols. (St. Louis, Mo.: Concordia Publishing House, 1955-), 1:79, 80.

60. Procopius, *History of the Wars,* 3.10.19.

61. C. W. Previté-Orton, *Shorter Cambridge Medieval History,* 2 vols. (Cambridge: University Press, 1953), 1:189.

62. Procopius, *History,* 5.16.11.

63. *Ibid.,* 6.20.27.

64. Charles Oman, *The Dark Ages, 476-916,* 4th ed. (London: Rivingtons, 1901), p. 106.

65. Previté-Orton, *Shorter Medieval History,* p. 192.

66. Thomas Hodgkin, *Italy and Her Invaders,* 2d ed., 8 vols. in 9 (Oxford: Clarendon Press, 1885-1899), 4:250.

Daniel 8
God and His Sanctuary

Introduction

During evening homework hours, how many parents have responded to the plaintive sigh of their children, "I just can't understand it!"

And how many parents have found that their children *could* have understood if they had read the explanation in the book!

In Daniel 8 we are invited to study yet another set of prophetic symbols; and, as for chapters 2 and 7, God provides the explanation so we can understand.

Indeed the word **"understand"** occurs so often from Daniel 8 onward that it becomes almost a motif for the balance of the book (see Daniel 8:16, 17; 9:23, 25; 10:12, 14; 11:33; 12:10).

But in Daniel 8, even though the interpretation begins right away just as it does in chapters 2 and 7, it is not completed within the limits of the chapter. It is continued at the end of chapter 9.

The prophetic symbols in Daniel 8 include beasts and horns as before and also a prophetic symbol of a period of time. While still in the vision Daniel hears a voice saying, **"Gabriel, make this man understand the vision,"** and immediately Gabriel comes to Daniel's side and bids him **"understand"** it. Verses 16 and 17.

But no sooner has Gabriel explained the beasts and horns than he finds he has to stop. The picture he has painted has caused Daniel, now an old man, to faint away. The vision ceases and Daniel says regretfully—almost like a child doing his homework—**"I was appalled by the vision and did not understand it."** Verse 27.

This is where Daniel 9 will fit in, a few years later. When Daniel gives himself heart and soul to the understanding of time prophecy, Gabriel will appear again, explaining that he has come to give Daniel **"wisdom and understanding."** Calling on him once more to **"understand the vision,"** the angel will start right in to resolve the time symbolism, just where he had left off at the end of Daniel 8.

It has often been pointed out that Jesus urged every one of us to "understand" Daniel 8 and 9 during His famous conversation with the disciples on the Mount of Olives (the "Olivet Discourse") a few nights before His crucifixion. Citing a key phrase from Daniel 9:27, similar to one in Daniel 8:13, Jesus said significantly, "Let the reader understand." Matthew 24:15.

It is attractive to assume that it was also *Jesus who commanded Gabriel to make Daniel understand the vision* in the first place. Daniel 8:15, 16 says:

When I, Daniel, had seen the vision [*of the beasts, horns, and time symbol*], **I sought to understand it; and behold, there stood before me *one having the appearance of a man.* And I heard a**

When God chose to represent Persia and Greece by a ram and a goat, animals of the sanctuary services, He called our attention to the centrality of the sanctuary in Daniel 8.

151

man's voice between the banks of the [river] Ulai, and it called, "Gabriel, make this man understand the vision."

The New Testament tells us in Luke 1.19 that Gabriel is the angel who stands "in the presence of God." Any being who can issue a command to Gabriel must rank very high in the administration of the universe. In the passage we just read, this exalted being is described as **"one having the appearance of a man."** Who could this being be but the same Person who in Daniel 7:13, is described as **"one like a son of man"**—that is, Jesus Christ, who is called the Son of man forty times in the Gospels (see p. 116)?

So Jesus our Saviour deeply desires us to understand the prophecy of Daniel 8 and 9.

And it is well worth our understanding. For it applies to the **"time of the end"** (Daniel 8:17), and it deals with the grandest theme of the ages.

Daniel 2 takes us through the rise and fall of nations and reaches its climax as Jesus Christ, the supernatural stone, sets up His kingdom of glory.

Daniel 7 takes us through the political scenes a second time, adding the tragic course of medieval Christianity, and reaches its climax as the judgment meets in heaven, where Christ receives His kingdom and graciously shares it with every "saint" found worthy.

Chapters 8 and 9 likewise take us through the political entities of history (omitting Babylon this time) and through medieval Christianity, but they point more directly to Christ's work of atonement and of salvation from sin which makes it possible for sinners to become saints so that they *can* inherit the kingdom.

Daniel 2 focuses on Christ our King.

Daniel 7 focuses on Christ our Judge.

Daniel 8 and 9 focus on Christ our High Priest, who died for our sins and is living again for our salvation.

As you read Daniel 8 (on the next page), see how much of it you can understand without further assistance. Then we'll discuss some of its aspects in detail.

CHAPTER 8

1 In the third year of the reign of King Belshazzar a vision appeared to me, Daniel, after that which appeared to me at the first. ² And I saw in the vision; and when I saw, I was in Susa the capital, which is in the province of Elam; and I saw in the vision, and I was at the river Ulai. ³ I raised my eyes and saw, and behold, a ram standing on the bank of the river. It had two horns; and both horns were high, but one was higher than the other, and the higher one came up last. ⁴ I saw the ram charging westward and northward and southward; no beast could stand before him, and there was no one who could rescue from his power; he did as he pleased and magnified himself.

5 As I was considering, behold, a he-goat came from the west across the face of the whole earth, without touching the ground; and the goat had a conspicuous horn between his eyes. ⁶ He came to the ram with the two horns, which I had seen standing on the bank of the river, and he ran at him in his mighty wrath. ⁷ I saw him come close to the ram, and he was enraged against him and struck the ram and broke his two horns; and the ram had no power to stand before him, but he cast him down to the ground and trampled upon him; and there was no one who could rescue the ram from his power. ⁸ Then the he-goat magnified himself exceedingly; but when he was strong, the great horn was broken, and instead of it there came up four conspicuous horns toward the four winds of heaven.

9 Out of one of them came forth a little horn, which grew exceedingly great toward the south, toward the east, and toward the glorious land. ¹⁰ It grew great, even to the host of heaven; and some of the host of the stars it cast down to the ground, and trampled upon them. ¹¹ It magnified itself, even up to the Prince of the host; and the continual burnt offering was taken away from him, and the place of his sanctuary was overthrown. ¹² And the host was given over to it together with the continual burnt offering through transgression; and truth was cast down to the ground, and the horn acted and prospered. ¹³ Then I heard a holy one speaking; and another holy one said to the one that spoke, "For how long is the vision concerning the continual burnt offering, the transgression that makes desolate, and the giving over of the sanctuary and host to be trampled under foot?" ¹⁴ And he said to him, "For two thousand and three hundred evenings and mornings; then the sanctuary shall be restored to its rightful state."

15 When I, Daniel, had seen the vision, I sought to understand it; and behold, there stood before me one having the appearance of a man. ¹⁶ And I heard a man's voice between the banks of the Ulai, and it called, "Gabriel, make this man understand the vision." ¹⁷ So he came near where I stood; and when he came, I was frightened and fell upon my face. But he said to me, "Understand, O son of man, that the vision is for the time of the end."

18 As he was speaking to me, I fell into a deep sleep with my face to the ground; but he touched me and set me on my feet. ¹⁹ He said, "Behold, I will make known to you what shall be at the latter end of the indignation; for it pertains to the appointed time of the end. ²⁰ As for the ram which you saw with the two horns, these are the kings of Media and Persia. ²¹ And the he-goat is the king of Greece; and the great horn between his eyes is the first king. ²² As for the horn that was broken, in place of which four others arose, four kingdoms shall arise from his nation, but not with his power. ²³ And at the latter end of their rule, when the transgressors have reached their full measure, a king of bold countenance, one who understands riddles, shall arise. ²⁴ His power shall be great, and he shall cause fearful destruction, and shall succeed in what he does, and destroy mighty men and the people of the saints. ²⁵ By his cunning he shall make deceit prosper under his hand, and in his own mind he shall magnify himself. Without warning he shall destroy many; and he shall even rise up against the

Prince of princes; but, by no human hand, he shall be broken. [26] The vision of the evenings and the mornings which has been told is true; but seal up the vision, for it pertains to many days hence.''

27 And I, Daniel, was overcome and lay sick for some days; then I rose and went about the king's business; but I was appalled by the vision and did not understand it.

The Message of Daniel 8

I. Two More Beasts Foreshadow the Future

"But, sir," shouted several of Alexander's soldiers, "look at their wagons! As soon as we climb up anywhere near them, they'll let the heavy things roll down and crush us. What can we do?"

"What can you do?" smiled Alexander. "You can lie down with your long shields covering your bodies and let the wagons roll over you. Then you can get up and finish the job."

The two beasts and their horns. We'll meet Alexander again in a moment. In the meantime we note with complete assurance the identification of the two beasts and their several horns in the first part of Daniel 8.

The ram with two horns, the shorter of which came to be the taller one, is specifically identified with Media and Persia. Daniel 8:20. The one-horned goat that flew over the ground and vanquished the ram is specifically called Greece. Daniel 8:21. Its single horn is defined (Daniel 8:22) as its **"first king,"** Alexander, or more properly as the kingdom of Alexander. (We have seen in Daniel 7:17, 23 that "king" equals "kingdom.") The four horns that rose when the single horn was broken are the four kingdoms (Daniel 8:22) into which Alexander's Hellenistic-Greek Empire was, for a time, divided, under Lysimachus, Cassander, Seleucus, and Ptolemy (see pages 109, 111).

The symbols are so apt that it is easy to forget that Daniel saw their fulfillment a long time in advance.

Now, Daniel 8:1, 2 says that in his vision Daniel seemed to be standing at the river Ulai (a canal 300 meters or about 900 feet wide) that used to flow near the ancient city of Susa. The point is that he was located at a community, Susa (or Shusha or Shushan), that would figure prominently as a treasure city and winter capital for the Medo-Persian Empire. In this symbolic way he was carried forward in time to the Medo-Persian period.

According to Daniel 8:1 the actual time of this vision was the third year of Belshazzar, 551 B.C., two years later than the vision of Daniel 7. The Babylonian Empire still had a dozen years to live, but a perceptive observer like Daniel could have discerned that its days were numbered. Nabonidus, its supreme king, was off in Tema developing a trade center and reviving moon worship. Belshazzar, the coregent, was allowing the economy of the capital to collapse. On the other hand Cyrus, the vigorous king of Persia, was out to conquer the world. God did not bother to include Babylon in this prophecy.

Cyrus is thought to have been the grandson of the final king of Media. At its height Media stretched through mountains from the river Halys in the northwest to the Persian Gulf in the southeast. By contrast Cyrus at first ruled only the tiny Median province of Persia. At that time the Median horn was much taller than the Persian horn.

But in 553, the year of the vision of Daniel 7, Cyrus rebelled against his grandfather, King Astyages, and soon subjugated Media under his own control. In 547, four years after the vision of Daniel 8, Cyrus would annex Lydia, extending his realm beyond the river Halys to the Aegean Sea. In 539 he would add Babylon. Thus the horn that came up second would find itself taller than the first one.

Broad-minded and generous, Cyrus treated the Medes as allies rather than as subjects, giving rise to the term "Medo-Persian Empire." In time, however, the Persian horn grew so tall that the empire was known simply as "Persian."

The Persian Empire enjoyed great leadership under several of its rulers besides Cyrus including, for example, Darius I (522-486) and Artaxerxes I (465-423), both of whom treated the Jews especially well and will deserve mention when we come to chapter 9. But Darius III (336-331), the final Persian emperor, was a weak ruler, certainly no match for Alexander the Great.

Alexander defeated Darius's immensely larger armies three times in three great military matches: first, by the river Granicus in Phrygia in 334; second, at the coast near Issus in Cilicia in 333; and third, on the plain of Arbela (or Gaugamela) in Syria in 331. Alexander's goat easily trounced Persia's ram, just as Daniel had foreseen two hundred years earlier.

God and Alexander's success. An article in the *Scientific American*[1] attributes Alexander's success partly to the Greek development of torsion artillery shortly before his time. Torsion artillery consisted of large catapults powered by heavy ropes of hair and sinew, twisted, like torsion springs with a ratchet and then released. They could shoot heavy stones repeatedly at a selected spot on a city wall until the wall gave way, and they could shoot oversized arrows into enemy ranks before the enemy archers were close enough to shoot their conventional weapons. Designed by highly skilled mathematician-engineers, they were remarkably accurate. A catapult constructed according to ancient specifications some years ago in Germany is reported actually to have split one of its arrows with a subsequent one, in the best style of Robin Hood.

Better known than his catapults are Alexander's personal qualifications for success. As we have seen in the case of the wagons, he seemed always to know what to do—when to attack or delay, whether to follow up a victory by chasing the enemy or to hold back and consolidate his position. He was physically brave. When one of his generals was killed at the siege of Tyre in the act of pressing through a breach in the city wall, Alexander unhesitatingly stepped into his place. And he could march all night. Once he led his cavalry with scarcely a pause on a chase that lasted for three days and *four* nights![2]

But in spite of Alexander's remarkable equipment and talents, we cannot escape the conviction that things might have turned out very differently if King Darius had not been such a notable coward. Darius's Persians vastly outnumbered the Greeks. At Arbela the Persians are said to have pitted a million men against Alexander's 47,000.[3] But at Granicus, Issus, and Arbela, King Darius lost his nerve at the first sign of a reverse, turned his chariot around, and fled for his life—a

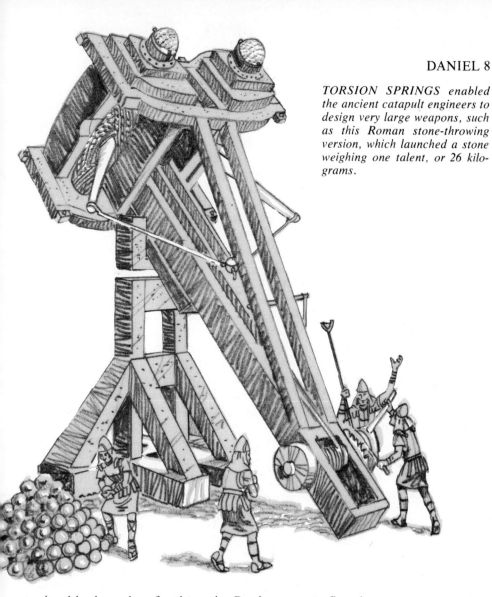

TORSION SPRINGS enabled the ancient catapult engineers to design very large weapons, such as this Roman stone-throwing version, which launched a stone weighing one talent, or 26 kilograms.

signal in those days for the entire Persian army to flee also.

In an unusually intriguing passage the Bible says that "the king's heart is a stream of water in the hand of the Lord; he turns it wherever he will." Proverbs 21:1. Historical accounts indicate that a single hour of courage on Darius's part in any one of his three great battles might well have saved his army and enabled it to annihilate Alexander's forces. Had God seen fit, He could easily have supplied Darius with this needed courage. He gave Daniel courage to face lions. He gave Daniel's friends courage to face a fiery furnace. But the Persian Empire had chosen to find its way without faith in the God of Israel, and in Persia's hour of crisis God allowed human weakness to run its course.

Daniel 7:6 says that dominion was **"given"** to the Greeks. Evidently the same

157

God who **"gave"** unrepentant Judah into the hands of Nebuchadnezzar (Daniel 1:2), and who **"gave"** decadent Babylon into the hands of Cyrus (Daniel 5:28), now **"gave"** the degenerate Persian Empire into the hands of Alexander. So does the "God who cares" oversee the affairs of men.

Three beasts "prolonged." Daniel 7:12 says that the lives of the first three beasts of chapter 7, unlike that of the fourth beast, were to be **"prolonged for a season and a time"** after their dominion had been taken away. In a symbolic gesture Alexander married a Bactrian princess, Roxane, and he enthusiastically endorsed the marriages of 10,000 of his Greek soldiers to Persian wives. Indeed Alexander revealed remarkably cosmopolitan statesmanship. He creatively set in motion a blending of the old Babylonian and Persian cultures with the Greek (or "Hellenic") culture, which was to stamp civilization as "Hellenistic" for centuries to come. Thus elements of Babylonian, Persian, and Greek civilizations persisted **"for a season and a time."** Indeed many of them influence us to this day.

"Of no other man can it be said with equal justice," observes a modern historian whose views are widely shared, "that he laid his mark upon all the civilizations that followed him in the lands where he had fought, and upon all those civilizations to the West which in turn took over from them."[4]

The "little horn" of Daniel 8:9-14. After Alexander's death his horn, that is, his kingdom, was divided into **"four conspicuous horns toward the four winds of heaven."** The narrative continues: **"Out of one of them came forth a little horn, which grew exceedingly great."**

Identification of this little horn will occupy our attention more or less during the next four sections. A word of clarification at this point will be helpful.

Readers of the English versions sometimes assume that when the Bible says that the little horn arose out of **"one of them,"** it means that it arose out of one of the four horns. What the Bible really means, however, is that the little horn arose out of one of the four winds; that is, that it arose out of one of the four directions of the compass. (We are dealing with an idiom.)

How can this be?

Nouns in Hebrew have grammatical gender. They are considered to be either masculine, feminine, or neuter. Many other languages also employ grammatical gender. And it is a rule in all of them that pronouns must agree with their antecedent nouns in being similarly masculine, feminine, or neuter. Even in English we think of a ship as feminine and refer to one with the feminine pronouns "she" and "her."

In the Hebrew for Daniel 8:8, 9, "horns" is feminine, and "winds" is either masculine or feminine. In the phrase "out of one of them," the pronoun "them" is masculine. This means that the antecedent noun for "them" cannot be "horns" but must be "winds."

Thus the little horn was to appear out of one of the four winds. It was to arise from one of the four directions of the compass.

It is cogent to our study that the Roman Empire, small at first, arose from a

158

point *westward* from the first three empires of prophecy. It is regrettable that some readers have supposed that the little horn of Daniel 8 was the strange little king, Antiochus Epiphanes.

II. The Horn That Trampled the Sanctuary

The little horn of Daniel 8 has been thought by some Bible students to be one of the Seleucid kings, Antiochus IV, commonly known as Antiochus Epiphanes (an-TIE-uh-kus e-PIF-uh-neez).*

Antiochus Epiphanes persecuted conservative Jews and suspended the temple services between the years 168 and 165 B.C. In discussing his activities, 1 and 2 Maccabees, two of the books in the Apocrypha, quote phrases from Daniel 8 and 9.

But of course the Bible doesn't *state* that the little horn of Daniel 8 is Antiochus Epiphanes, and there are many ways in which he does not fit the prophecy at all. Horns represent kingdoms, and he was only an individual king—a part of one of the four horns. He did not appear at the **"latter end"** of the Seleucid kingdom (Daniel 8:23) but approximately in the middle of the line of Seleucid kings. (The Seleucid dynasty ran from 312/311 to 65 B.C., and Antiochus Epiphanes reigned from 175 to 164 B.C.)

And he did not really **"prosper"** (verse 12) or grow **"exceedingly great"** (verse 9). His father, Antiochus III, was called "the Great," and rightly so, for he restored the original Seleucid dominions. Antiochus Epiphanes, on the other hand, was referred to sarcastically, by at least some of his contemporaries, as "Epimanes"—the mad man.[5] Antiochus Epiphanes, after a short-lived triumph in the "south" (Egypt), was totally defeated there when the Roman ambassador, C. Popilius Laenas, merely informed him that the Roman Senate wanted him to leave. The grim Roman drew a circle around Antiochus with his cane and demanded a decision before he stepped out of it.[6]

*"Seleucid" refers to the dynasty founded by Alexander's general, Seleucus. "Epiphanes" refers to the claim of Antiochus IV to be a manifestation, or epiphany, of God. The dates 168 and 165 B.C., used in this chapter for the interruption which Antiochus caused in the temple sacrifices, are based on the information in Parker and Dubberstein, *Babylonian Chronology*, p. 23. Some authorities prefer the dates 167 and 164 B.C.

In the **"east"** (Mesopotamia), Antiochus Epiphanes died under obscure and sorry circumstances. Even in the **"glorious land"** (Palestine), where at first he seemed successful, all his ambitions came to nothing within his lifetime.

Furthermore, all attempts to fit his desecration of the Jewish temple into **"2300 evenings and mornings"** have uniformly failed. The most nearly contemporary account, in Maccabees 1:54-59; 4:52-54, is overwhelmingly precise in stating that he interrupted the temple services for *three years and ten days* (from Chislev 15, 168, to Chislev 25, 165).

Now 1 Maccabees 1:54 applies the phrase **"desolating sacrilege"** (*bdelugma erēmōseōs,* Daniel 9:27, Greek) to what Antiochus Epiphanes did to the altar in the Jewish temple. (He evidently erected an idol on it and sacrificed a pig, to the horror of all devout Jews, for whom pigs have always been unfit for human touch.) But Jesus in the Olivet Discourse said that Daniel's **"desolating sacrilege"** was still future as of His day. Matthew 24:15. He added, "Let the reader understand." So, if we really want to understand the meaning of the little horn of Daniel 8, we shall have to conclude, with Jesus, that it cannot have been Antiochus Epiphanes, who died in 164 B.C., almost two hundred years prior to the Olivet Discourse. (For more information about Antiochus Epiphanes, see *Your Questions Answered,* pages 190-192.)

The little horn of Daniel 8 is Rome. The true fulfillment of the little horn of Daniel 8 can only be the Roman Empire and its successor, the Roman Church—purposely viewed, as in Daniel 7, from their darker aspects. The following considerations support this conclusion:

1. On the principle that succeeding visions in Daniel parallel and amplify earlier ones, we notice that in many ways the little horn of Daniel 8 parallels and increases our information about the little horn of Daniel 7 and the beast out of which it grew. In Daniel 2 and 7 Rome follows Greece; thus Rome follows Greece in Daniel 8 also.

2. Rome arose in the west, out of one of the "four winds" (see page 158).

3. We have already seen that, in their beastlike aspects, pagan and Christian Rome constituted a continuum. The Roman bishop was successor to the Roman emperor. Notice how a recent college textbook has expressed the matter:

> In the West, the Church took over the defense of Roman civilization. The emperor gave up the [pagan] title of Pontifex Maximus (high priest) because the Roman gods were no longer worshipped. The bishop of Rome assumed these priestly functions, and this is why the Pope today is sometimes referred to as the Pontiff. When the Huns, a fierce and savage tribe led by brutal Attila [AT-ih-luh], swept into Italy and threatened to take and destroy the city of Rome, it was the leader of the Christian Church, Pope Leo, not the emperor, who met the barbarian. Attila was so impressed with the Pope's spiritual power that he turned back. What Leo said to Attila remains unknown, but what is significant is the fact that it was the Pope and not the emperor who stood at the gates of Rome. The Roman Empire had become the Christian Church.[7]

Inasmuch as the Roman Church was a continuation of the Roman Empire, a single prominent horn appropriately represents both of them.

4. The Roman Empire, unlike Antiochus Epiphanes, successfully took control of the Middle East at the **"latter end"** (8:23) of the dominion of the Hellenistic kingdoms.

5. And in taking over the Middle East, the Roman Empire, unlike Antiochus Epiphanes, definitely **"grew exceedingly great toward the south, toward the east, and toward the glorious land."** Verse 9. Coming from the west, small at first like a **"little"** horn, Rome grew as it conquered Macedonia in 168 B.C., Syria in 65 B.C., Palestine in 63 B.C., and Egypt, too, after a long protectorate, in 30 B.C., making them all provinces of its own empire. Antioch in Syria, the former Seleucid capital, became in time a Roman capital second only to Rome and Constantinople. Alexandria, the former capital of Egypt under the Ptolemies, flourished richly as a Roman city.

6. Pagan Rome emphatically and tragically **"magnified itself"** against the **"Prince of the host."** Verse 11. Pontius Pilate and the soldiers who condemned and crucified Jesus were all Romans.

7. Both pagan and Christian Rome destroyed **"mighty men and the people of the saints"** (verse 24); that is, they both persecuted a large number of conscientious Christians and even tortured many of them in the process.

8. Both pagan and Christian Rome **"took away the continual burnt offering"** and **"overthrew the place of his sanctuary."** Verse 11. Pagan Rome did this literally—but only in a limited sense, as we shall see later—in A.D. 70 when soldiers under the Roman general (later emperor) Titus set the temple (or Jerusalem sanctuary) on fire, causing its complete destruction and forever terminating its services. In the 130s the Roman emperor Hadrian constructed a pagan temple in Jerusalem, renamed the city Aelia Capitolina, and went so far as to forbid Jews ever to live in the city—a rule that was enforced for centuries.

Christian Rome and the sanctuary. But did *Christian* Rome in any sense take away the continual burnt offering and overthrow the place of His sanctuary? The answer to this question will involve an analysis of Christ's ministry as our compassionate High Priest. It will also involve an understanding of the fascinating Hebrew word *tamid.*

III. Christ's All-of-the-Time Priesthood

I had known Ted well as a student in my classes. He was bright enough and had married a lovely girl. They had gone to a mission station in the Far East, and I had lost track of them.

Now here he was, walking into my office. At once I wanted to hear all the news about his family and his mission.

But he wanted to tell me that he no longer had a family and that he had been sent home from the mission. He had loved unwisely and had been discovered by some of the new Christians he had gone to serve. He had apologized repeatedly to

161

his wife, Esther. But Esther had been understandably hurt and had joined the mission director in advising him to go back to America. She had said that when she and the children got back, she would divorce him.

As things turned out, when Esther got back to America, she changed her mind and sweetly forgave her husband. At the time Ted walked into my office, however, things were very sad. Yet there was one bright gleam. Ted wanted to tell me that while he was getting ready to leave the country after Esther had put him out of the house, he had found a bed on somebody's back porch. Deeply repentant, he feared that he had sinned too seriously to be forgiven. When he awakened early one morning after a fitful night, he knew he could wait no longer to find out how he stood with God. Grabbing his Bible, he begged God to talk to him by directing his finger to an appropriate text.

He was well aware that this is not ordinarily a proper method of Bible study, and he could scarcely summon courage to open the pages for fear he would read something meaningless or, worse, something that would sound as though God had rejected him. At last, however, with his eyes squeezed shut, he did place his finger on a text and then, fearfully, opened his eyes again. And here is the text he was pointing to: "For I will be merciful to their unrighteousness, and their sins and their iniquities will I remember no more." Hebrews 8:12, K.J.V.

In my K.J.V. Bible I have written Ted's real name beside that verse to help me remember his experience with it as long as I live.

In Psalm 139 David describes how hard it is to find a *place* where we can get away from God: "If I . . . dwell in the uttermost parts of the sea, even there thy hand shall lead." Verses 9 and 10.

In Ted's experience I was reminded how hard it is to find a *time* when we can be away from God. In the gray light of dawn during the darkest period of his life, Ted found God dramatically ready to forgive and heal him.

> Just when I need Him, Jesus is near,
> Just when I falter, just when I fear;
> Ready to help me, ready to cheer,
> Just when I need Him most.[8]

Ted's experience effectively illustrates the real meaning of a vital Hebrew word in the heart of Daniel 8. This significant term is *tamid*. It is translated **"continual burnt offering"** in the R.S.V.:

It [*the little horn*] **magnified itself, even up to the Prince of the host; and the continual burnt offering** [*that is, the* tamid] **was taken away from him** [*the Prince of the host*]**, and the place of his sanctuary was overthrown.** Verse 11.

The tamid *of Daniel 8:13, 14 is symbolic.* It would be difficult to overemphasize the importance of understanding the term *"tamid"* and its far-reaching implications.

Those Bible readers who assume that the little horn of Daniel 8 is Antiochus Epiphanes interpret *tamid* in this passage as applying merely to the morning and evening sacrifices which Antiochus canceled between 168 and 165 B.C. Other Bible readers, who realize that the little horn is a symbol of a kingdom and cannot refer to any single king, point out that the sanctuary is also a symbol that cannot be restricted to the Jewish temple. In Daniel 2 and 7 metals and animals are symbols that stand for vast successive empires. Consistently, the *tamid* of Daniel 8:13, 14 is also a symbol. It stands for a reality far broader and richer than the offering of sacrifices twice a day in old Jerusalem.

As a matter of fact, *tamid* doesn't mean **"continual burnt offering."** *Tamid* means "continual" and is used in this passage to signify a continual something—without expressing what the something is. Translators have sometimes added the term **"burnt offering"** in an attempt to make the passage fit Antiochus Epiphanes.

Ted's experience and similar experiences of countless other Christians correctly encourage us to look away from Antiochus Epiphanes and to look instead at the symbolic *tamid* of Daniel 8 as representing the *continual*—that is, the all-of-the-time—*high-priestly ministry of Jesus Christ on our behalf in the heavenly sanctuary*.

The "continualness" of Christ's priestly ministry. That Jesus *is* our High Priest is the message of the book of Hebrews in the New Testament. Hebrews 3:1 invites us to "consider Jesus, the apostle and high priest of our confession."

That Jesus ministers *in the heavenly sanctuary* is stated clearly in Hebrews 8:1, 2, which says that "we have such a high priest, one who is seated at the right hand

Jesus, our High Priest, was represented by the high priest in the earthly sanctuary on the Day of Atonement.

of the throne of the Majesty in heaven, a minister *in the sanctuary* and the true tent [or 'tabernacle,' footnote] which is set up not by man but by the Lord.''

And that Jesus ministers on our behalf *continually* is emphasized in Hebrews 7:21-25, where His ministry is contrasted with the noncontinuous ministry of the Old Testament ''Levitical'' priests:

Those who formerly became [Levitical] priests took their office without an oath, but this one [Jesus Christ] was addressed with an oath,

''The Lord has sworn
and will not change his mind,
'Thou art a priest for ever.' ''

This makes Jesus the surety of a better covenant.

The former priests were many in number, because they were prevented by death from continuing in office; but he [Jesus] holds his priesthood permanently, because he continues for ever. Consequently he is able for all time to save those who draw near to God through him, since he always lives to make intercession for them. Hebrews 7:21-25.

Tamid *in the Old Testament*. The contrast which is drawn in Hebrews 7:21-25 between Christ's continuing priesthood and the noncontinuing ministry of the Old Testament priests is very much to the point. The Levitical priestly service was intended by God to be *just as continuous as it could humanly be*. In fact, it is in connection with what the Bible says about the continuousness of the Old Testament service that we discover the special meaning of the word *tamid*.

When used as an ordinary adjective, *tamid* describes a variety of things, such as *continual* employment (Ezekiel 39:14), *continual* sorrow (Psalm 38:17), and *continual* hope (Psalm 71:14).

Quite often, however, *tamid* is used in a technical sense to describe various basic aspects of the ritual associated with the Old Testament sanctuary. A dozen times (as in Numbers 28:3 and 1 Chronicles 16:40) it refers to the offering of a lamb, regularly, morning and evening, as a ''*continual* burnt offering.'' It also refers (as in Leviticus 24:2) to the lamps that were kept *continually* burning and (as in 2 Chronicles 2:4) to the ''*continual* offering of the showbread'' which was kept on display perpetually and was changed weekly. In Exodus 28:29, 30 *tamid* refers to the symbolically adorned breastpiece that the high priest wore *continually*, whenever his duties required him to enter the sanctuary. In 2 Chronicles 24:14 it refers to all the burnt offerings offered to God during a particular king's lifetime. And in 1 Chronicles 23:31 it refers to the special sacrifices offered regularly on Sabbaths, new moons, and feast days.

With this survey in mind, it becomes apparent that *tamid* took into account the entire continuing ministry of the Old Testament sanctuary and was by no means limited to the daily burnt offerings.

The original Old Testament sanctuary. To gain a fuller grasp of the Old Testament *tamid*—and through it a better understanding of Christ's heavenly ministry —it is helpful to get acquainted with the Levitical sanctuary and its services.

164

When God led the Israelites out of Egypt, He said to Moses, "Let them make me a sanctuary, that I may dwell in their midst." Exodus 25:8. On Mount Sinai He gave Moses precise instructions as to the sanctuary's design and rituals (see especially Exodus 25-30).

God's purpose in giving these directions was evidently to impress the people with (1) His holiness in contrast to their sinfulness, (2) His eagerness to forgive their sins in response to repentance, and (3) His desire—through the Holy Spirit—to dwell in and cleanse from sin their individual, personal "temples" (1 Corinthians 6:19, 20; Ephesians 2:21, 22; Revelation 3:20, 21).

Because at the time the Israelites were living like nomads on the Sinai peninsula, God said that the sanctuary should be constructed in the form of a tent, or "tabernacle," so it could be dismantled and moved whenever the people moved. It was to be 10 cubits by 30 (a cubit is about 46 centimeters or 18 inches) and divided into two rooms. The larger room was to be known as the "holy place," and the smaller, inner one, as the "most holy place." Two curtains or "veils" would serve as doors—the inner curtain being gorgeously embroidered with pictures of angels. A "court" surrounding the tabernacle was marked off with a linen fence.

God specified just how the tabernacle was to be furnished. Let's take a tour with Aaron, the high priest. The first item of furniture that he shows us, just inside the entrance to the court, is the large brass-plated "altar of burnt offering." As we walk beyond it, he shows us the brass "laver," a basin with water in it for ceremonial washings.

The tent-sanctuary, or tabernacle, that God directed Moses to build teaches us much about the heavenly sanctuary.

We step past the laver, and Aaron draws the first veil aside and leads the way out of the bright desert sun into the reverent dimness of the holy place. The air is fragrant. A fine column of smoke rises from incense burning on the exquisite little "golden altar"[9] directly ahead of us, in front of the second veil. Of course we can barely make it out, until our eyes get used to the place.

Our attention is attracted to the seven-branched "lampstand" on our left, near the south wall. Aaron tells us that it is made of solid gold and that at least some of its lamps are always burning. Now we notice that their light is reflected richly by the gold-plated frames that support the fabric-and-leather walls and roof. Behind the frames hangs a curtain richly decorated with angels.

Next to the north wall is a piece of gold-plated furniture about the size of a coffee table. Aaron says it is the "table of the bread of the Presence" (the "table of shewbread," K.J.V.). Twelve flat loaves, one for each tribe of Israel, are placed on it each Sabbath.

We admire the superb craftsmanship of the inner veil; then Aaron draws aside this second curtain and we enter the most holy place. In its center stands the "ark of the covenant," a gold-plated chest which, Aaron explains, contains the tablets of stone on which God engraved the Ten Commandments. The lid of the ark, called the "mercy seat," he tells us, is made of solid gold. Attached to it and beaten out of the same piece of gold are two angel-like carvings called "cherubim," looking down.

In real life, of course, we could never have entered the tabernacle. Only priests were allowed into the holy place; and only the high priest, one day a year, was allowed to enter the most holy place. Our imagination has served us well!*

After the Israelites settled in Palestine, the tabernacle became worn and battered. King Solomon replaced it with a stone temple in Jerusalem, based on the same plan as the tabernacle. It was Solomon's temple which Nebuchadnezzar razed to the ground more than three hundred years later.

After the Babylonian exile the Jews built a second temple on the same basic plan and on the same site as Solomon's temple. This second temple did not contain the ark, which was not seen again after Nebuchadnezzar's final attack. Its precincts did, at first, enclose the altar that Antiochus Epiphanes defiled in 168 B.C. Herod the Great, king at the time of Jesus' birth, so rebuilt and beautified this second temple that it came to be known as Herod's temple. Jesus taught in Herod's temple, and the Romans destroyed it in A.D. 70.

The Old Testament services. The sanctuary rituals which God required were impressive and varied. They were designed for an agricultural people who lived intimately with herds of cattle and flocks of sheep and goats. They symbolized Christ's death and heavenly ministry for the forgiveness of our sins in terms of the

---

*Ordinarily a brilliant, supernatural light which represented the presence of God shone between the cherubim. We made our imaginary tour just before the Israelites moved from one campsite to another in the wilderness, when the light was temporarily removed to permit the priest's Levitical assistants to wrap the furniture for moving. Otherwise the light would have overpowered us (see Genesis 3:24; Exodus 25:22; 1 Timothy 6:16; Exodus 40:34-38; Numbers 3:14-39).

death of valuable animals and the service of dedicated priests.

The basic ritual was the offering of a lamb each morning and evening. According to Leviticus 9:24 God Himself miraculously kindled the altar fire when the tabernacle was originally dedicated, and the priests were under strict instructions never to let it go out. "This is the law of the burnt offering. The burnt offering shall be on the hearth upon the altar all night until the morning, and the fire of the altar shall be kept burning on it. . . . It shall not go out." Leviticus 6:8-13.

Tradition later claimed that the original fire continued to burn from the time of Moses until Nebuchadnezzar destroyed the temple in 586 B.C., a total of over eight hundred years according to biblical chronology.

This continually burning sacrifice said a lot to the Israelites camped in the wilderness. At any moment when anyone felt remorse for his sinfulness, a glance at the tabernacle or at night a sniff of the air could bring reassurance that the sacrifice was in progress on his behalf. And the continuance of the sacrifice would remind him that the other basic functions of the priesthood were being maintained on his behalf also. The lamps were burning day and night, their steady glow reflecting from the gold-plated walls of the tabernacle. The bread was in its place on the golden table. And the high priest, as often at least as he was on duty, was carrying on his breastpiece the name of every tribe in the nation, thus symbolically carrying near his heart and in the presence of God the name of every individual in the encampment.

Later, when the Israelites settled in communities all over Palestine, and still later, when they settled all around the Roman Empire, it became impossible for them to visit the sanctuary every time they sinned or even as often as once a year. Even on the way home from a rare visit to Jerusalem, the worshiper would doubtless sin again and could not possibly return to the altar. But he had the comforting knowledge that the services were continuing on his behalf.

Behold, the Lamb of God. It was a lamb that was offered twice a day; and in the New Testament Jesus is often called a lamb, as in John 1:29 and 1 Peter 1:19. Jesus is called the Lamb 29 times in the book of Revelation. Isaiah 53 in the Old Testament speaks of a "lamb that is led to the slaughter," and Acts 8:32-35 in the New Testament applies the statement to Jesus. In 1 Corinthians 5:7 Paul alludes to the lamb sacrificed in the special Passover, or "Paschal," ritual and says, "Christ, our paschal lamb, has been sacrificed."

God did not limit the sacrifices to lambs. Sometimes He called for rams, bulls, calves, kids, and even doves and pigeons. Often "a cereal offering" was specified, as in Leviticus 2:1-11. But always when an animal sacrifice was offered for the forgiveness of sin, the person who offered the sacrifice led his animal to the tabernacle and, standing either at the entrance or beside the altar of burnt offering, laid his hands on the animal and personally took a knife and slew it. *The sinner himself slew the animal,* and the animal was "accepted for him, to make atonement for him." Leviticus 1:3, 4, 10, 11.

By laying his hands on the animal, the sinner symbolically transferred his own guilt to the innocent victim, and the animal became—in symbol—a substitute for him. As the *Jewish Encyclopedia* says, "The laying of hands upon the victim's head is an ordinary rite by which the substitution and the transfer of sins are effected." "In every sacrifice there is the idea of substitution; the victim takes the place of the human sinner."[10]

When John the Baptist saw Jesus for the first time, he called out to the crowds who had gathered to hear him preach, "Behold, the Lamb of God, *who takes away the sin of the world."* John 1:29. Years later Peter wrote in his first epistle, "He himself *bore our sins in his body."* 1 Peter 2:24.

The requirement that the sinner himself slay his substitute animal teaches a profound lesson that we still need to be reminded of. Every one of us can say, "If Christ died as my Substitute because He bore my sins, then it is my responsibility that He died. It is I who slew Christ."

> For guilt of my sin the nail drove in,
> When Him they crucified.[11]

And, of course, the sacrifice *died.* Every animal that died every day in every ritual gave its life to teach all of us the solemn truth that "the wages of sin is death." Romans 6:23. Sin causes death. Sin causes death so irrevocably and inevitably that God cannot merely overlook it. It has cost God something to forgive our sins. God "did not spare his own Son, but gave him up for us all." Romans 8:32. "God so loved . . . that he gave his only Son." John 3:16.

The cross in the Old Testament. God required the Levitical priests to perform a variety of rituals, for the reason that no single routine could adequately convey all the fullness of the gospel. Jesus, for example, could serve both as our Lamb and as our High Priest, because He returned to life after the crucifixion. No lamb or

The confession of sin on the head of a sacrificial lamb teaches us to lay our guilt on Jesus, our sacrificial Lamb.

bull or goat could illustrate the resurrection! Thus an animal *and* a human priest were required, and the animals were used in different ways at different times.

As a part of this variety the sacrifice was sometimes burned outside the camp instead of on the altar at the sanctuary. Hebrews 13:12, 13 reminds us that "Jesus also suffered outside the gate in order to sanctify the people through his own blood." Calvary, where Jesus died, was located outside Jerusalem. As a regular site for executions, it was a place of reproach—symbolic of the reproach that a person sometimes suffers who follows Jesus as a true disciple. Christian youth in high school know what this reproach is. So do husbands, wives, and close friends who suddenly decide to walk closer than before with their Lord. Hebrews 13:13 encourages us: "Therefore let us go forth to him outside the camp, bearing abuse for him."

The blood had to be applied. In the variety of rituals some of the blood from every sacrifice made for sin was sprinkled on or near one of the two altars. "It is the blood that makes atonement," says Leviticus 17:11. When the priest offered a sacrifice for himself, he took some of the animal's blood and sprinkled it on the golden altar in the holy place and on the floor in front of the inner curtain. By doing this he registered in the holy place a record of his *confessed and forgiven* sin (see Leviticus 4:2-6).

For obvious reasons blood from all the sacrifices could not possibly have been sprinkled in the holy place; so when the common people brought their sacrifices, God said for the priest to sprinkle some of the animal's blood on the large altar in the court. Then the priest was to cook a portion of the animal and eat it. In this way the priest, like Jesus—only symbolically of course—bore the "iniquity of the congregation" in his own body. Leviticus 10:17. When the priest again offered a sacrifice for himself, he carried into the holy place blood that now represented the people's sins as well as his own. Thus in one way or another a record of everyone's *confessed and forgiven* sins was preserved in the holy place.

It is of utmost importance to emphasize that forgiveness or "atonement" was not effected without both the *shedding* and the *application* of the blood. "Without the shedding of blood there is no forgiveness of sins," says Hebrews 9:22. Shedding of blood, however, was not enough. Some of the blood had to be applied to one of the altars by one of the priests in order for the symbolic ritual to be complete. In some cases *only* the applied blood is referred to, as in Exodus 30:10.

Many Christians overlook this fact. They speak gratefully about the act of salvation on the cross and about the blood which Jesus shed there, but they stop short and do not mention that in some sense Jesus had to "take blood" with Him into the heavenly sanctuary (Hebrews 9:12) in order to care adequately for our sins.

Many Christians think that Jesus only *died* in order to provide justification by faith. Romans 4:25, however, says that He was "put to death for our trespasses *and raised for our justification.*" Romans 5:10 says that "if while we were enemies we were reconciled to God by the death of his son, much more, now that we are reconciled, shall we be *saved by his life.''*

Hebrews 9:12 says that ''he entered once for all into the Holy Place, taking . . . his own blood, *thus* securing an eternal redemption.''

So the high-priestly ministry of Jesus Christ in the heavenly sanctuary is as vital to our salvation as was His death on the cross.

Indeed, to ask which is more important for our salvation—Christ's death on the cross or His living ministry in heaven—is almost like asking, ''Which is more important to the success of a jet plane: its engines or its wings?'' Engines and wings are both important in different ways, but both are absolutely, fundamentally, and irreplaceably essential.

Fully as essential as the cross is Christ's continual ministry, His *tamid,* in heaven.

The superiority of Christ's tamid. Even though the symbolism of the Levitical ministry provided rich reassurance and spiritual insight, it had no real value in itself. That is, it is obviously ''impossible that the blood of bulls and goats should take away sins''! Hebrews 10:4.

So the book of Hebrews traces Christ's superiority. Jesus is better, it says, than any Old Testament priest. Hebrews 7:11-16. Jesus is better than Moses, through whom God revealed the ritual. Hebrews 3. And He is better than the angels who assist in our salvation. Hebrews 1. Jesus offers better promises, a better covenant, and a better hope. Hebrews 8:6; 7:19. He serves in a better tabernacle. Hebrews 9:11. And He offered an immeasurably superior sacrifice. ''Sacrifices and offerings thou hast not desired,'' He said to His Father as He came into the world, ''but a body hast thou prepared for me.'' Hebrews 10:5.

And because Christ's sacrifice is immeasurably superior to the death of bulls and goats, *it does not need to be repeated.* Hebrews 9:25-28 is emphatic: ''Nor was it [necessary] to offer himself repeatedly, . . . But . . . he has appeared once for all . . . to put away sin by the sacrifice of himself. And just as it is appointed for men to die once, and after that comes judgment, so Christ, having been offered once to bear the sins of many, will appear a second time, not to deal with sin but to save those who are eagerly waiting for him.''

Because Christ does not die again, either sacrificially or from old age, His priesthood is marked by an immeasurable superiority in its *continual-ness.* As we read several pages back, ''The former priests were many in number, because they were prevented by death from continuing in office; but he holds his priesthood permanently, because he continues for ever.'' Hebrews 7:23, 24.

Thus Jesus ''is also able to save absolutely those who approach God through him; he is always living to plead on their behalf.'' Hebrews 7:24, N.E.B.

Christ and the New Covenant. We read a moment ago that Jesus offers a ''better covenant.'' Hebrews 7:22.

This better covenant, otherwise known as the new covenant (Hebrews 8:10-12; Jeremiah 31:31-34), is the gospel in a nugget. God promised it first to Adam after he sinned (see Genesis 3:15). He repeated it several times in the Old Testa-

170

ment using different words. It was ratified by Christ's death on the cross, and it is administered as an essential aspect of Christ's continuing priesthood.

Jeremiah and Ezekiel, Daniel's contemporary prophets, wrote about the new covenant several times. They showed that it offered three absolutely priceless gifts: (1) forgiveness of every sin, (2) power to live a changed life, and (3) membership among God's chosen people. Ezekiel expressed it once this way:

(1) I will sprinkle clean water upon you,
   and you shall be clean from all your uncleannesses. . . .
(2) A new heart I will give you,
   and a new spirit will I put within you. . . .
(3) You shall be my people,
   and I will be your God.
   Ezekiel 36:25-28.

Jeremiah arranged the same elements in this manner:

(2) I will put my law within them
   and I will write it upon their hearts;
(3) And I will be their God,
   and they shall be my people. . . .
(1) For I will forgive their iniquity,
   and I will remember their sin no more.
   Jeremiah 31:33-34.

The promise of new hearts with God's laws written on them reminds us that Jesus summarized the Ten Commandments as loving God with all our hearts and as loving our neighbors (good and bad) as much as we love ourselves (see Matthew 22:37-40).

When God asks us to love like this, He doesn't stand and bark orders like a drill sergeant. He offers to *give* us His kind of love. He cares!

And when we feel God's love astir inside us, it is much easier for us to treat our employees honestly, our competitors fairly, our parents honorably, and our spouses faithfully! When we love God because He inspires in us His own kind of love, we *want* to pray to Him and read and talk about Him. And we want to keep His Sabbath, because the Sabbath is His day—a special occasion for a rewarding relationship with so close a Friend.

It is a vital part of Christ's ongoing *tamid* ministry to change us, from the inside out. To help us to love things that are good for us and to love people who are bad to us. To help us become the kind of Christian that He was when He lived on earth.

The tamid *of Daniel 8*. The manifold superiority of Christ's continual priesthood—the reality of which the *tamid* of Daniel 8 is a symbol—is presented in Hebrews as providing a solid foundation for living faith. Inasmuch, then, as "we have a great high priest who has passed through the heavens, Jesus, the Son of

171

God, let us hold fast our confession. . . . Let us . . . with confidence draw near to the throne of grace, that we may receive mercy and find grace to help in time of need." Hebrews 4:14-16.

It is sad that some of the Jews, perhaps a majority of them, in Christ's day thought that their Levitical ritual was the true *tamid,* the ultimate expression of God's continuing concern for sinners. They did not look beyond the symbol to the reality. They did not discern that the lamb was but a shadow of the Lamb of God.

It is even more sad, in its own way, for anyone to suppose that the Old Testament ritual was the *tamid* about which God spoke in the grand prophecy of Daniel 8. Without a doubt the Old Testament *tamid* was important to God. He instituted it, and He was concerned that Antiochus Epiphanes would interrupt it briefly and that the Roman Empire would contribute to its demise.

But like the metals, beasts, and horns of Daniel's prophecies, which are symbols of empires and kingdoms, so the *tamid* of Daniel 8:13, 14 is a symbol. It is a symbol of the continual ministry of Jesus Christ in the heavenly sanctuary, forgiving our sins and providing power for us to live changed lives in fulfillment of the new covenant promises.

On a back porch one bleak morning nineteen hundred years *after* the Romans burned Herod's temple to the ground, it was Christ's *continuing* heavenly ministry and the words of His glorious new covenant that comforted my friend Ted.

IV. Christ's Priesthood Obscured

We asked ourselves several pages back (page 161) whether in any sense *Christian* Rome trampled on the continual ministry, the *tamid,* of Jesus Christ in the heavenly sanctuary.

For one answer to this vital question, we turn to the doctrinal decisions of the epochal Council of Trent. The Council of Trent (1545-1563) was convened to deal specifically with the Reformation started by Martin Luther. This council achieved a variety of ecclesiastical reforms and is considered a major element in the Catholic Counter-Reformation. But after lengthy debates on doctrine it voted to retain intact *almost all the basic traditional teachings of medieval Christendom.*

The doctrinal decisions of the Council of Trent are embodied in the popular Baltimore Catechism.[12] And because the Baltimore Catechism is readily available *and* is based on the Council of Trent, it provides convenient access to the traditional teachings of Christian Rome. Study of this catechism can help us answer our question.

Protestants who pick up a Baltimore Catechism for the first time are surprised to discover sensitive paragraphs describing Christian doctrines which they believe equally with their Catholic neighbors. They also discover teachings which some Christians have objected to since long before the Reformation.

Christians in the fifteenth century (for example) were taught to believe that if they hoped for forgiveness of mortal sins—sins like murder and staying home from mass—they had to confess them to an authorized priest, normally in a confes-

172

sional booth, and they had to perform every act of penance assigned to them after confession.—Baltimore Catechism, sec. 384, 408.

They were taught that at the Lord's Supper the "substance" of the bread undergoes a change, or "transubstantiation," into the body and blood of Christ[13] and that believers do not need to drink the wine as well as the bread because Christ's body *and* blood are "entirely present under the appearance of the bread" alone. They were taught that the mass is the "same sacrifice as the sacrifice of the cross," although in the mass there is no pain and—even though Christ's blood is present—the sacrifice is "unbloody."—Baltimore Catechism, sec. 350, 359, 360, 362.

Christians in the Middle Ages were taught that at death God assigns unrepentant sinners to hell, to writhe there forever with the devils in flames. Even repentant sinners are assigned by God at death to a place called purgatory, to suffer for unknown but often very extensive periods in preparation for heaven. Masses for souls in purgatory can be performed at the request of the living and serve to reduce their sufferings.—Baltimore Catechism, sec. 173, 184, 185.

They were also taught that the pope is the "supreme head" of the church, invested, as the vicar of Christ and successor of Peter, with full power to rule the church like a king.—Baltimore Catechism, sec. 137, 148, 162.

Changes since the Second Vatican Council. All of these beliefs, now many centuries old, have persisted in the Catholic Church until recent times. Since the second Vatican Council (1962-1965), however, thousands of Catholics have been asking whether they were ever really true. The controversial Dutch Catechism has concluded that at least some of them were not true. In its pages purgatory appears more as an experience than as a place, and the time required for a soul to spend in purgatory is reduced in some cases to as little as "months."[14] Hell, in the same book, no longer burns with literal flames but only with "dismay" at the recognition of one's "total perversion" and with the "inner remorse" sensed by an obstinate rebel in the presence of the "tender warmth of God's love."[15]

Catholics reading the Bible, as the Catholic Church now encourages them to do, are finding that the Bible nowhere says that masses benefit people in purgatory, that in fact, the Bible nowhere mentions purgatory. Neither does it call the eucharist a "sacrifice." The Bible calls it a "supper" (1 Corinthians 11:20) and portrays it as being eaten, not offered; and as being shared at the "table of the Lord" (1 Corinthians 10:21), never at an altar.

Catholics are finding that the Bible nowhere says that we must confess our sins to a priest. It says only that we must confess our sins and forsake them. 1 John 1:9; Proverbs 28:13. Through the Lord's Prayer the Bible teaches us to seek pardon directly from our Father in heaven. Matthew 6:12. The Bible does not require us to recite many "Our Fathers" and "Hail Marys," and it does warn against the danger inherent in repetitious prayer. Matthew 6:7.

Catholics are finding, also, that the Bible says that "Christ is *the* head of the church" (Ephesians 5:23); He is not one of the heads. The Bible nowhere says that the pope is the head of the church, not even its visible head.

Professor McKenzie, our friendly Jesuit at the University of Notre Dame (see page 128), unabashedly acknowledges that in justifying its official teachings about the authority of the pope, the Catholic Church does "not . . . claim that one can find in the New Testament, a statement of the same power in other words," or "that Peter thought of his own office in terms substantially identical [to the office of the pope]," or even that it can be proved, historically, that the pope really is the successor of Peter.[16]

And in view of the fact that "the New Testament is so explicit about both the bread and the wine," and in light of the fact that the use of both bread and wine by the laity "was certainly the most ancient practice," Professor McKenzie also says that "it is an obvious question . . . why Roman Catholics do not receive communion under both species." He admits wryly that if use of the wine were restored to Catholic worship, "no Roman Catholic who knows some of his history could feel entirely comfortable if the Roman Church adopted a liturgical practice for which it burnt John Hus[s] at Constance"; but he goes on to observe that at the present time "there is a serious movement within Roman Catholicism to restore the original sign in its integrity."[17]

The hints here that the Catholic Church may have erred in various ways, such as by withholding the wine and in burning John Huss, are especially troublesome to Roman Catholics, for their church teaches that

> it is unthinkable that an institution established by God for the salvation of souls could lead men into error and turn them away from God. If the Church could and did err in matters of faith or morals, it would not be a true teacher; it would fail in its ministry of sanctification and would not lead men to salvation but would be responsible for their condemnation.—Baltimore Catechism, sec. 163.

Catholics believe many things not found in the Bible on the simple basis that the Church teaches them and the Church cannot be wrong. But supposing the Church has been wrong?

Virtually all Christians in all the world, other than Roman Catholics, offer the wine to the laity. The Catholic Church itself offered the wine until about the twelfth century, and it is contemplating doing so again. Inasmuch as Jesus said "Drink of it, *all of you*" (Matthew 26:27), has it been wrong for the church to withhold the wine from millions of believers for so many years? Was it wrong for the Church to kill John Huss because he served it to his followers?

And if the Catholic Church can be wrong about the wine, is it possible that during mass the bread doesn't turn into the body of Christ? Was the church in error when it actually burned Wycliffe's followers because they insisted that the bread did not undergo such a change? Are Catholics, even today, wrong when they pray and sing hymns to the "reserved host" (the consecrated bread that is left over) in its golden tabernacle hanging in the church? Are they unwittingly worshiping a consecrated piece of bread?

174

If the church can be wrong, is it possible that it erred seriously in killing Lutherans when they insisted, among other matters, that it was not necessary to confess their sins to a priest and do penance?

Was the church wrong when it forbade people to keep the Sabbath on the seventh day of the week as taught in the Ten Commandments and said instead that they must observe Sunday, the first day of the week?

Is it any wonder that Catholics today face wrenching decisions? Is it any wonder that many of them are wandering away from all religion and that not a few are becoming Protestants?

When Catholics become Protestants under these searching circumstances, it is observed that they often make more dedicated Protestants than people born into Protestant homes.

Doubtful tradition and good motivation. Protestants need not suppose that covens of wizard bishops closeted themselves with the devil from time to time and deliberately concocted doctrines that couldn't be found in the Bible! Medieval Christian traditions may be said rather to have evolved from a gene pool of very defensible motivation.

We have already seen (pages 136-139) that many Christians in the second century abandoned the Sabbath of the Bible because the Jews seemed to keep it badly and because Sunday seemed to offer a more desirable memorial of Christ's death and resurrection.

The tradition that priests have the power to forgive sins developed in the third century after large numbers of church members apostatized in A.D. 250 during the short but sharp Decian persecution. A group of very strict bishops (the Novatianists) insisted that the apostates had sinned so mortally that they could never be forgiven. Other bishops, however, offered forgiveness to any apostate who confessed to them, in order to demonstrate that God forgives all contrite sinners.

Penance was also introduced about this same time—for the purpose of helping people not to take their mortal sins lightly. Penance at first consisted of standing conspicuously outside the church at meeting time for a number of years, then inside the church for several more years, and so on. When such rigorous penance proved counterproductive and people reasoned that they might as well be hanged for a sheep as for a lamb, less onerous options were offered, such as payments in cash and military service on a crusade. By this time an additional motive was at work. Profits from the sale of pardons and indulgences could be used to build beautiful churches to the glory of God.

When the wine at Communion came to be viewed as being the "blood of God," priests around the twelfth century stopped serving it to the laity for the excellent reason that no one wanted to commit the sacrilege of accidently spilling God on the floor.

In the thirteenth century officers of the papal Inquisition who handed heretics to the state to be burned did so on the allegedly merciful basis that if sinners suffered a short time in flames in this life, they would be spared far worse suffering in flames after death.

Doubtful traditions *can* develop from defensible motives. Jesus fully recognized the possibility of doing wrong for good reasons when He said, "The hour is coming when whoever kills you will think that he is offering service to God." John 16:2.

Addressing religious leaders, Jesus also remarked once, frighteningly and with more than a trace of irony, "You have a fine way of rejecting the commandment of God, in order to keep your tradition!" Mark 7:9. More plainly, on the same occasion He branded worship that is based on mere human authority as "vain" or useless. Mark 7:7.

Religion at the grass roots. Whatever the quality of a church's official teachings, there is usually a gap between what theologians write and what ordinary pastors and people believe and practice. Is there evidence that Christian Rome, during the long Middle Ages, did in fact separate church members from the continual priestly ministry, the *tamid* of Jesus Christ in the heavenly sanctuary? Did the church actually obscure the truth about His forgiveness and about His desire, through the Holy Spirit, to dwell victoriously in our hearts by faith?

The sad fact appears to be that in many medieval pulpits the gospel of Jesus Christ was hardly ever preached; indeed, that there were hardly any sermons on any subject. It was considered a reform measure when Archbishop Peckham in 1281 asked his priests to preach at least four times a year![18] And when the priests did preach, their messages tended to consist of fantastic miracle stories and of shocking illustrations of the seven deadly sins. As a natural consequence people tended to step outside the church during the sermon and to return only in time for the consecration of the bread during the ceremony of the mass. If they stayed inside for the sermon, they often acted indifferently or chatted with one another. Sometimes they played chess.[19]

With the people deprived, to a large extent, of the truth about Jesus Christ, it is little wonder that in the late Middle Ages traveling "pardoners" enjoyed great success—and occasioned great scandal. A pardoner was a kind of monk or friar who had received special authorization from the pope to hear confession and forgive sin for a fee. Pardoners did in actual fact hawk forgiveness;[20] and because they were allowed to keep part of the fee as their commission, they tended to forgive people who were not truly repentant. Drunks and fornicators loved them, but more thoughtful people took a different view. More than a century before Luther's birth, Geoffrey Chaucer, William Langland, and John Wycliffe denounced the pardoners as being opposed to true religion. Langland, in *Piers Plowman*, described them as "big loafers" who swarmed over the land with their bags and bellies full, hearing confession and forgiving any sinner for a price.[21]

A grotesque competition developed between the lenient, itinerant pardoners and the local parish priests. More than once a pardoner wrestled physically with a priest for the use of the priest's pulpit. Losing the contest, the pardoner might step to the back of the church and "preach" anyway, advertising his cheap indulgences and destroying the worship service.

But if the people were left unfed by the priest's preaching and were deceived by the pardoner's commercialized grace, they were also misled by the mass.

The priest stepped deep into the apse. He turned his back. He murmured in an unknown tongue. And when he rang his little bell and spoke the mystic phrase, *"Hoc est corpus meum"* ("This is my body," in Latin), the people believed that he begot Christ on the altar as surely as the virgin Mary gave Him birth in old Bethlehem. To exceptional, pious souls Communion constituted a moment of sweet consolation and of fellowship with the Crucified, but for the majority, attendance at mass was a kind of salvation by magic, an easy if irksome way to avoid untold years of agony in the flames of purgatory. Awareness that the real Christ was *alive,* ministering forgiveness in the heavenly sanctuary and longing to dwell victoriously—through the Holy Spirit—in people's hearts, was most certainly obscured.

All was not bad, however. Think of St. Francis and his love for the poor. Think of John Colet preaching on the epistles of Paul in Oxford and London. Think of Catholic missionary graves, numerous even before the sixteenth century.

Toward the end of the Middle Ages tracts were published to teach ordinary people what to say to someone who was dying. *Ars moriendi,* they were called: "On the Art of Dying." They taught the layfolk, in the absence of a priest, to encourage a dying person to believe in Jesus Christ as his personal Saviour—every ugly, tormenting doubt, appearance, and demon to the contrary notwithstanding. Even if God Himself should speak of wrath and judgment, the dying person should be encouraged to reply, "O God, I interpose between my sin and Thee the death of Jesus Christ."

All was not bad. But things were tragically far from what they should have

been. Prophecy purposely pointed to the dark side to show us God's concern for people and for their relationship to the ministry of our Lord in heaven.

Jesuit professor Robert E. McNally of Fordham University acknowledges that "the indulgence practice [of the pardoners] was an abuse which could and should have been corrected by ecclesiastical authority."[22] Indeed he emphasizes that "the old Church needed renewal and reform on all levels—morals, theology, spirituality, liturgy, and structure."

Both Protestants and modern Catholics alike can be pleased that earnest voices within the medieval church demanded change. "The question of Church reform was a burning question even a century before Luther," McNally continues. "The history of the period is filled with futile attempts on the part of good, discerning, capable, even saintly men, to reform the Church."[23] Luther, a devout and talented monk, provided a partial answer, McNally adds; but further reform—of both Catholicism and Protestantism—is needed still today.

Christian Rome and the tamid *of Daniel 8.* We have seen in earlier pages that pagan Rome **"magnified itsef . . . up to the Prince of the host,"** destroyed **"the people of the saints,"** and in a limited sense overthrew the **"sanctuary"** and took away the "tamid." It did these things when it crucified Jesus, persecuted Christians, demolished Herod's temple, and terminated the Old Testament ritual.

The medieval church assumed many of Christ's prerogatives as Prince of the host and obscured His high-priestly ministry in the heavenly sanctuary. It did so:

1. *By insisting on the pope's absolute kingship as the visible head of the church,* and persecuting people who said that the only head of the church is Jesus Christ. Ephesians 4:15; 5:23.

2. *By presenting the Lord's Supper in a manner that encouraged superstition,* and persecuting people (like the followers of John Wycliffe) who refused to teach that the bread turns into the actual body of Jesus.

3. *By withholding the wine at communion,* and persecuting people (like the Hussites) who requested the wine as a symbol of the new covenant in Christ's blood. Matthew 26:27, 28.

4. *By failing to preach the Word of God,* and burning at the stake people (like William Tyndale) who labored to make the Bible accessible to common people.

5. *By authorizing the purchase of pardons,* and excommunicating people (like Martin Luther) who said that justification is by grace alone through faith in Jesus Christ. Romans 3:24; Ephesians 2:5.

6. *By requiring confession to a priest and the performance of penance,* and persecuting people (like the Lutherans) who said that every Christian is a priest who can go directly to God through one Mediator, Jesus Christ. 1 Peter 2:9; 1 Timothy 2:5.

7. *By requiring that the first day of the week be observed in place of the seventh day,* even though God in the new covenant promised to write His law on people's hearts. Exodus 20:8-11; Hebrews 8:10-12.

These errors reflected the temper of the times. Today we live in a new time.

Thank God, the promise of Daniel 8 is that in our day Christ's high-priestly ministry, His *tamid,* is once more to become triumphantly available to all people.

V. Christ's Ministry Triumphant

Everything we have said so far about Daniel 8 has helped prepare us for our discussion of Daniel 8:14, the verse which has been called the peak and focus of the entire book.

In response to an anxious question about how long the priestly ministry (the *tamid*) would be trampled underfoot, the angel Gabriel replied, **"For* two thousand and three hundred evenings and mornings; then shall the sanctuary be restored to its rightful state."**

What enigmatic words—and how intriguing!

And we absolutely must remember that this verse is located in the *symbolic* portion of Daniel 8. The **"sanctuary"** and the **"evenings and mornings"** are no more literal than are the beasts and horns!

After Daniel looked at the beasts and horns and heard the prediction about the evenings and mornings and about the sanctuary, he naturally desired an explanation. Gabriel started to provide one, but what he said about the beasts and horns and their effect on Christ's heavenly ministry and on the people of God so overwhelmed Daniel that he fainted before Gabriel could deal specifically with verse 14.

Gabriel had been commissioned to **"make this man understand the vision."** True to his trust, he returned in Daniel 9 with an explanation of the evenings and mornings, which we shall study carefully in due course. Even so he did get in a few hints in Daniel 8. He said that the vision as a whole extended **"to the appointed time of the end"** (Daniel 8:19) and that **"it pertains to many days hence"** (verse 26). Thus he directed Daniel's (and our) attention to a restoration of the sanctuary *at the end of time.*

The "evenings and mornings" are days. In addition, we can discern from Daniel 8:14 itself that the 2300 evenings and mornings are really 2300 days. (They are *symbolic* days, of course. Just as the beasts stand for empires and the *tamid* symbolizes Christ's heavenly ministry, so the 2300 days of Daniel 8:14 are symbols that stand for 2300 years [see pages 238-240].)

Some commentators have interpreted the 2300 evenings and mornings to be only 1150 (literal) days. They explain that they have done this to make them fit as closely as possible to the three years and ten days that the temple was desecrated under Antiochus Epiphanes, and that they have assumed the phrase "evenings and mornings" to be an idiomatic abbreviation referring to the regular morning and evening burnt offerings which Antiochus Epiphanes interrupted.

For several reasons, however, 2300 is preferable to 1150. These reasons include the following:

---

*The Hebrew is literally "until," as in the Jerusalem Bible.

1. Even 1150 days *cannot* be fitted meaningfully into the experience of the Jews under Antiochus Epiphanes (see pages 190-192).

2. The expression **"evenings and mornings"** (literally, in Hebrew, "evening-morning") *cannot* be applied to the daily burnt offerings. In the sanctuary ritual special sacrifices were indeed offered twice a day, as we have seen (page 167), but they were never referred to as "evening and morning" sacrifices. They were always referred to as being offered "morning and evening." For example, "They offered to the Lord every morning and evening." 2 Chronicles 13:11. "The burnt offerings of morning and evening." 2 Chronicles 31:3. "Burnt offerings morning and evening." Ezra 3:3 (see also Numbers 28:4 and 2 Chronicles 2:4). In other words, it simply would not have occurred to a Jew to think of the daily sacrifices as "evening and morning" events.

3. On the other hand, the sequence "evening, morning" does occur in the Bible—not in connection with the daily burnt offerings, but in connection with the days of Creation. "There was evening and there was morning, one day," says Genesis 1:5. "There was evening and there was morning, a second day," adds Genesis 1:8. And so on. Jewish days were conceived to commence at sunset and continue to the following sunset. Thus the Sabbath began and ended at sunset (compare Leviticus 23:32 with Mark 1:32). A vestige of this practice is the contemporary custom of celebrating Christmas Eve *before* Christmas Day.

4. The Jewish scholars who prepared both of the principal ancient Greek versions of the Old Testament[24] did in fact understand the 2300 evenings and mornings to be 2300 days. Their translations both provide (in Greek, of course) "days of evening and morning, twenty-three hundred."

Carl F. Keil, who edited the widely used Keil and Delitzsch commentary more than a hundred years ago, was on firm ground when he wrote:[25]

> When the Hebrews wish to express separately day and night, the component parts of a day of a week, then the number of both is expressed. They say, e.g., forty days and forty nights (Gen vii:4, 12; Ex xxiv:18; 1 Kings xix:8), and three days and three nights (Jonah i:17; Matt xii:40), but not eighty or six days-and-nights, when they wish to speak of forty or three full days. A Hebrew reader could not possibly understand the period of time 2300 evening-mornings of 2300 half days or 1150 whole days, because evening and morning at the creation constituted not the half but the whole day. . . . We must therefore take the words as they are, *i.e.,* understand them of 2300 whole days.

Christian writers have perceived the "2300 evenings and mornings" to be 2300 days since at least the thirteenth century. Recent commentators who have drawn the same conclusion include Edward J. Young,[26] John F. Walvoord,[27] Leon Wood,[28] and S. J. Schwantes.[29]

Restored, victorious, or cleansed? Leaving further discussion of the time question until we get to Daniel 9, we turn to the "restoration of the sanctuary"—only to discover that Gabriel provided no specific explanation of it anywhere in the book.

Inasmuch as he had been told to **"make this man understand the vision,"** the conclusion is unmistakable that sufficient general information must be available in the Bible as a whole so that the term can be understood without additional specific interpretation.

When we look at the clause **"Then the sanctuary shall be restored to its rightful state,"** we find that translations vary widely. Today's English Version has "Then the Temple will be restored," which is fairly close to the R.S.V.; but The New English Bible has "Then the Holy Place shall emerge victorious." Monsignor Knox has "Ere the sanctuary is cleansed," and the K.J.V., at this point rather similar to Knox, provides "Then shall the sanctuary be cleansed."

The differences are occasioned in part by the fact that Gabriel spoke to Daniel in Hebrew, not English; and he said in Hebrew, "Then shall the sanctuary be *nitsdaq*," employing a word which occurs *only this one time* in the entire Hebrew part of the Bible.

Scholars know that *nitsdaq* is related to another Hebrew word, *tsadaq*, which is a rather common term. *Tsadaq* occurs in its various forms more than 250 times in the Bible and is normally translated into the English word, "righteousness." It is also translated into "to be righteous," "to be just" (in the Latin sense of "being righteous"), and "to justify" (meaning "to make something right" or "to make it appear to be right").

A literal translation of Daniel 8:14 quite possibly ought to be "Then shall the sanctuary be made righteous."

But the sanctuary is a building, and neither in English nor in Hebrew are buildings ordinarily made righteous! So some translators have struggled with the alternate words, "justified" and "just"; and when these haven't seemed to help much, they have tried synonyms and come up with "vindicate" and even "emerge victorious."

The editors of Today's English Version were quite sure that Daniel 8:14 refers to the restoration of the Jewish temple after its desecration by Antiochus Epiphanes. They translated *nitsdaq* with "restored" so as to make it fit their idea. But we have already seen that the rest of the chapter cannot possibly fit Antiochus Epiphanes; so it isn't helpful to compel this passage to do so.

Gabriel knew that Daniel could understand the passage without specific interpretation; so now we want to know *how other Jews who lived long ago* understood it. We are fascinated to discover that in both of the translations that were made into Greek in ancient times by Jewish scholars, the word *nitsdaq* is translated by an ordinary word meaning "cleansed," the same meaning as in the K.J.V. and in Monsignor Knox's version. Further, when the celebrated Christian scholar, Jerome, translated the passage into Latin around the year A.D. 400, after holding extensive conversations with a Jewish rabbi in regard to Old Testament idioms, he chose the Latin word that also means "cleansed."

The cleansing of the sanctuary. With this information from Jewish authorities before us, we begin to climb onto solid ground; for the annual highlight of the Old

181

Testament sanctuary ritual was a solemn ceremony in which the sanctuary was symbolically *cleansed!*

The day on which the sanctuary was cleansed is called in the R.S.V. and the K.J.V. the "day of atonement." It is well known even to nonreaders of the Bible by its Hebrew name, Yom Kippur.

Yom Kippur was and still is observed on the tenth day of the seventh month of the traditional Jewish year, a date that coincides roughly with the month of October. In Bible times the "day of atonement" was the most portentous day in the religious calendar. It was the only day when the high priest was permitted to enter the most holy place, the innermost compartment of the sanctuary.

As we saw on pages 167-170, when the people offered their personal sacrifices day by day, they placed their hands on their animals to transfer their guilt symbolically and then slew the animals as their symbolic substitutes. Subsequently, the priest made a record of their confessed *and forgiven* sins (Leviticus 4:20) by applying blood—immediately or later—to the golden altar in the holy place and to the floor nearby, in front of the inner veil.

Sin is so heinous that even the record of confessed sin contaminated the sanctuary. Thus on the Day of Atonement a unique ceremony was performed in order to cleanse it. The high priest was told that "he shall make atonement for the holy place, *because of the uncleannesses* of the people of Israel, and because of their transgressions, *all their sins;* and so he shall do for the tent of meeting, which abides with them in the midst of their *uncleannesses.*" Leviticus 16:16. Because this unique cleansing was not an ordinary housekeeping routine but was a cleansing from sin—that is, from unrighteousness—the cleansing was in fact a restoration to righteousness. Gabriel's use of *nitsdaq,* a unique form of the verb "to make righteous," is seen to be highly appropriate. Viewed in *this* light, the R.S.V. is correct when it uses the phrase, "restored to its rightful state."

According to Leviticus 16, on the Day of Atonement the high priest cast lots over two carefully selected goats in order to distinguish the "Lord's goat" from the "scapegoat" (K.J.V.). He then slew the Lord's goat and carried some of its blood through the holy place into the most holy place, where he sprinkled it on the floor in front of the ark of the covenant and on the ark itself. (It is helpful to notice that Leviticus 16 calls the most holy place simply the "holy place" and calls the sanctuary as a whole the "tent of meeting.")

In the original tabernacle a brilliant, supernatural light—later known as the "shekinah"—shone above the ark as a symbol of the presence of God (see page 166). It was a solemn moment when the high priest drew aside the inner veil and stepped into God's presence!

The gospel and the Day of Atonement. On no other day of the year was the gospel so fully proclaimed in the temple ritual. The Day of Atonement started, as did every other day, with the sacrifice of the lamb that symbolized the Lamb of God. As on every other day the "bread of the Presence" in the holy place represented Jesus, the Bread of Life. John 6:35. The seven-branched lampstand represented

183

On the annual Day of Atonement, the High Priest entered the most holy place.

Jesus, the Light of the world. John 8:12. And the priests represented Christ in His heavenly ministry. But in addition to these regular features, on the Day of Atonement blood that represented the blood of Christ was applied directly, in the presence of God, to the ark containing the Ten Commandments. This blood served as an impressive symbol of the price that our sins have cost and which Jesus has been willing to pay. Specifically, the blood was applied to the golden lid of the ark, the "mercy seat." God Himself provided the place, in His own presence, where sins could be forgiven.

The fact that on the Day of Atonement the high priest stepped into God's presence to atone for sin points up the personal nature of sin and its atonement. When we sin, we sin against God. When we seek forgiveness, we seek it through His Son. By faith we enter together with the Son into the presence of the Father. And when we do this, we find that the Father has been waiting to receive us. He has already prepared a "mercy seat."

The Day of Atonement provided persuasive evidence that God is not a tyrant. He hates sin, but He loves sinners, and He longs to lead us to repentance so He can forgive us. As Paul wrote in 2 Corinthians 5:19, "*In Christ God* was reconciling the world to himself." The word "reconcile" is a synonym for "atone." On the Day of Atonement, God revealed Himself as a person who is busy "at-one-ing" people —reconciling people—to Himself.

Having applied the blood in the most holy place, the high priest passed back out of the sanctuary, on the way applying blood to the golden altar in the holy place and to the altar of burnt offering in the court. During the year both altars had been sprinkled with blood representing confessed sin.

Thus, says the Bible, he "made an end of atoning for the holy place [that is, for the most holy place] and the tent of meeting [that is, the sanctuary as a whole] and the altar." Leviticus 16:20.

After he had *finished* making the atonement for the entire sanctuary, the high priest laid his hands on the live goat, which was then led to an uninhabited area in the wilderness and allowed to escape (hence the name, "scapegoat").

The people's part. It is most important to learn that the people of Israel were expected to become deeply involved in the religious meaning of the Day of Atonement.

To alert the Israelites to the great day just ahead, the priests summoned them to

Trumpets on Rosh Hashanah (New Year's Day) announced the soon arrival of the Day of Atonement/Day of Judgment.

a sacred meeting on the *first* day of the seventh month (Rosh Hashanah) by blowing an alarm on their long, straight, silver trumpets.[30] Leviticus 23:23-25; Numbers 10:1-10. These trumpets seem always to have been used in pairs. As their mellow tones rose, clear as sunbeams, above the noisiness of a community, the children no doubt ran home to shout, "They're blowing the trumpets. Listen, everyone!"

Nine days for preparation followed. The Day of Atonement, the tenth day of the seventh month, could, like our Christmas, fall on any day of the week. But whatever day it fell on, it was as sacred as the weekly Sabbath day. Leviticus 23:26-32. Whereas, however, the Sabbath was a day for joy (Isaiah 58:13, 14), the Day of Atonement was an occasion for the people to "afflict" themselves. They were to engage in deep spiritual self-examination. A custom arose of fasting on the day.*

The purpose of the Day of Atonement was the removal of sin, ceremonially from the sanctuary and truly from the people. Through Moses, God told the Israelites that the high priest entered the most holy place not only to "make atonement for the sanctuary" but also to make atonement "for *you,* to cleanse *you,*" so that *"from all your sins you shall be clean before the Lord"* (see Leviticus 16:30-33).

Leviticus 16:29, 30 specifically states that this removal of sin was the reason they were to afflict themselves. They were to afflict themselves "for"—that is, *because*—an atonement was being made for them.

It was taught very clearly that the atonement would not benefit the people if they did not afflict themselves. The Day of Atonement offered no magic and encouraged no superstition. The people were taught that "whoever is not afflicted on this same day shall be cut off from his people." Leviticus 23:29. To make the point dramatically urgent, God added, "Whoever does any work on this same day [that is, whoever refuses to keep it as a sacred, solemn Sabbath], that person I will destroy from among his people."

It was a day for at-one-ment. God had appointed the day; He had designed the mercy seat, consecrated the high priest, and provided the atoning blood. Those who refused reconciliation evidently chose separation, and God honored their decision.

Day of Atonement/Day of Judgment. The requirement that persons who refused to take the day seriously should be "cut off" implies that the Day of Atonement *was also a day of judgment.* Any Israelite who refused to enter seriously into the religious promise of the day was to be investigated by the elders, tried, sentenced, and punished.

Jewish rabbis have long described the day as one of judgment. In fact, Jewish

---

*The requirement to "afflict" themselves was at first a completely spiritual one. The people were expected to observe the Day of Atonement as a very sacred occasion on which to worship God, pray earnestly, confess sin, and make wrongs right. They were to afflict their souls by probing their memories and their motives to see if they were really sincere in their religious profession.

tradition has expanded the concept of judgment to include the first day of the month (Rosh Hashanah) as well, and even all the days in between, with final sentence being pronounced on Yom Kippur.[31] "The idea of a universal day of judgment," says *The Universal Jewish Encyclopedia,* dominates the ten-day penitential season and "is expressed particularly in the Unethanneh Tokef prayer of Yom Kippur."[32]

With the Day of Atonement seen to be a day of judgment, we sense immediately that the cleansing of the sanctuary in Daniel 8:14 is closely parallel to the judgment scene of Daniel 7 and to the arrival of the supernatural stone in Daniel 2. We are on firm ground. Unfolding parallelism is one of the principal keys to understanding the book of Daniel.

The judgment in Daniel 7 compares readily with the entry of Christ as High Priest into heaven's most holy place at the commencement of the celestial Day of Atonement/Day of Judgment:

> **Thrones were placed** [*symbolized by the ark in the most holy place*]
> **and one that was ancient of days** [*God the Father*]
> **took his seat** [*on heaven's "mercy seat"*]; . . .
> **ten thousand times ten thousand stood before him** [*the angels, represented in the tabernacle by the cherubim above the ark*];
> **the court sat in judgment** [*heaven's Day of Atonement*],
> **and the books were opened.**
>
> **I saw in the night visions, and behold, with the clouds of heaven there came** [*passing into heaven's "most holy place" like the earthly high priest on the Day of Atonement*]
> **one like a son of man** [*Jesus, our heavenly High Priest*],
> **and he came to the Ancient of Days. . . .**
>
> **And to him was given dominion and glory and kingdom.** [*At the close of this heavenly judgment, Christ will receive a kingdom that is peopled entirely with "saints" who have been fully cleansed from sin and who have chosen at-one-ment with God and with one another.*] Daniel 7:9-14.

Here is the cleansing of the sanctuary as viewed, not merely on the portable TV of the Old Testament tabernacle, but on the wide, wide screen of infinity and eternity. The cleansing of the tabernacle was only a "shadow" (Hebrews 8:5) of something that far transcended it. As a place, the heavenly sanctuary is glorious enough for the throne of Deity, vast enough for millions of angels. It is cleansed, not by the blood of bulls and goats, but by the life and death and blood of Jesus.

Can heaven be "cleansed"? But can we really conceive of a "cleansing" of the sanctuary in heaven? Can anything in heaven need to be cleaned?

Hebrews 9:22, 23 answers Yes. "It was necessary for the copies of the heavenly things to be purified with these rites, but the heavenly things themselves with better sacrifices than these." J. B. Phillips translates the passage a little more clearly: "It was necessary for the earthly reproductions of heavenly realities to be purified by such methods, but the actual heavenly things could only be made pure in God's sight by higher sacrifices than these."[33]

In our study of Daniel 9 (and of Revelation 14 in *God Cares, II*), we shall try to learn much more about the precise meaning of the **"cleansing of the sanctuary"** in heaven.

But we have already seen enough to know that the symbolic language of Daniel 8:14 is not directed to the strange behavior of Antiochus Epiphanes (see *Your Questions Answered*, pages 190-192). *The language of Daniel 8:14 is symbolic.* It transports us to the cosmic courtroom, to the universal assize of Daniel 7.

Restored, victorious, AND cleansed! Gabriel's choice of the unique word *nitsdaq* has provided us very appropriately with the concept of "cleansing" and of "restoring to righteousness (or purity) after defilement." The New English Bible has yet another translation, "emerge victorious" (page 181). Well, there is a distinct sense in which "emerge victorious" is appropriate also.

For ages Christ's *tamid,* His priestly ministry in heaven, was to be **"trampled under foot,"** in some sense even **"taken away from him."** And the prophecy has been fulfilled. For many centuries the truth about Jesus has been maligned. His freedom to help people has been limited by the false theories of paganism and secularism and even by the mistaken emphases of certain Christian doctrines. Not to mention evil men, well-intentioned men have so misrepresented the fatherly character of God and the amazing grace of Christ that millions of people have preferred to depend on earthly priests, to accumulate their own good works, or to take their chances with Lady Luck rather than to trust Jesus for forgiveness and let His Spirit transform their lives.

To put the matter bluntly, "Rome" has misrepresented Christ's ministry with a false sacrifice (the mass), a false priesthood, a false head of the church, and a false method of salvation.

In the judgment God puts a stop to this state of affairs and sets all things right. It is a day of victory for Him and for His way of doing things.

Heaven's jubilee. The sanctuary is God's court of justice.

The Day of Judgment is His "Day of Atonement," when He vindicates and cleanses everyone who sincerely desires to be at-one with Him and when He removes everyone who separates himself from Him.

When God has finished doing this, a shout of victory will ring from galaxy to galaxy across the starry sky. God's patience with wicked people has been a mercy to the wicked, but it has been a trial to the saints. In their woe they have often cried out, "O Sovereign Lord, how long?" Revelation 6:10. When at last God brings the wicked to their end, the righteous universe will exclaim in praise, "We give thanks to thee, Lord God Almighty, . . . that thou hast taken thy great power and begun to reign." Revelation 11:17.

Indeed, although the ancient Day of Atonement began with solemnity, it too ended with joy. Village maidens clothed in white danced over the fields, exulting in the happiness of renewed innocence.[34]

187

God provided for another source of joy in addition to renewed innocence. In the afternoon of the Day of Atonement every fiftieth year, at the conclusion of seven cycles of seven years, the "shofar" trumpets announced the beginning of a Year of Jubilee. Leviticus 25.

Heralds were to "proclaim liberty throughout all the land unto all the inhabitants thereof." Leviticus 25:10, K.J.V. Hebrew slaves were to be released. All land that had been bought or sold since the previous jubilee was to be returned to the descendants of the original owners. It was a plan for curing social inequity. It taught that God, not man, is the real owner of the earth.

What an illustration for the book of Daniel! At the close of heaven's Day of Atonement/Day of Judgment, the trumpet of the Lord will sound, God will declare His Son King of kings and Lord of lords, the supernatural stone will smite the image, and the earth will be taken from those who destroy it (Revelation 11:18) and given to the saints of the Most High. The meek will inherit the earth. Matthew 5:5.

> **The court shall sit in judgment** [*on heaven's Day of Atonement*]
> **and his** [*the little horn's*]
> **dominion** [*his self-assumed authority to trample on Christ's* tamid *and on His truth and people*]
> **shall be taken away to be consumed and destroyed to the end. . . .**
> **And the greatness of the kingdoms . . . shall be given to the people of the saints of the Most High** [*at the commencement of heaven's Year of Jubilee*]." Daniel 7:26, 27.

The Day of Atonement and you. The personal message of Daniel 8:14 is that God wants *you!* He cares enough to draw you to Himself at any cost to Himself. "The Father himself loves you." John 16:27. And He wants you to examine yourself deeply to see if any sin separates you from Him and separates you from other people whom He also loves.

A God who calls the Day of Judgment a Day of Atonement must be a very wonderful God.

So we want to know *when* the heavenly sanctuary will triumph, *when* it will be cleansed and restored to its rightful state.

In chapter 9 Gabriel will come back and "make us understand" many things, including the mystery of the "two thousand and three hundred evenings and mornings," which are 2300 days.

Further Interesting Reading

In Arthur S. Maxwell, *The Bible Story,* vol. 6:
   "Gabriel's Glorious Secret," beginning on p. 66.
In *Bible Readings for the Home:*
   The chapters entitled "The Prophetic Symbols of Daniel 8,"
   "The Atonement in Type and Antitype," and "The Judgment."

DANIEL 8:9-12: SYMBOLIC PREDICTION

9. **Out of one of them** [*the four winds of heaven, the four directions of the compass*] **came forth a little horn** [*Rome*] **which grew exceedingly great toward the south** [*Africa*], **toward the east** [*Greece, Asia Minor, and Syria*], **and toward the glorious land** [*Palestine*].

10. **And it grew great, even to the host of heaven** [*the people of God, Jewish and Christian*]; **and some of the host of the stars** [*God's people*] **it cast down to the ground.**

11. **and trampled upon them** [*persecuted them*]. **It magnified itself, even up to the Prince of the host** [*Jesus Christ, whom pagan Rome crucified and Christian Rome often misinterpreted*], **and the continual burnt offering** [*the tamid, the continual ministry of Christ in heaven and the symbol of it in the Old Testament ritual*] **was taken away from him, and the place of his sanctuary was overthrown** [*partially at the destruction of Herod's temple by pagan Rome and much more fully through the misrepresentations of Christian Rome*].

12. **And the host** [*the people of God*] **was given over to it** [*Rome, the little horn*] **together with the continual burnt offering** [*the* tamid] **through transgression** [*God permitting the forces of evil to reveal themselves so that error could be seen in its sinfulness and people would be persuaded to turn away from it*]; **and truth** [*about the Ten Commandments, Christ's heavenly ministry, and righteousness by faith*] **was cast down to the ground, and the horn** [*Rome*] **acted and prospered.**

DANIEL 8:23-25: GABRIEL'S INTERPRETATIVE PREDICTION

23. **And at the latter end of their rule** [*at the end of the Hellenistic kingdoms symbolized by the four horns, around 65 B.C.*], **when the transgressors have reached their full measure** [*when human wickedness is at a peak*], **a king of bold countenance** [*Rome*], **one who understands riddles** [*"skilled in intrigue," N.A.S.B.; "A master of stratagem" N.E.B., referring to pagan and Christian Rome as masters of international and religious diplomacy*], **shall arise.**

24. **His power shall be great, and he shall cause fearful destruction, and shall succeed in what he does, and destroy mighty men** [*political enemies*] **and the people of the saints** [*the persecuted people of God*].

25. **By his cunning he shall make deceit prosper under his hand** [*persuading millions to follow pagan and medieval traditions*], **and in his own mind he shall magnify himself** [*the emperor as a divine being, the medieval pope as "another God on earth"*]. **Without warning he shall destroy many** [*for example, in the St. Bartholomew's Day massacre*]; **and he shall even rise up against the Prince of princes** [*Jesus Christ, on the cross and as our royal priest in heaven*]; **but, by no human hand** [*that is, by the providence of God in human affairs, by clearer perception of truth, by the Day of Judgment in heaven, and finally by the second coming of Christ*], **he shall be broken.**

189

8

Your Questions Answered

Who was Antiochus Epiphanes? We have frequently referred to Antiochus Epiphanes (see e.g. pages 159, 160). Much more can be said, however, to anyone who is intersted.

To begin with: Probably the reason that many Christians have assumed that Antiochus Epiphanes fulfilled the prophecy of Daniel 8 is that their acquaintance with him has been limited to a few paragraphs in books on prophecy and to brief notes in study Bibles. If they knew more about him, they would recognize that he could not be the little horn of Daniel 8.

Antiochus Epiphanes was the eighth king (175-164 B.C.) in the Seleucid dynasty of the Hellenistic kingdom that came to be known as Syria. He is mentioned by the Roman historian Livy *(History of Rome,* books 44, 45), the Greek historian Polybius *(The Histories,* books 26, 27), and the anonymous Jewish historians who wrote 1 and 2 Maccabees in the Apocrypha. He scarcely strides out of their pages as a legendary antichrist. He emerges as a born loser, a really tragic little man.

His father, Antiochus III the Great, pushed back the boundaries of the Seleucid kingdom to their original position. But at the Battle of Magnesia, 190 B.C., even he lost much of the territory—all of Asia Minor—to the Romans, a power newly arising in the west.

The Romans liberated the area they confiscated from Antiochus III and did not take direct control of it. Rome was still a **"little horn,"** developing slowly from the direction of **"one of the four winds."** Daniel 8:8, 9. Roman envoys, however, sailing east from Rome, clearly dominated international politics in the Middle East.

To make sure that Antiochus III honored the treaty imposed on him after his bitter defeat at Magnesia, the Romans took hostage one of his youthful sons, the later Antiochus Epiphanes. At Rome, and later during a visit to Greece, young Antiochus became saturated with the kind of Hellenistic culture which the Romans were then adopting. At his father's death the Romans allowed the young man to accede to the throne, and he returned to Antioch determined to make a name for himself by (1) spreading Hellenism—Greek thought and customs—at any cost and (2) enlarging his domains in imitation of his dad's exploits.

We have already seen (page 159) how his military dreams were shattered when a Roman envoy drew a circle around him. His cultural dreams succeeded a little better, but ultimately they led to his downfall. He attempted to spread Hellenism by granting sufficient money to various cities so that they could build Greek temples and Greek gymnasiums. In the process he reduced his nation to bankruptcy. He died while on a campaign to recoup his finances by robbing the treasure of an ancient eastern temple, as earlier (see page 191) he had raided the treasure of the Jewish temple.

Both his cultural and his military dreams led to his notorious relationship with the Jews. As 1 Maccabees 1:11-15; 2:43-52 reveals, *a group of liberal, Hellenizing Jews* led by the Jewish *high priest,* Jason, *took the initiative* in applying to Antiochus for a grant to build a Greek gymnasium in Jerusalem.

In a Greek gymnasium athletes (all male) practiced and competed with each other without any clothes on. (The word "gymnasium" means "a place of nakedness.") The ostensible reason behind this custom was to honor manliness. When even the priests, at the instigation of the high priest, neglected their temple duties in order to work out nude at the gym (2 Maccabees 4:17-27), the more conservative Jews were scandalized.

Antiochus was a playful fellow when he wasn't angry. He enjoyed, for example, dressing up like a commoner and running for election. It is not clear that the opposition of the conservative Jews would have led to a confrontation with him had Antiochus not been turned out of Egypt by the Roman envoy. It had cost Antiochus much to organize his army for the invasion of Egypt, and suddenly the whole enterprise had become a dead loss. He was setting out for home when he learned that the priest Jason (he, again!) was engaged in an attack against his fellow Jews. Confounded and sore from his treatment in Egypt, Antiochus attacked the Jews as an outlet for his private rage. Then he robbed the temple as a means of recovering the cost of his Egyptian campaign. Even so he might not have robbed the temple if he had not been guided by Menelaus, a Hellenizing Jew who had promised Antiochus a large bribe in exchange for being allowed to replace Jason as high priest.

It was after this unfortunate series of events, in which renegade Jews played a very prominent role, that Antiochus shifted from voluntary cultural uniformity to required religious uniformity.

As a part of the new order of things, on Chislev 15, 168 B.C., a statue of the Greek god Zeus was erected upon the altar of burnt offering. First Maccabees 1 indicates that once more liberal Jews assisted in the process. Ten days later, on Chislev 25, they began to sacrifice "unclean" animals on the altar, most likely including swine. 2 Maccabees 6:5.

The conservative Jews now rallied around Judas Maccabeeus, under whose intrepid leadership they secured a series of victories over the armies which Antiochus sent against them. Antiochus's Judean campaign was as much a failure as the rest of his pitiable career.

Safe at last from the mad king's hostility and from the machinations of the liberal Jews, the devout Jews removed the old altar and dedicated a new one three years to the day after the offering of unclean sacrifices had begun, three years and ten days after the statue of Zeus had been erected. Chislev 25 occurs in the Jewish calendar close to Christmas in the Gregorian calendar. It is today honored as "Hanukkah," celebrating the "dedication" of the new altar in 165 B.C. In the New Testament John 10:22, 23 dates an episode in Christ's life with a

191

reference to this annual feast: "It was the feast of the Dedication at Jerusalem; it was winter."

There is no doubt that Antiochus interrupted the temple services, but all attempts to fit his interruption into the 2300 **"evenings and mornings"** of Daniel 8:14 have uniformly failed. There is simply no way they *can* be fitted into three years, or even into three years and ten days!

And it should be noted that the desolation of the temple was as largely due to the disloyalty of Jews as to the madness of Antiochus. Sooner or later the liberal Jews might well have desolated the temple on their own had Antiochus not required them to do so. They were already neglecting the ritual in order to practice naked in the gym, and they had already secured the king's support for Hellenizing Jerusalem.

As long ago as 1733, Sir Isaac Newton, the celebrated scientist who first explained the operation of gravity, wrote the following notice about Daniel 9 and Antiochus Epiphanes:

> This last horn is by some taken for ANTIOCHUS EPIPHANES, but not very judiciously. A horn of a Beast is never taken for a single person: it always signifies a new kingdom, and the kingdom of ANTIOCHUS was an old one. ANTIOCHUS reigned over one of the four horns, and the little horn was a fifth under its proper kings. This horn was at first a little one, and waxed exceeding great, but so did not ANTIOCHUS. It is described great above all the former horns, and so was not ANTIOCHUS. His kingdom on the contrary was weak, and tributary to the ROMANS, and he did not enlarge it. The horn was a King of fierce countenance, and destroyed wonderfully, and prospered and practised; that is, he prospered in his practices against the holy people: but ANTIOCHUS was frightened out of EGYPT by a mere message of the ROMANS, and afterwards routed and baffled by the JEWS. The horn was mighty by another's power, ANTIOCHUS acted by his own. The horn stood up against the Prince of the Host of heaven, the Prince of Princes; and this is the character not of ANTIOCHUS but of ANTICHRIST. The horn cast down the Sanctuary to the ground, and so did not ANTIOCHUS; he left it standing. The Sanctuary and Host were trampled under foot 2300 days; and in DANIEL'S Prophecies days are put for years: but the profanation of the Temple in the reign of ANTIOCHUS did not last for so many natural days. These were to last till the time of the end, till the last end of the indignation against the JEWS; and this indignation is not yet at an end. They were to last till the Sanctuary which had been cast down should be cleansed, and the Sanctuary is not yet cleansed.[35]

Sir Isaac Newton's observations contrast sharply with the note to Daniel 8:1 in the 1967 edition of the Scofield Reference Bible, which refers to the *"remarkably precise* predictions in chapters 8 and 11 about the reign, character, and antecedents of Antiochus Epiphanes."

References

1. Werner Soedel and Vernard Foley, "Ancient Catapults," *Scientific American*, March 1979, pp. 150-160.

2. J. B. Bury, *A History of Greece to the Death of Alexander the Great*, The Modern

Library (New York: Random House, n.d.), pp. 769, 770.

3. *Ibid.*, pp. 761, 762.

4. Stewart C. Easton, *The Western Heritage from the Earliest Times to the Present* (New York: Holt, Rinehart, and Winston, 1961), p. 81.

5. See Polybius, *The Histories*, 26.1.

6. The classic account is in Livy, *History of Rome*, 45.12.

7. Harry A. Dawe, *Ancient Greece and Rome*, World Cultures in Perspective (Columbus, Ohio: Charles E. Merrill Publishing Co., 1970), p. 188.

8. William Poole et al., compilers, *Rodeheaver's Gospel Solos and Duets Number 3* (Chicago: The Rodeheaver Hall-Mack Co., 1938), no. 131.

9. Hebrews 9:3, 4 and 1 Kings 6:22 identify the golden altar with the most holy place, not because it was located in the most holy place, for it was located immediately outside of it; but because the incense rising from the golden altar was offered to God, whose presence was manifested most markedly above the ark in the most holy place, the golden altar was sometimes thought of as "belonging to" the most holy place. Exodus 40:26 makes plain that it was indeed located in the holy place (here called the "tent of meeting"). Exodus 30:1-10 manifests a clear awareness of the close relationship between the golden altar and the ark, but by requiring Aaron to burn incense on the golden altar twice a day this passage also shows that it was located in the holy place, for Aaron was permitted to enter the most holy place only once a year.

10. *The Jewish Encyclopedia*, art., "Atonement, Day of."

11. L. M. Hollingworth, "The Cross Was His Own."

12. The selections from the Baltimore Catechism are taken from *This We Believe, By This We Live: Revised Edition of the Baltimore Catechism, No. 3* (n.p.: Confraternity of Christian Doctrine, 1957).

13. In order to be faithful to the Fourth Lateran Council, to Thomas Aquinas, and to the Council of Trent, the Baltimore Catechism ought to say that the *substance* of the bread is transformed into the *substance* of the body and blood of Christ. The meaning of "substance" is not our ordinary understanding of the word in common use but a philosophical one, referring to the essential nature or self-existence of a thing. One useful rendering of the assumed change is, "The 'breadness' of the bread changes into the 'bodyness' and 'bloodness' of Christ." McKenzie, *Catholic Church*, p. 147, says that "the relation of the bread and wine to the body and blood of Jesus Christ is one of the most intricate theological propositions within the Roman Catholic system, and it is difficult even for a trained theologian to state it accurately."

14. *A New Catechism* (New York: Herder and Herder, 1967), pp. 176, 177.

15. *Ibid.*, pp. 480, 481.

16. McKenzie, *Catholic Church*, pp. 10, 4. What Catholics do believe about papal claims, he says, is that they are a "legitimate extension" of New Testament doctrine.

17. *Ibid.*, pp. 150, 151.

18. Thomas Frederick Simmons and Henry Edward Nolloth, eds., *The Lay Folks Catechism*, with intro. notes, and glossary, original series, no. 118 (London: Early English Text Society, 1901), intro.

19. For items in this paragraph and below see, among other sources, Gordon Hall Gerould, ed., *The North England Homily Collection* (published privately, 1902); and G. R. Owst, *Preaching in Medieval England* (Cambridge: Cambridge University Press, 1926).

20. "In the later Middle Ages, the right to share in an indulgence was hawked around Europe by the 'Pardoners.' . . . Pardons were a source of great profit to the ecclesiastical authorities and were frequently used to obtain money for building purposes, as for St. Peter's, Rome, and the completion of York Minster."—*Oxford Dictionary of the Christian Church*, art. "Pardon."

193

21. Walter W. Skeat, ed., *The Vision of William Concerning Piers the Plowman in Three Parallel Texts Together With Richard the Redeless,* 2 vols. (Oxford: Clarendon Press, 1886), B text, prologue and passus kk.

22. Robert E. McNally, S.J., "The Reformation: A Catholic Reappraisal," in *Luther, Erasmus and the Reformation: A Catholic-Protestant Reappraisal,* ed. John C. Olin, James D. Smart, and Robert McNally, S.J. (New York: Fordham University Press, 1969), p. 39.

23. *Ibid.,* p. 32.

24. The two principal ancient Jewish translations of the Old Testament into Greek are the Septuagint (LXX) and the one by Theodotian, which is of higher quality. The LXX is generally agreed to have been completed around 150 B.C. The translation of Theodotian has generally been supposed to have been made around A.D. 180 in response to the rise of Christianity. Recently, however, study of the Dead Sea Scrolls has suggested strongly that the Theodotian translation was made around 150 B.C. also. See documentation and arguments in Gerhard F. Hasel, "Daniel Survives the Critics' Den," *Ministry,* January 1979, pp. 9-11.

25. Keil, *Daniel,* pp. 303, 304.

26. Edward J. Young, *The Prophecy of Daniel: A Commentary* (Grand Rapids, Mich.: Wm. B. Eerdmans Publishing Co., 1949), pp. 174, 175.

27. John F. Walvoord, *Daniel: The Key to Prophetic Revelation, A Commentary* (Chicago: Moody Press, 1971), pp. 189, 190.

28. Leon Wood, *A Commentary on Daniel* (Grand Rapids, Mich.: Zondervan Publishing House, 1973), p. 218.

29. S. J. Schwantes, " 'Ereb Bōqer of Daniel 8:14 Re-examined," *Andrews University Seminary Studies* 16 (1978):375-385. A very helpful article.

30. In spite of the instructions in Numbers 10 that silver trumpets were to be used on the first day of the month, the Jewish ritualists at some point in history chose to blow "shofar" trumpets instead. Shofar trumpets were adapted animal horns. Instead of the clear tone of metal trumpets, they produced tones that resembled throaty bleats and blasts. They are still employed in Jewish ritual today (see, e.g., *Encyclopedia Judaica,* art. "Shofar").

31. See, e.g., *The Jewish Encyclopedia,* art. "Day of Judgment," and *Encyclopaedica Judaica,* art. "Day of Atonement."

32. *The Universal Jewish Encyclopedia,* art. "Day of Judgment."

33. The book of Hebrews is here possibly speaking of the dedication of the tabernacle; but the point is clear that heavenly things can stand in need of cleansing.

34. See, e.g., *Encyclopaedica Judaica,* art. "Day of Atonement"; and Mishnah *Ta'anith* 4.8, trans. in *The Babylonian Talmud,* Soncino ed., 35 vols. (London: The Soncino Press, 1935-1952), *Ta'anith* 26b, p. 139.

35. *Sir Isaac Newton's Daniel and the Apocalypse,* ed., Sir William Whitla (London: John Murray, 1922), p. 222.

Daniel 9
God Schedules the Atonement

Introduction

Daniel 9 is one of the most Christ-centered chapters in the Old Testament. The fulfillment of its precise predictions concerning the first coming of Jesus has fascinated Christians since the early days of the church. Furthermore, insights gained over the past two hundred years have led some Bible students to believe that this chapter, when linked to Daniel 7:9-14 and 8:13, 14, dates the judgment which precedes the second coming of Christ. They are right, for Daniel 7-9 shows that we are already living in the hour of judgment.

At the close of Daniel 8, we left Daniel in distress. The vision of the little horn and of the trampled sanctuary had made him ill. He returned to his government responsibilities after spending a few days in bed; but, he says, **"I was appalled by the vision and did not understand it."** Daniel 8:27.

His failure to understand the vision of Daniel 8 was in conflict with Gabriel's commission to **"make this man understand the vision."** Daniel 8:16. Therefore in chapter 9 Gabriel returned to continue his interrupted explanation.

Actually thirteen active years (551-538 B.C.) elapsed between chapters 8 and 9. You will recall from page 107 that *fifty* years (603-553) elapsed

between chapters 2 and 7.

In the interim Belshazzar's corrupt kingship had coasted to its close, Babylon had fallen to a Medo-Persian army led by Darius the Mede (probably Gubaru, or Gobryas (see pages 104, 105), and King Cyrus the Great had entered the city in triumph. Darius was now serving as vassal king of Babylon under King Cyrus and would continue a little over a year, from October 539 to his death in November 538. During this year Daniel was appointed chairman of the presidents—and was also sentenced to a night in the lions' den. Daniel 6.

Inasmuch as the events of Daniel 9 occurred during Darius's one-year reign, we can calculate that Daniel's experience with the angel who protected him from the lions occurred either shortly before or shortly after his visit from the angel Gabriel.

As you read Daniel 9, you will notice that the chapter falls into three clear divisions: (1) Daniel's "diary" reference to his study of the writings of Jeremiah, (2) Daniel's heartfelt prayer, and (3) Gabriel's further prediction explaining Daniel 8:14.

Daniel's diary. **"In the first year of Darius,"** Daniel says, **"I . . . perceived in the books the number of years which, according to the word of the Lord to Jeremiah the prophet, must pass before the end of the desolations of Jerusalem, namely, seventy years."** Verses 1-3.

195

Daniel was concerned about Daniel 8:14 and its symbolic prediction, **"for two thousand and three hundred evenings and mornings, then the sanctuary shall be restored to its rightful state."** He had good reason to know that it referred to the spiritual restoration or "cleansing" associated with the annual Day of Atonement (see pages 181-188). But what about the 2300 evenings and mornings? The temple in Jerusalem was in ruins. An "evening and morning" is a *day* according to Genesis 1 (see page 180), and Daniel quite likely knew that his contemporary, the prophet Ezekiel, had been shown in long-time visions that a *day symbolizes a year*. Ezekiel 4:6. Was it possible, then, he must have wondered, that the sanctuary in Jerusalem would not be restored for *2300 years?*

Daniel had known Jeremiah the prophet during his childhood in Jerusalem. He cherished a copy of the older man's writings. In these writings Jeremiah said something about the time during which Jerusalem would lie desolate. Daniel decided to look at the passages in Jeremiah again.

Unrolling the scroll, Daniel read that *after seventy years* God would "punish the king of Babylon and . . . the Chaldeans for their iniquity." Jeremiah 25: 11, 12. This was encouraging—for Babylon by now had been punished by the Medes and Persians, and Jerusalem had been subjugated for sixty-eight years (605-538, counted inclusively). The seventy years were almost at an end! But Jerusalem and its temple were in ruins; and nothing, apparently, was being done toward rebuilding them. Had Jeremiah, after all, been wrong? Would the sanctuary, perhaps, lie waste for 2300 years?

Daniel unrolled the scroll further and read again:

For thus says the Lord:
When *seventy years* are completed for Babylon
I will visit you, and
I will fulfill to you my promise and
Bring you back to this place [Jerusalem].

"Seventy weeks (490 years) are determined upon thy people."

7 weeks — 62 weeks — one week

457 B.C.	408 B.C.	A.D. 27	A.D. 31
The Decree to Restore Jerusalem	Restoration of Jerusalem	Baptism of Jesus Christ	Crucifixion of Jesus Christ

For I know the plans I have for you, says the Lord,
plans for welfare and not for evil,
to give you a future and a hope.

Then you will call upon me and come and pray to me, and
I will hear you.

You will seek me and find me;
when you seek me with all your heart,
I will be found of you,
says the Lord, and

I will restore your fortunes
and gather you from all the nations
and all the places where I have driven you,
says the Lord,
and I will bring you back to the place
from which I sent you into exile.
Jeremiah 29:10-14.

Such beautiful words! Such comforting promises! Such a gracious picture of God.

But the passage was also a call to prayer—earnest, solemn, penetrating prayer. "When you seek me with all your heart, I will be found of you."

Daniel's prayer. And so Daniel prayed. Most of Daniel 9 consists of his prayer. And what a prayer it is. As Norman Porteous says,[1] "If this was indeed how men prayed in those days, then we are in a position to understand how the faithful among the Jews came through the storms and stresses" of their day.

Gabriel's explanation. While he was still praying, God gave a signal to Gabriel; and the great, friendly angel came once more to explain the vision. He arrived **"at the time of the evening sacrifice."** Daniel 9:21. No lamb had been offered in Jerusalem for almost fifty years, but God honored the time of day when a lamb would have been offered if the sanctuary had still been standing. Gabriel arrived at a most appropriate time to explain a prophecy about the sanctuary.

1810 years to the sanctuary cleansing

The 2300 Days (Years) of Amazing Bible Prophecy

JOE MANISCALCO, ARTIST, © 1981 PPPA

A.D. 34
Stoning of Stephen
Gospel to the Gentiles

A.D. 1844
Cleansing of
Heavenly Sanctuary
Begun

9

CHAPTER 9

1 In the first year of Darius the son of Ahasuerus, by birth a Mede, who became king over the realm of the Chaldeans— ² in the first year of his reign, I, Daniel, perceived in the books the number of years which, according to the word of the LORD to Jeremiah the prophet, must pass before the end of the desolations of Jerusalem, namely, seventy years.

3 Then I turned my face to the Lord God, seeking him by prayer and supplications with fasting and sackcloth and ashes. ⁴ I prayed to the LORD my God and made confession, saying, "O Lord, the great and terrible God, who keepest covenant and steadfast love with those who love him and keep his commandments, ⁵ we have sinned and done wrong and acted wickedly and rebelled, turning aside from thy commandments and ordinances; ⁶ we have not listened to thy servants the prophets, who spoke in thy name to our kings, our princes, and our fathers, and to all the people of the land. ⁷ To thee, O Lord, belongs righteousness, but to us confusion of face, as at this day, to the men of Judah, to the inhabitants of Jerusalem, and to all Israel, those that are near and those that are far away, in all the lands to which thou hast driven them, because of the treachery which they have committed against thee. ⁸ To us, O Lord, belongs confusion of face, to our kings, to our princes, and to our fathers, because we have sinned against thee. ⁹ To the Lord our God belong mercy and forgiveness; because we have rebelled against him, ¹⁰ and have not obeyed the voice of the LORD our God by following his laws, which he set before us by his servants the prophets. ¹¹ All Israel has transgressed thy law and turned aside, refusing to obey thy voice. And the curse and oath which are written in the law of Moses the servant of God have been poured out upon us, because we have sinned against him. ¹² He has confirmed his words, which he spoke against us and against our rulers who ruled us, by bringing upon us a great calamity; for under the whole heaven there has not been done the like of what has been done against Jerusalem. ¹³ As it is written in the law of Moses, all this calamity has come upon us, yet we have not entreated the favor of the LORD our God, turning from our iniquities and giving heed to thy truth. ¹⁴ Therefore the LORD has kept ready the calamity and has brought it upon us; for the LORD our God is righteous in all the works which he has done, and we have not obeyed his voice. ¹⁵ And now, O Lord our God, who didst bring thy people out of the land of Egypt with a mighty hand, and hast made thee a name, as at this day, we have sinned, we have done wickedly. ¹⁶ O Lord, according to all thy righteous acts, let thy anger and thy wrath turn away from thy city Jerusalem, thy holy hill; because for our sins, and for the iniquities of our fathers, Jerusalem and thy people have become a byword among all who are round about us. ¹⁷ Now therefore, O our God, hearken to the prayer of thy servant and to his supplications, and for thy own sake, O Lord, cause thy face to shine upon thy sanctuary, which is desolate. ¹⁸ O my God, incline thy ear and hear; open thy eyes and behold our desolations, and the city which is called by thy name; for we do not present our supplications before thee on the ground of our righteousness, but on the ground of thy great mercy. ¹⁹ O LORD, hear; O LORD, forgive; O LORD, give heed and act; delay not, for thy own sake, O my God, because thy city and thy people are called by thy name."

20 While I was speaking and praying, confessing my sin and the sin of my people Israel, and presenting my supplication before the LORD my God for the holy hill of my God; ²¹ while I was speaking in prayer, the man Gabriel, whom I had seen in the vision at the first, came to me in swift flight at the time of the evening sacrifice. ²² He came and he said to me, "O Daniel, I have now come out to give you wisdom and understanding. ²³ At the beginning of your supplications a word went forth, and I have come to tell it to you, for you are greatly

198

beloved; therefore consider the word and understand the vision.

24 "Seventy weeks of years are decreed concerning your people and your holy city, to finish the transgression, to put an end to sin, and to atone for iniquity, to bring in everlasting righteousness, to seal both vision and prophet, and to anoint a most holy place. [25] Know therefore and understand that from the going forth of the word to restore and build Jerusalem to the coming of an anointed one, a prince, there shall be seven weeks. Then for sixty-two weeks it shall be built again with squares and moat, but in a troubled time. [26] And after the sixty-two weeks, an anointed one shall be cut off, and shall have nothing; and the people of the prince who is to come shall destroy the city and the sanctuary. Its end shall come with a flood, and to the end there shall be war; desolations are decreed. [27] And he shall make a strong covenant with many for one week; and for half of the week he shall cause sacrifice and offering to cease; and upon the wing of abominations shall come one who makes desolate, until the decreed end is poured out on the desolator."

The Message of Daniel 9

I. A Prayer That God Could Answer

Daniel must have been pleased to see Gabriel arrive while he was still praying.

We all want to have our prayers answered; so, before looking at what Gabriel told Daniel, let us see what we can learn about this prayer that God answered so remarkably. No doubt Heaven preserved it for us so we would study it with this in mind.

We have already learned a lot about Daniel's prayer life (see pages 101-103). In this present prayer Daniel did at least six things that deserve our attention.

1. He prayed very much in earnest.
2. He depended on God's righteousness, not his own.
3. He used the Bible.
4. He confessed his own sins *and* the sins of his group.
5. He sought the glory of God and of His sanctuary.
6. He claimed God's promises.

Like all human communication, effective prayer involves both words and attitude. "Take with you words and return to the Lord," says Hosea 14:2. "Seek me with all your heart," adds Jeremiah 29:13.

In harmony with the customs of his day Daniel emphasized the deep longing of his soul not only with the choice of appropriate words but also with **"fasting"** and the use of **"sackcloth and ashes."** Daniel 9:3. Sackcloth was a coarse fabric of goat or camel hair. It was worn in times of great sorrow or deep spiritual agitation (see, for example, 2 Samuel 3:31 and 2 Kings 19:1, 2). Drab and unattractive, sackcloth expressed a person's heartfelt humility. Dirtying one's face with ashes intensified the sense of self-abasement.

Daniel's fasting suggests that his prayer, as we have it in Daniel 9, may be a summary of prayers offered over an extensive period. Daniel 10:2, 3 describes another fast that Daniel observed about two years later and that lasted for three weeks.

Nothing indicates that Daniel felt that his fasting, sackcloth, and ashes could earn merit points. They helped express his earnestness and no doubt actually deepened it. But he didn't call God's attention to them. He said, **"We do not present our supplications before thee on the ground of our righteousness, but on the ground of thy great mercy."** Daniel 9:18.

James 5:16 says that "the prayer of a righteous man has great power in its effects"; but Paul reminds us, "None is righteous, no, not one." Romans 3:10. So what are we to do? Do what Daniel did! Come before God in our sinfulness. It is the only way we *can* come. Confess that we are sinners, and ask God to hear us on the grounds of His mercy and righteousness. Jesus invites us to come in *His* name. John 14:13, 14.

Daniel used the Bible in his prayer. His words show that he must have been

Daniel prayed "in sackcloth and ashes," a custom of his day in times of great sorrow and self-abasement.

JOHN STEEL, ARTIST © 1980 PPPA

reading three passages written especially for exiles: (1) Moses' counsel to future exiles (Leviticus 26); (2) Solomon's prayer for future exiles, offered during the dedication of the same temple which now lay in ruins (1 Kings 8:46-53); (3) Jeremiah's letter to contemporary Babylonian exiles (Jeremiah 29:15-20).

Each of these passages indicates that the cause of exile is sin. God wanted the Israelites to enjoy the Land of Palestine, and He promised it to them in perpetuity. If the Israelites persisted in sinning God would allow them to be carried into exile; but if they confessed their sins in the foreign land, He would forgive them and bring them home. Leviticus 26 specified that the exiles must confess the sins of their ancestors: "But if they [the exiles] confess their iniquity *and the iniquity of their fathers* in their treachery which they committed against me, and also in walking contrary to me, . . . and they make amends for their iniquity; then I will remember my covenant with Jacob, . . . and I will remember the land." Verses 40-42.

Responding to this instruction, Daniel prayed, **"We have sinned and done wrong and acted wickedly and rebelled, turning aside from thy commandments and ordinances; *we* have not listened to thy servants the prophets. . . . *All Israel* has transgressed thy law and turned aside, refusing to obey thy voice."** Daniel 9:5-11.

It is absolutely astonishing that Daniel offered a prayer like this. Even his enemies, when they set themselves to find a reason for killing him, could find nothing improper in his conduct. Daniel 6:4. Yet Daniel said, **"*We* have sinned and done wrong and acted wickedly and rebelled."**

Daniel was not lying. He was not playing games. He was identifying himself with his group, with the social unit of which he was a member. As a whole the group was in exile because as a whole the group had sinned.

It is fashionable in some quarters today to say that our church—or our nation, or our school, or whatever—doesn't accomplish what it might because our bishops, or our congressmen, or our administrators have been corrupt and lazy. In this way we blame our leaders instead of ourselves. Daniel, however, said, **"To us, O Lord, belongs confusion of face, to our kings, to our princes, and to our fathers, because *we* have sinned against thee."** Daniel 9:8.

Seeing a drunk staggering along, a famous evangelist is reputed to have said, "There, but for the grace of God, go I." When in prayer we admit that *we* have sinned, we acknowledge that we are made of the same stuff as our leaders, and that if we were in their shoes, we would likely make the same mistakes or worse. Indeed in our families and among our acquaintances we do make similar mistakes. "You have no excuse, O man, whoever you are, when you judge another," warns Romans 2:1, "because you, the judge, are doing the very same things."

If we had lived five hundred years ago or a thousand, who is to say we would have done any better than our ancestors?

"O God, forgive my family. *We* quarrel so much. We have so much time for TV trivia and so little time for things that matter."

"O God, forgive my corporation. *We* have such unhappy tensions between management and labor and so little regard for quality.''

"O God, forgive my nation. *We* are so materialistic, so racially separate."

"O God, forgive my club. *We* are so exclusive and flippant."

"O God, forgive my church, the Christian church. Through the ages we have persecuted one another, we have compelled people to believe as we do, we have disregarded Your prophets and trampled on Your commandments. As Christians we have failed to let You give us victory over pride, greed, and lust. We have often given non-Christians the impression that God Himself cannot really help people. To us belongs confusion of face as we see Islam and astrology and eastern cults make more converts than the church of Christ.

"O God, bring in a new day. Bring it soon. Let Your church be changed into Your likeness. Make us clean, generous, kind. Take away our adultery, racism, and Sabbath breaking. In the words of Daniel, **'O Lord, hear; O Lord, forgive; O Lord, give heed and act; delay not, for thy own sake, O my God, because thy city and thy people are called by thy name.'** Daniel 9:19."

Those last words from Daniel point up another priority in prevailing prayer. Daniel sought God's glory and the glory of His sanctuary. If every Christian—if one billion Christians of all denominations—were pleading with God today like Daniel, asking Him to forgive our collective sins and to make His church a true credit to His name, how God could bless us! How impressed the non-Christians would be!

If that is too much to hope for, how about a prayer-study group on your own street? Women who stay home with children and who see few adults besides their husbands need and greatly enjoy such fellowship with other women. Men and couples likewise get together frequently in prayer-study groups. At a prayer-study group, or even in your own family, you could start out by studying prayer. At the end of this section are lists of selected prayers and lists of things the Bible says about prayer. You could then analyze them, find the principles involved, and apply them to your own prayer life. All Bible prayers are different. We find no single verbal package to employ when approaching God. Then you could pray that God would use you as a group to bless others.

One more thing. Daniel knew from the Bible that God is a "covenant-keeping" deity—a God who keeps His promises. At the beginning of his prayer he addressed God as the One who **"keepest covenant and steadfast love with those who love him and keep his commandments."** Daniel 9:4.

Solomon's prayer at the dedication of the temple began with a reference to God as One who keeps covenant (1 Kings 8:23), and Leviticus 26 also refers to God's covenant. Daniel was acquainted with these passages. He had also read about God's covenants in Jeremiah 31.

William Tyndale, who lost his life translating the Bible in the sixteenth century, gave a splendid definition of prayer in his comment on Jacob's prayer in Genesis 32:9-12. It reminds us to remember God's promises when we pray:

> Prayer is to cleave unto the promises of God
>   with a strong faith,
> And to beseech God
>   with a fervent desire
> That he will fulfill them
>   for his truth and mercy only.

It's a good definition. Remembering as we begin our prayers that God keeps His promises helps us to have the kind of faith He can respond to.

Now that we have looked at Daniel's notable prayer, let us look on the next page at the answer God sent him.

PRAYER IN THE BIBLE

Some notable prayers in the Bible
Moses' prayer of intercession. Exodus 32:31, 32.
Hannah's prayer for a child. 1 Samuel 1:4-18.
David's prayer of confession. Psalm 51.
Some other prayer psalms. Psalms 17; 86; 90; 102.
Solomon's prayer at the dedication of the temple. 1 Kings 8:22-53.
Elijah's prayer on Mount Carmel. 1 Kings 18:36, 37.
Elisha's prayer in Dothan. 2 Kings 6:17.
Jehoshaphat's prayer in crisis. 2 Chronicles 20:5-12.
Christ's sample prayer (the Lord's Prayer, Our Father). Matthew 9:9-13.
Christ's intercessory prayer. John 17.
Christ's prayer in Gethsemane. Matthew 26:36-46.
Christ's prayer on the cross. Luke 23:46.
The disciples prayer at sea. Matthew 8:25.
The last prayers in the Bible. Revelation 22:20, 21.

Other notable references to prayer

Old Testament	*New Testament*	
Leviticus 26:40-45	Matthew 5:44	Romans 10:1
1 Samuel 7:5	Matthew 6:5-8	2 Corinthians 12:7-10
1 Kings 18:41-46	Luke 1:13; 6:12	Ephesians 1:16
2 Chronicles 33:13	Acts 1:14	Philippians 1:19
Jeremiah 29:7	Acts 16:25	James 5:14-18

Principles of effective prayer
Faith in God and His promises. Matthew 21:21, 22; Hebrews 11:6.
Persistence. Luke 11:5-13; 18:1-8.
Earnestness. Jeremiah 29:13, 14.
Forgiving spirit. Matthew 6:14, 15.
Right home relationship. 1 Peter 3:7.
Humility. Luke 18:10-14.
Unselfishness. James 4:3.
Attitude of obedience to God. Proverbs 15:29; 28:9.
Submission to God's will. Matthew 6:10; 26:39.
Dependence on Jesus Christ. John 14:13, 14.
Desire for advance of God's kingdom. Matthew 6:9, 10.

Kinds of prayer
Prayers express praise, gratitude, complaint, submission, as well as request.

II. Date of the Cross Foretold

When the Lord Jesus Christ strode into the villages of Galilee, He electrified the people with His dramatic proclamation, "The time is fulfilled, and the kingdom of God is at hand." Mark 1:15.

We want to know, What did Jesus mean by the words, *"The time is fulfilled"*?

What did Paul mean by saying, *"When the time had fully come,* God sent forth his Son, born of a woman"? Galatians 4:4.

And what did Paul have in mind when he spoke about the new, eternal life which God "promised ages ago and at *the proper time* manifested in his word"? Titus 1:2, 3.

Jesus and Paul were aware that God had appointed a set time, and they knew that it had arrived. The angel Gabriel had announced this set time in the astonishingly accurate prediction which he gave to Daniel at the close of Daniel 9.

More than half a millennium in advance, Gabriel's daring prophecy had foretold the very year in which Jesus would be baptized and also when He would be crucified! Much more even than that, it explained *why* Jesus would come. He would come to have success with a covenant with His people. He would die to put an end to sin and would bring in everlasting righteousness. Even His resurrection was implied in the prophecy, for after making an end of sin He would **"anoint a most holy place."**

But we must not get ahead of ourselves. Let us advance perceptively a step at a time.

The link between Daniel 8 and Daniel 9. It is basic to keep on remembering that Daniel 9 explains Daniel 8:14, and that Daniel 8 and 9 form a unit.

When Gabriel appeared, Daniel recognized that he was the same person **"whom I had seen in the vision at the first."**

Gabriel's opening sentence was, **"O Daniel, I have now come out to give you wisdom and *understanding.*"**

After paying Daniel the compliment of calling him a man **"greatly beloved,"** Gabriel added, **"therefore consider the word and *understand* the vision."**

Gabriel had been commissioned to **"make this man understand the vision"** of chapter 8. He had, within that chapter, explained everything except verse 14, with its references to the cleansing of the sanctuary and to the 2300 evening-and-morning days. Daniel had not needed an explanation of the cleansing of the sanctuary, but the 2300 days perplexed him. Were they literal days (as he must have hoped), or were they symbolic like the other items in Daniel 8:3-14 and like the days in Ezekiel 4:6? And if they did refer to 2300 *years,* was God saying that the *tamid* services at the Jerusalem temple would not be restored for 2300 years? If so, what about Jeremiah's prophecy of only 70 years?

Daniel was concerned about the calculation of time.

Gabriel began his explanation with a statement about time.

The seventy weeks cut off. Said Gabriel, **"Seventy weeks of years are decreed**

205

concerning your people and your holy city, to finish the transgression, to put an end to sin, and to atone for iniquity, to bring in everlasting righteousness, to seal both vision and prophet, and to anoint a most holy place.'' Daniel 9:24.

Seventy *weeks* of years! Daniel had been looking at a prophecy by Jeremiah that talked about seventy years. Now Gabriel was speaking about a period seven times as long. Commentators are virtually unanimous in saying that Gabriel meant 490 years (70 x 7 years).[2]

And these 490 years where **"decreed,"** says the R.S.V. The New English Bible has **"marked out."** The K.J.V. has **"determined."**

The underlying Hebrew term is *chathak* (kah-thak). It is another once-in-the-Bible word, like *nitsdaq* (page 175).

But even though *chathak* is used only this once in the Bible, it is well known to scholars from its usage outside the Bible. The well-known Hebrew-English dictionary by Gesenius says that properly it means to "cut" or to "divide." Ancient rabbis used it as meaning to "amputate."[3]

Translators know that *chathak* means to cut, divide, and amputate, but they haven't always understood how to make sense out of a literal translation, and so they have proposed a variety of alternatives, including not only "marked out" and "determined" and "decreed" but also "foreshortened," and others.

It is best to let the word be itself. Gabriel had come to explain the 2300 days. He began his explanation by announcing that 490 years were to be "cut" or "ampu-

While Daniel was still praying, Gabriel arrived to answer his request about the restoration of the sanctuary.

tated'' from the longer period. The matter is as simple as that.

Here is the answer to Daniel's lingering question about the length of the 2300 days. Inasmuch as 490 years cannot be "cut" away from 2300 literal days, which add up to less than 7 years, the solution is clear. The 2300 days are indeed symbolic and stand for 2300 actual years.

Daniel of course still wanted to know when the 2300 years were to begin, in order to calculate when they would end. Certainly we want to have this information too.

Gabriel would provide it in a moment.

The seventy weeks segmented. First, though, we need to note that in verses 25 to 27 Gabriel trisected the 70 weeks into three unequal segments consisting of 7 weeks (49 years), 62 weeks (434 years), and 1 week (7 years). He subdivided the final week further into halves (3½ years each). A diagram can help:

70 WEEKS

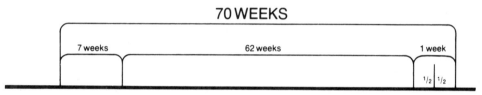

The seventy weeks begun. Verse 25 says, **"Know therefore and *understand"*–** there is that crucial verb again, **"understand"—"that from the going forth of the word to restore and build Jerusalem to the coming of an anointed one, a prince, there shall be seven weeks."**

Daniel must have been encouraged to learn that there really would be a decree issued some day authorizing the restoration of Jerusalem! Can we find out anything more about this decree?

Yes; in fact we need to look at three decrees, all preserved for us by Ezra the scribe.

1. The first of these three decrees, issued in 538 (or possibly 537) by Cyrus the Great, permitted a resettlement of the Jewish exiles in their homeland and empowered them to build for God "a house at Jerusalem." Ezra 1:2-4. In connection with this decree Cyrus released the sacred utensils that Nebuchadnezzar had carried to Babylon—and which Belshazzar had blasphemously drunk from on the night when Cyrus defeated him, only a year or two prior to this decree. There were 5469 of them. Ezra 1:7-11.

Some fifty thousand Jews returned to Palestine within a year. They ran into stiff opposition from the non-Jewish inhabitants of the area. The record in the books of Ezra and Nehemiah sounds almost like a modern newscast from the Middle East!

In the face of this opposition, work on the temple dragged (see Ezra, chapters 2 to 5).

2. The second of the three decrees was issued around 519 by Darius I Hys-

taspes (not to be confused with Darius the Mede). Shortly after Darius began to reign, he received a letter asking him to confirm the original decree made by Cyrus. Darius ordered a thorough search of the Persian archives in Babylonia and Ecbatana, and when an official memo of the decree was at last recovered (Ezra 6:1-5), he cheerfully issued the requested confirmation (Ezra 6:6-12).

3. The third decree was issued by Artaxerxes I Longimanus. ("Longimanus" refers to the length of his hands.) Qualitatively, this third decree (Ezra 7:11-26) was superior to the first two, for it commissioned Ezra to appoint magistrates and judges with full political and religious authority to try cases under both Jewish and Persian law and to impose capital punishment. Said Artaxerxes:

> You, Ezra, according to the wisdom of your God which is in your hand, *appoint magistrates and judges* who may judge all the people in the province Beyond the River, all such as know the laws of your God; and those who do not know them, you shall teach. Whoever will not obey *the law of your God and the law of the king,* let judgment be strictly executed upon him, whether for death or for banishment or for confiscation of his goods or for imprisonment. Ezra 7:25, 26.

In his report Ezra says that he gathered together a group of potential leaders, traveled with them from Babylonia to Jerusalem, arrived in Palestine in the fifth month of Artaxerxes's seventh year, and, at some unspecified time thereafter,

When implemented in 457 B.C., the decree Ezra received from Artaxerxes marked the beginning of the seventy weeks and the 2300 year-days.

"delivered the king's commissions to the king's satraps and to the governors of the province Beyond the River." Ezra 8:36. He also says that the temple was finally completed according to the *"decree* of Cyrus, and Darius, and Artaxerxes." Ezra 6:14. His reference to the three documents by the singular word "decree" indicates the unity of the decrees. It also calls attention to the third one, without which the first two were incomplete.

For it was this third decree—the decree of the seventh year of Artaxerxes—which gave Jerusalem its legal rebirth. It was this third decree, authorizing the appointment of magistrates and judges and, in particular, reestablishing Jewish law as a basis of local government, which made possible the restoration of Jerusalem as a capital.

Hence it was this third decree that Gabriel had in mind when he spoke of a decree to **"restore and build Jerusalem."**

Now, can this decree be dated?

Beyond a doubt.

As we have seen, Ezra implemented the decree at some time after his arrival in Palestine in the fifth month of the seventh year of Artaxerxes's reign. Because the Jewish months were numbered from spring to spring (see pages 45-47), the fifth month in old Jerusalem fell somewhere between mid-July and mid-September on our calendar (depending on the timing of New Year's day in any given year; see pages 257-263). The fifth month of the seventh year of Artaxerxes fell in the late summer or early autumn of 457 B.C., and the decree was implemented soon afterward.

We now have the date when the seventy weeks began: the autumn of 457 B.C.

With this anchor secured, it is a simple matter to calculate each of the other dates for our chart. Seven weeks (49 years) from 457 B.C. bring us to 408 B.C. Seventy weeks (490 years) from the autumn of 457 B.C. bring us to A.D. 34. Counting one week (7 years) back from A.D. 34 brings us to A.D. 27. Counting forward again 3½ years bring us to A.D. 31.*

70 WEEKS-490 YEARS

We will return to these dates shortly and examine the evidence for fulfillment in each case. First, though, we'll need to understand more about the purpose of the seventy weeks and about the events which were to occur on the different dates.

In view of his deeply spiritual prayer, Daniel had reason to anticipate a deeply

*For more on the calculation of A.D. 31 (and on a different dating of the seventy weeks from another decree in 445 or 444) see *Your Questions Answered,* pages 251-253. If your private calculations say that the 490 years ran from 457 B.C. to A.D. 33 instead of the A.D. 34, see *Your Questions Answered,* page 254.

209

spiritual answer. He was not disappointed. As we shall see, Gabriel's response in Daniel 9:24-27 went far beyond anything Daniel had requested.

Daniel 9:24-27 is an inspired passage of such great vitality and informational density that we shall want to analyze it very closely.

Daniel 9:24 as introduction. Daniel 9:24 separates itself naturally from the rest of the passage. It is an introduction to verses 25-27. It states, in extremely terse language, what it was that God planned to achieve during the seventy weeks. **"Seventy weeks of years,"** it says, **"are decreed** [*amputated, cut off*] **concerning your people and your holy city, to finish the transgression, to put an end to sin, and to atone for iniquity, to bring in everlasting righteousness, to seal both vision and prophet, and to anoint a most holy place."**

We have reminded ourselves several times already that Daniel 9:24-27 was given to help explain the prophecy of Daniel 8:14, which said that at the end of 2300 days the sanctuary would be **"restored to its rightful state,"** or cleansed. We have already mentioned that the time period, 70 weeks, throws light on the time period, 2300 days. Now we notice that the phrases **"put an end to sin,"** **"atone for iniquity,"** and **"anoint a most holy place"** are plainly sanctuary language. Gabriel *is* truly helping us to understand the sanctuary prophecy of Daniel 8:14!

Daniel 9:24 as work of art. If you could read Hebrew (and it may be that you can), you would be delighted by the precision with which Daniel 9:24 has been crafted.[4] It is subdivided into two parallel groups, one consisting of two-word units and the other of three-word units.* Further, between the two groups is a remarkable wordplay, or serious pun. Let me *paraphrase* the verse in an attempt to carry its literary form into English.

Two-word Units		Three-word Units	
	Seventy weeks of years are decreed [cut off] concerning		
	your people		*your holy city*
	to—		to—
A	finish transgression	B	introduce everlasting righteousness
A'	seal† sins	B'	seal† vision, prophet
A"	expiate iniquity‡	B"	anoint holy sanctuary

But let us catch our breath. We want to study prophecy, and we find ourselves doing linguistics!

In Daniel 8 we studied *tamid* in order to understand the continual ministry of Christ which the medieval church obscured. We also studied *nitsdaq* in order to

---

The R.S.V. attempts to convey the presence of the two groups by the dual use of the conjunction "and" in the middle of the verse ("and* to atone for iniquity") and at the end of the verse (*"and* to anoint a most holy place").

†Wordplay, or serious pun. ("To seal sins" is a literal translation of the Hebrew words translated "to put an end to sin" in the R.S.V.)

‡"Expiate Iniquity" is a paraphrase for "atone for iniquity."

understand how the sanctuary was to be made right, restored, or cleansed. Without word studies like these, many people over the centuries have supposed that Daniel 8 focuses on the heathen king Antiochus Epiphanes rather than on our great High Priest, Jesus Christ!

And by not learning about the literary structure of Daniel 9:24-27, some people today teach that something very important will be done *against* God's saints in the *future* by *antichrist* that was actually done *for* them *nineteen hundred years ago* by *Jesus Christ!*

If a few moments with word study and literary structure can help us avoid misunderstandings like these, the effort is eminently worth our while!

Basic principles of Hebrew literary style. Very well, let us devote a few brief moments to five basic aspects of Hebrew literary style involved in an understanding of the seventy-week prophecy. Remember that Hebrew people loved their language. They found great beauty in its inner rhythms. When they were the most earnest, they paid the closest attention to style. Their greatest prophets were great poets. They even punned seriously.

One of the most pleasant ways for you to introduce yourself to Hebrew literary form, in preparation for a serious analysis of Daniel 9:24-27, would be to get a group of people together—your own family would be fine—and read a few psalms out loud the way the Israelites did years ago. As a starter, Psalm 107:23-32, 43 is printed for you on page 212, arranged as you might use it in a religion class or in your home. I have chosen the K.J.V. because its translation of this passage is so famous.

If you *can* arrange to have a group read Bible poetry with you, you may like to help them visualize themselves standing in two groups facing each other under the Palestinian sun, with the leader standing at one end of the space between them backed by musicians with trumpets and cymbals. Rendering a passage back and

With a little planning, group reading of the Psalms reveals the exquisite literary organization of Hebrew poetry.

forth by two groups is called "antiphonal," from a Greek word that means "voice over against voice."

Antiphonal grouping is no gimmick! The musical heart of Hebrew is the parallel representation of an idea in two or more adjacent lines. When two groups of people do the reading, one group reads the first statement of an idea and the other group reads its parallel. The attractive parallel repetitions come in different kinds. Some examples will make them clear.

1. *Synonymous parallels.* In the most common kind of parallel the idea is simply restated in different words. For instance:

> *A*   He maketh the storm a calm,
> *A'*   so that the waves thereof are still.

PSALM 107:23-32, 43, K.J.V.

Boys: They that go down to the sea in ships,
  Girls: that do business in great waters;
Boys: These see the works of the Lord,
  Girls: and his wonders in the deep.
Boys: For he commandeth, and raiseth the stormy wind,
  Girls: Which lifteth up the waves thereof.
Boy A: They mount up to the heaven,
Boy B: They go down again to the depths:
  Girls: Their soul is melted because of trouble.
Boy A: They reel to and fro.
Boy B: and stagger like a drunken man,
  Girls: and are at their wit's end.

Girl A: He maketh the storm a calm,
  Girl B: so that the waves thereof are still.
Girl A: Then are they glad because they be quiet;
  Girl B: so he bringeth them unto their haven desired.

Boy A: Let them exalt him also in the congregation of the people,
  Boy B: and praise him in the assembly of the elders.

Leader: Whoso is wise, and will observe these things,
         even they shall understand the lovingkindness of the Lord.

---

2. *Antithetical Parallels.* Sometimes the second line *contrasts* with the first. Psalm 1:6 is a good example:

A   The Lord knows the way of the righteous,
B   but the way of the wicked will perish.

3. *Synthetic parallels.* Sometimes the second line simply *adds* to or *completes* the thought of the first line.

4. *Alternating parallels.* As you become more aware of what to look for, you will often find two related ideas *alternating* with each other and *extending through* several verses. Psalm 37:3-5 provides an illustration.

A   Trust in the Lord, and do good;
B   so you will dwell in the land, and enjoy security.

A'   Take delight in the Lord,
B'   and he will give you the desires of your heart.

A"   Commit your way to the Lord; trust in him,
B"   and he will act.

Perhaps you would like to reread our selection from Psalm 107 just now and see how expert you have already become at recognizing the different kinds of parallels. If you haven't mastered their technical names yet, look for pairs and other groups of lines that are (1) similar, (2) contrasting, (3) completing, and (4) alternating.

After you have begun to find your way through the book of Psalms, you will want to look at the prophetic books like Isaiah and Jeremiah. You will find that large portions of them are written in the same style as the book of Psalms. Isaiah 53, a spiritual gem anyway, takes on new pathos and depth when you are conscious of its poetic parallel structure. On pages 72, 73 we discussed the fact that Nebuchadnezzar used poetic style in Daniel 4 and in some of his known official cuneiform inscriptions.

5. *Chiasms.* Once in awhile, as you read your Bible, you will discover, with the joy of a Frenchman finding truffles, that you have happened onto a chiasm. A "chiasm" (pronounced KIE-asm) consists of a pair of contrasting ideas that suddenly reverse their direction, like partners at a square dance. There are two exquisite chiasms in Daniel 9:24-27; but since an understanding of them is not essential to an understanding of the seventy-week prophecy, they are not discussed here but are taken up in *Your Questions Answered,* pages 255, 256.

The purpose of the seventy weeks. With this brief introduction behind us, let us look again at Daniel 9:24, *paraphrased* as we did it a moment ago in order to bring out its literary structure:

Seventy weeks of years are decreed [cut off] concerning

your people		*your holy city*
to—		to—
A	finish transgression	B	introduce everlasting righteousness
A'	seal* sins	B'	seal* vision, prophet
A"	expiate iniquity†	B"	anoint holy sanctuary

As we look at the verse again now, we are struck by the relationships that exist among the various lines. For instance, the *B* lines answer to the *A* lines either by "contrast" or by "completion." The purpose of the seventy weeks is shown as *A* to finish transgression and *B* to begin everlasting righteousness; *A'* to seal sins and *B'* to seal the vision and the prophet; *A"* to atone for iniquity and *B"* to anoint the holy sanctuary.

We also notice a "synonymous parallel" relationship among the *A* lines and among the *B* lines. The three parallel clauses in the *A* section form a single repeated statement. They say that all kinds of sins (transgression, sin, and iniquity—see Leviticus 16:21) are to be finished and sealed off by means of the atonement. How often our compassionate God has repeated His promise to take away the sins of the world (John 1:29), to remove our sins as far as the east is from the west (Psalm 103:12), and to make our scarlet sins as white as snow (Isaiah 1:18)! God's basic purpose for the seventy weeks is *atonement*.

The *B* section of Daniel 9:24 appears at first glance to be more complex than the *A* section, but it still conveys a unified concept. It does not deal merely with the Jewish temple that Daniel had been praying about! It deals also with the heavenly holy city, New Jerusalem (Revelation 21:2), the "mother of us all" (Galatians 4:26, K.J.V.).

It *must* deal with the heavenly sanctuary and the *tamid* (priestly ministry) which Jesus performs there! Christ's heavenly ministry, along with His death on the cross, is essential to the "everlasting righteousness" of verse 24. The heavenly sanctuary is the principal focus of the vision of Daniel 8, which Daniel 9:24-27 is intended to explain. And it is the heavenly sanctuary, not the Jerusalem temple, which Jesus purifies with His blood. Hebrews 9:11-26.

The book of Hebrews is a great help to the understanding of Daniel 9:24. Hebrews 9:26 speaks about Jesus as having to *"put away sin* by the sacrifice of himself." This statement corresponds obviously to the *A* part of Daniel 9:24, **"to finish the transgression, to put an end to sin, and to atone for iniquity."** Hebrews also reminds us to look to Jesus Christ as the "source of eternal salvation" (Hebrews 5:9)—counsel that corresponds to God's promise in Daniel 9:24 that the Messiah would **"bring in everlasting righteousness."**

The book of Hebrews teaches too that Jesus, after His resurrection, ascended

*Wordplay, or serious pun. ("To seal sins" is a literal translation of the Hebrew words translated "to put an end to sin" in the R.S.V.)

†Remember that "expiate iniquity" is a paraphrase for "atone for iniquity."

214

to serve as our High Priest in the heavenly sanctuary. Before the priests commenced their service in the earthly sanctuary, the sanctuary was "anointed" in a special ceremony. Leviticus 8:10, 11. Similarly we may understand from Daniel 9:24 that as Jesus commenced His ministry in the heavenly sanctuary, He first undertook to **"anoint a most holy place."**

The R.S.V. translation **"anoint a most holy place"** does not mean that Jesus anointed only the innermost area of the heavenly sanctuary (see pages 181-184). The word "place" is not used in the *original* language of Daniel 9:24. In the Bible many things associated with the sanctuary are called "most holy," including the altar of burnt offering (Exodus 29:37), the golden altar (Exodus 30:10), sin offerings (Leviticus 6:29), and incense (Exodus 30:36). What Jesus anointed upon His ascension to heaven after His resurrection was the heavenly sanctuary as a whole.

Before we leave the literary structure of Daniel 9:24, we must satisfy our curiosity about the wordplay, or pun, in lines A' and B'. In Line A' "seal" is used in the sense of sealing an envelope in order to show that the letter is finished. When Jesus applies His more-than-sufficient atonement, sins are finished with. In line B' "seal" is used in the sense of sealing a document to guarantee its authenticity. The fulfillment of the seventy-week prophecy as outlined in verses 25-27 was to be so spiritually significant and so strikingly timely that it would confirm, or guarantee, or "seal," the fulfillment of the 2300-day prophecy of which it is a part.

Daniel sought a spiritual answer to his prayer, and he received a spiritual answer beyond his expectations. He asked forgiveness for the Jewish sins that had caused the demolition of Solomon's temple. God promised forgiveness and removal of *all* His people's sins. Daniel prayed for the restoration of the Jewish temple. God pointed him to the anointing of the heavenly sanctuary which Christ would accomplish in connection with His atonement.

Reduced to a single sentence, the A part of Daniel 9:24 tells us that within the seventy-week period atonement for all sins would be provided for. Reduced to a single sentence, the B part tells us that just as surely as the seventy-week prophecy would be fulfilled, Jesus would anoint a new sanctuary and provide a high-priestly ministry that would offer eternal righteousness.

These concepts will become clearer as we continue our study. As we do so, let us remember that the promise of Daniel 9:24 is for us today. In Christ we can die to habitual sin and taste everlasting righteousness right now. Christ puts selfishness to death and gives us altogether new lives.

"Do you not know that all of us who have been baptized into Christ Jesus were baptized into his death? We were buried therefore with him by baptism into death, so that as Christ was raised from the dead by the glory of the Father, we too might walk in newness of life." Romans 6:3, 4.

Do you feel that you have been "kidnapped" by some unhealthful or immoral habit? Jesus paid your "ransom" at Calvary. 1 Timothy 2:6. Go free—and as you walk in faith, your confidence in His promises will increase, and you will gain more consistent victories.

Is your marriage in trouble? Christ can save it. He came long ago to forgive; He lives today to help. He can put an end to bickering and jealousy. As you trust Him to answer your prayers, He will give you a new ability to love and forgive. In Christ we do not need to go looking for new spouses. He can turn us into renewed spouses.

"If any one is in Christ, he is a new creation." 2 Corinthians 5:17.

The events of the seventy weeks. We have looked at verse 24, which states God's purposes for the seventy weeks. Now let us look at verses 25-27 which outline the events for the seventy weeks along with other events that are not confined to the seventy weeks but are related to them.

The R.S.V. is for the most part an excellent translation of the Bible. Unfortunately it is flawed in its translation of the "seven weeks" and the "sixty-two weeks" (see *Your Questions Answered,* pages 254, 255). Because of this weakness in the R.S.V., the New American Standard Bible (N.A.S.B.) is at this point more useful:

25. So you are to know and discern that from the issuing of a decree to restore and rebuild Jerusalem until Messiah the Prince there will be seven weeks and sixty-two weeks; it will be built again, with plaza and moat, even in times of distress.

26. Then after the sixty-two weeks the Messiah will be cut off and have nothing, and the people of the prince who is to come will destroy the city and the sanctuary. And its end will come with a flood; even to the end there will be war; desolations are determined.

27. And he will make a firm covenant with the many for one week, but in the middle of the week he will put a stop to sacrifice and grain offering*; and on the wing of abominations will come one who makes desolate, even until a complete destruction, one that is decreed, is poured out on the one who makes desolate. Daniel 9:25-27, N.A.S.B.

Now let us look at this passage laid out with appropriate headings so as to expose its literary organization. It is well worth rereading in any case. The lines under the *A* headings constitute the first half of each of the three verses; the *B* lines are the second half. You will notice quickly that although the passage is not Hebrew *poetry,* it makes use of the extended alternating parallels, wordplays, and other stylistic features of the Hebrew language. These will be of considerable assistance as we attempt to discover what the passage means.

A   Messiah Prince to come
[*1*] So you are to know and discern that from the issuing
        of a decree to restore and rebuild Jerusalem
        until Messiah the Prince

---

*Cereal, or grain offerings were often required, either along with or at least at the time when an animal was offered. They consisted some times of a baked loaf or of ingredients for making a loaf (see, for example, Leviticus 2:1-11; 6:14-19, etc.).

[2] there will be seven weeks*
   and sixty-two weeks;
        B   *The city to be rebuilt*
          [1] it will be built again, with plaza and moat,†
          [2] even in times of distress.
A' Messiah to be cut off
[2] Then after sixty-two weeks*
[1] the Messiah will be cut off and have nothing,
        B' Desolater prince to destroy the city
          [1] and the people of the prince who is to come
             will destroy the city and the sanctuary.
          [2] And its end will come with a flood;
             even to the end there will be war;
             desolations are determined.†
A" Messiah to terminate sacrifices
[1] And he will make [keep] a firm covenant with the many
[2] for one week,*
[2']but in the middle of the week*
[1']he will put a stop to
   sacrifice and grain offering;
        B" The desolater prince to be destroyed
          [2] and on the wing of abominations
             will come one who makes desolate,
          [1] even until a complete destruction,
             one that is decreed,†
             is poured out on the one who makes desolate.

Do you see how the sections under the *B* headings alternate and contrast with the sections under the *A* headings? Do you also see that each of the *A* sections is subdivided into statements [1] about the Messiah and [2] about "weeks"? And that the *B* sections, which introduce us to the desolater prince, are subdivided into statements [1] about construction and destruction and [2] about distress and desolation?

The unity of the *A* sections is enhanced by a play on the word **"week,"** which appears in each verse and which comes through very clearly in translation. In the *B* sections there is a play on the Hebrew word for "cut," which, unfortunately, doesn't come through at all in translation. Believe it or not, **"moat," "determined,"** and **"decreed"** are all translated from the same Hebrew root meaning "cut."

Did you observe the sequence [1] [2] [2'] [1'] in the *A* section of verse 27? A complex chiasm is lurking there. You can read about it, if you like, under *Your Questions Answered,* pages 255, 256.

*Wordplay in Hebrew   †Wordplay in Hebrew

We have seen enough to recognize that the two columns, A and B, though related to each other, are *sufficiently independent to stand alone*. The A column says that at predetermined times during the seventieth week the Messiah Prince will arrive on the scene, will keep covenant with many people, will be killed, and will cause sacrifices to cease. The B column says that the history of Jerusalem will be a troubled one. Its rebuilding will be accompanied by distress. A desolater prince will destroy it again, and then the desolater himself will be destroyed in a predetermined destruction.

The events in the A column are unmistakably and intimately related to the seventy weeks. They are expressly dated to the seventy weeks, and they fit the *spiritual* purposes of the seventy weeks as announced in verse 24. The events in the B column, however, are not expressly timed to the seventy weeks. They imply that the Holy City, Jerusalem, will be rebuilt within the alloted time, providing a place for Messiah to appear; but they are not explicitly dated.* Neither do they directly fulfill the spiritual purposes of the seventy weeks as announced in verse 24.

Because the B sections of verses 25-27 are so much in contrast to the A sections and to verse 24, we can helpfully organize the four verses of Gabriel's prophecy, in simplified fashion, to look like this:

THE SEVENTY WEEKS (DANIEL 9:24-27) ANALYZED

GOD'S PURPOSE (9:24)

A Termination of sin through atonement
B Introduction of everlasting rightousness [through the cross at Jerusalem and the sanctuary in heaven]

A EVENTS FOR THE MESSIAH DURING THE 70 WEEKS (9:25-27)	B EVENTS RELATED TO THE 70 WEEKS BUT NOT CONFINED TO THEM (9:25-27)
At the end of 7+62 weeks Messiah to arrive *After the 7+62 weeks* Messiah to be cut off *During the 70th week* Messiah to keep covenant *In the middle of the 70th week* Messiah to stop sacrifices	*Jerusalem to be restored in difficult times* *Jerusalem to be destroyed by a desolater prince* *The desolater prince himself to be destoyed*

---

*Some commentaries hold that the year 408, at the close of the "seven" weeks, marks the completion of the restoration of Jerusalem. Unfortunately historical records from Palestine for the period around 408 are too scanty for this concept to be verified. In any case the angel did not say that the city would be finished at the end of the seven weeks. In fact he gave no specific event to mark the close of either the seven weeks or the seventy weeks.

218

Two princes in conflict. One of the principal advantages we can gain from our literary study of Daniel 9:24-27 is the proper identification of the person referred to by the pronoun **"he"** in verse 27, who keeps covenant and stops sacrifices.

Verse 25 promises the arrival of the Messiah Prince, and verse 26 speaks of a prince whose people will destroy the city and the sanctuary. It is not surprising that some Bible students have confused the two princes and assumed that they were one and the same. But when we lay out the passage according to the laws of Hebrew literary style we can instantly differentiate two separate princes. The *A* sections of verses 25-27 promise a Messiah Prince, and the *B* sections warn of a desolater prince. Sections *A* and *B* are parallel but *contrasting.*

In verse 27 Gabriel says that *"he* **will make a firm covenant with the many for one week,"** and that in the middle of the week *"he* **will put a stop to sacrifice and grain offering."** Again it is not surprising that through the centuries some Bible students have made the mistake of supposing that this **"he"** is the desolater prince rather than the Messiah Prince. Even the well-known Roman commentator Hippolytus made this mistake in the third century, concluding that it was a future antichrist rather than Jesus Christ who would stop the sacrifices.[5] It is regrettable that Hippolytus's error is sometimes cited today as if it were the truth.

You know better! You know that the **"he"** who keeps covenant and stops sacrifices is found in the *A* column, along with the references to the seventy weeks. He is not found in the *B* column. He is the Messiah Prince, our Saviour; He is not the desolater. He is Jesus Christ; He is not a future antichrist.

Jesus Christ as the Messiah Prince. We have taken for granted that the Messiah Prince was Jesus Christ. The time has come to show that He really was.

A "prince" in the Bible is a prominent leader. Jesus is "God" and "Son of God"; hence He is a prince preeminent. Prince Jesus technically became the Messiah *on the occasion of His baptism.* The Hebrew word "messiah" means "an anointed person." The Greek word "christ" also means "an anointed person." It was customary in Bible times for individuals who were selected for prominent leadership to be ordained to their roles by being anointed with oil. For example, David was anointed by Samuel to be a *king* (1 Samuel 16:1, 13), Aaron was anointed by Moses to be a *priest* (Exodus 30:30), and Elisha was anointed by Elijah to be a *prophet* (1 Kings 19:16).

Jesus, who was both a king, a priest, and a prophet, was anointed by God at His baptism in the River Jordan when the Holy Spirit descended upon Him in the shape of a dove. Luke 3:21, 22; Acts 10:37, 38. One of John the Baptist's disciples soon searched out his brother Peter and announced with conviction, "We have found the Messiah." John 1:41, 42. A little later when preaching one Sabbath in the Nazareth synagogue, Jesus applied to Himself the Messianic prophecy of Isaiah 61:1, 2.

> The *Spirit of the Lord* is upon me
> Because he has *anointed* me
>   to preach good news to the poor.

> He has sent me
>> to proclaim release to the captives
>> and recovering of sight to the blind,
>> to set at liberty those who are oppressed,
>> to proclaim the acceptable year of the Lord. Luke 4:18, 19.

Inasmuch as God anointed Jesus to proclaim liberty, to restore sight, and to preach the good news of forgiveness and a fresh start, it is no wonder that Hebrews 1:9 says that God anointed Him with the "oil of gladness." Joy is a "fruit of the Spirit" (Galatians 5:22), and Jesus was *"full* of the Holy Spirit" (Luke 4:1). Wherever Jesus went, He brought joy.

Everyone suffering from disease or a handicap rejoiced at His touch. Mourners rejoiced when He resurrected their dead. Guilt-plagued people breathed sighs of relief. Everywhere Jesus made people happy. He was anointed with the oil of gladness. He was the Messiah of happiness!

When the woman at Jacob's well said, "I know that Messiah is coming," Jesus responded, "I who speak to you am he." John 4:25, 26.

So we have His word for it. Jesus was the Messiah promised in the Old Testament. And because the name "Christ" means the same as "Messiah," every time we call Him, "Jesus *Christ,"* we acknowledge the fact that He is the Messiah.

Jesus as the terminator of sacrifices. We have seen that in Daniel 9:24-27 Gabriel predicted that the Messiah would **"put a stop to sacrifice and grain offering"** (N.A.S.B.); in other words, that He would **"cause sacrifice and offering to cease"** (R.S.V.).

You may wonder how this prophecy can have been fulfilled by Jesus in view of the fact that Jewish priests continued to burn sacrifices and to make other types of offerings until the Romans destroyed their temple in A.D. 70, almost forty years after the crucifixion.

The book of Hebrews gives the answer. It describes Jesus as truly the terminator of sacrifices. It says that through His incarnation and death He "abolishes" the old sacrifices. Weymouth says that He "does away with" them. The New English Bible has, He "annuls" them. Hebrews 10:4-9 leaves no doubt about this:

> For it is impossible that the blood of bulls and goats
> should take away sins. Consequently, when Christ
> came into the world, he said,
>> "Sacrifices and offerings thou hast not desired,
>> but a body hast thou prepared for me;
>> in burnt offerings and sin offerings
>> thou hast taken no pleasure.
>> Then I said,
>> 'Lo, I have come to do thy will, O God,'
>> as it is written of me in the roll of the book."

When he said above,
"Thou hast neither desired, nor taken pleasure
in sacrifices and offerings and burnt offerings
and sin offerings:
(these are offered according to the law),
then he added,
"Lo, I have come to do thy will."
He abolishes the first in order to establish the second.

The author of the book of Hebrews says here that Jesus Christ "abolishes the first [ritual] in order to establish the second."

But didn't he know that sacrifices continued to be offered in Jerusalem for many years after Jesus died?

Of course he did! As a matter of fact, he wrote Hebrews while the temple was still very much in use. In the passage we just read he said that the sacrifices and the offerings *"are* offered [present tense] according to the law." Hebrews 10:8. In Hebrews 10:11 he said that "every priest *stands* daily [present tense] at his service, offering repeatedly the same sacrifices."

Certainly, yes, the priests did continue to repeat the age-old ritual, and the author of Hebrews was well aware of the fact. But he was also well aware, as an inspired spokesman for God, that their sacrifices *no longer mattered.* They provided religious drama, devoid of saving spiritual significance.

Not to press the matter unduly, we may remind ourselves that various non-Christian religions have continued to offer animal sacrifices until the present day. By His death Jesus did not make the offering of sacrifices impossible. God does not compel anyone to stop the religious burning of animals. But in the sight of heaven Christ's cross was the Sacrifice to end all sacrifices. With the death of Jesus no ritual sacrifice, Jewish or otherwise, has significance anymore for salvation.

A startling miracle should have taught this lesson to the Jewish priests even though the teachings of the prophets failed to do so. At the very moment when Jesus had "breathed his last," "the curtain of the temple was torn in two, from top to bottom"! Mark 15:38.

Until that precise instant, entrance into the most holy place had been restricted to the high priest once a year. Now, theoretically, it was open to everyone at any time.

With such dramatic symbolism as this, Heaven said to all the world, "You do not need the Jewish priesthood anymore. Helpful in countless ways as rabbis and Christian priests and ministers may be, you do not *need* them either in order to enter the presence of God. There is only one Mediator between God and men, the Man Christ Jesus" (see Hebrews 9:15 and 1 Timothy 2:5).

During the seventieth week of Daniel 9 Jesus Christ amply fulfilled the prophecy, **"He shall cause sacrifice and offering to cease."**

What we are studying sheds light on the possible future course of Jewish sacrifices. Many people are wondering whether it is likely that during a short period just prior to Christ's second coming, God will ask the Jews, in memory of the cross, to restore their animal sacrifices.

The answer from our study of Daniel 9:24-27 is that He most certainly will not. Jesus has done away with animal sacrifices. He has annulled them. He has abolished them. He has **"caused sacrifice and offering to *cease*."**

The date of Christ's baptism foretold. One of the most intriguing aspects of the seventy-week prophecy is its timely fulfillment. According to our chart on page 209 the Messiah was to arrive in the year A.D. 27 and was to cause sacrifice and offering to cease three and a half years later, in the year A.D. 31. So we want to know whether Jesus really was baptized/anointed in A.D. 27 and whether His crucifixion did occur in A.D. 31.

We should notice, incidentally, that Gabriel foretold no specific event to mark the close of the seventy weeks in A.D. 34. We'll discuss A.D. 34 in our next section, "Jesus Kept His Promise."

As soon as we look into the dates 27 and 31, we are struck with something quite remarkable among Bible students. We find a vigorous dispute about the precise dates involved, but a solidly reassuring consensus in respect to the very short period within which all suggested dates are found to fall. A recent investigator from Dallas Theological Seminary has listed more than twenty writers, represent-

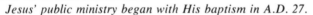

Jesus' public ministry began with His baptism in A.D. 27.

ing widely different schools of thought. In spite of their differences, with only one exception, their dates for the crucifixion all fall within the nine-year period, A.D. 27-36.[6] Scholars have no choice except to place the crucifixion into this short period because, indisputably, Jesus was crucified under Pontius Pilate. Even the second-century pagan historian Tacitus says in his *Annals of the Roman Empire,* 15. 44, that Jesus was "executed in Tiberius's reign by the governor of Judaea, Pontius Pilatus." The Bible, of course, indicates the same. Luke 3:1; 23:24.

Pilate served as administrator (sometimes called "procurator") of Judea between the years 26 and 36, and this is the obvious reason that scholars agree on the general period for Christ's death.

Now, the year 31 falls right in the middle of Pilate's term as procurator. If we knew nothing more about the date of the cross than simply that it came near the middle of Pilate's incumbency, we would say that Gabriel's prediction, made from a distance of more than 500 years, was very, very close.

But we do know more than this. Before finalizing on a date for the cross, however, let us look closely at the date of Christ's baptism/anointing.

Jesus was baptized by John the Baptist; and, according to Luke 3:1, John the Baptist commenced his brilliant but very brief ministry in "the fifteenth year of the reign of Tiberius Caesar."

Tiberius Caesar succeeded the famous Roman emperor Augustus, who died on August 19, A.D. 14. (The month of August was named for Augustus.) Even without a master's degree in historical chronology, a person can calculate that the fifteenth year of Tiberius, the year when John the Baptist commenced his ministry, must have begun no later than A.D. 28. And A.D. 28 is very close to A.D. 27, the year we posited a while ago for Christ's baptism/anointing.

But people who specialize in historical chronology tell us that there is good reason to conclude that the fifteenth year of Tiberius began in A.D. 27. You will remember from our discussion on pages 45-47 that the reigns of kings were usually counted differently in ancient times from the way they are in our own, and that different countries used different seasons (either spring or fall) for beginning each of the years of a reign. As for the Jews, even though they began their *religious* year from the first day of the month Nisan in the spring (sometime in March or April), in the era we are talking about they began the reigns of non-Jewish kings on the Jewish *civil* New Year's Day (Tishri 1, Rosh Hashanah) in the autumn, following the new moon of either September or October. They had also adopted the custom of considering a king's "first year" as the interval between the day he began to reign and the arrival of the following autumn New Year's Day. Jewish clerks, like the clerks in several other eastern Mediterranean lands, began to date documents by a new emperor's "first year" as soon as they heard the news that he had begun to rule.

Tiberius began to rule upon the death of Augustus, which occurred on August 19, A.D. 14. The next Jewish New Year's Day came somewhere between mid-September and mid-October. There was plenty of time for news about the installa-

223

tion of the new emperor to reach Palestine and for the "first year" of his rule to commence there before Jewish New Year's. So it was, according to a custom recorded in the Jewish Mishnah, that the *"second year"* of Tiberius must have begun in Palestine on New Year's Day in September or October A.D. 14 even though by then Tiberius had been in power for no more than about two months!*

Fantastic as such a phenomenon may appear to be to Western minds, it is a custom in some Oriental countries even today for children to be considered a year old in the year of their birth and to be *two* years old on the subsequent New Year's Day. This custom is followed, even if New Year's comes only a day or two after a child is born. Western tourists are puzzled to learn that children who appear to be only six years old, for example, claim to be eight.

On this basis, the *"fifteenth* year . . . of Tiberius" (Luke 3:1) did not begin in August A.D. 28 as we might suppose on the basis of modern Western calculations. Reckoned "Jewish fashion," as the *Interpreter's Dictionary of the Bible* describes the process we have followed here,[7] Tiberius's fifteenth year began in September or October A.D. 27.

*Archaeologists have found many Palestinian coins from various years of Tiberius's reign, but they have found no Palestinian coins dated in his "first year." This absence of first-year coins can be explained by the extreme shortness of his first year.

Correlations of Events in the Life of Christ and the Reign of Tiberius

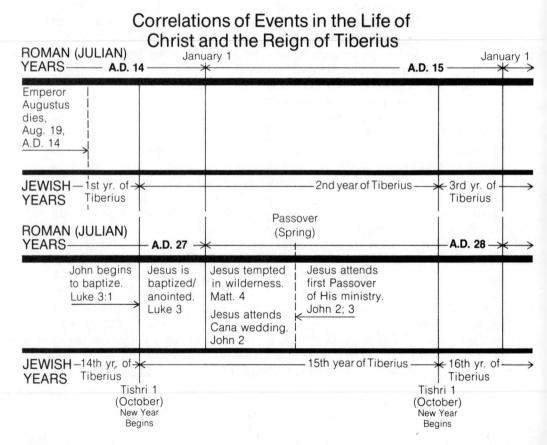

Inasmuch as Jesus was baptized shortly after John began to preach and inasmuch as between His baptism and His first Passover (in the following spring) He spent six weeks in the wilderness of temptation, gathered disciples here and there, and attended the Cana wedding feast, it is perfectly safe to conclude that He was baptized within the year 27. Gabriel's prediction about 69 weeks to the anointing of the Messiah at His baptism in A.D. 27 was fulfilled with astonishing precision.

The date of the cross foretold. We return now to the date of Christ's crucifixion. Is there any evidence that Jesus' death occurred in the year that we calculated it would, that is, in A.D. 31?

The forthright answer is that, in the present state of expertise, there is no *absolute* contemporary proof that it did. The Bible provides a clear dateline for His baptism, the "fifteenth year . . . of Tiberius," but it does not expressly identify the date of His death. This is one reason why the commentators do not all agree.

But we have already noted that their differences amount to scarcely a year or two either way. All commentators take into account that the crucifixion occurred, in general, while Pontius Pilate was procurator (A.D. 26-36) and, in particular, at a Passover that fell no more than three or four years later than His baptism.

We are thus very certainly *close* to A.D. 31. A margin of error—if one should even think to call it an error—of only a single year in a prophecy spanning half a millennium would still be deeply impressive. It would represent less than one quarter of one percent!

But it isn't necessary to accept even this slight possible discrepancy, as we shall see as we go along.

Those scholars who settle on the year 30 rather than on the year 31 do so partly by appealing to astronomy. They assume that the Passover always fell on the first full moon after the spring equinox, and they know that astronomers can calculate any full moon in history without much difficulty.

But astronomers themselves insist that they cannot provide the information needed to settle the question of the calendar year of the cross! Either 30 or 31 is possible, they say, depending on a variety of factors. For a discussion of astronomy and the date of the cross, see *Your Questions Answered,* pages 257-263.

If we cannot properly depend on astronomy, the Bible itself provides valuable evidence that we certainly do not want to overlook, and A.D. 31 fits this evidence. For instance, Daniel 9 indicates that the interval between the Messiah's anointing (at His baptism) and the time of His death would be **"half of the week,"** or three and a half years. The Gospel of John, by recording the annual Passovers that Jesus attended, provides evidence that three and a half years did indeed elapse between Christ's baptism and His death.

John 2 and 3 tell about a Passover during which Jesus talked at night with Nicodemus and told him that he must be born again.

John 5:1 tells of a feast, most probably a Passover, in connection with which Jesus healed a man who had suffered thirty-eight years from paralysis.

225

John 6:4 tells of a Passover season during which Jesus fed a very large crowd with a boy's small lunch.

John 12:1 introduces the Passover season during which Jesus died.

We have seen that Christ's baptism occurred near the end of A.D. 27. So His first (or "Nicodemus") Passover occurred in the spring of A.D. 28. Then His second (or "paralytic") Passover fell in the spring of A.D. 29, His third (or "large-meal") Passover came in the spring of A.D. 30—and His final (or "crucifixion") Passover occurred three and a half years after His baptism, that is to say, *in the spring of A.D. 31,* just as Gabriel had indicated.

If Gabriel were an athlete instead of an angel, we would stand to our feet and cheer!

Gabriel's dependability reminds us that according to Daniel 9:24 one of the purposes of the seventy weeks was to *"seal* **up the vision and prophecy"** (K.J.V.) of the 2300 days. Because the shorter prophecy was so stunningly fulfilled, we have reason to depend on the longer one.

Of course what Jesus *did* during the seventieth week accomplished far more than chronology ever could to seal the vision and prophecy. We'll speak about what He did and its bearing on the 2300 days in the following two sections.

III. Jesus Kept His Promise

When I was a teenager, I went through periods of reading and memorizing the Bible. I was working in the Psalms once when something exceptional struck me. I went to see my father in his study at bedtime and showed him Psalm 15, K.J.V.

> Lord, who shall abide in thy tabernacle?
>   Who shall dwell in thy holy hill?
> He that walketh uprightly,
>   and worketh righteousness,
>   and speaketh the truth in his heart. . . .
> He that sweareth to his own hurt, and changeth not.

I pointed to the last line, "He that sweareth to his own hurt, and changeth not." "Does it mean that when you promise something, you ought to do it *anyway?"* I asked.

My dad answered simply, "That's the way it looks to me," and I was profoundly impressed.

"He that sweareth to his own hurt, and changeth not."

The New International Version has "Who keeps his oath even when it hurts." The Jerusalem Bible has "Who stands by his pledge at any cost." The Living Bible, Paraphrased reads this way: who "keeps a promise even if it ruins him."

I feel quite certain about something. When by the grace of God you who read these lines are permitted to live in God's "holy hill," you will be pleased to have as neighbors people who in this life had lived like this. People who bought your used

226

car and met all the payments, even though the engine burned out. People who ordered a hundred cases of whatever line it was you carried and didn't cancel when a competitor offered them a better deal. People who agreed to sponsor your child's early-teen club and didn't resign when the assistant moved away. People who married for better or for worse and never wavered.

If anyone in all history swore to his own hurt and kept his promise anyway, it was Jesus. In Gethsemane, stretched on the ground in agony the night before the cross, He pleaded with God to find an easier way to save the human race. He did not want to be crucified.

Crucifixion was an excessively brutal way to die. Romans reserved crucifixion for traitors and robbers and most of all for slaves. They conducted crucifixions publicly for their deterrent effect. They stripped a convict naked and flogged him till his chest and back were in ribbons. Then they arranged his legs uncomfortably and drove blunt nails through his ankles and wrists* into a wooden frame.[8]

But far more distressing even than the torture of crucifixion was, for Jesus, His anticipation of separation from the Father. In poignant anguish on the cross He would shout the prayer, "My God, my God, why hast thou forsaken me?" Matthew 27:46. God would not actually forsake Him (see John 16:32). But in order to serve as our Substitute and Saviour, our Lord Jesus in some mysterious manner had to be caused to experience the dreadful anguish that all unrepentant sinners will share in the judgment. That final penalty of the wicked when they realize that, by their own choice, they are God-forsaken and lost forever.

In order to save us, Jesus identified Himself with us. He who "knew no sin" was *"made . . . to be sin"* for our sakes! 2 Corinthians 5:21. Sin separates us from God. Isaiah 59:2. As the responsibility of our sinfulness was laid on Jesus in Gethsemane, He sensed Himself being separated like a sinner from His Father. This estrangement, this ugly alienation, was to Him utterly heartrending and abhorrent. Himself our Intercessor, He longed for an intercessor of His own.

Jesus also became oppressed with apprehension that—with the union between Himself and God broken up—He would be unable to bear with patience and compassion the appalling insults and agonies of the trial and crucifixion. To be our Atonement and Sin Bearer, He must remain absolutely free from any sin of His own. If He surrendered in any way to the insinuating temptations of Satan, He knew that the human race, which He loved with all His heart, would be lost forever.

No wonder Jesus prayed in Gethsemane, "My Father, if it be possible, let this cup pass from me." Matthew 26:39.

But lying prostrate in the garden, clutching the weeds with His hands, wrestling feverishly with God as blood forced its way through His skin and mingled with the cold sweat of fear that was forming on His forehead (Luke 22:44), Jesus

---

*If, as most Christians believe, Christ's palms rather than His wrists were pierced by nails, the Romans first tied ropes around His wrists to help support His weight. The small bones in the palms could not otherwise have supported Him.

realized that the human race would be lost unless He agreed to die.

His prayer now breathed only submission. "Not as I will, but as thou wilt."

He would keep His promise. He would die for humanity, though even His best friends didn't care enough to stay awake with Him on a night like this. Matthew 26:40-46. He would die for the Jews, even though their corrupt leaders would demand His death.

Jesus was a promise-keeping Saviour, a "covenant-keeping" God.

Daniel 9:27 foretold that He would behave this way. It says that the Messiah would **"make a strong covenant with many for one week."** R.S.V.

Definition of terms. We need to define our terms. **"To make a strong covenant"** is an unusual phrase in English. It is an attempt to translate a very unusual expression in Gabriel's Hebrew.

In every instance when the Old Testament tells about someone's merely "making a covenant" (or "ratifying one"—the meaning is the same), the Hebrew idiom employed is "cutting a covenant."* But the phrase "to make a strong covenant" is translated from quite a different set of words.

Now, Jesus most certainly did make or ratify a covenant while He lived on the earth. At the Last Supper He lifted a cup of wine and said to His disciples, "This is my blood of the covenant, which is poured out for many for the forgiveness of sins." Matthew 26:28. His use of the word "covenant" and of the phrase "for many" shows that at the Last Supper He was thinking of Daniel 9:27, **"He will make a strong *covenant* with *many* for one week."** The reference to His blood means that the covenant could become effective only as He sacrificed Himself on the cross.† "Without the shedding of blood there is no forgiveness of sins." Hebrews 9:22.

The covenant which Jesus ratified at the Last Supper was, of course, the glorious "new covenant" (Ezekiel 36:25-28; Jeremiah 31:31-34; Hebrews 8:10, 11) which we discussed on pages 170, 171. It offers (1) forgiveness of every sin, (2) membership among God's chosen people, and (3) power from God to live a changed life in harmony with His laws of love.

Jesus without doubt made or ratified this covenant at Calvary, but Daniel 9:27 does not say merely that He would "make a covenant." Professor Edward Young has correctly observed:[9]

> The writer [of the book of Daniel] does not mean to say that he will make a covenant. The ordinary idiom to express such a thought is "to cut a covenant," and

*The idiom seems to be based on an ancient custom of cutting up several sacrificial animals and placing their parts on different altars. The parties making the covenant then walked between the altars (see Genesis 15). The significance seems to have been, "If either of us breaks this covenant, may he be cut apart like these animals."

†When a wealthy person promises to mention a friend in his "last will and testament," the friend feels sure he can count on inheriting something, but only after the wealthy person dies. Galatians 3:15-18 and Hebrews 9:15-17 compare the new covenant to a last will and testament. The new covenant was dependable from the moment God first gave it, because God cannot lie (Hebrews 6:18) and because Jesus was determined to die for us at any cost to Himself. But such is the nature of sin that God *could* not ever have provided forgiveness without the death of Jesus. The effectiveness of the new covenant required Christ's death.

this idiom is not used here. Now, if the writer had wished to state that a covenant would be *made,* why did he not employ the ordinary Hebrew idiom for expressing such a thought? Why did he use this strange phrase, "cause to prevail" which appears in only one other passage in the OT, Ps. 12:4 [where it refers to the persuasive power of flattery]?

The R.S.V. translation, **"he will make a strong covenant,"** is one attempt to take the difference into account, but it really misses the point. Gabriel's Hebrew uses a verb based on the Hebrew root, *gabar,* a term that connotes "to prevail," meaning to persist, to predominate, to win, to have real success (see, for example, Genesis 7:18; 49:26; Exodus 17:11; Lamentations 1:16). For Daniel 9:27 Professor Young suggests "cause to prevail," and the Modern Language Bible has almost the same—"make the covenant to prevail."

Perhaps the simplest way to express the meaning is to say that Jesus would energetically *honor His covenant under any circumstances.*

A covenant is a promise. The "new covenant" is the supreme "new promise." Repeatedly in the Old Testament God promised to make or keep this new promise. Thus a dual promise was involved, a promise to keep a promise. And when Jesus, as God's representative, came into the world, He said to His Father, "Lo, I have come to do thy will, O God." Hebrews 10:7.

Having arrived in the world, Jesus the Messiah honored Heaven's solemn pledge in the face of every contrary circumstance. No matter what combination of mockery, threat, torture, dread, and death—of fightings without and fears within—rose up against Him, Christ saw to it that His covenant prevailed. He caused His promise to triumph over all.

Having sworn to His own hurt, He refused to change. He ratified the promise at any cost to Himself, and He then applied it to even the most wicked sinners who sought out its benefits.

Keeping the covenant for a week. Daniel 9:27 says that Messiah would keep His promise, come what may, **"for one week."** The week here is the final one of the seventy weeks allotted in a special sense to the Jews. It was to come **"after"** the sixty-nine weeks. In the **"middle of the week"*** Jesus was to cause sacrifices to cease—that is, with three and a half years of the final seven left to run, Jesus was to be killed—and then He was going to go on keeping the promise nonetheless. The

---

*The R.S.V. translation, "for half of a week," is based unfortunately on the assumption that the prophecy refers merely to Antiochus Epiphanes. In "The Seventy Weeks of Daniel 9: An Exegetical Study" (*Andrews University Seminary Studies* 17 [1979]:13) Professor Jacques Doukhan has pointed out that, although the Hebrew word *"chatsi"* does mean "half" in some other settings, yet when it is used in grammatical construction with a period of time (here a "week"), it always means "middle of" *not* "half of." See Exodus 12:29; Judges 16:3; and Ruth 3:8, where it means the "middle of the night," or "midnight," and Jeremiah 17:11 and Psalm 102:24, where it means the "middle of one's life," or "mid-life." In Joshua 10:13 *"chatsi"* refers to the middle of the sky. The meaning in Daniel 9:27 is not that Antiochus Epiphanes would suspend Jewish sacrifices for three and a half years—something that Antiochus Epiphanes in fact never did. (According to 1 Maccabees 1:54, 59; 4:52-54, he stopped them for only three years and ten days.) The meaning is that in the middle of the seventieth week Messiah would "abolish," "annul," "terminate" the significance of Jewish sacrifices forever.

prophecy implies His resurrection. It shows that He intended to go on keeping His promise to the Jews even after they crucified Him!

The Bible record shows that He actually did this. A few hours *before* His death an unruly mob shouted angrily, "His blood be on us and on our children." Matthew 27:25. Six weeks *after* the cross, on the Day of Pentecost, Peter, citing the promise of God, offered forgiveness to these same people and their same children! Said Peter, "Repent, and be baptized every one of you in the name of Jesus Christ for the forgiveness of your sins; and you shall receive the gift of the Holy Spirit. For the *promise,*" Peter concluded, "is to *you* and to *your children* and to all that are far off, every one whom the Lord our God calls to him." Acts 2:38, 39.

Three thousand Jews accepted the provisions of the promise on that occasion. Acts 2:41. A little later five thousand men, in addition to women and children, accepted Jesus when Peter told them, *"You* are the sons of the prophets and of the *covenant* which God gave to your fathers. . . . God, *having raised up* his servant [Jesus Christ], *sent him to you first,* to *bless you* in turning every one of you from your wickedness." Acts 3:25, 26.

So persuasive was this superlative sort of love, so attractive was the appeal of a God who kept His promise in spite of rejection and crucifixion, that "the word of God increased; and the number of disciples multiplied greatly in Jerusalem, and a great many of the *priests* were obedient to the faith." Acts 6:7.

The priests had led the people in their opposition. But Christ's determination to forgive and save was so intense and undaunted that He caused His covenant to prevail even in *their* wayward and cruel hearts.

Thus in the years immediately following the cross, thousands of Jews accepted the threefold benefits of the new covenant: (1) forgiveness of every sin, (2) power to live changed lives, and (3) membership in God's special people.

The new covenant and your family. "The promise is to you and to your children," Peter said on the Day of Pentecost. Acts 2:39.

We all hope some day to "abide in God's tabernacle," to "dwell on His holy hill" (Psalm 15); but we know that we are completely unworthy. We do not always speak the truth or work righteousness or keep our word. We don't treat people— even the members of our families—with consistent kindness. Sometimes we are terribly mean.

The new covenant is for us. Let us believe that it is for us, and let us trust it and allow it to go to work inside us.

Alone or at family worship, let us talk about the sacrifice and patience of Jesus until we *know* that He cares deeply about each one of us. As the realization of His love takes hold, we can but bow our heads and say, "Lord, we know You care; we know You love. O Lord, forgive us; forgive our children. In Your wonderful, mysterious way keep Your promise to fill us with Your power to help us keep Your commandments and to be kind and dependable and good like You are. Accept us, please, into Your chosen people."

He will certainly answer our prayer. He really keeps His promises.

230

IV. God's New Israel

The temple desolated. In our discussion on pages 19-22 we reminded ourselves that in the early days of their history, God selected the Israelites to be His special people whose chief responsibility was to reveal to the other people of the world His generous kindness. Gabriel's words in Daniel 9:24, **"Seventy weeks of years are decreed** [*amputated or cut off*] **concerning your people,"** imply that God, foreseeing all human activity, knew sadly, in advance, that at the close of the seventy weeks He would have to depend on a different people.

Addressing a large crowd in the temple courts on the Tuesday afternoon before He died, Jesus indicated that the time for this change of people had drawn very close. With deep pathos choking His voice, He declared to the Jews, "Your house is left unto you desolate."

Desolate!

"Desolate" is one of the key words in Daniel 9:24-27. Jesus knew that in A.D. 70, some forty years in the future, the Roman general Titus, son of the Roman emperor Vespasian, would violently storm the walls of Jerusalem. Titus's soldiers*—the **"people of the prince who is to come"** (Daniel 9:26)—would set the temple on fire. The idol-worshiping Roman soldiers—the "desolating sacrilege spoken of by the prophet Daniel" (Matthew 24:15)—would ruin the entire city and leave it uninhabited and desolate. But on this Sunday afternoon at the climax of the triumphal entry, nearly forty years before the Roman armies destroyed the city, Jesus announced to the Jewish people that their temple was already desolate!

A temple is a symbol of God's presence. Either God is, in some deep spiritual sense, present in a temple, or it is only an empty shell.

When Jesus said that the temple was desolate, His words did not make it so. He had left heaven in order to bring to the temple the unparalleled privilege of His physical presence. Suppose the high priest had recognized Him as the Son of God. Suppose he had accepted Him instead of accusing Him—had crowned Him instead of crucifying Him!

Suppose, on behalf of the Jewish people, the high priest had knelt before Jesus and prayed like Daniel, "We have sinned! O Lord, hear! O Lord, forgive."

Alas, John 1:11, K.J.V., says of Christ, "He came unto his own, and his own received him not." The New English Bible says, "He entered his own realm, and his own would not receive him." The R.S.V. reads, "He came to his own home, and his own people received him not."

---

*The Jewish historian, Josephus, who was present at the siege of Jerusalem, insists that after holding a council with his generals, Titus determined to save the temple as a priceless ornament of the Roman Empire. Josephus's account, which has not gone unchallenged by modern historians, says in part that in spite of Titus's decision, during the excitement of the attack "one of the soldiers, awaiting no orders and with no horror of so dread a deed, . . . snatched a brand . . . , and, hoisted up by one of his comrades, flung the fiery missile through a low golden door. . . . As the flame shot up, a cry, as poignant as the tragedy, arose from the Jews, who flocked to the rescue, lost to all thought of self-preservation, . . . now that the object of all their past vigilance was vanishing."—*Jewish War*, 6.236-253; translation by H. St. J. Thackeray in Loeb Classical Library.

The temple was desolate because Jesus Christ, the Son of God and the Son of man, had come to His temple and had been "rejected by the elders and chief priests and scribes." Luke 9:22.

The King and His kingdom. But can we be certain that this is what Jesus had in mind? During His triumphal entry into Jerusalem only two days before He announced that the temple was desolate, had not the Jews regaled Him with thunderous cheers, "Blessed is the King who comes in the name of the Lord"? Luke 19:38.

True enough. But on Friday morning, a few days later, many from the same crowd would shout, "Crucify him!"

The explanation is that the Jews really wanted Jesus to be their king—but they wanted Him to be their kind of king. They wanted Him to lead them in overthrowing the Romans and in making Jerusalem, not Rome, the capital of the world. They did not want a king who could say to Pilate, on the night of His trial, "My kingship is not of this world." John 18:36.

In His public and private presentations Jesus very often referred to the "kingdom of God" and to the "kingdom of heaven" (see, for example, Matthew 3:2; 6:33; Mark 10:14). Subjugated by the Romans, the Jews listened eagerly. Their pulses quickened as they dreamed of their glorious days as a nation under Kings David and Solomon. They recalled the so-called "kingdom prophecies"* which predicted world leadership for the Jewish people. They interpreted these prophecies in a materialistic sense and longed for a leader who could guarantee international prestige and economic prosperity. They wanted a Saviour from Rome but not necessarily from their sins.

But when a wealthy young leader asked how he could be sure to gain eternal life, Jesus didn't reply, Help Me reestablish the Israelite kingdom. He told him instead to keep the commandments, give away his possessions, and "follow me." Matthew 19:16-22.

When Nicodemus came at night, Jesus said that if he wanted to enter the kingdom, he must first be "born again." John 3:1-5, K.J.V.

Most people don't want to "follow Christ" or be "born again"! The wealthy young leader walked away, sorrowful. Even Nicodemus surrendered fully only when Jesus died on the cross.

Many Jews claimed the kingdom promises without caring about the kingdom qualifications. They forgot that in Daniel 7 God promised the kingdom only to the "saints." They forgot Psalm 15:1-4, K.J.V.:

> Lord, who shall abide in thy tabernacle?
> Who shall dwell in thy holy hill?
> He that walketh uprightly,

*Some "kingdom prophecies" are found in 2 Samuel 7:8-16; Isaiah 2:2-4; 4:3-6; Jeremiah 23:5-8; Zechariah 12; 14. The conditional nature of even 2 Samuel 7:8-16 is revealed in 1 Kings 2:3, 4 and Psalm 132:10-12. The promised "son of David" king was, of course, Jesus Christ. In rejecting the promised King, the people of Israel forfeited their promised world leadership.

233

Nearly forty years before Roman armies destroyed Jerusalem Jesus announced that the Jewish temple was already desolate.

and worketh righteousness,
and speaketh the truth in his heart. . . .
He that sweareth to his own hurt, and changeth not.

Many Jews in Jesus' day forgot that to many of the kingdom prophecies there was a conditional aspect. "If at any time I declare concerning a nation or a kingdom that I will build and plant it," says the Lord through Jeremiah 18:9, 10, "if it does evil in my sight, not listening to my voice, then I will repent of the good which I had intended to do to it."

Many Jews forgot that under the new covenant God offers power for the changed life that qualifies a person for membership among His special people. Chafing under Roman oppression, these Jews wanted power to conquer their enemies. They were not interested when Christ offered them power to conquer themselves.

Even today millions of Christians would rather rule others than control themselves. Like the Jews of old, they too want Christ to be their own kind of king.

The vineyard reassigned. The very morning after the triumphal entry Jesus stood in the temple and in story form warned the Jews that because they had refused to let God help them live *His* kind of life, the "kingdom" was about to be given to someone else.

In His story Jesus told of a businessman who planted a vineyard at a distance from his home and rented it to tenant farmers. "When the season of fruit drew near," Jesus said, "he sent his servants to the tenants, to get his fruit; and the tenants took his servants and beat one, killed another, and stoned another. Again he sent other servants, more than the first; and they did the same to them.

"Afterward," Jesus went on, "he sent his son to them saying, 'They will respect my son.'

"But when the tenants saw the son," Jesus continued, "they said to themselves, 'This is the heir; come, let us kill him and have his inheritance.' And they took him and cast him out of the vineyard, and killed him.

"When therefore the owner of the vineyard comes," Jesus asked His audience, "what will he do to those tenants?"

The crowd was caught up in the story and felt a swell of righteous indignation. They replied heatedly, "He will put those wretches to a miserable death, and let out the vineyard to other tenants who will give him the fruits in their seasons."

Immediately Jesus came to the point. Explaining that the "son" in the story was Himself, whom the priests were about to murder, He said to the Jews, "Therefore I tell you, the kingdom of God will be taken away from you and given to a nation producing the fruits of it." Matthew 21:33-43. The new nation, as we shall see in a moment, was to be the fellowship of true Christians drawn out of all races.

The end of the seventy weeks. For the termination of the seventy weeks, Gabriel in Daniel 9:24-27 prescribed no specific event. Gabriel did not say what particular act or transaction, if any, marked the close of the prophetic period which, for 490 years, had counted out the privileges of the Jewish nation.

We do know, however, that a few years after the cross—and various commentators[10] have placed the event around A.D. 34—the Jewish leadership confirmed its rebellion against God by creating the first Christian martyr. The Sanhedrin, the highest governing body in the Jewish commonwealth, officially stoned Stephen.

In killing Christ the Jewish leaders had persuaded the Romans to commit the murder for them. In killing Stephen they threw rocks with their own hands, employing the traditional Jewish procedure for execution. The symbolism was devastating.

Ever since Christ's baptism/anointing in A.D. 27, God had caused the covenant with Israel to triumph in the public ministry of Jesus—a unique demonstration of patient, forgiving love. Now the vineyard was to be taken from Israel and offered to a different "nation."

But just as God didn't *make* the temple desolate, so now He didn't arbitrarily deprive the Jewish nation of its privileges in order to bestow them on the Gentiles. The antichristian Jewish leaders launched a "great persecution" against the Christian Jews, which compelled them to leave Jerusalem. Acts 8:1, 2.

Harassed by this persecution, the Jerusalem Christians "went everywhere preaching the word." Acts 8:4, K.J.V. Philip preached Christ in Samaria. Acts 8:5. Peter, divinely guided, opened the gospel to the Roman military officer, Cornelius, in Caesarea. Acts 10. Most amazing, one of the leading Jewish persecutors, Saul of Tarsus (later known as Paul the Apostle), became convinced of God's goodness by watching the forgiving spirit of his own victims. Born again through the grace of God, Paul heard the voice of God summon him to "carry my name before the Gentiles and kings and the sons of Israel." Acts 9:15. "Depart," said the heavenly voice, "for I will send you far away to the Gentiles." Acts 22:21.

Thus the rejection of Christ which was epitomized in the stoning of Stephen led directly to the proclamation of the gospel in the non-Jewish world.

God's "Israel" today. Very soon Gentile Christian congregations sprang into existence all the way from Jerusalem to Rome. Some of their names are preserved in the titles of New Testament books: Romans, Corinthians, Galatians, Ephesians, Philippians, Colossians, Thessalonians.

Contemplating these new congregations, Paul perceived the fulfillment of the prophecy of Hosea 2:23, "Those who were not my people I will call 'my people.' " Romans 9:25.

In Paul's day every Jew still cherished God's promise found in Exodus 19:5, 6. It constituted a kind of national charter: "If you will obey my voice and keep my covenant, you shall be my own possession among all peoples; . . . and you shall be to me a kingdom of priests and a holy nation." But in 1 Peter 2:9, God told the new Christian membership that *they* were now the "chosen race, a royal priesthood, a holy nation, God's own people."

The vineyard had been assigned to its new tenants.

But the new tenants were not exclusively Gentile! The founders of the new nation, Christ and His apostles, were all Jews, and its members were a mixture of Gentiles and Jews. Let us never forget this.

Said Paul to the Gentiles in Ephesians 2:12-14, "You [Gentiles] were at that time [before the cross] separated from Christ, alienated from the commonwealth of Israel, and strangers to the covenants of promise, having no hope and without God in the world. But now in Christ you who once were far off have been brought near in the blood of Christ. For he is our peace, who has made *us both* [Jews and Gentiles] *one,* and has broken down the dividing wall of hostility."

In Christ, "Gentile" needs no longer to be distinguished from "Jew." "In Christ Jesus you are all sons of God, through faith. . . . There is neither Jew nor Greek, . . . for you are *all one* in Christ Jesus. And if you are Christ's, then you are Abraham's offspring, heirs according to promise." Galatians 3:26-29.

The covenant promises apply equally to all. Everyone is urged to receive (1) forgiveness of every sin, (2) power to be changed, and (3) membership in God's chosen people. *All* the **"saints of the Most High"** (Daniel 7:18) are assured entry into His everlasting kingdom.

The success of the gospel among non-Jews led some Christians in Paul's day to wonder if perhaps the kingdom would never again be restored to the Jews. God had promised the kingdom to King David's dynasty in perpetuity. 2 Samuel 7:8-16. Had God now failed? they asked.

They need not have worried. God can be trusted! For one thing, Jesus, the supreme "son of David" (Matthew 22:42), was already sitting on the throne of the universe (Revelation 3:21)! For another, they needed to *define the term "Jew."*

"He is not a real Jew who is one outwardly," Paul explained in Romans 2:28, 29. "He is a Jew who is one inwardly." Being a real Jew is not a matter of inheriting genes from Father Abraham! "It is not the children of the flesh who are the children of God," Paul said in Romans 9:8, "but the children of the promise are reckoned as [Abraham's] descendents." In God's sight "there is no distinction between Jew and Greek. . . . For 'every one who calls upon the name of the Lord will be saved.' " Romans 10:12, 13.

God's kingdom promises cannot fail! Indeed, in Christ their value is enhanced. The Old Testament prophets could not hope that more than a "remnant" (a small minority) of literal Israel would ever accept the covenant and be saved into God's kingdom. Romans 9:27; 11:14. But as the gospel reaches the Gentiles as well as the Jews, as God's new "Israel" becomes every true believer in every part of the whole wide world, Paul can reach the triumphant conclusion, "And so *all Israel* will be saved"! Romans 11:26.

"The kingdom and the dominion and the greatness of the kingdoms under the whole heaven shall be given to the . . . saints of the Most High"—including you and your spouse and your parents and your children, and anyone else who accepts the promises of the new covenant—and **"their kingdom shall be an everlasting kingdom."** Daniel 7:27.

V. The Judgment Has Begun

For the moment he must have been the happiest man on earth.

But only for the moment.

He was an important servant of a wealthy lord. In telling about him in Matthew 18:23-35 Jesus indicated that this servant had borrowed ten thousand talents—a very large sum—and that he had been unable to pay it back. Perhaps he had invested it in a shipload of ceramics from Italy and the ship had gone down, or in a caravan of eastern silks, and bandits had made off with the lot.

Anyway, when the lord had found out that the servant couldn't pay, he had ordered him and his family sold as slaves and their value applied to his account.

Horrified, the servant had fallen on his knees. "Lord, have patience with me," he begged, "and I will pay you everything."

"Out of pity for him," Jesus says, "the lord of that servant released him and forgave him the debt." It was most generous of him.

At that particular moment the servant must have felt happy indeed. But as he walked out of his lord's office, he met a fellow employee who happened to owe him a "hundred denarii" (worth perhaps twenty dollars, more or less). Incredibly he grabbed his petty debtor by the throat and yelled at him to pay up.

The employee wrenched himself loose and fell to his knees. "Have patience with me," he begged, "and I will pay you."

If the 10,000-talent debtor had wanted to stay *forgiven, he should have forgiven his 100-penny debtor.*

But the servant, angered at having to wait for his money, had the man thrown in prison.

When the other employees heard what had happened, they complained to the lord—who immediately called his servant in and talked to him with considerable feeling. "You wicked servant!" he said. "I forgave you all that debt because you besought me; and should you not have had mercy on your fellow servant, as I had mercy on you?" And he had *him* thrown in prison.

Jesus concluded His story with this sensible but sobering message: "So also my heavenly Father will do to every one of you, if you do not forgive your brother from your heart." Matthew 18:35.

Let's keep this story in mind as we continue our study of Daniel 8 and 9. We will return to it specifically on page 246. It has a very direct bearing on the prophecy of the 2300 days.

The 2300 days dated. Fascinating and significant as the seventy weeks are when they are studied alone, we must remind ourselves again that they are mentioned by Gabriel as a means of focusing light on the 2300 days of Daniel 8:14.

"For two thousand and three hundred evenings and mornings [that is, for 2300 days*]**,"** said the angel in Daniel 8:14, **"then the sanctuary shall be restored to its rightful state."**

"Make this man understand the vision," came the command to Gabriel a moment later, and Gabriel immediately attempted to comply. But after he had explained the beasts and horns that were also part of the vision, he had to stop, for Daniel fainted, and the 2300 days went unexplained.

About thirteen years later Gabriel returned to Daniel and invited him to **"understand the vision."** Right off he talked about time. **"Seventy weeks of years,"** he began, **"are decreed** [amputated or cut off] **concerning your people."** Daniel 9:24.

We have seen that the exact fulfillment of Gabriel's seventy-week prophecy in the first advent of Christ contributes to an understanding of the 2300 days partly by proving that the 2300 days represent *2300 years*. For example, it would be impossible to amputate 490 years from 2300 ordinary days!

We have been guided to this conclusion about *2300 years,* by recognizing these points also:

1. The 2300 days are introduced in the *symbolic* part of Daniel 8, revealing that they are as certainly symbolic as are the beasts, horns, 1260 days, and

2. Ezekiel, Daniel's contemporary prophet, fellow exile, and neighbor in Babylonia, was specifically informed in a symbolic prophecy that a day stands for a year. Ezekiel 4:6.

We might also have considered that in the earliest years of the Jewish nation, while the Israelites were still on their way from Egypt to Palestine, God through Moses related forty *days* of disobedience to forty *years* of punishment. Numbers 14:34. In this way God established the "day for a year" concept in the Jewish mentality from the start.

*See pages 179, 180.

The Jewish scholar Nahawendi wrote about the "2300 *years*" in the ninth century A.D.[11] Arnold of Villanova, a brilliant physician who treated popes and kings and who battled Paris theologians, argued in 1292 that when Daniel "says 'two thousand three hundred days' it must be said that by days he understands *years*." "It is not unaccustomed, in the Scripture of God," Villanova went on, "for days to understand years. . . . The Spirit in Ezekiel testified: 'A day for a year I have reckoned to you.' "[12]

Daniel 8:17 says that the vision of the 2300 days applied to *"the time of the end."*

Assured from Scripture that the 2300 days are 2300 years, we still want to understand when they were to begin so that we can calculate when they were to end. The clue, again, must lie in the prophecy of the seventy weeks. How else could the seventy weeks help us adequately to **"understand"** the 2300 days? Therefore Gabriel's pronouncement **"From the going forth of the word to restore and build Jerusalem to the coming of an anointed one, a prince"** *dates the beginning of the 2300 days as surely as it dates the beginning of the seventy weeks.*

We have found that the seventy weeks began in 457 B.C. Thus it follows that the 2300 days also began in 457 B.C.

So, when did they end?

The 490 years ended in A.D. 34. When we cut off or amputate 490 years from

At the commencement of the Day of Atonement/Day of Judgment, at the close of the 2300 year-days, Jesus moved on "clouds" to the "Ancient of Days" in heaven.

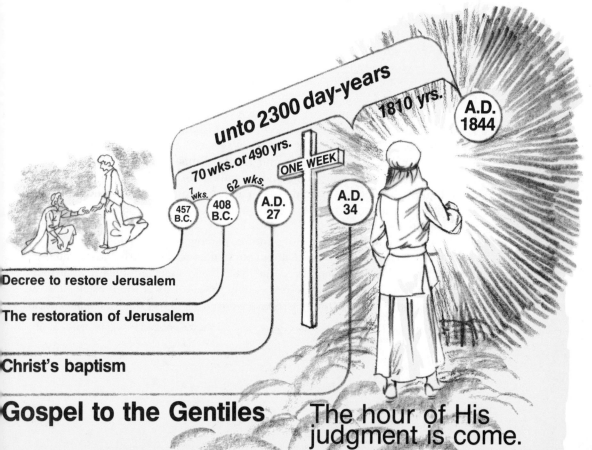

Decree to restore Jerusalem

The restoration of Jerusalem

Christ's baptism

Gospel to the Gentiles   The hour of His judgment is come.

2300 years, 1810 years are left. So, the 2300 years were to extend 1810 years after A.D. 34. Thus the 2300 days ended in the year 1844.

The 2300 year-days ran from 457 B.C. to A.D. 1844.

What happened in 1844? You are curious and wonder what happened in 1844. You do not remember reading anything appropriate in a history book.

The angel said, in effect, that in 1844 the "sanctuary" would be restored to its rightful state. As we have seen, the sanctuary he was talking about is that "sanctuary . . . which is set up not by man but by the Lord," the one that is located in heaven where Jesus ministers as our faithful High Priest. Hebrews 8:1, 2.

The process which marked the close of the 2300 days began *in heaven* in 1844. This is why you have not read about it in history books!*   •

On pages 181-188 we saw that the words **"then shall the sanctuary be restored to its rightful state,"** when studied carefully in their context and in the light of the undering Hebrew, connote at least four related processes and events:

1. The exoneration of Christ's *tamid,* His high-priestly ministry, after a long period when it was "trampled under foot."

2. The final cleansing of the sanctuary, and of the people who worship at the sanctuary, from all sin.

3. In connection with this cleansing, an act of judgment.

4. Following this cleansing and act of judgment, a sounding of the jubilee trumpet, the destruction of nations by the supernatural stone, and the inheritance of Christ's kingdom by His saints.

Exoneration of Christ's tamid. The high-priestly ministry of Jesus was obscured in the Middle Ages by ministers who neglected to preach the gospel and who imposed confession and penance on people, threatening with excommunication or even execution all who wouldn't comply (see pages 172-179). The unveiling of the truth about Christ's heavenly priesthood began around 1517 when Martin Luther rediscovered the biblical teaching that salvation is a *gift* of God which we may enjoy through *faith* in Jesus. "By grace you have been saved through faith; and this is not your own doing, it is the gift of God—not because of works, lest any man should boast." Ephesians 2:8, 9. "The wages of sin is death, but the free gift of God is eternal life in Christ Jesus our Lord." Romans 6:23.

A further vast enrichment in the understanding of Christ's heavenly ministry occurred during the period around 1844. You are reading some of it now! Much more will be discussed in our comments on the book of Revelation.

All Christians believe in the Christ of history, hanging on the cross. Many Christians believe in the Christ of the future, coming on the clouds. But a great many Christians do not know much about our contemporary Christ, performing a very special work which commenced in 1844. Everyone should learn what the Bible says about the work that Jesus is doing for all of us at the present time.

The sanctuary and the Day of Judgment. On pages 115-119 we saw that Daniel

---

*On pages 218 and 234 we observed that Gabriel also specified no on-earth event for the close of either the seven weeks or the seventy weeks.

7:9-14 pictures the initial phase of the final judgment. The special work that Jesus is doing for us at the present time involves His participation in this early phase of the judgment in addition to His normal services as our High Priest.

In the vision of Daniel 7 the Ancient of Days takes a seat and **"one like a son of man"** approaches Him on the **"clouds of heaven."** The Ancient of Days is God the Father and the Son of man is Jesus, but in Daniel 7:13 Christ's coming **"with the clouds of heaven"** is not what Christians refer to as the second coming. At the second coming Jesus comes "in the clouds" (1 Thessalonians 4:17) to the earth to rescue His saints. In Daniel 7 He appears before the Ancient of Days to make up His roster of saints before coming to rescue them.

This traveling of Jesus from one place to another at judgment time is not unique. He journeyed from heaven to earth when the time came in the seventy-week prophecy for Him to be born and slain as our Redeemer. He will again journey from heaven to earth when the time comes for Him to reign in glory as our King of kings. Likewise, in 1844, at the close of the 2300 year-days, He is portrayed as passing from one part of heaven to another when the time came for Him to make a significant transition in His service as our High Priest.

In symbolic, sanctuary language we may say that in 1844 Jesus passed from the holy place of heaven's sanctuary to its most holy place* (see pages 181-183).

On page 186 we saw that the judgment in Daniel 7 is the same event as the cleansing/restoring of the sanctuary in Daniel 8:14. This cleansing/restoring/judging *precedes the second coming.* In Revelation 14:6, 7 John says, "I saw another angel fly in midheaven, with an eternal *gospel* to proclaim to those who dwell on the earth . . . ; and he said with a loud voice, . . . *The hour of his judgment has come."* Inasmuch as the gospel is being preached after the hour of judgment has arrived, the judgment must commence before the work of the gospel closes. It begins before the second coming.

Indeed! The gospel has seen its *widest* application to human need since the commencement of the judgment in 1844.†

Four phases of final judgment. To avoid confusion we ought to notice that the Bible refers to the final judgment in a variety of ways. Sometimes it seems to speak of a single divine act. "God will bring every deed into judgment, with every secret thing." Ecclesiastes 12:14. God "has fixed a day on which he will judge the world." Acts 17:31. "We shall all stand before the judgment seat of God." Romans 14:10.

*Hebrews 6:19 R.S.V. and Hebrews 9:8 K.J.V. sound as though Jesus were already at work in heaven's most holy place during the first century, when the book of Hebrews was written. The underlying Greek for Hebrews 6:19, however, says only that Jesus had entered "within the veil," as in the K.J.V. and N.A.S.B. There were two veils or curtains (Hebrews 9:3), and Hebrews 6:19—as also Hebrews 8:2; 9:12, 24, 25; 10:19; and 13:11—tells us simply about the "holy places" or "sanctuary." The book of Hebrews is concerned to tell us that Jesus is at work in the heavenly sanctuary, but it is not concerned to say in which area of the sanctuary He is working.

†In his famous *History of Christianity,* page 1345, Kenneth Scott Latourette selects the nineteenth century as the "great century" for the gospel. Christianity closed the century, he observes, "on a rising tide and with mounting momentum, more widely spread geographically than at any previous time, . . . and . . . making its impression upon more of mankind than ever before."

But in addition to referring to the final judgment in general terms like these, the Bible also designates at least four phases of the final judgment, one before, one at, and two after the second coming.

1. *Judgment before the second coming:* The Son of man comes to the Ancient of Days (Daniel 7:9-15, 26, 27), cleanses the sanctuary (Daniel 8:14), and *investigates* the books (Daniel 7:10) to disclose who is qualified to be retained in the book of life.

2. *Judgment at the second coming:* The Son of man, seated in glory, *separates* the sheep from the goats. Matthew 25:31-46.

3. *Judgments after the second coming:*

a. During the 1000 years the saints sit on thrones, and judgment is committed to them as they *examine* the records of the world and of the fallen angels. Revelation 20:4; 1 Corinthians 6:2, 3.

b. At the close of the 1000 years, sentence is pronounced and judgment is *executed* against the unsaved. They and death itself are thrown into the lake of fire. Revelation 20:12-15.

Although the terms are not used in the Bible, for convenience we can speak of phases of the final judgment that deal with "investigation," "separation," "examination," and "execution." The phase which began in 1844—the first of the four phases of the final judgment—is the "investigative judgment," or, more simply perhaps, the "pre-advent* judgment."

The Bible also mentions other moments of judgment besides the final judgment. King Belshazzar was "weighed in the balances and found wanting" on October 12, 539 B.C. (see pages 86-88). Israel was judged at the close of the seventy weeks, when her unique privilege as God's most favored nation was assigned to a new Israel, which was to be composed of "real Jews" of all races (Galatians 3:28, 29), the spiritual descendants of Abraham.

Day of Judgment/Day of Atonement. On pages 183-185 we saw that the symbolic cleansing of the Old Testament sanctuary (Leviticus 16 and 23) occurred on the symbolic Day of Atonement, which was also a symbolic Day of Judgment. By reasoning in the reverse direction, we learn that the current day of judgment (since 1844) is also a Day of Atonement.

This is a precious insight.

God's principal purpose in this first phase of the final judgment is not to condemn but to acquit. In "cleansing the sanctuary" God seeks to remove sin so thoroughly that even the record of confessed sin is blotted out. Sin separates. Isaiah 59:2. Removal of sin makes reconciliation (at-one-ment) a reality. Removal of the last memory of sin ("I will remember their sin no more," Jeremiah 31:34) renders reconciliation absolute and permanent.

---

*"Advent" means "coming." Christ's first advent was His coming to earth as a baby. His second advent will be His second coming on the clouds. "Pre-advent" is here used to mean "prior to the second coming."

God is searching the "books," not to expose the people who have failed, but to disclose those who have remained faithful. The fearful judgment at the end of the 1000 years concludes with those who are unsaved being condemned to the punishment of eternal death. But the pre-advent judgment that began in 1844—the great final Day of Atonement that fulfills the symbolic Day of Atonement of Leviticus 16—evidently culminates with the thrilling pronouncement: "Clean from all your sins before the Lord." Leviticus 16:30, K.J.V. At its close Jesus departs from heaven to earth to gather His saints and to crown them with eternal life.

A further parallel with the Old Testament now appears meaningful. The only persons whose lives came in review on the old Day of Atonement were the Israelites, God's special people. This was so because the only sins that were blotted out on that day were the sins of the people who had offered sacrifices during the preceding year. The godless tribes beyond the bounds of Israel were presumed lost without examination, at least from the human standpoint.

So today. God seeks His faithful among the "real Jews" who have joined His true Israel through the centuries. Jesus Christ is the "true light that enlightens every man." John 1:9. The people who are being examined in the present investigative, pre-advent phase of the judgment are those who, in some way or other, at some time or other, have responded favorably to this Light. "There is salvation in no one else, for there is no other name under heaven given among men by which we must be saved." Acts 4:12.

Atonement includes more than the cross. Perhaps you are accustomed to thinking of the "atonement" as including only the cross and not the pre-advent judgment as well.

The cross was indeed supreme, a unique act of atonement made on our behalf. Our gracious, loving, eternal, holy God suffered the horrible punishment of a traitor, robber, and slave. As our Substitute He shed His blood for us. We bow our heads and our hearts. Uncomprehending, we ask, "O God, do You care this much for us?"

And He replies, "Yes, I care this much—and more."

We learned on page 169 that in order for the *shed* blood of a sacrifice to accomplish atonement it had to be *applied* to an altar in the sanctuary by a priest. And before atonement could be ultimate and final, blood had to be applied again by a priest, in the most holy place.*

It may come as a surprise to discover that the older versions of the Bible, such as the K.J.V., never used the English word "atonement" to refer to Christ's death. They used it almost exclusively in connection with sanctuary activities that *follow* the slaying of a sacrifice.

The atonement involves even more than the cross!

*Sin does not need to be forgiven twice (see Hebrews 10). The second application of blood, made on the Day of Atonement, represented the removal of the record of confessed sin and also the fact that the repentant sinner had *chosen to remain in a faith relationship with God* and *still* desired to be at-one with Him.

Jesus, our Sacrifice, died for us once; but think how long He has *suffered* for us. In all the afflictions of ancient Israel, He was afflicted. Isaiah 63:9. He is pained when a sparrow falls. Matthew 10:29. For thousands of years "he has borne our griefs and carried our sorrows." Isaiah 53:4.

Jesus died for us, but He was *raised* for our justification. Romans 4:25. And He "always lives to make intercession" for us. Hebrews 7:25.

It is good to remember at all times that Jesus is still eager to "cause the covenant to prevail" in our lives at any personal cost.

"Atonement" is God's entire program for meeting our needs and for reconciling us to Himself. The cross and the post-1844 cleansing/judgment, each very different and each essential, are two major, unique events in the grand drama of the plan of salvation (see pages 169, 170).

Faithful to the end. Are you accustomed to thinking that you are already "clean from all your sins before the Lord" in view of God's promise in 1 John 1:9?

In truth, when we confess our sins, we *are* forgiven—just as the Old Testament Jew was forgiven as soon as his animal's blood was applied to an altar. Leviticus 4:35. In 1 John 1:9 God assures us that "if we confess our sins, he is faithful and just, and will forgive our sins and cleanse us from all unrighteousness."

But God is not arbitrary. If, say, a teen-age girl accepts Jesus as her Saviour during a gospel revival but later chooses not to live as a Christian, God will not

"If we confess our sins, He is faithful and just, and will forgive our sins and cleanse us from all unrighteousness." 1 John 1:9.

compel her to live with Him forever. How uncomfortable that would be for both of them!

It is unthinkable, besides, that God will save all the people who merely think well of Him for an hour once a week in church but who refuse to live like Christians during the rest of the week. What sort of neighbors would they make in the new kingdom?

"He who endures to the end will be saved," says Jesus in Matthew 24:13. Hebrews 3:14 cautions us that "we share in Christ, if only we hold our first confidence firm to the end." Paul warns the Gentile "branches" that have been grafted into the "olive tree" of God's true Israel that they may yet be broken off. "If God did not spare the natural branches [i.e., Jews by nationality], neither will he spare you," he says. God will continue to be kind to you, "provided you continue in his kindness." Romans 11:20-22.

In order to be pronounced clean in the end, we must continue to the end to "abide" in Him (see John 15:1-11).

When we recognize our sinfulness and come to God "just as we are," we are (1) immediately forgiven and (2) accepted into Heaven's family, God's true Israel, The new covenant promises this. There is no waiting in line and no price to pay.

But the new covenant also promises (3) power to help us to change—to obey His commandments and to develop kindly ways and an upright character. "I will put my law within them, and I will write it upon their hearts." Jeremiah 31:33. God really wants us to qualify in the judgment.

One of the primary functions of the ongoing pre-advent judgment is to disclose the people who have accepted God's proffered power *as well as* His promised pardon.

Forgivable, forgiven, forgiving. God cannot overlook selfishness. He cares too much for our happiness to populate His beautiful new earth with stubborn sinners.

Take only one of His judgment criteria as an example: In His Sermon on the Mount, at the close of the Lord's prayer, Jesus laid down this principle, "If you forgive men their trespasses, your heavenly Father also will forgive you; but if you do not forgive men their trespasses, neither will your Father forgive your trespasses." Matthew 6:14, 15.

If this rule is placed alongside the promise of 1 John 1:9, the picture emerges that God forgives us freely as soon as we say we're sorry for our sins against Him; but if we aren't sorry enough to forgive the people who sin against us, then after a while His forgiveness of us doesn't count anymore. In other words, in order to stay forgiven we must be both forgivable and forgiving.

But it's hard to forgive people who have been unfair to us!

Indeed it is. But the only people we *can* forgive are people who have been unfair to us. No one else has done anything to be forgiven for.

Here is a practical application for the new covenant. God promises to write His law of love in our hearts. He wants to help us to be forgiving. He actually promises to give us His spirit of love. It is ours for the asking and for the believing. For the *looking* too. By beholding we become changed. 2 Corinthians 3:18. If in imagination we look at Christ dying for our sins and living again for our salvation, it becomes easier for us to forgive the people who hurt us. We find ourselves saying with Jesus, "Father, forgive them; for they know not what they do." Luke 23:34.

In Christ's story with which we began this section, the forgiven but unforgiving servant needed to feel God's love in his heart.

I doubt very much that this man's problem was ingratitude. I assume that he was very thankful for being forgiven ten thousand talents. But he completely misinterpreted what his lord had done. He assumed, evidently, that he was forgiven because he was such an important servant that his lord couldn't very well get along without him. I believe he swaggered out of the office.

And when he met the poor chap who couldn't instantly hand over his twenty dollars, he got very angry—because the man's refusal seemed like an insult to his dignity.

He was grateful that the lord had forgiven him. He ought to have been grateful that his lord had forgiven *even* him.

And who is this unforgiving servant? You and I, I fear, unless we see ourselves unworthy of even the least of His favors, so humbled by His goodness and our sinfulness that we want to be as nice to everybody as He has been to us.

How can we Christians sing "Amazing Grace" in church and then fight with our spouses in divorce courts to see who gets the camera and who gets the TV? Jesus Christ died and lives again to make atonement—to provide forgiveness and reconciliation. How, then, can Christians demand apologies, harbor grudges, and sue each other? How can we do these things and hope to be declared, in the end, "clean from all your sins before the Lord"?

May God help us!

And that is just what God wants to do; He wants to help us now, during this end-of-time Day of Atonement. The Day of Judgment/Day of Atonement is in session at this present moment! Under the new covenant those who in the end will be (1) clean from all their sins before the Lord, and who will be (2) privileged to live among God's people in a sinless world, will be those who (3) have not only confessed their sins but have also accepted His power to live helpfully and healingly in this sinful world.

Grace to forgive an enemy. Corrie ten Boom, who suffered terribly in a concentration camp because she helped Jews during World War II and who has become well known through her book and movie *The Hiding Place,* testifies that the Lord does provide grace to help us be forgiving.

"It was at a church service in Munich," she says, "that I saw him, the former S.S. man who had stood guard at the shower room door in the processing center at Ravensbruck. He was the first of our actual jailers that I had seen since that time. And suddenly it was all there—the roomful of mocking men, the heaps of clothing, Betsie's pain-blanched face.

246

"He came up to me as the church was emptying, beaming and bowing. 'How grateful I am for your message, *Fräulein*,' he said. 'To think that, as you say, He has washed my sins away!'

"His hand was thrust out to shake mine. And I, who had preached so often to the people in Bloemendaal the need to forgive, kept my hand at my side.

"Even as the angry, vengeful thoughts boiled through me, I saw the sin of them. Jesus Christ had died for this man; was I going to ask for more? Lord Jesus, I prayed, forgive me and help me to forgive him.

"I tried to smile. I struggled to raise my hand. I could not. I felt nothing, not the slightest spark of warmth or charity. And so again I breathed a silent prayer. Jesus, I cannot forgive him. Give me Your forgiveness.

"As I took his hand the most incredible thing happened. From my shoulder along my arm and through my hand a current seemed to pass from me to him, while into my heart sprang a love for this stranger that almost overwhelmed me.

"And so I discovered that it is not on our forgiveness any more than on our goodness that the world's healing hinges, but on His. When He tells us to love our enemies, He gives, along with the command, the love itself."[13]

VI. The Vision Understood and Sealed

God instructed Gabriel to make Daniel understand the vision of the 2300 days. After our extensive study of Daniel 9:13, 14 and Daniel 9:24-27, we too are able to understand, at least in part. A summary will crystallize our discoveries thus far. First, Daniel 9:24-27, N.A.S.B.:

> 24. **Seventy weeks** [*70 × 7 = 490 years*]
> **have been decreed** [*cut off from the 2300 year-days*]
> **for your people** [*the Jews, who continued to be God's chosen nation until A.D. 34*]
> **and your holy city** [*Jerusalem, where Christ was to die, and the New Jerusalem with its heavenly sanctuary, where, within the seventy weeks, Jesus would "anoint the most holy place"*]
> **to finish transgression, to make an end of sin, to make atonement for iniquity, to bring in everlasting righteousness** [*all provided for at the cross and made effective through Christ's heavenly priesthood*]
> **to seal up vision and prophecy** [*to guarantee fulfillment of the 2300 day prophecy (a) by fulfilling time elements so accurately that we can depend also on the date 1844 and (b) by providing at the cross the essential basis for Christ's heavenly ministry, which culminates in the pre-advent (pre-second-coming) Day of Atonement/Day of Judgment*],
> **and to anoint the most holy place** [*to dedicate the heavenly sanctuary*].
>
> 25. **So you are to know and discern that from the issuing of a decree to restore and rebuild Jerusalem** [*from the decree of Artaxerxes in 457 B.C. which restored Jerusalem to capital-city status and necessitated its reconstruction*]
> **until Messiah the Prince** [*Jesus, at His baptism/anointing*]
> **there will be seven weeks and sixty-two weeks** [*69 weeks = 483 years, from the decree of 457 B.C. to Christ's baptism in A.D. 27*],
> **it** [*Jerusalem*]

shall be built again, with plaza and moat, even in times of distress [*adjacent nations opposed Israel's resettlement in Palestine*].

26. **Then after the sixty-two weeks** [*that is, at some point after His baptism in A.D. 27*]
the Messiah will be cut off and have nothing [*Jesus was crucified virtually alone and without even His clothes*]
and the people of the prince who is to come [*Rome, represented by at least Titus and his soldiers, who fought Jerusalem in the first Jewish War, A.D. 66-73*]
will destroy the city and the sanctuary. [*The soldiers of Titus burned Herod's temple and demolished Jerusalem.*]
And its end will come with a flood, even to the end there will be war; desolations are determined. [*In the Jewish War, 66-73, half a million Jews are said to have died, almost depopulating Palestine.*]

27. **And he** [*Jesus, the Messiah Prince*]
will make a firm covenant with many for one week [*Jesus "caused His covenant to prevail" with many of the Jews for the entire seventieth week, A.D. 27-34, even though Jewish leaders executed Him*],
but in the middle of the week [*Passover, A.D. 31*]
he will put a stop to sacrifice and grain offerings [*by His supreme Sacrifice, He abolished the significance of the temple sacrifices*],
and on the wing of abomination will come one who makes desolate [*here is Christ's prediction of the Roman "desolating sacrilege"**]
even until a complete destruction, one that is decreed, is poured out on the one who makes desolate [*Daniel 7:11 foretold complete destruction of both pagan and Christian Rome*].

With these insights freshly reviewed, we're ready for Daniel 8:13, 14.

13. **"For how long is the vision** [*that is, the vision that Gabriel was told to make Daniel understand*]
concerning the continual burnt offering [*Christ's continual tamid ministry as our High Priest in the heavenly sanctuary*],
the transgression that makes desolate [*the sinners who have opposed God's truth and people, especially pagan and Christian Rome, the "desolating sacrilege" which Jesus spoke about*]
and the giving of the sanctuary and host to be trampled under foot [*the obscuring of Christ's high-priestly ministry, portrayed as extending in a notable sense until 1844*]?"

14. **And he said to him, "For two thousand and three hundred evenings and mornings** [*2300 years*]

---

*The little horn of Daniel 8 represents Rome in two phases: (1) the pagan Roman Empire and (2) the Christian Roman Church (see pages 159-161). Necessarily the "transgression that makes desolate" (Daniel 8:13) also has a two-phase fulfillment: (1) the military attack by pagan Roman soldiers on Jerusalem in A.D. 70, leaving the temple totally destroyed, and (2) the long-continued spiritual teachings of Christian Rome, deflecting worshipers away from Christ's priesthood in the heavenly sanctuary to its own substitute priesthood. The phrase "the transgression that makes desolate" is paralleled by "upon the wing of abominations shall come one who makes desolate" (Daniel 9:27), "the abomination that makes desolate" (Daniel 11:31; 12:11), and "the desolating sacrilege" (Matthew 24:15). "Transgression," "abomination," or "sacrilege" is, in this case, an erroneous system of worship (see, e.g., 1 Kings 11:5-7; 2 Kings 23:13).

248

then [*in 1844, which was 2300 years after 457 B.C. when the seventy weeks began*]
the sanctuary [*in heaven, where Christ ministers*]
shall be restored to its rightful state [*cleansed and vindicated in the pre-advent Day of Atonement/Day of Judgment*]."

The chart on page 250 shows the parallel nature of Daniel's prophecies and provides a convenient review.

The judgment is now. The Bible has many more things to say about the Day of Atonement/Day of Judgment that is transpiring in heaven and about the current role Jesus is playing in our salvation. We'll have occasion to refer to them often in our expositions of Revelation in *God Cares, II*.

God cares. It was important to Him to tell us in advance when Jesus would fulfill the atonement on the cross (A.D. 31) and when He would commence the pre-advent Day of Atonement/Day of Judgment in heaven (1844). He wanted us to know, because these events are vital to the plan of salvation.

It is wonderful to know that soon the books will have been investigated and God will declare to the universe that His roster of saints has been made up, containing all the people who have been found clean from all their sins before the Lord. Leviticus 16:30.

Yet it is a solemn thought that the judgment has been in progress more than a century. It is in session now.

How important that we "afflict ourselves" as the Israelites did on the old Day of Atonement (Leviticus 23:27)—that is, that we "examine ourselves" to see whether we are holding on to the faith (2 Corinthians 13:5), and with earnest prayer and Bible study seek to know God's will for us and obey it.

"Fear [that is, reverence] God, and keep His commandments," says Ecclesiastes 12:13, 14, "for God will bring every deed into judgment, with every secret thing."

God longs to write His commandments, His law of love, on our hearts. Have we let Him? Are our thoughts victorious over immorality? Are our business practices above dishonesty? Are our social relations free from hypocrisy? Are we kind to our children? Do we honor our parents? Do we worship God sincerely and keep His Sabbath holy? Do we really help people who are in need? Do we forgive as we have been forgiven?

Do we love the Lord? Are we abiding in Him (John 15:1-11)? Or do we think more about TV entertainers than about our Lord and Saviour?

"I know the plans I have for you, says the Lord, plans for welfare and not for evil, to give you a future and a hope. Then you will call upon me and come and pray to me, and I will hear you. You will seek me and find me; when you seek me with all your heart." Jeremiah 29:11, 12.

Further Interesting Reading

In *Bible Readings for the Home:*
The chapter entitled "The Hour of God's Judgment."

PARALLELS IN DANIEL'S VISIONS—2

DANIEL 2	DANIEL 7	DANIEL 8	DANIEL 9
BABYLON *gold head*	**BABYLON** *lion*		
PERSIA* *silver chest*	**PERSIA*** *bear: one shoulder higher*	**PERSIA*** *ram: one horn higher*	**DECREE, 457 B.C.,** *to restore Jerusalem*
GREECE** *brass thighs*	**GREECE**** *leopard: with four heads*	**GREECE**** *goat: one horn becomes four*	**70 WEEKS** (457 B.C.-A.D. 34)
ROMAN EMPIRE *iron legs*	**ROMAN EMPIRE** *monster*	**ROMAN EMPIRE** *little horn from the west*	*baptism/anointing, A.D. 27* *crucifixion, A.D. 31* *new "Israel," A.D. 34*
			DESOLATING SACRILEGE *the destroyer prince destroys temple and Jerusalem A.D. 70*
EUROPE AS DIVIDED ROME *iron and clay feet and toes*	**EUROPE AS DIVIDED ROME** *ten horns on monster* A.D. 538		
extension of Roman iron from legs into feet symbolizes continuation in Europe of characteristic Roman concepts	**ROMAN CHURCH** *little horn on monster* *persecutes saints speaks vs. God*	**ROMAN CHURCH** *little horn* *tramples host and heavenly* <u>*tamid*</u>	**DESOLATING SACRILEGE** *the destroyer prince* *desolates saints and sanctuary*
	1798	*1844*	
	JUDGMENT SITS *Son of Man comes to Ancient of Days*	**SANCTUARY "RESTORED"** *Day of Atonement pre-advent Day of Judgment*	
NEW KINGDOM *stone becomes a mountain*	**NEW KINGDOM** *Son of Man gives dominion to saints.*		**DESOLATING SACRILEGE** *destroyed completely*

1260 DAYS (538-1798) — with ★ at A.D. 538 and ★ at 1798

2300 DAYS (457 B.C.-A.D. 1844) — with ★ at Persia/ram and ★ at 1844

*For the early years after Cyrus conquered Babylon, "Persia" may be considered an abbreviation for "Medo-Persian Empire."

**"Greece" is an abbreviation for Alexander's "Greco-Macedonian Empire" and for the group of "Hellenistic," or "Macedonian," kingdoms that developed out of it. Says, M. Cary, A History of the Greek World, p. 10: "Alexander conquered for Greece rather than for Macedon. Hellenistic history is therefore essentially an extension of Greek history, . . . "

Your Questions Answered

1. A number of Bible students start the seventy weeks in 444 B.C. rather than in 457 B.C. as advocated on pages 196, 209. Are there good reasons for preferring one date above another?

The dates 457 B.C. and 444 B.C.* represent two separate authorizations for the restoration of Jerusalem issued by the Persian emperor Artaxerxes (465-423 B.C.). The first authorization, which was very broad in scope, was issued in the seventh year of his reign, 457 B.C. The second, a relatively limited one, was issued in his twentieth year, 444 B.C. (see Ezra 7 and Nehemiah 2).

It will aid us materially in settling on the better of these two dates if we realize to begin with that Artaxerxes was in some respects a fickle man. For example, when a quick-witted friend saved him once from an attack by an angry lion, he "rewarded" his friend by banishing him![14] On another occasion his representative and brother-in-law, Megabyzus, solemnly assured an Egyptian rebel named Inarus that if Inarus surrendered, his life would be spared. But a few years later, Artaxerxes executed Inarus anyway.[15]

Persian decrees were supposed to be irreversible (see Daniel 6:8 and Esther 8:8). The changeableness and unpredictability of Artaxerxes I keenly embarrassed Megabyzus and led him and many of his fellow Persians into an open revolt against Artaxerxes that came near to wrecking the empire.

The fact that Artaxerxes had to issue a *second* authorization for the restoration of Jerusalem, when, under Persian law, one alone should have been enough, was a consequence both of his fickleness and of the rebellion of Megabyzus. Further, it is important to our study to know that Megabyzus, at the time of his large-scale rebellion, was serving as governor of Beyond the River—the province that included Syria and Palestine and in which Jerusalem was located.

Now, the books of Ezra and Nehemiah reveal that the Jews experienced a great deal of trouble in the course of rebuilding their temple and of restoring Jerusalem. Ezra 4:4-6, 24 tells about various difficulties the Jews encountered during the reigns of Cyrus (539-530 B.C.), Darius (522-486), and Ahasuerus (486-465). Ezra 4:7-23 reports, somewhat out of order, how next a group of Samaritans complained to Artaxerxes (465-423) about the rebuilding of Jerusalem and how, in response, fickle Artaxerxes reversed his decree of 457 B.C. and ordered that the rebuilding be suspended.

This complaint of the Samaritans was addressed directly to King Artaxerxes by local officials, and the king's reply was, in turn, addressed directly to the local officials (see Ezra 4:7, 8, 17). Both the local officials and the king in this

---

*Bible commentators have sometimes dated these two authorizations in 458 and 445 respectively. The discovery of dated papyri from a Jewish garrison town on the island of Elephantine in the river Nile, and especially of a double-dated papyrus known as "Kraeling 6," has established the accuracy of 457 and 444 (see Horn and Wood, *The Chronology of Ezra 7*).

instance avoided the ordinary custom of communicating with each other through the governor of the province. But their procedure in this case is not hard to understand if the governor, Megabyzus, was in open revolt against the king at the time!

Let us project a survey of the period onto our mental screens.

In 538 or 537 Cyrus issued a decree for rebuilding the temple and for resettlement of Jews in Palestine. Ezra 1.

Around 520 a governor of Beyond the River named Tattenai (whose name has been found on a cuneiform tablet) investigated progress at the temple, which had been going on by then for some sixteen years, and wrote to Darius asking him to check the archives to see if the Jews had indeed received authority from Cyrus to rebuild the temple. Ezra 3:3-17.

Around 519 Darius graciously issued a new decree, confirming the earlier one of Cyrus. Ezra 4:1-12. No mention was made by Cyrus, Darius, or Tattenai of rebuilding the city itself; only of rebuilding the temple.

In 457 Artaxerxes I issued the third decree, this one authorizing the restoration of Jerusalem to capital-city status. That is, he authorized the appointment of magistrates and judges and the application of Jewish and Persian law to local government. Ezra 7:12-26. His decree implied, of course, the construction of buildings to house the government officials and their offices and courts and also the construction of city walls to protect the new officials, offices, and courts, and the construction of forts to house and headquarter the soldiers who would be needed to enforce the decisions of the magistrates and the verdicts of the judges. Without such buildings, walls, and forts, the appointment of magistrates and judges would have been meaningless.

Ezra traveled to Palestine at once and led the people into the long, long work of restoring the ancient city. Ezra 7:1-10.

It was apparently about a decade later, perhaps around 448 B.C., that Megabyzus, as governor of Beyond the River, sprang the very serious revolt that we referred to earlier. The Samaritans took advantage of the new situation to make Artaxerxes believe that the Jews were fortifying their city so that they, too, could rebel. In the touchy context of the times, *the changeable Artaxerxes replied directly to the Samaritans that they should see to it that the Jews stopped their rebuilding efforts at once.* Ezra 4:7-23. The Samaritans were only too happy to oblige the king, and in their zeal went beyond his orders. They did not merely stop the work; they *broke down some of the walls and burned the wooden city gates and temple doors.*

Meanwhile, back at Susa, one of the capital cities of the Persian Empire (and Daniel's apparent location during the vision of Daniel 8 more than a century earlier), Nehemiah was as worried as any other Jew. Nehemiah was the king's "cupbearer." Nehemiah 1:11. He was certainly aware of the serious revolt in Palestine. He probably also knew about the king's order requiring the rebuilding of the city to be stopped. He feared the worst.

Nehemiah had a brother (apparently a blood brother, according to Nehemiah 7:2) who was living in Palestine. If only Hanani would come back to Persia, Nehemiah could find out from him what was really going on there.

Then one day, Hanani, Nehemiah's brother, did appear in Susa. Nehemiah eagerly questioned him about conditions in Jerusalem. What Hanani told him filled him with dismay.

Said Hanani, "The survivors there in the province who escaped exile are in great trouble and shame; the wall of Jerusalem is broken down, and its gates are destroyed by fire." Nehemiah 1:3.

"When I heard these words," says Nehemiah, "I sat down and wept, and mourned for days." Nehemiah 1:4.

Nehemiah was so taken back and disheartened by the news that his brother had brought him that he couldn't throw off his gloom for some three or four months (compare Nehemiah 1:1 with 2:1). King Artaxerxes was away at the time on business in other parts of the empire. When at last he returned, Nehemiah, the king's cupbearer, still could not compose himself sufficiently to appear happy in his presence.

Artaxerxes, providentially in a good mood, asked him what his trouble was. When Nehemiah explained, the king at once issued a series of valuable executive memos and told Nehemiah to take them west with him to the new governor of Beyond the River, Sanballat by name, and personally to supervise the repair of the walls of Jerusalem at state expense.

Some commentators have supposed that Nehemiah was plunged into despair at news from his brother Hanani that virtually the entire city, except for the recently rebuilt temple, was still lying on the ground as it had been left by Nebuchadnezzar in 586 B.C. 142 years earlier. This is hard to believe. As a boy and as a young man Nehemiah had known all about the destruction under Nebuchadnezzar. News from his brother in 444 B.C. stating that "the walls of Jerusalem were broken down" could scarcely have surprised Nehemiah *unless he had known about a substantial rebuilding of the city and its walls in the meantime.*

Those Bible students who say that it was not until 444 that the rebuilding of the walls of Jerusalem was first authorized, overlook or do not know about many of the data that we have discussed here. The decree of 457, which authorized the restoration of Jerusalem to capital-city status, with the inescapable restoration of the defensive and enforcing mechanisms essential to supporting such a status, qualifies as the starting point for the 490 years much better than 444 does.

2. How is it that 490 years from 457 B.C. extend to A.D. 34 rather than to A.D. 33? If your pocket calculator says that the 490 years from 457 B.C. extend to A.D. 33 instead of to A.D. 34, there are two reasons.

1. Your calculator doesn't know that the 490 years began in the autumn of 457 B.C. and so have to extend to at least the autumn 490 years later.

2. Your calculator is programmed to deal with *cardinal* numbers (like "one," "two," "three," etc.) and not with *ordinal* numbers (like "first," "second," "third," etc.). The years B.C. and A.D. are *ordinal* numbers. They help us to locate events that took place within the "first" year, "second" year, "third" year, etc., before or after the birth of Christ.

In school we are taught to add and subtract cardinal numbers almost exclusively, because our contemporary culture uses cardinal numbers almost exclusively. In ancient times greater use was made of ordinal numbers.

Now, between the cardinal numbers +1 and −1 there is a zero. Pocket calculators are programmed—and children in school are taught—to assume this zero. But between "the first year after" the birth of Jesus and "the first year before" the birth of Jesus, there was no twelve-month-long zero year. Between the first year before *you* were born and the first year after you were born there was no such zero year either!

This chart will help you calculate ten years from B.C. 7 to A.D. 4. Analagous calculations will take you successfully from B.C. 457 to A.D. 34.

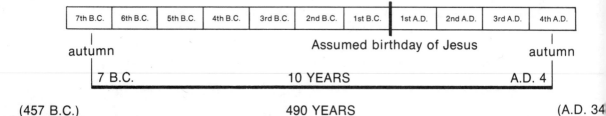

3. **Why is the R.S.V. punctuation for the "seven weeks and sixty-two weeks" different from that in some other versions?** Some versions, including the R.S.V. and The New English Bible, make a division between the seven weeks and the sixty-two weeks. The R.S.V. reads as follows: **"To the coming of an anointed one, a prince, there shall be seven weeks. Then for sixty-two weeks it shall be built again. . . . And after the sixty-two weeks, an anointed one shall be cut off."** The inference is that there are *two* anointed persons, one of them coming after seven weeks and the other, after an additional sixty-two.

The R.S.V. translation differs sharply from the N.A.S.B. version used in our study on pages 216, 217, which links the seven weeks and the sixty-two weeks together. Versions that agree with the N.A.S.B. include the K.J.V., the American Standard Version, the New International Version, the Jerusalem Bible, the Modern Language Bible, and the version of Monsignor Knox.

It must be remembered that, like the rest of the Old Testament autographs,* the original manuscript which Daniel prepared contained no punctuation. At some unknown early period, scribes introduced punctuation into the

*An "autograph" is the original handwritten material. A "manuscript" can be a later handwritten copy, either of the autograph or of another manuscript.

translation known as the Septuagint and the one by Theodotian. The famous Latin Vulgate version made around A.D. 400 also used punctuation. Later, between 600 and 1400, punctuation was introduced into Hebrew manuscripts by Jewish scribes called Masoretes.[16]

The translators of the N.A.S.B., K.J.V., American Standard Version, and so on, chose to follow the early punctuation used by Theodotian, the Septuagint, and the Latin Vulgate. The R.S.V. and The New English Bible translators elected to follow the later Masoretic punctuation.

The punctuation mark that causes the difference is known as an *athnach*. It looks like this: ˆ . In many cases it has the force of an English colon or semicolon. Here is a rather literal translation of the pertinent portion of Daniel 9:25 showing the location of the Masoretic *athnach* but omitting all other punctuation:

> **. . . to the coming of messiah prince there shall be seven weeks ˆ sixty-two weeks it shall be restored and built with squares and moat but in a troubled time.**

Now, although the *athnach* often has the force of an English comma or semicolon, it sometimes doesn't have any more value than a comma, and sometimes it seems to have no value at all. Here are three examples[17] from the book of Daniel. In the first the *athnach* seems to be a comma, but in the second and third examples it has little if any value.

> **Daniel became distinguished above all the other presidents and satraps ˆbecause an excellent spirit was in him.** Daniel 6:3.
>
> **These men came by agreement and found Daniel ˆmaking petition and supplication.** Daniel 6:11.
>
> **I, Daniel, perceived in the books ˆ the number of years.** Daniel 9:2.

Inasmuch as the Masoretic punctuation was supplied more than a thousand years after Daniel was written, and inasmuch as the *athnach*, even when present, does not always signify an important pause, we are fully justified in accepting the translations in the N.A.S.B., K.J.V., Jerusalem Bible, and so on, in preference to the translation in the R.S.V.

4. Where are the chiasms in Daniel 9:24-27? A "chiasm" (KIE-asm) is a sophisticated literary device in which two pairs of parallel lines are arranged in the order *Y Z, Z′ Y′*. To aid the eye, the lines can be printed in an hourglass or "X" configuration. It is from the Greek letter X, often pronounced "KIE," that the chiasm got its name. To prepare for Daniel 9:24-27, here is a chiasm from another part of Daniel, Daniel 12:10:

> *Y*   **Many shall purify themselves, and make themselves white, and be refined;**
> *Z*   **but the wicked shall do wickedly;**

Z'   and none of the wicked shall understand;
Y'   But those who are wise shall understand.

The initial two lines of this chiasm speak Y about the pure and Z about the wicked. In the second pair of lines, the order is *reversed*. The wicked Z' are mentioned first, and then Y' the wise. We are not expressly informed that the wise people of the last line are the same as the pure people of the first line, but an English reader guesses at the identification (the wise equal the pure) intuitively. The Hebrew reader in ancient times knew without doubt that the wise were the same as the pure, because he was familiar with the Y Z, Z' Y' sequence of chiasms. As soon as he noticed the *reversal* in the middle lines, he leaped to the correct conclusion.

There is a jewel of a chiasm in the first section of Daniel 9:27. Quoting from the N.A.S.B. we get

Y   He [Messiah] will make a firm covenant with the many
Z   for one week, but
Z'   in the middle of the week
Y'   He will put a stop to sacrifice and grain offering.

The Y Y' lines speak of the Messiah's activities, while the Z Z' lines talk about a week and the middle of a week. Again, by the laws of the chiasm, we know there is a definite relationship between the fourth line and the first. In this case we know that the Messiah puts a stop to the sacrifices in connection with His success with the covenant. Through His death as the ultimate Sacrifice, He renders all animal and cereal sacrifices meaningless.

Daniel 9:26, 27 presents a fine, complex chiasm. Simplified a bit it looks like this:

Y   The Messiah will be cut off with no one to help.
Z   The sanctuary will be terminated [destroyed]
     by the desolater prince.
Z'   The sacrifices will be terminated [stopped]
     by the Messiah.
Y'   The desolater prince will be destroyed.

In the Z Z' lines reference is made to the sanctuary and its sacrifices. In the Y Y' lines, the two princes are referred to, and the implication is that the desolater prince will be destroyed because he first of all cut off the Messiah.

Look more closely, and you will find a wordplay. The verb **"destroy"** or a snyonym ("cut off," "stop") is found in each line. And references to the princes bounce back and forth—Messiah, desolater, Messiah, desolater—like a ball in a game of tennis.

256

Analysis of these chiasms helps confirm our confidence in the literary analysis of Daniel 9:24-27, which we undertook on pages 213-218.

5. Why cannot astronomers date the crucifixion? Before we look at some of the reasons why astronomers cannot date the crucifixion, we need to know a few things about Passover, and we need to think about the moon.

The observance of Passover. In Exodus 12 Moses stipulated that Passover lambs should be killed on the fourteenth day of the first month of the Jewish religious year; that is, on Nisan 14, in the spring. Passover commemorated the miraculous deliverance of the Israelites from Egypt at the time of the Exodus. For the celebration in Christ's day, each large family, or group of small families, had a lamb slain at the temple during the afternoon of the fourteenth and then roasted it at home. After dark that night they ate the lamb along with bitter herbs and unleavened bread.

Because Jewish days began at sunset, the afternoon on which the Passover lamb was slain came near the end of Nisan 14; and the evening, when the lamb was eaten, was actually the beginning of Nisan 15.

Moses stipulated in Leviticus 23:6 that no leavened bread should be eaten for a whole week. Thus Nisan 15 was known as the First Day of Unleavened Bread. (In time the whole period from the slaying of the lamb to the last day of Unleavened Bread came to be known loosely as "Passover" and "The Feast of Unleavened Bread.") Whatever day of the week the *First* Day of Unleavened Bread fell on was regarded as a sabbath, the annual Passover sabbath (see Leviticus 23:7 and the *Jewish Encyclopedia*).

On the day following the First Day of Unleavened Bread—that is, on the day following Passover sabbath—Moses said (in Leviticus 23:9-15) that a sheaf of new, ripened grain should be waved before the Lord by a priest in the temple. Waving this sheaf of "first fruits" was a gesture of praise to God for the entire crop. It marked the moment when the barley harvest could begin. Paul used it as a symbol of Christ's resurrection as the "first fruits of those who have fallen asleep." 1 Corinthians 15:20.

SPECIAL DAYS OF CRUCIFIXION WEEK

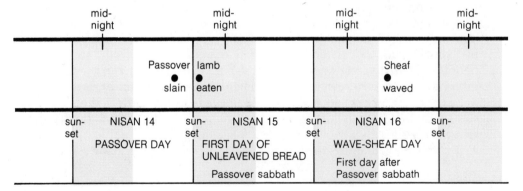

A few observations about the moon. To twentieth-century urban dwellers, the celebrated orb of night is a pleasant but largely dispensable luxury. If we happen to notice it, surging up from the eastern horizon, orange and strangely oversize at the time of full moon; or if we happen to notice it in the west, a fragile crescent suspended in the ruddy glow of sunset, we may be enchanted for a moment, but that is all.

We don't feel we need the moon. We have electric lights to see by at night; we have printed calendars to tell the date by, and quartz-crystal digital watches to tell the time by.

Go back a couple of centuries, however, and the moon provided virtually all the night light that most people could afford. Go back two thousand years, and most calendars were conscientiously regulated by the appearance of the moon.

The word "month" comes from the word "moon." Originally a month was the twenty-nine or thirty days between the first appearance of a crescent moon at sunset and the first appearance of the next crescent moon.

The twenty-nine or thirty days! Twelve months of twenty-nine or thirty days each equal only about 354 days, which is eleven or twelve days short of the 365¼ days in the solar year. Because of the shortness of the so-called "lunar year," based on the moon alone, it was necessary in ancient times to insert a thirteenth month every second or third year. The result was a lunisolar calendar with some years about 354 days long and others about 383 days long.

Although the process seems awkward to us, the people then were used to it. By at least the fourth century B.C. Babylonian astronomers had developed a "nineteen-year cycle" that showed in advance just when to insert the extra months (seven times in the nineteen years) in order to keep the months more or less in step with the seasons and thus achieve optimum synchronization with the sun. After the Romans forbade the Jews to live in Jerusalem (about A.D. 135), Jewish observations from Jerusalem became impossible, and the Jews developed a cycle similar but not identical to the Babylonian one.

Have you noticed that when the moon is full it rises in the east at almost the very time when the sun sets in the west? Because the full moon is on the *opposite* side of the earth as compared to the sun, it is said to be in "opposition" to the sun.

The converse of a full moon is a "new moon." Whereas a full moon is in opposition to the sun, a new moon, which is located on the *same* side of the earth as the sun, is described as being in "conjunction" with the sun. Many people think that a crescent moon is the same as a new moon, but it isn't. A full moon is all light and a new moon has *no* light (except for a trace of earthshine). Because a new moon is located on the same side of the earth as the sun, the sun's light falls entirely on the side we cannot see and a new moon is to us virtually *invisible*.

But the moon is always restlessly changing its relationship to the sun and to

258

the earth. So it comes about that in several hours after new moon—or within a day, or two days, or even up to nearly four days (see page 261)—the moon so shifts its position in the sky that we are able to see a slender crescent of it hanging once again above the western horizon soon after sunset.

Among the Jews, Passover was timed to occur at or near a full moon at the beginning of the barley harvest; that is, soon after the spring equinox. It is known from the Gospels that Jesus died on a Passover (Nisan 14) that fell on a *Friday* in the early years of the procuratorship of Pontius Pilate. Astronomers are assumed to have unlimited capacity to calculate the motions of the heavenly bodies. To some Bible students,[18] therefore, it appears a simple matter to ask astronomers to give us the dates for the first full moon after the spring equinox in the years 29-33 and then to conclude that whichever full moon falls on a Friday must be the Passover of the crucifixion.

Of course, astronomers *can* readily supply all the new moons we need, and, for that matter, all the full moons we may desire as well. Indeed, subtle and complicated though the necessary calculations are, in 1973 Herman H. Goldstine taught an IBM 360 Model 91 computer to figure out all the new moons and all the full moons between 1001 B.C. and A.D. 1651! And the computer calculated them—all 65,600 of them—in only 132 seconds.[19]

But how valuable are these staggering calculations for our purposes? They do help a little; but the problem is that we have to take into account several other vital factors, each of which, unfortunately, is imponderable and unknowable in the present state of astronomy and archaeology.

a. **The law of the barley harvest.** If the priests were required to wave a sheaf of fresh-cut barley (the first grain to ripen in Palestine) in the temple the day after Passover sabbath as a signal for the barley harvest to commence, the weather had to have been warm enough for a few weeks prior to Passover in order for the barley to be ripe.

The climate in Jerusalem can be bone-chilling cold as late as the end of March. I know this from experience. Because the twelve-month lunar year was so short compared to the 365¼ day solar year, Passover was frequently in danger of coming too early for the barley. Thus a thirteenth month often had to be inserted in March in order to lengthen the old year and to postpone the Passover and the day of Wave Sheaf. With this extra month inserted, Passover might come close to the *second* full moon after the equinox rather than to the first one. At our great distance from the time of Christ, no astronomer or archaeologist knows which years contained this thirteenth month.

b. **The Babylonian or the barley-harvest cycle?** We mentioned a moment ago that the Babylonians had a nineteen-year cycle under which the thirteen-month years were all arranged in advance. Archaeologists have learned what this cycle was and how to relate it to the Julian-Gregorian calendar that we use today. If we knew for certain that the Jews in Jerusalem followed the Babylonian cycle in the time of Jesus, we could easily transfer the Babylonian data to

Jerusalem and know without doubt which years contained the extra month. But we do not know that Jerusalem Jews were following the Babylonian cycle at the time, and there is evidence that they were not.[20] The Babylonian cycle would have placed Passover in some years *a month too early* for the barley harvest.

The Interpreter's Bible, in its comment on Matthew 26:17, is commendably cautious when it says that A.D. 30 may be considered the date of the crucifixion *"if"* the Palestinian Jews were, at the time, following the Babylonian cycle—which, quite evidently, they were not. On the contrary, A.D. 31 is as possible as A.D. 30 if atmospheric and astronomical conditions combined to place Nisan 1 that year at a maximum interval after the new moon.

c. **Visibility of the crescent.** According to ancient custom, before a crescent moon could be counted as marking the commencement of a month, it had actually to be seen and reported to a committee of priests. Official observers stood on vantage points at sunset on the 29th of a month and scanned the western sky eagerly. The earliest crescent often cannot be seen until the sun has set long enough for the dusk to be somewhat advanced, and often it is so close to the horizon by then that it drops out of sight after being visible to a trained eye for only a few minutes.

If there were a low-lying cloud, if merely a denser-than-average haze polluted the horizon at Jerusalem, the anticipated crescent would not be observed. The current month would be continued an additional day, making it thirty days long. And the new month would commence on the following night, even if the crescent were still obscured. (Remember that Jewish days and, hence, Jewish months and years, began at sunset.)

Nisan 14 commenced at sunset on the fourteenth night, counted "inclusively," after the official announcement of the crescent.

Even if modern astronomers were able to tell us the precise evenings when the new spring crescents were most likely to have been seen at Jerusalem in A.D. 30 to 33, they still could not tell us for sure that they were actually seen on those nights, because they have no way of knowing what atmospheric conditions prevailed there at the time. Consequently, even if they could give us the true nights when the crescent moon should have been seen, they still could not tell us whether that night was actually counted as Nisan 1 or as the 30th of the preceding month. And this weakness is crucial, because in order to locate the Friday of the crucifixion, which was a Nisan 14, the 1st of Nisan must of course be known precisely.

We are looking for a Passover—that is, for a Nisan 14—that occurred on a Friday sometime in the years 30 to 33; and we are expecting, from the "midst of the week" prediction, to find it in A.D. 31. The point we are making is that it is impossible to prove from astronomy which of these years actually had a Nisan 14 Friday.

Was Friday, April 7, A.D. 30, the Passover Day of Christ's crucifixion, as many commentators have assumed? It may have been, *if* the crescent appeared after sunset on Friday, March 24, fourteen nights earlier. But if the crescent was obscured on March 24 and the month had to begin a day late, then Nisan 14, Passover Day, did not come on Friday, April 7 but on Saturday, April 8—and the year A.D. 30 is disqualified. Or, perhaps in this particular year the weather was cold, the barley was slow, and Nisan was required to commence on the night of the new crescent a month later; then Nisan 14 fell on a Sunday or Monday, and, once more, A.D. 30 is disqualified.

d. **The interval between new moon and the crescent.** We mentioned on page 259 that the interval between new moon and the crescent can be as short as a few hours or as long as almost four days. Here is one of the most perplexing of problems. Some commentators who presume to tell us the exact Friday on which the crucifixion fell assume that the crescent always appeared either on the same day as new moon or on the following day. They think they can tell the evening of the first crescent just by glancing at Goldstine's list of new moons. They do not realize the *variability* of the interval between new moon (conjunction) and the visible crescent.

Achilles Tatianus in the sixth century A.D. observed that the crescent moon appears up to "three or four days after [the] birth [of the moon] . . . and not at the same time she was born."[21]

Joannes Hevelius in the seventeenth century warned that "the first rising of the moon does not generally happen on the first day after conjunction, but at length on the second, often also on the third and fourth."[22]

And an ancient astronomer named Geminus has been quoted as saying "that when the moon is in *perigee,* and her motion quickest, she does not *usually* appear until the second day, nor in *apogee,* when slowest, until the fourth. The exception in the former case intimating that she might sometimes be seen on the first day."[23]

Fully in harmony with these statements, there is reason to believe that in the year A.D. 30 the crescent may not have appeared on March 24 (see above), even if the weather had been fine, for the interval between the new moon of March 22 and its subsequent crescent may well have been longer than two days; and, if so, Nisan 14 would not have occurred on a Friday. But a Nisan that starts as late as March 25 is still quite early for the barley harvest; so it is likely that it started twenty-nine or thirty days later, in April, making a Friday Nisan in A.D. 30 quite impossible.

e. **Sectarian differences.** A fifth matter for concern in dating the crucifixion by the moon is evidence in the Gospels that in the time of Jesus the Jews themselves, even in Jerusalem, were not agreed on how to calculate the Passover! The priests may even have used calculations partly independent of the moon!

Although on the week Christ died the official slaying of Passover lambs took place on Friday afternoon and the feast on Friday night, Jesus and His disciples

261

prepared their Passover lamb on Thursday afternoon and ate it on Thursday night. And the account in the Gospels leaves the impression that what Jesus and the disciples did many other people were doing, for it appears to have occasioned no surprise.

There is, moreover, evidence from the Dead Sea Scrolls[24] that the Essene community taught that Passover should always be celebrated on a Wednesday, without regard either to the moon or to Nisan 14!

It is possible, therefore, that Passover was observed in Palestine by different groups on *Tuesday, Thursday, and Friday nights* in the year when Jesus died! If the Jews could not agree on how to calculate Passover in terms of the moon, truly we do not have any positive way of determining the date of Christ's death by asking astronomers to pick out a Friday, Nisan 14.

Professional astronomers warn us that they are indeed incompetent to date the crucifixion. For example, D. H. Sadler, superintendent of the *Nautical Almanac* office in the Royal Greenwich Observatory in England, states that "purely local conditions can invalidate even the most careful work in respect of a particular observation of the lunar crescent."[25]

Nonastronomers are properly impressed by the ability of astronomers to predict eclipses. But in contrast to the reliability of eclipse calculations, Professor O. Neugebauer, expert on ancient astronomy at Brown University, says that "exactly the opposite, however, is the case in the problem of first visibility [of the crescent moon]. All modern tables have to make arbitrary assumptions as to the visibility conditions in antiquity in general or in specific localities. These assumptions are highly arbitrary, and even for modern times, extremely unreliable. Since the phenomenon of first visibility is connected with sunset, all such tables involve inaccuracies of one full day."[26]

Specifically in reference to the subject of our present quest, G. M. Clemence of the U.S. Naval Observatory wrote that "the interval from new moon to the appearance of the crescent cannot be calculated from theory alone. Criteria must be established empirically for each individual geographical locality. Different writers have not always agreed completely on these criteria; and, moreover, some allowance presumably must be made for variations due to local practices and circumstances at the time of each observation. . . . *The dates of Nisan 14 in the years of the first century of the Christian era cannot possibly be determined by any astronomical calculation; they can be fixed, if by any means at all, only by the study and interpretation of contemporary records.*"[27]

So, when all is said that can be said by astronomy, we are best off to accept the biblical statement that Jesus would "cause sacrifice and offering to cease" "in the midst of the week."

There is no reason *not* to take A.D. 31 as the year of the crucifixion.

6. Was a Passover Friday possible at all in A.D. 31? Mindful of every caution in the previous answer, curious readers may still hanker to know whether astronomy can in *any* way discern a Friday crucifixion in A.D. 31.

The answer is that, yes, a Friday crucifixion in A.D. 31 is entirely "possible" according to astronomical calculations (for whatever they may be worth), granted a few unprovable yet reasonable assumptions.

We assume to begin with that the March 12 new moon (conjunction) was too early for the barley-harvest requirement. (Dated Jewish papyri found at Elephantine do not allow Nisan to begin as early as March 14, and neither did the Babylonian cycle.) So, with March 12 regarded as too early, the new moon prior to Nisan 1 in the year 31 becomes the one listed as number 12755 on page 86 of Goldstine's computer printout, for Tuesday afternoon, April 10. Goldstine's time for the new moon is 2:45 p.m. in Babylon. In Jerusalem, some 850 kilometers or 525 miles to the west, the new moon occurred thirty-seven minutes earlier, local time.

If the interval between this April 10 new moon and the first visibility of the crescent moon at Jerusalem was a very long 3.19 days, as it could have been, or if it was shorter but was obscured the first night, the crescent was observed at sunset on Friday, April 13.

With the observation of the crescent, the month of Nisan commenced at once and Nisan 1 should be dated in our Julian-Gregorian calendar as the Saturday, April 14, which followed at midnight. The fourteenth night thereafter, counting the evening of the crescent (inclusive reckoning), brought Jerusalem to the commencement of Nisan 14 at sunset on April 26, a Thursday. Thus April 27, the Passover day on which Jesus died, was a Friday—Friday, Nisan 14, A.D. 31.

A diagram may help to make this statement clearer.

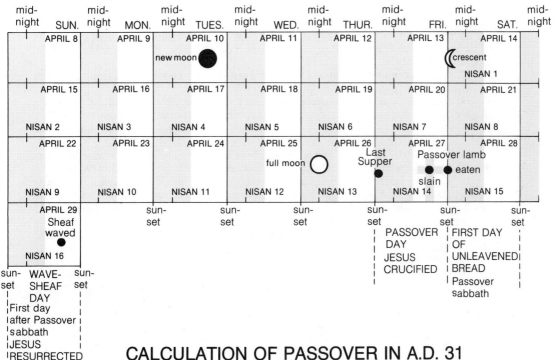

CALCULATION OF PASSOVER IN A.D. 31

References

1. Porteous, *Daniel,* p. 134.

2. Gerhard F. Hasel, "The Seventy Weeks of Daniel 9:24-27," *Ministry,* May 1976, insert. Hasel claims to know only two commentators who have suggested any other interpretation.

3. Jacques Doukhan, "The Seventy Weeks of Daniel 9: An Exegetical Study," *Andrews University Seminary Studies* 17 (1979):1-22.

4. *Ibid.* This article provides an excellent analysis of the literary structure of Daniel 9:24-27.

5. Hippolytus, *Commentary on Daniel,* frag. 2.39, 40; ANF, 5:184.

6. Harold W. Hoehner, *Chronological Aspects of the Life of Christ* (Grand Rapids, Mich.: Zondervan Publishing House, 1975), pp. 95-98.

7. G. B. Caird, "Chronology of the N.T., The," *The Interpreter's Dictionary of the Bible.*

8. Martin Hengel, *Crucifixion in the Ancient World, and the Folly of the Message of the Cross* (Philadelphia: Fortress Press, 1977); H. Haas, "Anthropological Observations on the Skeletal Remains from Giv'at ha'Mivtar," *Israel Exploration Journal* 20 (1970):38, 39; Anthony F. Sava, M.D., "The Wounds of Christ," *The Catholic Biblical Quarterly* 16 (1954):438-443.

9. Young, *Daniel,* p. 209.

10. See, e.g., W. R. Thompson, "Chronology of the New Testament," *The Zondervan Pictorial Encyclopedia of the Bible,* which recommends A.D. 33 or 34 for the conversion of Paul, and *The Westminster Dictionary of the Bible,* rev. ed., art. "Paul," which suggests A.D. 35. The stoning of Stephen occurred at some point prior to Paul's conversion.

11. See Froom, *Prophetic Faith,* 2:196.

12. See *ibid.,* 1:750.

13. Corrie ten Boom with John and Elizabeth Sherrill, *The Hiding Place* (Washington Depot, Conn.: Chosen Books, 1971), chap. 15.

14. A. T. Olmstead, *History of the Persian Empire* (Chicago: University of Chicago Press, 1948), p. 344.

15. *Ibid.,* pp. 308, 312.

16. For a survey of the work of the Masoretes (sometimes spelled, "Massoretes") see F. F. Bruce, *The Books and the Parchments,* 3d rev. ed. (London: Pickering & Inglis, 1963), pp. 40-42, 117-124.

17. These examples are from Desmond Ford, *Daniel* (Nashville, Tenn.: Southern Publishing Association, 1978), p. 229.

18. See, e.g., Caird, "Chronology." Roger Rusk, "The Day He Died," *Christianity Today,* March 1974, pp. 720-722, appeals to astronomy for a Thursday full moon in A.D. 30.

19. Herman H. Goldstine, *New and Full Moons, 1001 B.C. to A.D. 1651* (Philadelphia: American Philosophical Society, 1973).

20. Siegfried H. Horn and Lynn H. Wood, *The Chronology of Ezra 7,* rev. ed. (Washington, D.C.: Review and Herald Publishing Association), 1970, pp. 47n, 83, 119, 156.

21. Achilles Tatianus, "Isagogue," *Uranologion,* 141, in Grace Amadon, "Ancient Jewish Calendation," *Journal of Biblical Literature* 61 (1942):260. (The Amadon article must be read with care, as it combines commendable research with some insupportable speculation.)

22. Joannes Hevelius, *Selenographia* (Gedani, 1647), p. 274, in Amadon, "Ancient Jewish Calendation," p. 260.

23. In William Hales, *New Analysis of Chronology* (London, 1830), 1:67.

24. The evidence is summarized briefly in Earle Hilgert, "The Jubilees Calendar and the Origin of Sunday Observance," *Andrews University Seminary Studies* 1 (1963):44-51.

25. D. H. Sadler to Francis D. Nichol, January 24, 1956, in *Seventh-day Adventist Bible Commentary,* ed. Francis D. Nichol, 7 vols. (Washington, D.C.: Review and Herald Publishing Association, 1953-1957), 5:263.

26. O. Neugebauer to Francis D. Nichol, January 19, 1956, in *Seventh-day Adventist Bible Commentary,* ed. Francis D. Nichol, 7 vols. (Washington, D.C.: Review and Herald Publishing Association, 1953-1957), 5:263, 264.

27. G. M. Clemence to Francis D. Nichol, January 24, 1956, in *Seventh-day Adventist Bible Commentary,* ed. Francis D. Nichol, 7 vols. (Washington, D.C.: Review and Herald Publishing Association, 1953-1957), 5:262. Emphasis supplied.

Daniel 10
God's Angels Care for Us

Introduction

If you think that Daniel has already taught us so much that there is little left to learn, you're in for a surprise.

Chapters 10, 11, and 12 form a new unit. Chapter 10 is the introduction, and it offers one of the most fascinating behind-the-scenes revelations of all time.

Daniel and his attendants were walking beside the river Tigris (or Hiddekel, K.J.V.), which at one point flowed only about 55 kilometers (35 miles) from Babylon. The time was spring in the **"third year of King Cyrus,"** probably 535 B.C.* Seventy years had passed since Daniel had been compelled to accompany Nebuchadnezzar's army on its march from Jerusalem to Babylon. He had been about seventeen then. He was nearing ninety now.

God had been good. He had cared for Daniel in every crisis, answering his prayers, keeping him physically fit (Daniel 10:8), and using him to bless his generation.

But now a crisis had developed again. Work on the Jerusalem temple, so recently launched in response to Cyrus's authorization, had run into stiff opposition from surrounding tribesmen. Ezra 4:5 indicates that hos-

*Assuming that Daniel reckoned the year according to the Jewish civil calendar, beginning it in the autumn.

tile Samaritans had even "hired counselors" against the Jews, probably meaning that they had bribed government officials to influence King Cyrus to rescind his decree. With only the altar completed so far, further restoration of God's only temple in the entire world was imperiled. Characteristically, Daniel had taken to his knees.

What a praying person he was!

Daniel had prayed, instead of complaining, when threatened with execution in Daniel 2. He had given thanks three times a day when faced with hungry lions. While studying Jeremiah's seventy-year prophecy, he had confessed his sins and those of his people. Now we find him praying again.

Very much in earnest, this time he fasted for **"three weeks,"** from the fourth to the twenty-fourth of the **"first month"** of the year (see Daniel 10:2-4). His fast thus occupied most of Nisan and included the seven days of unleavened bread which followed Passover (Nisan 14). Passover had reminded him of God's mighty power in delivering Israel from Egypt nearly a thousand years before. So Daniel found a secluded place on the Tigris where he could beseech God to reveal His mighty power on Israel's behalf again. For three weeks he ate only plain things, avoiding rich foods and desserts, so his mind could be as clear as possible for communing with Heaven.

Jesus Himself appeared to Daniel by the Tigris to reassure him that Jerusalem would be rebuilt.

God answered Daniel's prayers as wonderfully when he was old as when he was young. In fact, more so. In Daniel 2 He answered by replaying Nebuchadnezzar's image dream. In Daniel 6 He sent an angel to tame the lions. In Daniel 9 He sent His highest created angel, Gabriel. In Daniel 10 He *sent His Son*.

A glorious vision of Jesus. That the glorious Being who appeared to Daniel on the banks of the Tigris in this, his fifth vision,* *was* Jesus, the Son of God, is proved by comparing Daniel's account of what he saw with the description John wrote of the glorified Jesus who appears in his vision on the island of Patmos. Revelation 1:13-16.

Both John and Daniel saw a Being of transcendent beauty and ineffable radiance, robed like a priest. The complex metaphors they used to describe Him were appropriate to Hebrew poetic thought. (Compare, for instance, the description of a beautiful woman in Song of Solomon 4:1-8.) The same Christ is described in simpler language as He appeared to Peter, James, and John in sublime majesty on the mount of transfiguration:

> He was transfigured before
>   them,
> and his face shone like the sun,
> and his garments became white
>   as light. . .
> glistening, intensely white.
> Matthew 17:2; Mark 9:3.

When the three disciples saw Jesus glorified, they "fell on their faces and were filled with awe." Soon Jesus touched them and said, "Rise, and have no fear." Matthew 17:6, 7. When John saw Jesus in vision, he "fell at his feet as one dead," but Jesus laid a hand on him and said, "Fear not." Revelation 1:17. When Daniel saw Jesus, he too fell to the ground, until a hand touched him and a voice said, **"Fear not."** Daniel 10:10-12.

Daniel was almost overpowered *three* times. For a while he even stopped breathing. Three times he was encouraged. At last he was significantly **"strengthened"** (verses 18, 19) and enabled to observe the vision as it continued.

When Paul, nearing Damascus, experienced *his* vision of Christ, he and his companions fell to the ground, but he alone discerned the full impact of the vision (see Acts 9:1-19; 22:4-16; 26:9-18). In Daniel's case **"great trembling"** took hold of the attendants who accompanied him; and like Paul, **"Daniel, alone saw the vision."** Daniel 10:7.

At His second coming Jesus will once more appear in His glory, and "all the tribes of the earth will mourn." Matthew 25:31; 24:30. His saints, however, will rejoice and shout, "This is our God; we have waited for him . . .; let us be glad and rejoice in his salvation." Isaiah 25:9.

"Blessed are the pure in heart, for they shall see God." Matthew 5:8.

Daniel's prayer answered. After seeing the vision of Jesus in His glory, and after being reassured, Daniel learned from an angel—whom many assume to have again been Gabriel, who appeared to him in the visions of chapters 8 and 9—that his three-week-long prayer had begun to be answered on the first day he began to pray! Said the angel, **"Fear not, Daniel, for from**

---

*Daniel's five visions are as follows: (1) the repetition of Nebuchadnezzar's dream (Daniel 2:19); (2) the vision of the four beasts, little horn, and judgment scene (Daniel 7); (3) the vision of the two beasts, little horn, and 2300 days (Daniel 8); (4) the seventy weeks (Daniel 9); and (5) the history of God's people till the end of time (Daniel 10-12).

the *first day* that you set your mind to understand and humbled yourself before your God, your words have been heard, and I have come because of your words." Daniel 10:12.

Angels in conflict with demons. Then the angel added, **"The prince of the kingdom of Persia withstood me twenty-one days; but Michael, one of the chief princes, came to help me."** Verse 13.

Who was this **"prince of the kingdom of Persia"** who dared to resist an angel of God for three full weeks?

He was not King Cyrus, whose titles included Great King, King of Babylon, and King of Lands. This person was the **"prince"** of Persia, and he is introduced to us as occupying a capacity analogous in some way to that of the other "princes" who are mentioned in this chapter—the **"prince of Greece"** in verse 20 and Michael **"your prince"** in verse 21. In Daniel 12:1 Michael is

further introduced as **"the great prince who has charge of your people."**

The prince of Persia was evidently an angel-prince who identified himself with the Persian Empire. Because he opposed an angel of God for three weeks, we conclude that he was an evil angel. Second Peter 2:4 speaks of angels who sinned and were cast out of heaven. Paul says that the gods whom the nations of his day worshiped were in reality demons. 1 Corinthians 10:20. Paul also disclosed that our real enemies are not ordinary people made of "flesh and blood" but are the "principalities" and "powers," the "spiritual hosts of wickedness," and the "world rulers of this present darkness." Ephesians 6:12. Jesus three times identified Satan as the "prince" (K.J.V.) or "ruler" (R.S.V.) of this present world. John 12:31; 14:30; 16:11.

So The New English Bible and To-

When Daniel was overcome by the brightness of Jesus' glory, Gabriel touched him graciously to reassure him.

day's English Version of Daniel 10:13 both speak about **"the angel prince of the kingdom of Persia."** The Interpreter's Bible[1] refers to the **"angel patron of Persia,"** and The Anchor Bible[2] speaks of "the tutelary spirit of guardian angel of the Persian kingdom, as the rabbis and most Christian commentators have rightly acknowledged." John F. Walvoord[3] concludes, "This 'prince' is not the king of the kingdom of Persia but rather the angelic leader of Persia, a fallen angel under the direction of Satan, in contrast to the angelic prince Michael who leads and protects Israel."

Suddenly the TV of Scripture has flashed to a totally unexpected scene. Behind the visible realm, for three weeks day and night, an angel of God has been wrestling with a determined and powerful demon in an attempt to countervail his influence and to prevent Cyrus from rescinding his all-important decree. At last Michael—who defeated the entire army of demons on another occasion (Revelation 12:7)—reinforces Gabriel. The demon is routed, and the king of Persia makes the right decision. Cyrus refuses to acquiesce in the Samaritan scheme to shut down the temple reconstruction. And he will never waver on this matter again.

We are greatly intrigued by this supernatural struggle. It eclipses any Super Bowl game on planet Earth. The stakes are not an annual pennant but the future of mankind.

With this introduction—a vision of the glorified Jesus and a revelation of the great controversy that goes on hour by hour behind the scenes—the angel will proceed in chapters 11 and 12 to outline events of history to the end of time.

CHAPTER 10

1 In the third year of Cyrus king of Persia a word was revealed to Daniel, who was named Belteshazzar. And the word was true, and it was a great conflict. And he understood the word and had understanding of the vision.

2 In those days I, Daniel, was mourning for three weeks. ³ I ate no delicacies, no meat or wine entered my mouth, nor did I anoint myself at all, for the full three weeks. ⁴ On the twenty-fourth day of the first month, as I was standing on the bank of the great river, that is, the Tigris, ⁵ I lifted up my eyes and looked, and behold, a man clothed in linen, whose loins were girded with gold of Uphaz. ⁶ His body was like beryl, his face like the appearance of lightning, his eyes like flaming torches, his arms and legs like the gleam of burnished bronze, and the sound of his words like the noise of a multitude. ⁷ And I, Daniel, alone saw the vision, for the men who were with me did not see the vision, but a great trembling fell upon them, and they fled to hide themselves. ⁸ So I was left alone and saw this great vision, and no strength was left in me; my radiant appearance was fearfully changed, and I retained no strength. ⁹ Then I heard the sound of his words; and when I heard the sound of his words, I fell on my face in a deep sleep with my face to the ground.

10 And behold, a hand touched me and set me trembling on my hands and knees. ¹¹ And he said to me, "O Daniel, man greatly beloved, give heed to the words that I speak to you, and stand upright, for now I have been sent to you." While he was speaking this word to me, I stood up trembling. ¹² Then he said to me, "Fear not, Daniel, for from the first day that you set your mind to understand and humbled yourself before your God, your words have been heard, and I have come because of your words. ¹³ The prince of the kingdom of Persia withstood me twenty-one days; but Michael, one of the chief princes, came to help me, so I left him there with the prince of the kingdom of Persia ¹⁴ and came to make you understand what is to befall your people in the latter days. For the vision is for days yet to come."

15 When he had spoken to me according to these words, I turned my face toward the ground and was dumb. ¹⁶ And behold, one in the likeness of the sons of men touched my lips; then I opened my mouth and spoke. I said to him who stood before me, "O my lord, by reason of the vision pains have come upon me, and I retain no strength. ¹⁷ How can my lord's servant talk with my lord? For now no strength remains in me, and no breath is left in me."

18 Again one having the appearance of a man touched me and strengthened me. ¹⁹ And he said, "O man greatly beloved, fear not, peace be with you; be strong and of good courage." And when he spoke to me, I was strengthened and said, "Let my lord speak, for you have strengthened me." ²⁰ Then he said, "Do you know why I have come to you? But now I will return to fight against the prince of Persia; and when I am through with him, lo, the prince of Greece will come. ²¹ But I will tell you what is inscribed in the book of truth: there is none who contends by my side against these except Michael, your prince.

The Message of Daniel 10

Michael Champions God's People

Would you like to know what else the Bible says about Michael, the **"great prince"** who could so readily rout the demon prince of Persia? Who is this formidable but friendly person?

Daniel 10:13 calls him **"one of the chief princes"**; but according to what the Bible says elsewhere, this identification is an understatement.

Jude 9 calls Michael "the archangel" an expression that means "the chief angel." Michael is "the" archangel, *the* chief angel. Folk stories have created several "archangels"; but in the Bible there is only one, the archangel Michael.

Michael, a holy Being. In the Hebrew language the name Michael is a question: "Who is like God?" According to Revelation 12:7, in the celestial, invisible warfare that began long ago to be waged between right and wrong, Michael commanded the angels of God in driving the angels of Satan out of heaven.

Joshua met this same Commander of the angels prior to the battle of Jericho and learned that He is a very holy Person. Seeking help through prayer previous to his assault on Jericho, Joshua suddenly observed a soldier standing ahead of him, sword in hand. "Are you for us, or for our adversaries?" he challenged. And the soldier replied, "As commander of the army of the Lord I have now come. . . . Put off your shoes from your feet; for *the place where you stand is holy.*" Joshua 5:13-15.

You already know that Moses was once told to take off *his* shoes because the ground he occupied was holy. Moses was standing by a blazing shrub that miraculously didn't burn up. A voice from the fire commanded him, "Put off your shoes from your feet, for the place on which you are standing is holy ground." Exodus 3:5.

Michael, the LORD (Yahweh). In the conversation that followed at the shrub, the Person in the flames identified Himself to Moses as "the God of your fathers, the God of Abraham, the God of Isaac, and the God of Jacob." Exodus 3:6. He also identified Himself as "I AM WHO I AM"—that is, as the Lord, Yahweh, or Jehovah. Exodus 3:14, 16. But Exodus 3:2, in introducing the account of this great event, states that it was "the *angel* of the LORD" who appeared to Moses in the flaming bush.

Can an angel be God? Can God be an angel?

What *is* an angel? The word "angel" literally means "messenger." God has many messengers. You and I, erring humans, can be angels in this sense! The spies whom Joshua sent to examine Jericho in preparation for his attack are called "messengers" in English but "angels" in Greek. James 2:25.

The supreme Messenger, the supreme Person sent to earth with a message, is Jesus Christ. In His prayer on the way to the cross (John 17), He referred to

Himself as "Jesus Christ whom thou [God] hast *sent.*" Verse 3. In the same prayer He referred to Himself and the Father as being "one." Verse 11. In the heavenly Trinity, Jesus, God's Son, is as truly divine as God the Father is. Both are eternal and both bear the "family" name, Yahweh, Jehovah, I AM. But Jesus is the Messenger, the very special "Angel," sent out by the Father.

Jesus is the Angel of His presence (Isaiah 63:9) and the Angel who redeems us (Genesis 48:16).

At the second coming the *voice of the archangel* signals the resurrection of the dead, according to 1 Thessalonians 4:16. And according to John 5:28, 29, it is the *"voice of the Son of God"* that raises the dead. Daniel 12:1-4 says that when Michael arises at the end of time, **"many of those who sleep in the dust shall awake."**

Michael, the archangel whose voice will raise the dead, is Jesus the Son of God, our Saviour. And being both God and an Angel (in a very special sense), He is inevitably, ex officio, the chief of the angels—the Archangel.

Michael, the glorified Christ. Now, if the Lord Jesus is Michael, then the magnificent Being whose brightness almost overpowered Daniel at the opening of the vision of Daniel 10 was also Michael.

The fact of His being Michael is obscured in the R.S.V. by a regrettable rendering of Daniel 10:13, which seems to say that in order for Gabriel to make his visit to Daniel, he had to leave Michael for a while to continue the fight with the prince of Persia. The implication in the R.S.V. is that Gabriel came by himself to see Daniel. A further unfortunate implication is that the bright Being in the vision was not Michael but Gabriel.

The Interpreter's Bible[4] rightly points out that the simplest translation of the Hebrew is "seeing that I was left there," meaning that the verse says nothing at all about Gabriel's leaving Michael alone but instead that Gabriel had been working alone until Michael came to help him. Happily, a number of versions do translate the verse this way. **"For *I* [Gabriel] had been left there with the kings of Persia"** is the translation in the N.A.S.B. **"Because I was detained there with the king of Persia,"** says the New International Version. **"Because I had been left alone in Persia,"** reads Today's English Version.

The value of knowing this. And what is the value of knowing that Michael is not a created being but is, in fact, our divine Lord and Saviour, Jesus Christ?

For one thing, this knowledge helps us to keep the vision of Daniel 10-12 in proper perspective. The vision begins with a revelation of Jesus in His glory. It ends with a revelation about Jesus at the second coming. The history (of the world) here presented begins and ends with the Lord of history. Once more we are reminded that God cares, that He is in control.

Knowing that Michael is Jesus also helps us to remember that the principal focus of Daniel's prophecies is neither on Antiochus Epiphanes nor on the antichrist. We must never forget this, or we are in danger of strange and unnecessary blunders. The focus is always on Jesus Christ. Jesus is the supernatural stone of

273

Daniel 2. He is the Son of man who comes on the clouds in Daniel 7. He is the Messiah Prince who is cut off in the seventy-week prophecy, who nonetheless causes His covenant to prevail.

And isn't it good to know that when the angel in Daniel 10:21 calls Michael **"your prince,"** he means that Jesus is *our* Prince? And when in Daniel 12:1 he calls Michael **"the great prince who has charge of your people,"** he is reminding us that the Son of God Himself has the affairs of His church in hand?

It's good to be on the side of the winner. It's good to remember that our Leader is not merely a world champion; He is the universal Champion! He is also a General who has never lost a war and who never will!

Even this isn't all. If Jesus is the *chief* Angel, the General of heaven's armies, He is in command of heaven's countless angels, some millions of whom Daniel observed assembling in the heavenly sanctuary at the beginning of the pre-advent judgment. Daniel 7:9, 10. Hebrews 1:14 tells us that the good angels are "ministering spirits *sent forth to serve,* for the sake of those who are to obtain salvation."

This is good news. To think that powerful, friendly angels are sent to answer our prayers, just as they were sent to answer Daniel's prayers long ago.

The bad news is that Satan, too, leads an army of angels (Revelation 12:7)—fallen, evil angels—and that at their head he "prowls around like a roaring lion, seeking someone to devour." 1 Peter 5:8.

We have seen that demon spirits seek to dominate the affairs of nations. It is not fanciful to assume that Satan assigns angels to be demon princes of cities as well. Isaiah 14 talks about the "king," that is, the demon prince, of the city of Babylon. Ezekiel 28 talks about the "king," or demon prince, of the city of Tyre.

No wonder Paul urges us to pray, as a matter of first importance, for everyone in a position of community leadership. 1 Timothy 2:1-4. Every Christian ought to be a Daniel, praying regularly and earnestly that Jesus Christ (that is, Michael) will commission angels to contend with the demons who every day seek to control the nation and city where he lives.

And the home where he lives too.

Have you ever wondered why you speak angrily to the people you love the best? Or why your children are at times unbearably rude? Have you ever wondered if the paperbacks you read and the TV shows your family watches are not so many doorways through which demons invade your home?

Because of the "spiritual hosts of wickedness" who try to control us, Paul urges every Christian to clothe himself in the whole armor of God (see Ephesians 6:12-18). He adds in verse 18, "Pray at all times in the Spirit, with all prayer and supplication. . . . Keep alert with all perseverance, making supplication for all the saints."

"Keep alert with all perseverance." Satan's angels can be determined and very stubborn. One resisted Gabriel for three weeks. It is good that Daniel kept on praying.

In Bible times an enemy army encircled the city of Dothan by night, hoping in a

274

few days to breach the walls, plunder the place, and enslave the population. Elisha the prophet lived in Dothan and, like Daniel, was a man of prayer.

When Elisha's young servant got up at daybreak, he saw the enemy tents and chariots and dashed back indoors. "Alas, my master!" he shouted. "What shall we do?"

"Fear not," replied Elisha. *"Those who are with us are more than those who are with them."*

It was time for Elisha's morning prayer. Compassionately he asked the Lord to "open his [servant's] eyes." When they rose from their knees and looked outdoors, to the young man's utter joy and total wonderment, he saw that on this side of the city and on that side of the city and in whatever direction he looked "the mountain was full of horses and chariots of fire round about Elisha." 2 Kings 6:15-17.

Jesus has angels to outnumber any force Satan can bring against us! And He'll send them at once to our rescue as He did for Daniel. If we pray, the words will become true in our case as they were in Elisha's, "Those who are with *us* are more than those who are with them."

God has not promised to keep us from all harm (see pages 53-56), but He has promised to sustain us in every trial (Isaiah 41:10) and to help us avoid falling into sin (Jude 24).

"Keep alert with all perseverance, making supplication."

Every morning, before anyone leaves for the day, should not your family bow in prayer? Together, with the children, if at all possible? And again at bedside before going to sleep at night?

Your prayer at first can be simple, but it should be in earnest. To build faith it should contain a Bible promise or some reflection on God's goodness.

"Dear Father in heaven," you might say.

"We thank You for telling us in the Bible about Your love and about how much You care for us.

"Forgive us for not responding as we should.

"Bless our family today. Help us to be cheerful, like Daniel, when people are unkind to us. Help us to be consistently thoughtful and honest and true.

"Please send Your mighty angels to protect us, all day in all danger, and to keep us from every sin.

"What we ask for ourselves, we ask also for every Christian, for our nation, and for the city where we live.

"We ask it, trusting in Jesus as our Saviour.

"Amen."

Further Interesting Reading

In Ellen G. White, *Triumph of God's Love:*
"The Origin of Evil," beginning on p. 492,
"Agency of Evil Spirits," beginning on p. 511.
In *Bible Readings for the Home:*
The chapters entitled "Origin, History, and Destiny of Satan,"
"The Ministration of Good Angels,"
"The Dark Ministry of Evil Angels."

References

1. Gerald Kennedy, expository comments on Daniel 10:13, The Interpreter's Bible, ed. George Buttrick, 12 vols. (New York: Abingdom Press, 1952-1957), 6:506.
2. Alexander A. Di Lella, commentary on Daniel 10, The Anchor Bible, 23:282.
3. Walvoord, *Daniel*, p. 246.
4. Kennedy, comments on Daniel 10:13, The Interpreter's Bible, 6:507.

Daniel 11
God and Human Hostility

Introduction

Among the most helpful passages in the book of Daniel may be Daniel 11:6. At first the verse sounds like unintelligible ancient history. In actual fact it contains a gripping human-interest story that reveals a great deal about God.

> After some years they shall make an alliance,
> and the daughter of the king of the south
> shall come to the king of the north to make peace;
> but she shall not retain the strength of her arm,
> and he and her offspring shall not endure;
> but she shall be given up,
> and her attendants,
> her child,
> and he who got possession of her.

Whatever does it mean?

We shall see on page 286 that around 250 B.C., King Ptolemy Philadelphus of Egypt and King Antiochus Theos of Syria attempted to guarantee peace between their countries by having King Antiochus marry King Ptolemy's daughter, Berenice.

Antiochus already had a wife, called Laodice. It was part of the deal that he divorce her.

So the divorce was arranged, the new marriage was celebrated, and in due course a baby boy arrived who could someday be the next king. Unfortunately Antiochus soon found that he didn't like Berenice very well. He kept making comparisons between her and his first wife. And when Berenice's father, the king of Egypt, died, Antiochus divorced her and took Laodice back again.

But Laodice had become bitter. She was afraid, too, of what her husband might do next. So using her royal powers in a manner all too common in those days, she had Antiochus, Berenice, and Berenice's attendants and little son all murdered.

It's not a pretty story. Think of the tears these women shed. Think of the rejection, insecurity, and hostility that they felt.

Then remember that the angel told Daniel about the whole situation *almost three hundred years before it happened.*

"Jesus Christ is the same yesterday and today and forever." Hebrews 13:8.

God knows about every broken heart and broken home. He knows the crushing pain that human hostility induces. And in Daniel 10-12 Jesus appears at the beginning and end of prophecy to teach us that *if we'll let Him,* He'll comfort, encourage, and guide us in every personal tragedy.

277

The human race as hostile. But Daniel 11 deals with more than personal tragedy. It ranges over history, as if the angel who spoke it were a kind of cosmic Walter Cronkite reviewing headlines on TV and signing off, "So that's the way it is"—or rather, since this is predictive prophecy, "So that's the way it will be."

And like the evening headlines, almost every act reported in this chapter is a hostile one. Every actor appears in a bad light, fighting or preparing to fight someone. Except that, near the end, a few **"wise"** persons appear, who stand firmly for God under heavy provocation.

God knows all about us; and what He knows for the most part isn't good, "since all have sinned and fall short of the glory of God." Romans 3:23. Sin is always committed against somebody, either our neighbor or the Lord. In this chapter hostile humans are portrayed as cheating, undercutting, and killing one another, then turning their practiced pride and rage against God Himself.

In the context of so much human hostility, this fifth vision of Daniel teaches us that God is present to heal whenever we seek Him.

It also teaches that God is present to blow the whistle on our nasty contests. Verses 27, 29, and 35 refer to "appointed" times. The apostle Paul was similarly aware of God's stopwatch when he said in Acts 17:26, 27,

And he [God] made from one
    [man] every nation of men
to live on all the face of the earth,
*having determined allotted
    periods*
    and the boundaries of their
    habitations,
that they should seek God,

in the hope that they might feel
    after him
and find him.
*Yet he is not far from each one
    of us.*

The language of Daniel 11. The language of Daniel 11 is considered to be "literal" in that it isn't symbolic in the same way that the language of chapters 2, 7, and 8 is. There are no multi-element images, no beasts or horns. Just the same, its language is far from easy. It is cryptic, almost like a code. Each sentence condenses quantities of information. Many metaphors are employed. Many pronouns do not seem, at first, to have clear antecedents. The underlying Hebrew presents problems.

Our first reaction is to wish that God had made the story plainer. Then we reflect that He told the story in this manner for our sakes. The prophecy is for us, and He chose to express it as He did, knowing His way was best.

Numerous interpretations. The cryptic quality of Daniel 11 has led to a variety of interpretations.

But, by intentionally omitting the names of people and the dates of major events, God has encouraged us to study the course of history and to make our own comparisons between what He said and what we find. For some Christians, matching history to this particular prophecy has become a religious diversion, even a lifelong passion, more fascinating and far more rewarding than doing jigsaw pictures or crossword puzzles.

The most popular interpretation has always been that the heart of the chapter (verses 21-39) deals with Antiochus Epiphanes, of whom we have heard before (see pages 190-192). Josephus, the famous Jewish historian, held this interpretation in the first century A.D. It is possible that Christ's disciples did also.

If the disciples did hold this view, they must have been very surprised to hear Jesus say that the **"abomination that makes desolate"** (translated "desolating sacrilege" in Matthew 24:15) that was "spoken" of by Daniel the prophet (in Daniel 8:13 and 11:31) was still to be fulfilled in the future (see footnote, page 248). Their surprise must have grown when they heard Jesus add, "Let the reader [of Daniel] understand." **"Understand"** is a key word in the book of Daniel.

Jesus was present when the angel gave Daniel the contents of chapter 11. The fact that *He* considered the Antiochus Epiphanes interpretation to be inadequate is significant.

There is no doubt that the interpretation which applies verses 21-39 to Antiochus Epiphanes is very old. But is this a good recommendation for it? At the close of the vision the angel told Daniel to **"shut up the words, and seal the book, until the time of the end."** Then another angel commented, **"The wise will understand."**

In other words, old interpretations are *bound to be inadequate.* Only interpretations made in relatively recent years have any chance of getting the real issues straight. The vision was sealed until the time of the end.

No doubt God would be happy to see you working on your own interpretation of Daniel 11. You would need to read history books, pray earnestly, and consult with other studious, praying Christians. "You must understand this, that no prophecy of scripture is a matter of one's own interpretation." 2 Peter 1:20.

But don't be misled by any single translation, and be wary of brief footnotes in study Bibles. Scholars wrestling with the linguistic difficulties involved have sometimes adapted the Hebrew and tailored their translations to fit a cherished interpretation when they really shouldn't have done so. Years ago the well-known Charles H. H. Wright warned that "these modern attempts to correct the text of Daniel so as to bring it into closer harmony with the records of the Maccabean times are . . . highly suspicious. If the Patristic, mediaeval, and post-Reformation writers have twisted sentences of Daniel to make them express the meaning those commentators desired them to convey, all such writers have been far outshone in that particular point by modern critics."[1]

Aids to interpretation. Before attempting to find out what the angel tried to tell Daniel (and us) in chapter 11, it will be helpful to set down a number of observations to influence us as we go along.

1. *Study helps.* In harmony with what we have been saying, we should expect to study history books and to examine more than one Bible translation.

2. *Long time.* Daniel 11 begins with a reference to King Cyrus, who was reigning at the time, and ends at the **"time of the end,"** when Michael will stand up and raise the dead. Thus we should expect the interpretation of Daniel 11 to lead us over long periods of time.

3. *Landmarks.* Spotted along this time period are a few prominent markers to guide us on our way, as buoys guide ships and omnitransmitters guide planes. The most important of these markers are (a) the **"prince of the covenant"** in verse 22 and (b) the **"abomination that makes desolate"** in verse 31. The Hebrew

279

word for **"prince"** is not the common word *"sar"* but the relatively rare *"nagid"* and is identical to the word for the **"prince"** who **"causes the covenant to prevail"** in Daniel 9:24-27. The **"prince of the covenant"** is *Jesus Christ* (see page 219); hence, by the time we reach verse 22 in our interpretation of Daniel 11, we must be down at least to the time of Christ. And as for the **"abomination that makes desolate"** (verse 31), Jesus indicated in Matthew 24:15 that it was future to His day. By the time we reach verse 31 we must be well into the Christian era.

4. *Parallels.* We have learned that the great prophetic panoramas of Daniel 2, 7, 8, and 9 not only parallel but also augment each other. We will expect Daniel 11 also to introduce new material while at the same time running parallel to the other visions (see page 295).

5. *Christian history.* We have seen that Daniel 7 and 9 deal largely with the course of the Christian church. The little horn of Daniel 7 represents Christian Rome trampling on God's law and persecuting His saints during a specially designated 1260 years, 538-1798. The little horn of Daniel 8 represents both pagan and Christian Rome, contributing to that misrepresentation of Christ's heavenly ministry which is pictured as ending in 1844, at the close of the 2300 year-days. We will anticipate, then, that Daniel 11 will probably also deal some of the time with the Christian church.

6. *"Your people."* We are supported in this expectation when we hear the angel tell Daniel that the message concerns **"your people."** Daniel 10:14. In our study of Daniel 9:19, 24 we learned that the term **"your people"** means ethnic Israel until the close of the seventy weeks (A.D. 34) and after that Christian Israel—the church of all believers in Jesus, both Jew and Gentile (see pages 231-234).

Encouragement about details. Daniel 11 contains many details. If you don't like details, you may prefer to come back and read the chapter later; but do not be dismayed. God loves details.

Scientists tell us that each drop of rainwater that falls during a thunderstorm contains at least 100 billion billion atoms. And that each atom is composed of protons, neutrons, and electrons. And that each proton and neutron is most likely composed, in turn, of as many as three infinitesimally tiny, rapidly spinning, toplike particles called quarks.

There are over four billion people in our world. Each has his or her own set of social, economic, and family problems. How good it is that the God of raindrops knows all there is to know about everyone's concerns and the hostilities they generate, that He has known about them for centuries in advance, and that He "is not far from each one of us." Acts 17:27.

The fact that man has walked on the moon doesn't mean nearly so much as the fact that, in a very practical sense, God walks on the earth. Think about this as you read Daniel 11 and be encouraged.

CHAPTER 11

1 And as for me, in the first year of Darius the Mede, I stood up to confirm and strengthen him.

2 "And now I will show you the truth. Behold, three more kings shall arise in Persia; and a fourth shall be far richer than all of them; and when he has become strong through his riches, he shall stir up all against the kingdom of Greece. ³ Then a mighty king shall arise, who shall rule with great dominion and do according to his will. ⁴ And when he has arisen, his kingdom shall be broken and divided toward the four winds of heaven, but not to his posterity, nor according to the dominion with which he ruled; for his kingdom shall be plucked up and go to others besides these.

5 "Then the king of the south shall be strong, but one of his princes shall be stronger than he and his dominion shall be a great dominion. ⁶ After some years they shall make an alliance, and the daughter of the king of the south shall come to the king of the north to make peace; but she shall not retain the strength of her arm, and he and his offspring shall not endure; but she shall be given up, and her attendants, her child, and he who got possession of her.

7 "In those times a branch from her roots shall arise in his place; he shall come against the army and enter the fortress of the king of the north, and he shall deal with them and shall prevail. ⁸ He shall also carry off to Egypt their gods with their molten images and with their precious vessels of silver and of gold; and for some years he shall refrain from attacking the king of the north. ⁹ Then the latter shall come into the realm of the king of the south but shall return into his own land.

10 "His sons shall wage war and assemble a multitude of great forces, which shall come on and overflow and pass through, and again shall carry the war as far as his fortress. ¹¹ Then the king of the south, moved with anger, shall come out and fight with the king of the north; and he shall raise a great multitude, but it shall be given into his hand. ¹² And when the multitude is taken, his heart shall be exalted, and he shall cast down tens of thousands, but he shall not prevail. ¹³ For the king of the north shall again raise a multitude, greater than the former; and after some years he shall come on with a great army and abundant supplies.

14 "In those times many shall rise against the king of the south; and the men of violence among your own people shall lift themselves up in order to fulfil the vision; but they shall fail. ¹⁵ Then the king of the north shall come and throw up siegeworks, and take a well-fortified city. And the forces of the south shall not stand, or even his picked troops, for there shall be no strength to stand. ¹⁶ But he who comes against him shall do according to his own will, and none shall stand before him; and he shall stand in the glorious land, and all of it shall be in his power. ¹⁷ He shall set his face to come with the strength of his whole kingdom, and he shall bring terms of peace and perform them. He shall give him the daughter of women to destroy the kingdom; but it shall not stand or be to his advantage. ¹⁸ Afterward he shall turn his face to the coastlands, and shall take many of them; but a commander shall put an end to his insolence; indeed he shall turn his insolence back upon him. ¹⁹ Then he shall turn his face back toward the fortresses of his own land; but he shall stumble and fall, and shall not be found.

20 "Then shall arise in his place one who shall send an exactor of tribute through the glory of the kingdom; but within a few days he shall be broken, neither in anger nor in battle. ²¹ In his place shall arise a contemptible person to whom royal majesty has not been given; he shall come in without warning and obtain the kingdom by flatteries. ²² Armies shall be utterly swept away before him and broken, and the prince of the covenant also. ²³ And from the time that an alliance is made with him he shall act deceitfully; and he shall become strong with a small people. ²⁴ Without warning he shall come into the richest parts of the province;

and he shall do what neither his fathers nor his fathers' fathers have done, scattering among them plunder, spoil, and goods. He shall devise plans against strongholds, but only for a time. ²⁵ And he shall stir up his power and his courage against the king of the south with a great army; and the king of the south shall wage war with an exceedingly great and mighty army; but he shall not stand, for plots shall be devised against him. ²⁶ Even those who eat his rich food shall be his undoing; his army shall be swept away, and many shall fall down slain. ²⁷ And as for the two kings, their minds shall be bent on mischief; they shall speak lies at the same table, but to no avail; for the end is yet to be at the time appointed. ²⁸ And he shall return to his land with great substance, but his heart shall be set against the holy covenant. And he shall work his will, and return to his own land.

29 "At the time appointed he shall return and come into the south; but it shall not be this time as it was before. ³⁰ For ships of Kittim shall come against him, and he shall be afraid and withdraw, and shall turn back and be enraged and take action against the holy covenant. He shall turn back and give heed to those who forsake the holy covenant. ³¹ Forces from him shall appear and profane the temple and fortress, and shall take away the continual burnt offering. And they shall set up the abomination that makes desolate. ³² He shall seduce with flattery those who violate the covenant; but the people who know their God shall stand firm and take action. ³³ And those among the people who are wise shall make many understand, though they shall fall by sword and flame, by captivity and plunder, for some days. ³⁴ When they fall, they shall receive a little help. And many shall join themselves to them with flattery; ³⁵ and some of those who are wise shall fall, to refine and to cleanse them and to make

them white, until the time of the end, for it is yet for the time appointed.

36 "And the king shall do according to his will; he shall exalt himself and magnify himself above every god, and shall speak astonishing things against the God of gods. He shall prosper till the indignation is accomplished; for what is determined shall be done. ³⁷ He shall give no heed to the gods of his fathers, or to the one beloved by women; he shall not give heed to any other god, for he shall magnify himself above all. ³⁸ He shall honor the god of fortresses instead of these; a god whom his fathers did not know he shall honor with gold and silver, with precious stones and costly gifts. ³⁹ He shall deal with the strongest fortresses by the help of a foreign god; those who acknowledge him he shall magnify with honor. He shall make them rulers over many and shall divide the land for a price.

40 "At the time of the end the king of the south shall attack him; but the king of the north shall rush upon him like a whirlwind, with chariots and horsemen, and with many ships; and he shall come into countries and shall overflow and pass through. ⁴¹ He shall come into the glorious land. And tens of thousands shall fall, but these shall be delivered out of his hand: Edom and Moab and the main part of the Ammonites. ⁴² He shall stretch out his hand against the countries, and the land of Egypt shall not escape. ⁴³ He shall become ruler of the treasures of gold and of silver, and all the precious things of Egypt; and the Libyans and the Ethiopians shall follow in his train. ⁴⁴ But tidings from the east and the north shall alarm him, and he shall go forth with great fury to exterminate and utterly destroy many. ⁴⁵ And he shall pitch his palatial tents between the sea and the glorious holy mountain; yet he shall come to his end, with none to help him.

The Message of Daniel 11

God Knows All About Us

A principal difference between the vision of Daniel 11 and the other visions in the book is that, whereas the others deal with the sweep of empires, this one often talks about individuals. In the other visions, **"king"** means "kingdom." In Daniel 11, **"king"** often means "king."

You have read the chapter and likely you haven't known what to do with it. Now let's look at it again and see how specific events in history match specific phrases in the prophecy.

The common interpretation of verses 1-13. There is hardly any disagreement among Bible students about the first thirteen verses. Let's go over this first part slowly enough so we can see how accurately it has been fulfilled.

1. **And as for me** [*Gabriel*],
   in the first year of Darius the Mede,
   I stood up to confirm and strengthen him.

Gabriel, whom we assume the angel to be, here says that a year or two before this vision he had personally assisted Darius the Mede (not King Darius I) in his administration of Babylon. This information helps explain why Darius was so friendly to Daniel in the matter of the lions' den.

2. **And now I will show you the truth.**
   Behold, three more kings shall arise in Persia,
   and a fourth shall be far richer than all of them.
   And when he has become strong through his riches,
   he shall stir up all against the kingdom of Greece.

After the death of King Cyrus, who was reigning at the time of the vision, the next three kings of Persia were Cambyses (530-522), a usurper called the False Smerdis or Bardiya (522), and Darius I (522-486). Cyrus and Darius I both issued decrees to rebuild the temple.

The fourth king was Xerxes (486-465), known in the Bible as Ahasuerus and the husband of Queen Esther. He spent four full years stockpiling supplies and assembling manpower for a military expedition against Greece, just as the angel had predicted. He truly stirred up **"all."** His army teemed with contingents from forty nations—Persians sporting turbans, Assyrians wearing brass helmets, Colchians with wooden hats, Thracians with fox-skin caps, Ethiopians draped in leopard skins, and so on and on.[2] Together they marched, perhaps 300,000[3] of them, mostly on foot, all the way from their homelands to the battles of Salamis (480) and Plataea (479) in Greece—and to complete defeat.

3. **Then a mighty king** [*Alexander*] **shall arise**
   who shall rule with great dominion
   and do according to his will.

283

Victory over the Great King of Persia was a heady tonic for citizens of the little city-states of Greece. Dreams of conquering the Persian Empire began to dance in their heads. Eventually Alexander, son of King Philip of Macedonia, united most of the Greeks, then crossed the Hellespont into Asia and, as we saw earlier (pages 156, 157), completely conquered the empire of the Great King.

4. **And when he [*Alexander*] has arisen, his kingdom shall be broken
and divided toward the four winds of heaven,
but not to his posterity,
nor according to the dominion with which he ruled;
for his kingdom shall be plucked up
and go to others besides these.**

Alexander was just settling into the task of building the capital of his new empire at the site of old Babylon, when swamp fever overtook him. He died in June 323 B.C. at the age of 32 and was survived by a brain-damaged half brother, Philip, and by an infant son, born actually after Alexander's death. His leading generals fought with each other, eliminated the brother and the son, and in 301 sliced up the empire four ways. The far west went to Cassander, the north to Lysimachus, the east to Seleucus, and the south to Ptolemy.

5. **The king of the south [*Ptolemy*] shall be strong,
but one of his princes shall be stronger than he
and his dominion shall be a great dominion.**

The terms **"king of the north"** and **"king of the south"** appear frequently in Daniel 11. They designate, at first, the persons who controlled Syria and Egypt, countries lying *north* and *south* of Jerusalem. The actual areas controlled by these kings varied from time to time. Sometimes the northern (Seleucid) kingdom reached from the Aegean Sea to India, and sometimes it consisted of only a few city-states. The king of (Ptolemaic) Egypt annexed Libya and also certain areas on the coast of Asia Minor. During much of the early period covered by Daniel 11, Egypt also controlled Lebanon, Cyprus, and Judea. See map on page 285.

The capital of Egypt under the Ptolemies was not Cairo but Alexandria, a flourishing community founded by Alexander. The principal capital of the Seleucid kingdom was Antioch, in Syria, near to the Mediterranean.

All the kings of Egypt carried the name Ptolemy (TOL-uh-mee), and all the kings of Syria who are referred to in Daniel 11 were called either Antiochus or Seleucus. Because so many had the same names, each was distinguished in ancient times by a second name chosen by the king himself or given to him by his people. Today we give them numbers as well. The result is admittedly a series of "jawbreakers"!

In verse 5 the angel said that the **"king of the south"** would be **"strong."** Ptolemy I Soter (323-280) was, in fact, strong right from the start. Egypt was immensely wealthy and rather easy to protect. The **"prince"** who became **"stronger than he"** was Seleucus I Nicator, the general who originally won the eastern part of

Alexander's empire. Seleucus was driven out of the east by yet another one of Alexander's generals and fled to Egypt for safety. Ptolemy gave him special status and helped him outfit a new army.

Quickly successful in driving his rival out of the east, Seleucus followed through by pushing Lysimachus out of Syria and Asia Minor, thus making himself **"king of the north"**—and the master of most of Alexander's former empire, from the Aegean to India. He would have liked to control Judea too, taking it away from Egypt; but Ptolemy reminded Seleucus that without his help in the first place, he could never have staged his comeback.

6. **After some years they** [*Antiochus II and Ptolemy II*] **shall make an alliance,
    and the daughter of the king of the south
    shall come to the king of the north to make peace;
    but she shall not retain the strength of her arm,
    and he and her offspring shall not endure;
    but she shall be given up,
    and her attendants,
    her child,
    and he who got possession of her.**

When Alexander's "horn" kingdom was "broken," it was divided into four (later three) "horn" kingdoms, each led at first by one of Alexander's four generals.

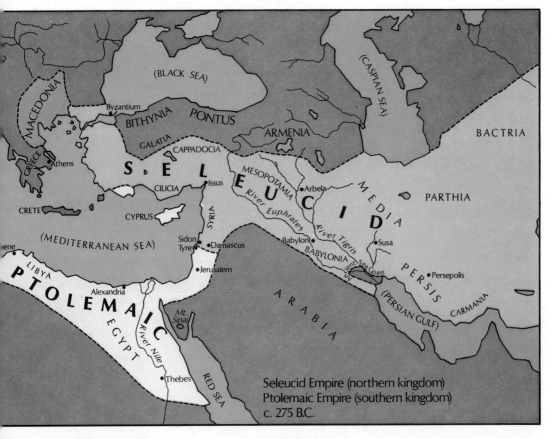

Seleucid Empire (northern kingdom)
Ptolemaic Empire (southern kingdom)
c. 275 B.C.

KINGS OF THE SOUTH AND KINGS OF THE NORTH

THE PTOLEMIES		THE SELEUCIDS	
Ptolemy I Soter	*323-282	Seleucus I Nicator	312-281
Ptolemy II Philadelphus	285-246	Antiochus I Soter	281-261
		Antiochus II Theos	261-246
Ptolemy III Euergetes	246-221	Seleucus II Callinicos	246-225
		Seleucus III Ceraunos	225-223
Ptolemy IV Epiphanes	221-203	Antiochus III the Great	223-187
Ptolemy V Epiphanes	203-181	Seleucus IV Philopater	187-175
Ptolemy VI Eupator	181	Antiochus IV Epiphanes	175-164
Ptolemy VII Philometer	181-145	Antiochus V Eupator	164-150
Etc. to B.C. 51		Etc., to B.C. 65	
Cleopatra VI	51-30		

*Ptolemy I Soter was designated "satrap," 323-305, but after 305 his new title as "king" was made retroactive to 323.

Ptolemaic dates from Edwyn Bevan, *The House of Ptolemy*. Seleucid dates from Parker and Dubberstein, *Babylonian Chronology*, 2d ed.

We looked at this verse on page 277. We have to remind ourselves that all these details were revealed by God almost three hundred years in advance. The **"they"** at the beginning of the verse refers to Antiochus II Theos (261-246) and Ptolemy II Philadelphus (285-246). Antiochus II, you recall, divorced Laodice in order to marry Berenice, daughter of Ptolemy II. When Ptolemy II died, Antiochus took Laodice back, but she had Antiochus and Berenice and Berenice's baby and attendants all killed.

Breaking his relationship with his wife was a strange basis for a king to adopt for building a new relationship with a foreign king.

> 7. **In those times a branch from her roots** [*Ptolemy III*]
>   **shall arise in his place;**
>   **he shall come against the army and enter the fortress**
>   **of the king of the north** [*Antiochus II*],
>   **and he shall deal with them and shall prevail.**

By his divorce and remarriage Antiochus II lost far more than he could have hoped to gain. For the next king of Egypt, Ptolemy III (246-221), a brother of Berenice's, determined to avenge Berenice's death by invading Syria. He took his army all the way to Babylon and beyond before voluntarily pulling back![4] His navy occupied Seleucia, the port that served Antioch, the capital of Syria, and for some time Egyptian shipping dominated the eastern Mediterranean.

> 8. **He** [*Ptolemy III*] **shall also carry off to Egypt**
>   **their gods with their molten images**
>   **and with their precious vessels of silver and gold;**

286

> **and for some years he shall refrain from**
> **attacking the king of the north.**

In the process of his triumphant Syrian campaign, Ptolemy III captured 2500 gold and silver images, many of them being Egyptian gods that had been stolen by a succession of conquerors over the centuries. Watching him carry these lifeless idols south through Palestine on his way home to Egypt, the Jews must have smiled in contempt. But the Egyptians were delighted at what their Greek king had achieved for them, and they hailed him as their benefactor. In Greek "benefactor" is *"euergetes"*; hence Ptolemy III *Euergetes*.

Ptolemy III Euergetes was quite satisfied with himself after his profitable foray, and he didn't attack the Syrians again as long as he lived.

> 9. **Then the latter** [*a new king of the north, Seleucus II*]
> **shall come into the realm of the king of the south**
> **but shall return into his own land.**

The Ptolemies and Seleucids resumed their quarrel, like feuding Hatfields and McCoys. For well over a century the Jews apprehensively observed their armies marching north and south through Palestine, knowing that victory or defeat could change their overlords and their liberties and taxes too.

In the year 242 Seleucus II Callinicus attempted to avenge himself for Egypt's deep penetration of his ancestral lands, but his army was vanquished and his navy blown away. He returned to Antioch badly bloodied and empty-handed.

> 10. **His sons** [*the two sons of Seleucus II, namely Seleucus III,*
> *who was assassinated after a short reign (225-223) and*
> *Antiochus III the Great (223-187)*]
> **shall wage war and assemble a multitude of great forces,**
> **which shall come and overflow and pass through,**
> **and again shall carry the war as far as his fortress.**
> 11. **Then the king of the south** [*Ptolemy IV*],
> **moved with anger,**
> **shall come out and fight with the king of the north** [*Antiochus III*];
> **and he** [*Antiochus III*] **shall raise a great multitude,**
> **but it shall be given into his** [*Ptolemy's*] **hand.**
> 12. **But when the multitude is taken** [*that is, the army defeated*]
> **his heart** [*Ptolemy's*] **shall be exalted,**
> **and he shall cast down tens of thousands,**
> **but he shall not prevail.**

These three verses deal principally with the battle of Raphia, June 22, 217 B.C., as if God chose to pay special attention to this particular battle as an evidence of His interest in every battle.

But why should God be concerned about a battle?

At Raphia in 217 B.C. approximately 70,000 foot soldiers and 5000 cavalry

287

were committed on each side. The body count next day showed that Antiochus III had lost 10,000 killed and 4000 taken prisoner. Ptolemy's losses were lighter but still significant. When hostility is so rampant and so many men suffer and die, should not God care?

It is a point of interest that both armies at Raphia, like armies at some other major battles, deployed trained elephants to confuse the cavalry and to provide elevated mobile fortresses. Wrote a later Roman war reporter, Ammianus Marcellinus: "Elephants, frightful with their wrinkled bodies and loaded with armed men, [are] a hideous spectacle, dreadful beyond every form of horror."[5] The Egyptians used 73 of the big beasts, herded in from Somalia, and the Syrians, 102, brought all the way from India. Despite their numerical disadvantage, Egypt won the battle, for Antiochus lacked discipline.

Yet victory gained Ptolemy little in the long run. He was a notorious debauchee. He failed to follow up the success his generals had handed him—and Antiochus III was eager for a rematch.

13. **For the king of the north** [*Antiochus III*]
    shall again raise a multitude, greater than the former;
    and after some years
    he shall come on with a great army and abundant supplies.

Resilient as a tennis ball, Antiochus III bounced high after his defeat at Raphia. He led his army to India in the east and to the Aegean in the west, making the **"king of the north"** once more nominal master of most of Alexander's former empire. Hoping to be master of it all, he prepared for a second attack on Egypt.

The timing seemed propitious, for the new king of the south was Ptolemy V Epiphanes, a boy of six. Besides, there was unrest along the Nile, Egyptians defying and even rioting against their Greek overlords. It is of interest to know that the famous Rosetta Stone, now housed in the British Museum, records concessions made to the restless Egyptian people by the regents of the boy king, Ptolemy V, in an effort to prevent further trouble.

Interpretation of Daniel 11:14, 15. When I was a boy, one of my teachers observed that "prophecy is history written in advance." I hope you have enjoyed seeing how the first thirteen verses of Daniel 11 have been minutely fulfilled.

These opening verses are interpreted rather unanimously; verses 14-39, however, have occasioned a variety of expositions. Let us look first at verses 14 and 15.

14. **In those times**
    many shall rise against the king of the south;
    and the men of violence among your own people
    shall lift themselves up in order to fulfill the vision;
    but they shall fail.

Among the **"many"** who were to **"rise against the king of the south"** were those Egyptians we mentioned a moment ago who were rebelling against their Greek overlords. In addition, Antiochus III, a determined enemy, secured an alliance with

288

Both armies at the battle of Raphia, 217 B.C., deployed elephants to provide elevated mobile fortresses.   JOHN STEEL, ARTIST, © 1980 PPPA

The Rosetta Stone preserves concessions wrung from the boy-king Ptolemy V when "many" rose up against him.

KEYSTONE

Philip of Macedon, the current successor to Cassander in the west. *All* these rose in hostility against the king of the south.

But who were the **"men of violence among your own people"** who would **"lift themselves up in order to fulfill the vision"** but who would **"fail"**? Some commentators speculate that a party of militants must have gathered around a Jewish fanatic, impressed by some wild vision of his that the time was ripe to break free while Syria and Egypt were at war. Such a group may have existed, but so far *no record of one has come to light.*

The K.J.V. has, for this part of verse 14, **"The robbers of thy people shall exalt themselves to establish the vision; but they shall fall."**

The underlying Hebrew means, literally, "the breakers of your people," and the R.S.V. *interprets* this phrase to refer to violent people among the Jews. Obviously the Hebrew can just as well refer to *outsiders who come in* to rob or break the Jews.

So who are the **"robbers"** or **"breakers"** of God's people? In the vision of

290

Daniel 7 the fourth beast *"devoured* and *broke* **in pieces, and** *stamped* **the residue."** Daniel 7:7. In Daniel 8:13 the little horn **"trampled"** the sanctuary underfoot. The fourth beast and the little horn are *Rome;* so the angel's real meaning in Daniel 11:14 is that the Romans would enter the story at this point in fulfillment of the visions of Daniel 7 and 8 and—also in fulfillment of Daniel 7 and 8—that they would in the course of time trample on God's people and, ultimately, fall. Verse 14 wraps up Roman history in a concise prophetic nugget.

As a fact, it *was* in the days of Antiochus III that the Romans *did* enter the history of the eastern Mediterranean. When they learned that Antiochus III had made an alliance with Philip of Macedon against Ptolemy V of Egypt, they feared the development of a new superpower in the Middle East and warned Philip and Antiochus III to *stay out of Egypt.* Their warning amounted to a kind of Mediterranean "Monroe Doctrine" or "Cuban Policy."

Antiochus III, Ptolemy IV, and Philip had all come to the throne between 221 and 223 B.C., and all were young men (aged 17-23) at the time, observes historian E. R. Bevan. "The world in which their reigns began was the Graeco-Macedonian world as it had been constituted by the conquests of Alexander the Great; *the world in which they ended was a new world over which was flung the shadow of Rome."* [6] The prophecy of Daniel 11 takes into account this momentous transition in human events.

15. **Then the king of the north** [*Antiochus III*]
    shall come and throw up siegeworks,
    and take a well-fortified city.
    And the forces of the south shall not stand,
    or even his picked troops,
    for there shall be no strength to stand.

Heedless of Rome's admonition to stay out of Egypt, Antiochus III went ahead with his aggression. North of the Sea of Galilee, near the site of the later city called Caesarea Philippi, where Peter recognized Jesus as the Son of God (Matthew 16:13-20), Antiochus trounced a well-trained army led by Scopas, a skilled and experienced general in the service of Egypt. The defeated troops retired to Tyre, but Antiochus followed them and laid siege. When the fighting was over, the king of the north had a firm grip on the Jewish homeland of Judea, and Ptolemaic Egypt never owned it again.

Having now examined fifteen verses of Daniel 11 in detail in order to illustrate the method of interpretation, we can afford to be more cursory with the rest.

The common interpretation of verses 16-39. The interpretation that applies verses 16-39 to the career of Antiochus Epiphanes is so widely available that it need not be repeated here. Unfortunately it misses the two basic landmarks (in verses 22 and 31) that we discussed on pages 279 and 280. It supposes that the **"prince of the covenant"** is merely the obscure priest, Onias III, instead of our Saviour, Jesus Christ, and it assumes that the **"abomination that makes desolate"** ap-

291

peared more than 160 years *before* the days of Jesus, even though in Matthew 24:15 Jesus indicated that it would appear *after* His day. This interpretation also assumes that the person in verse 20 who was to be **"broken, neither in anger nor in battle,"** was Seleucus IV Philopater. But according to the best available evidence,[7] Seleucus IV Philopater was murdered.

In spite of its shortcomings, the Antiochus Epiphanes interpretation bore such an apparent relationship to the career of the little king that it seems to have been believed by many Jews in the time of Christ. As we note on pages 278 and 279, it is possible that even the disciples believed it. If so, they were startled when—sitting with Jesus on the Mount of Olives overlooking the Jerusalem temple on a cool spring night shortly before the crucifixion—they heard Jesus invite them to "understand' that the "abomination that makes desolate" was still in the future (see footnote, page 248).

A broader interpretation of verses 14-39. With a vast hindsight which we enjoy today but which the disciples on the Mount of Olives did not possess, we now reread verses 14-39, looking for the new "understanding" that Jesus recommended. And now we notice that the climax verses, 31-39, definitely point to something or someone far bigger than Antiochus Epiphanes and his three-year persecution in tiny Judea. They sound instead as if God is dealing with a universal phenomenon.

Impelled by Christ's remarks, we look for other people, places, and events that match the prophetic panorama far better.

Reminding ourselves that the **"robbers of thy people"** (verse 15, K.J.V.) are the Romans, we now perceive that verse 16 outlines the conquest of **"the glorious land"** of Palestine by the Roman general, Pompey. Verses 16-19 portray the famous Roman Julius Caesar and his affair with **"the daughter of women,"** Queen Cleopatra of Egypt, and his later exploits in frontier areas, **"the coastlands."**

Subsequently Julius Caesar was assassinated on the Ides of March, 44 B.C., at the hands of sixty fellow Romans led by G. Cassius Longinus, the **"commander"** who **"put an end to his insolence."** Verse 18. Yes, Julius Caesar was one of the world's more insufferably insolent men. Gifted with extraordinary capacity for hard work, he abused his talent at times with military butchery in order to achieve personal ambition. Once he launched a foreign war "deliberately, gratuitously and illegally" for his own personal aggrandizement, during which he claimed, "with some, but not total exaggeration," that his army had killed 430,000 Germans in one day.[8] His "insolent" attempt to replace the Roman republican form of government with a personal dictatorship led directly to his death—which was predicted twice for emphasis in verses 18 and 19 (just as some events are apparently repeated in verses 11 and 12).

Julius Caesar was followed (verse 20) by Caesar Augustus, the founder of the Roman Empire and the issuer of that famous "decree that all the world should be taxed" (Luke 2:1 K.J.V.), or "enrolled" (R.S.V.) for tax purposes, at the time when Jesus Christ was born.

There being no punctuation or paragraph divisions anywhere in the Hebrew of this chapter, we can assume a major paragraph break between verses 20 and 21.

Augustus founded not only the Roman Empire but also the *position of Roman emperor*. Because of this, the word "augustus" quickly became a synonym for "emperor," and every emperor was known as an augustus. As we saw on page 154, in the fifth and sixth centuries after Christ, the head of the Roman state was succeeded by the head of the Roman Church; that is, the "augustus" was succeeded by the "Holy Father." The **"contemptible person,"** then, who was to arise in the place of Augustus, was the medieval pope—viewed, like all other leaders in Daniel 11, from the angle only of his hostilities.

Remember: In Daniel 11 everyone is hostile, except for the **"wise"** people in verses 32-34 who stand firmly for God in time of persecution. "All have sinned and come short of the glory of God." Romans 3:23.

Thus the medieval papacy grows to strength from an early position of smallness (verse 23), makes and breaks treaties (verse 23), and plunders the rich in order to reward its friends in unprecedented fashion (verse 24).

In this interpretation verses 25-30 foreshadow the era of the crusades—a momentous phenomenon and one of the most prominent examples of Roman Christianity as hostility. Initiated vigorously by the persuasive oratory of Pope Urban II, the era of the crusades saw Western Europe setting out no fewer than seven times within approximately 150 years (1095-1250) to wrest the Holy Land from the Muslims and render it safe for Christian pilgrims.

293

The Muslims who controlled Jerusalem at the time of the first crusade, and who regained control from time to time thereafter, were headed by the caliphs (or, later, the sultans) in *Egypt*.[9] So the first crusade was a great attack against the **"king of the south"** (verses 24, 25). And it was a great success—of sorts. Jerusalem was taken on July 15, 1099. In their religious zeal the invading Christians ran their consecrated swords through every Muslim and even every Jew they found inside the walls. "Men waded in blood up to their ankles."[10] The slaughter was "as horrible as any recorded in history."[11]

For a victory such as this, reports a contemporary, the Christians knelt in worship and with tears of joy gave thanks.[12]

The sixth crusade was unique. King Frederick II, who could speak several languages including Arabic, secured Jerusalem, Bethlehem, and Nazareth by negotiation, without shedding a drop of blood.

But the crusades were not uniformly successful. Some of them, notably the children's crusade, were disasters. The seventh also was **"not this time as it was before."** Verse 29. In this, the final crusade to the Middle East, the pious monarch, Louis IX, was actually taken prisoner at Cairo, Egypt. Ten years later, the Egyptian sultan and his general, Baibans, drove the Christians out of Palestine to stay (until 1917).

During the crusades the Muslims hired Greek naval vessels to assist them in opposing the crusaders. Here are the **"ships from Kittim."** Verse 30. ("From Kittim" signifies "from the west.") Although Roman Christianity ultimately lost the crusades, trade between Europe and the east was greatly stimulated by them; and Italian merchants in Venice and Genoa were especially enriched. Verse 28. Europeans learned to enjoy sugar, cotton, glass mirrors, diapers, and many other products of the east.

The **"two kings"** who **"speak lies at the same table, but to no avail"** (verse 27) epitomize the perfidy and hypocrisy that conspicuously characterized the crusade experience. Historians call attention to the mutual mistrust of the allies on both sides, principally on the Christian side. More specifically, these "kings" may represent Christian leaders like Reginald of Chatillon and Guy de Lusignon who eagerly violated solemn peace treaties made with the generous Islamic sultan, Saladin.[13] They may also represent various other Christian and Muslim leaders who made and broke treaties as opportunity suggested, and also several of the crusaders who promised safety to Muslim townspeople if they would surrender, only to break their word and massacre them without mercy.[14] In the hope of finding gold that the Muslims might have swallowed, the Christians sometimes ripped open their stomachs.

Tragically, the papacy bears the primary responsibility for the crusades and their ghastly atrocities. Pope Urban II launched the first one. If he may be partly excused on the assumption that he did not fully anticipate its barbarous outcome, what can be said for Pope Eugene III, Pope Gregory VIII, Pope Clement III, Pope Innocent III, and Pope Gregory IX, who enthusiastically encouraged later

PARALLELS IN DANIEL'S VISIONS—3

DANIEL 7		DANIEL 8		DANIEL 11	
PERSIA, the bear	v. 5	PERSIA, the ram	vs. 3, 20	PERSIA, king	v. 2
GREECE, the leopard	v. 6	GREECE, the he-goat	vs. 5, 21	GREECE	v. 3; cf. v. 2
		was strong	v. 8	a mighty king	v. 3
dominion given	v. 6			rules with great	
				dominion	v. 3
		great horn broken	v. 8	kingdom broken	v. 4
		toward four winds of		toward four winds of	
four heads	v. 6	heaven	v. 8	heaven	v. 4
PAGAN ROME,		PAGAN ROME		PAGAN ROME	
the terrible beast		the little horn	v. 9	robbers of thy people	
	vs. 7, 11, 19, 23	trampled on the host	v. 10		v. 14 K.J.V.
exceedingly strong				a contemptible person	v. 21
break in pieces				a small people	v. 23
		toward glorious land	v. 9	in glorious land	v. 16
		prince of the host	v. 11	prince of the covenant	v. 22
CHRISTIAN ROME,	vs. 8	CHRISTIAN ROME		CHRISTIAN ROME	
the little horn	20-26	the little horn	v. 9		
		burnt offering taken away	v. 11	burnt offering taken away	v. 31
		sanctuary cast down	v. 11	sanctuary profaned	v. 31
change times and law	v. 25	cast down truth to		works deceitfully	v. 23
		ground	v. 12		
		practiced and prospered	v. 12	prospers	v. 36
		transgression of the		abomination that makes	
		desolation	v. 13	desolate	v. 31
				how long?	(12:7)
		time of the end	v. 17	time of the end	vs. 35, 40
		transgressor come to			(12:4, 9)
		full measure	v. 23	wicked do wickedly	(12:10)
		end of indignation	v. 19	indignation accomplished	
					v. 36
three and half time	v. 25	end at time appointed	v. 19	end at time appointed	
					vs. 27, 35
		becomes mighty	v. 24	becomes strong with a small	
		destroys wonderfully	v. 24	people	v. 23
				great fury to destroy	v. 44
wear out saints	v. 25	destroys the holy people	v. 24	wise fall by sword	v. 33
		causes craft to prosper	v. 25	corrupts by flatteries	v. 32
		magnifies himself	v. 25	magnifies himself	
				and	vs. 36, 37
speak words against God	v. 25			speaks against God	v. 14
dominion taken away					
	vs. 11, 26				
consumed to end	vs. 11, 26				

crusades even though they well knew what was likely to happen? Indeed the papacy was emboldened by the spirit of the Middle East crusades to initiate similarly frightful European crusades against Christian "heretics." Many of these "heretics" were sincere believers in God's **"holy covenant."** Verses 28, 30. If ever Roman Christianity obscured the *tamid* ministry of our compassionate High Priest in the heavenly sanctuary (see pages 172-178), it did so during the era of the crusades.

No wonder Muslims, who are not ignorant of this history, still hesitate to accept Jesus Christ.

No wonder, either, that medieval Christianity shows up badly in the book of Daniel.

Within a setting like this the **"abomination that makes desolate"** (verse 30) clearly cannot be confined to a metal idol erected temporarily by Antiochus Epiphanes on a stone altar in old Jerusalem. Instead it is seen to be that vast system of belief and practice which for a thousand years or more led people away from the priestly ministry of Jesus, depriving them of access to the **"prince of the covenant"** mentioned in verse 22 (see pages 172, 173). The **"wise"** who fell **"by sword and flame, by captivity and plunder"** (verse 33) were the brave people of God such as the Waldenses, Lollards, Hussites, Lutherans, Anabaptists, and Huguenots, who chose to be hanged or drowned or burned at the stake or tortured or imprisoned rather than give up their living faith (see page 132). They also likely included devout Roman Catholics who held loyally to God when Protestants, in the spirit of medieval tyranny, inflicted counterpersecution.

The king who was to **"exalt himself and magnify himself above every God"** (verse 36) was the medieval papacy! Not that any pope ever intended to do such a thing. No pope intended to place himself above God. But when popes claimed the right to kill people whom God loved and to change the Ten Commandments that God delivered on Mount Sinai, did they not honor themselves above God (see pages 133-135)?

When medieval popes hired armies to achieve their political ends, when Julius II (who styled himself "Julius Caesar II") led his own armies into battle, was not the papacy putting its trust in the **"god of fortresses"**? Verse 38. And the new god who was to be honored with gold and silver and precious stones (verse 38)—was she not the Blessed Virgin, who, with all her purity and motherly compassion, has often occupied in Catholic devotion a more prominent place than her divine Son?

When we remember that the **"prince of the covenant"** is Jesus rather than merely Onias III and that the **"abomination that makes desolate"** was still future in Christ's day, we realize that the message of Daniel 11 is the same, ultimately, as the message of Daniel 7 and 8. In Daniel 11 God warns us that out of the secular empires of earth a politico-religious entity was to arise that would (1) replace Christ's priestly ministry with a counterfeit Christian ministry and (2) persecute the people who attempted to maintain faith in the true Christ.

Insofar as medieval teachings persist in the various denominations of Christianity today, obscuring Christ's heavenly ministry, ignoring the special judgment that is already in session, and persuading people that they do not need to keep all of the Ten Commandments, the **"abomination that makes desolate"** is still at work. The warning of Daniel 11 is *current* evidence that God cares enough to alert us to danger and direct us to Himself.

What about Daniel 11:40-45? We have said nothing so far about verses 40-45. The last of these verses apparently parallels in part the career and demise of Roman Christianity.

As we have seen (pages 172-177), the greatest fault of Roman Christianity has been that it obscures the work of Jesus Christ in the heavenly sanctuary. In Daniel 7 Roman Christianity is symbolized by a little horn on the head of a very unattractive symbolic animal. By way of punishment for its misleading activity, this animal is selected for special mention in Daniel 7:11 and 26, in connection with the pre-advent judgment. It is scheduled to have **"its body destroyed and given over to be burned with fire."** For **"the court shall sit in judgment, and his dominion shall be taken away, to be consumed and destroyed to the end."**

In Daniel 11:45 the latter-day "king of the north" will **"pitch his palatial tents between the sea and the glorious holy mountain; yet he shall come to his end, with none to help him."** The **"glorious holy mountain"** appears to be a metaphor for the Jerusalem temple which, in turn, symbolizes the heavenly sanctuary. Pitching **"palatial tents"** between the Mediterranean Sea and the Jerusalem temple symbolizes the encroachment of the king of the north on the prerogatives of Christ's sanctuary ministry. As a consequence of this encroachment the king of the north will be punished so that, like the little-horn animal of Daniel 7 that he parallels, he will **"come to his end, with none to help him."** The little horn-power and the king of the north seem to represent the same earthly power.

Some of these matters will come clearer when we study the book of Revelation in *God Cares, II.* But as to the precise events on earth that will accompany their fulfillment, wisdom suggests we may not know them until they actually take place.

The purpose of prophecy is not always to provide prior knowledge of specific future events. Many Bible prophecies were given with the intention that they would be understood—and build faith—only after they were fulfilled. Thus Jesus said about a certain prediction He made concerning Himself, "I have told you before it takes place, so that when it does take place, you may believe." John 14:29; compare John 13:19; 16:4.

The impulse to schedule the future in detail has embarrassed many earnest Christians over the centuries. Armageddon, for instance, has probably been slated for more dates by enthusiastic Bible students than any other world event. Can you imagine the excitement that pulsed in millions of Christian breasts when in 1918 the newspapers daily plotted the progress of General E. H. Allenby as he approached the Ottoman army camped at Megiddo in Palestine? Megiddo is the traditional site of Armageddon!

In the meantime, we are in good company when we *desire* to schedule the future! Christ's own disciples, it appears, temporarily forgot His warning about the future-ness of the abomination of desolation. With only moments to go before His ascension, they asked Him if He were going right then to establish His everlasting kingdom!

Jesus replied that it was not for them to know the "times and seasons" which God chooses to keep secret. Acts 1:7. In the few remaining seconds that He was able to spend with them on earth, He diverted their attention from schedules about the kingdom to a promise-prophecy that He evidently valued as being far more important. "You shall receive power," He said, "when the Holy Spirit has come upon you; and you shall be my witnesses in Jerusalem and in all Judea and Samaria and to the end of the earth." Acts 1:8.

Jesus, who knows all there is to know about us, knew then and evidently knows now that the only remedy for our human hostilities is the new covenant, with its promises of (1) forgiveness, (2) power to change, and (3) a place among God's people (see pages 170, 171). He *wants us to introduce this covenant to everyone, everywhere,* in the power of His Spirit.

The inference is obvious. When this good news about the kingdom has been carried in the power of the Spirit "throughout the whole world," then and only then "the end will come." Matthew 24:14.

Further Interesting Reading

In *Bible Readings for the Home:*
The chapters entitled "Trials and Their Object," "Confessing Faults and Forgiving One Another," "Meekness and Humility," and "The Game of Life."

References

1. Charles H. H. Wright, *Daniel and His Prophecies* (London: William and Norgate, 1906), p. 305.

2. Herodotus, *Persian Wars,* 7.61-80.

3. J. B. Bury, *A History of Greece to the Death of Alexander the Great,* The Modern Library (New York: Random House, n.d.), pp. 255, 256.

4. Edwyn Bevan, *The House of Ptolemy: A History of Egypt Under the Ptolemaic Dynasty* (Chicago: Argonaut, 1968), p. 196.

5. Ammianus Marcellinus, *History,* 19.2.3; text and trans. by John C. Rolfe, *Ammianus Marcellinus: With an English Translation,* 3 vols., Loeb Classical Library (London: William Heinemann, 1956-1958), 1:476, 477.

6. Bevan, *The House of Ptolemy,* pp. 217, 218. Emphasis supplied.

7. Edwyn Robert Bevan, *The House of Seleucus,* 2 vols. (London: Edward Arnold, 1902), 1:125, citing Appian, *Roman History,* 11:8.

8. Michael Grant, *The Twelve Caesars* (London: Weidenfeld and Nicholson, 1975), p. 33.

9. Previté-Orton, *Medieval History,* p. 522.

10. Thompson and Johnson, *Medieval Europe,* p. 528.

11. William Ragsdale Cannon, *History of Christianity in the Middle Ages: From the Fall of Rome to the Fall of Constantinople* (New York: Abingdon Press, 1960), p. 172.

12. Thompson and Johnson, *Medieval Europe,* p. 529.

13. Previté-Orton, *Medieval History,* pp. 529-531.

14. Thompson and Johnson, *Medieval Europe,* p. 530.

Daniel 12
God's "Prince" Is on Our Side

Introduction

Daniel 12 may be separated into four divisions: events at the time of the end, verses 1-4; questions and answers, verses 5-10; days and blessings, verses 11, 12; and a personal promise in parting, verse 13.

Events at the time of the end. The first four verses of Daniel 12 constitute Gabriel's conclusion to the long vision which begins in Daniel 10:5 and which occupies all of chapter 11.

The latter-day **"king of the north"** has been observed rampaging against the saints until he comes to ruin. Now the camera focuses on Jesus Christ (see page 273). **"At that time,"** says Gabriel, **"shall arise Michael, the great prince who has charge of your people. And there shall be a time of trouble, such as never has been since there was a nation till that time; but at that time your people shall be delivered, every one whose name shall be found written in the book."** Daniel 12:1.

The events listed do not occur in an instant. They occupy an interval of time, though a relatively brief one. The rising up of Michael, the period of tribulation, and the raising of the dead take place **"at that time,"** that is, when the great persecutor of Daniel 11:40-45 is coming to his end.

The rising up of Michael reveals that the pre-second-coming judgment foreshadowed in Daniel 7:9-14 and in Daniel 8:14 is now completed. The books have been investigated. In full view of onlooking millions throughout the universe, Jesus, our High Priest of the heavenly sanctuary, has time and again raised His crucifixion-wounded hands on behalf of repentant, loyal believers, imparted to them overcoming power, and claimed for them salvation full and complete. Now this phase of His work of atonement is done. Jesus can come at last as the supernatural stone to strike the image and set up His everlasting kingdom.

The time of trouble that occurs in connection with Christ's coming is the reverse of an earlier tribulation described in the words of Matthew 24:9, "They will deliver you up to tribulation, and put you to death." In this earlier tribulation the saints are delivered *to* death. In the final tribulation the saints are delivered *from* death.

Revelation 2:10 speaks of the earlier tribulation. "You will have tribulation. Be faithful unto death, and I will give you the crown of life." Revelation 3:10 speaks of the final tribulation. "Because you have kept my word of patient endurance, I will keep you from the hour of trial which is coming on the whole world."

In the resurrection which Daniel 12:1, 2 says will accompany the deliverance of God's people, **"many of those who sleep in the dust of the earth shall awake, some to everlasting life,**

and some to shame and everlasting contempt." The "many" resurrected at this time include all of the people who are being saved—"every one whose name shall be found written in the book." The "many" also include *some* of the unsaved. The rest of the unsaved will be resurrected later on. Revelation 20 speaks of two general resurrections —the first, of all the righteous, and the second, a millennium later, of the unrighteous.

Who are the unrighteous persons who are raised, along with the righteous, in Daniel 12:1-2? We get a hint from the answer Jesus returned to the high priest when the high priest put Him on oath at His trial and required Him to state whether or not He was the Son of God. In His answer Jesus directed the high priest's attention to the Son of man in Daniel 7 and added, "Hereafter *you will see* the Son of man . . . coming on the clouds of heaven." Matthew 26:64.

Jesus is portrayed as traveling on clouds to the judgment at the close of the 2300 year-days. Daniel 7:13; 8:14. When that judgment is completed, He will "arise" and travel on clouds to the earth. The high priest and, evidently, the other people who also contributed directly to His crucifixion will be raised at the second coming in order to experience the fulfillment of Christ's prophecy. "Behold," says Revelation 1:7, K.J.V., "he cometh with clouds; and every eye shall see him, and *they also which pierced him.*"

In Daniel 12:3 Gabriel promised that the wise shall shine like the stars (see page 306). Then he said, **"But you, Daniel, shut up the words, and seal the book, until the time of the end. Many shall run to and fro, and knowledge shall increase."**

It is very likely that the visions could have ceased at this point; but Daniel appears to have been startled at being told to **"shut up the words."** He wanted eagerly to **"understand,"** and in his visions he had frequently been encouraged to do so. Now he learns that something has to remain locked up until almost the end of the world.

Gabriel cannot have meant that all the information in the book of Daniel was to be **"shut up"** until the time of the end. The identity of the head of gold as Babylon and of the ram as "Media and Persia" and of the goat as Greece is stated explicitly within the book, beyond all doubt or mystery. But Babylon, Persia, and Greece were empires which ruled in Daniel's own day and in his immediate future. The events to be "shut up" were only those that would occur near the end.

Questions and answers. At the very moment when Daniel was told to **"seal the book, until the time of the end,"** the same Person **"clothed in linen,"** whom he had seen at the beginning of the vision, appeared again. He was Michael, of course (see pages 272-275). He was standing above the river Tigris, flanked by an angel honor guard.

Seeing Him, Daniel asked earnestly, **"How long shall it be till the end of these wonders?" "O my lord, what shall be the issue of these things?"**

Michael declined completely to answer the second question, and this is surely significant. **"Go your way, Daniel,"** He said, **"for the words are shut up and sealed until the time of the end."** Daniel wasn't living in the time of the end; so he didn't need to understand all the details of end-of-time developments. Michael's answer teaches us that prophecy is provided for practical purposes. It is not given to arouse speculation or to satisfy needless curiosity, no matter how spiritual and

The redeemed will be resurrected to meet Jesus at His return, an event foretold in Nebuchadnezzar's vision of chapter two.

Christ-centered our curiosity may be.

Although Michael didn't answer Daniel's second question, He did answer his first one, and He did so in striking fashion. **"The man clothed in linen, who was above the waters of the stream, raised his right hand and his left hand toward heaven; and I heard him,"** says Daniel, **"swear by him who lives for ever that it would be for a time, two times, and half a time; and that when the shattering of the power of the holy people comes to an end all these things would be accomplished."**

Michael raised His hands and swore a solemn oath. When the Son of God swears by the Living God, the message that follows is important. The message in this case was that at the *end* of the 1260 years of Daniel 7:25 (see page 130), years characterized by a great persecution of the saints of God, wonderful new light would dawn on the end-of-time prophecies in the book of Daniel.

You will be interested to know that the Being of Daniel 12:7 appears again in Revelation 10. Once more, with uplifted hand, He swears by "him who lives for ever."

There are differences between Revelation 10 and Daniel 12, as well as similarities. The same book which in Daniel 12 is described as closed in Revelation 10 is seen to be open. And whereas the Being of Daniel 12 states how long the book would be closed, the Angel of Revelation 10 swears that there would be "no more delay." In other words, the Angel of Revelation 10 calls attention to the book of Daniel as finally being opened for the last days.

In Revelation 10 John, who sees the vision, is invited to eat the little open book. He does so and finds that it tastes very sweet, but it gives him a sour stomach. In spite of this disappointment he is told that he must keep on prophesying.

Portions of Daniel's book (or scroll) dealing with long-term prophecies were sealed (that is, not to be fully understood), "until the time of the end."

Thus, in symbolic language, Revelation 10 adds immeasurably to the picture painted in Daniel 12; for Daniel says only that at the opening of the book **"knowledge shall increase,"** **"many shall run to and fro,"** **"the wicked shall do wickedly,"** and the **"wise shall understand."** Revelation adds by implication that before the wise completely understand, they will first misunderstand! They will "eat" the opened prophecies of Daniel with keen anticipation, only to find their first joy turn to ashes, their delight to disappointment. How this was actually fulfilled we'll see when we study Revelation, chapters 10-14, in *God Cares, II.*

The prediction that **"many shall run to and fro, and knowledge shall increase"** is fascinating. Does it refer to the explosions in travel and in information which the world has witnessed since the close of the 1260 years?

With our rushing highways and crowded universities, it is difficult to imagine what life was like when most people could neither read nor write and spent their entire lives within the confines of a single county—or when the invention of the stirrup and an improvement in the moldboard plow could alter the direction of European history![1]

Airplanes date only from 1903. Automobiles were first mass produced in 1909. Millions of adults can still remember life without television. I can still remember, vividly, the sense of wondrous fantasy that came over me when, in my boyhood, my older brother told me, with all the assurance and authority of an older brother, that if a ball were hit hard enough, it would sail in orbit around the earth. Now astronauts sail in orbit around the earth and around the moon.

Today knowledge is increasing so quickly that information in many areas of research is said to double every few years. Sensitive portions of superfast computers are cooled close to absolute zero (-273.16 Celsius), because the speed of electrons at higher temperatures isn't rapid enough for needed computations.

Although the words of Daniel 12:4 have been used to describe this explosion of travel and knowledge, they more likely refer to the increased understanding of Bible prophecy which the chapter says was to occur in the end of time. The two concepts are not unrelated. Increase in knowledge and in transportation has vastly increased the number of people who can read and write, the distribution of missionaries, and the printing of God's Word. With vastly more people praying over and contemplating the book of Daniel, greater understanding of its messages was bound to take place.

We'll have much more to say about this increased understanding when we come to Revelation, chapters 10-14.

Days and blessings. In Daniel 12:11, 12 the Angel speaks of 1290 days and of the blessedness of a person who waits to the end of 1335 days. Inasmuch as the Angel does not provide any event for the close of the 1290 days and none for either the beginning or the ending of the 1335 days, it is not yet possible to state with certainty the manner in which these two time prophecies were to be fulfilled.

A personal promise in parting. It is a pleasure to see the book of Daniel close with a personal promise for elderly Daniel himself. **"You shall rest, and shall stand in your allotted place at the end of days."**

Daniel would rest. He would spend the years that intervened between his passing and the rising up of Michael asleep in the grave. And when Michael rose up, Daniel would be assured of a place among the saints in the brand-new kingdom of God.

The promise is for us too. It implies that Daniel's messages and prophecies would fill the place God intended them to fill at the end of the age.

That this prediction is now being fulfilled is revealed in part by the fact that you and I and countless others are studying the book of Daniel today and gaining from it a great new understanding of the love of God and of how much He cares for us.

The incredible increase of knowledge in modern times has opened the world to almost instant communication of the gospel and thus to a more complete understanding of Daniel's prophecies.

CHAPTER 12

1 "At that time shall arise Michael, the great prince who has charge of your people. And there shall be a time of trouble, such as never has been since there was a nation till that time; but at that time your people shall be delivered, every one whose name shall be found written in the book. 2 And many of those who sleep in the dust of the earth shall awake, some to everlasting life, and some to shame and everlasting contempt. 3 And those who are wise shall shine like the brightness of the firmament; and those who turn many to righteousness, like the stars for ever and ever. 4 But you, Daniel, shut up the words, and seal the book, until the time of the end. Many shall run to and fro, and knowledge shall increase."

5 Then I Daniel looked, and behold, two others stood, one on this bank of the stream and one on that bank of the stream. 6 And I said to the man clothed in linen, who was above the waters of the stream, "How long shall it be till the end of these wonders?" 7 The man clothed in linen, who was above the waters of the stream, raised his right hand and his left hand toward heaven; and I heard him swear by him who lives for ever that it would be for a time, two times, and half a time; and that when the shattering of the power of the holy people comes to an end all these things would be accomplished. 8 I heard, but I did not understand. Then I said, "O my lord, what shall be the issue of these things?" 9 He said, "Go your way, Daniel, for the words are shut up and sealed until the time of the end. 10 Many shall purify themselves, and make themselves white, and be refined; but the wicked shall do wickedly; and none of the wicked shall understand; but those who are wise shall understand. 11 And from the time that the continual burnt offering is taken away, and the abomination that makes desolate is set up, there shall be a thousand two hundred and ninety days. 12 Blessed is he who waits and comes to the thousand three hundred and thirty-five days. 13 But go your way till the end; and you shall rest, and shall stand in your allotted place at the end of the days."

20—G.C.-1

The Message of Daniel 12

The Wise Shall Shine Like the Stars

It's a beautiful promise. Since childhood I have enjoyed its sound. They shall **"shine." "Like the stars." "For ever."** It's a poetic picture of the happiness awaiting God's saints and of its permanence.

> **And those who are wise shall shine**
> **like the brightness of the firmament;**
> **and those who turn many to righteousness,**
> **like the stars for ever and ever.** Daniel 12:3.

The joy everlasting which God has in store for His people is one of the major themes of the book of Daniel. **"The kingdom and the dominion and the greatness of the kingdoms under the whole heaven shall be given to the people of the saints of the Most High; their kingdom shall be an everlasting kingdom."** Daniel 7:27.

"Those who are wise shall shine . . . like the stars for ever and ever."

Who are the wise? But who are these wise persons who are to shine forever? We hope that they are not wise in doing wrong! To spend eternity with clever cutthroats and experienced swindlers doesn't seem attractive. We hope to have honest neighbors and to be honest ourselves.

Daniel 12:3 is Hebrew poetry. The **"wise"** in the first line, therefore, are the same as **"those who turn many to righteousness"** in the third line. Daniel 12:10 also speaks of the wise. It defines them as those who **"understand,"** that is, as the people who understand the practical meaning of the prophecies of the book of Daniel. In a reverse parallelism known as a chiasm (see page 255), the same verse identifies the **"wise"** as those who **"purify themselves"** and **"make themselves white"** and become **"refined."**

So the wise of Daniel 12—those who will shine like the stars forever and ever—are people who study the prophecies of Daniel till they *understand* them, who *share* their understanding with others, and who become *pure*.

What is there to understand and share? What then is there in Daniel to understand and share? Beasts and horns; weeks and days; Seleucids and Ptolemies; angels, one at a time and in throngs uncountable; and much more!

You now can explain the image and its metals, the sequence of the four beasts, the rise and progress of the little horns, the events of the seventy weeks, the commencement and close of the 2300 year-days. It is valuable that you can explain them. All the symbols are important, or God would not have placed them in His Word.

But symbols are symbols. They say something about something else. The symbols in Daniel convey a message about God. And, as we have found repeatedly, the message they convey is good news. For example:

306

1. It's good news that God knows everyone and everything—past, present, and future. He knows **"what will be in the latter days."** He is never surprised. He always has a solution prepared for every problem.

2. It's good news that God is constantly monitoring empires and individuals—and nations and corporations and families—and that He will bring them all alike into judgment. No act of injustice ever goes unnoticed.

3. It's good news that, in fact, the first phase of the final judgment is in session already. Jesus, the Son of man, our High Priest, is disclosing to the onlooking universe the identity of His repentant, faithful followers and retaining their names in the book of life.

4. It's good news that, whenever He deems it best, God *can* deliver us from lions and fiery furnaces and irascible executives; and that one day soon He will certainly deliver us from all earthly terrors and disappointments and from death as well.

5. It's good news that Christ is eager to "cause His covenant to prevail," even at infinite cost to Himself; and that through His covenant He wants to provide forgiveness, power for a changed life, and membership in His special people.

6. It's good news that God cares for us so much that He cannot visualize a moment, even in the remotest future, when He would prefer to live without us. He desires His saints to shine like the stars, forever, with Him.

How do the wise become pure? So the book of Daniel is full of good news. It offers much for us to understand and share. But how do the wise become *pure?*

The answer is found, first of all, I think, in Daniel 12:1, **"At that time shall arise Michael, the great prince** *who has charge of your people."*

In famous phrases Martin Luther once expressed the basic thought in this way:

> Did we in our own strength confide,
>   Our striving would be losing,
> Were not the right man on our side,
>   The man of God's own choosing.
> Dost ask who that may be?
>   Christ Jesus, it is He.

The saints become pure because they have the right Man on their side. The High Priest of the heavenly sanctuary ever lives to make intercession for them. Hebrews 7:25. This is His ordinary work. And on the Day of Atonement/Day of Judgment, in an especially gracious sense, He undertakes a work of final cleansing so that He can say at the end of it, "You are clean from all your sins before the Lord." Leviticus 16:30 (see pages 168-172).

But Daniel 12:10 says that the saints purify *themselves* and make *themselves* white. Is this, perhaps, an instance of bygone legalism, of outdated do-it-yourself paganism?

Not in the least. The New Testament, too, says that the saints "have washed their robes and made them white." Revelation 7:14. But it also says where they have washed them. In the only effective place. "In the blood of the Lamb."

Jesus offers His new covenant promises of (1) forgiveness, (2) power to change, and (3) membership in His kingdom to everyone—even to those who crucified Him. But His promises are effective for us only as we accept them for ourselves by faith. John 3:16.

And our faith must be dynamic, responsive, willing.

Jesus taught the importance of obedience in a passage near the close of the Sermon on the Mount. This passage, like Daniel 12, also defines a **"wise"** person. Jesus here likens a "wise man" to "everyone . . . who *hears* these words of mine and *does* them." Matthew 7:24.

As a boy Daniel heard that God wanted His people to eat only healthful foods. In the royal college of Babylon, in spite of great pressure from peers and officers, he remembered God's words and did them.

Daniel's friends knew that, for their own happiness, God asked them to worship Him alone and not any other god. Caught between patriotic nation worship and a fiery furnace, Daniel's friends remembered the Ten Commandments and did them.

Daniel also obeyed God when threatened with the lions.

But Daniel and his friends could have done nothing unless God had helped them. God **"gave"** Daniel favor with the personnel officer in the royal college.

Christ on the cross is the supreme revelation of how much GOD CARES and of how earnestly He desires to have people of all races become "His people" for ever.

God gave Daniel the vision about Nebuchadnezzar's dream and its interpretation. God's Son walked with the three men in the fire. God's angel guarded Daniel in the den.

It must have been a thrill for Daniel to have the school officials become friendly to him and then to find himself at the top of his class. He must have been glad a hundred times that he had taken his stand for what God taught.

Have you wondered how Daniel would have felt if he hadn't taken such a stand?

We know it was a tremendous joy for Daniel to have God repeat Nebuchadnezzar's dream to him. He was able to save his own life and the lives of the wise men and also to please the king. He must have been very glad that from the start he had held to a firm decision to be God's man in Babylon.

Suppose, however, that he hadn't!

It must have brought Daniel a serene sense of achievement and satisfaction to see Nebuchadnezzar in his later years issue a decree in honor of the God of heaven. He must have thanked God every day for the privilege of playing a part in such a grand development.

Suppose, however, that Daniel had misrepresented God by acting, even now and then, "just like everyone else."

When Michael rises up (Daniel 12:1) with all the other saints who rise from the dust, I can see in my mind's eye Oswald Glait and Mr. and Mrs. Andreas Fischer (whom we read about on page 139) coming up to shine like the stars forever. They understood the prophecy of Daniel 7. They saw that the little horn had tried to change God's law about the seventh-day Sabbath. They determined, by God's grace, to keep His true Sabbath at any price. They paid the full price. And now and throughout eternity they will be so very glad that, when they heard His word, they did it.

The Day of Atonement/Day of Judgment is in session. Jesus is still lifting up His crucifixion-wounded hands in your behalf. Now is the especially opportune time to "afflict your soul"—to make certain that everything is at peace between you and Him and, insofar as it is possible, between you and everyone else. This is the "day of at-one-ment." You have been forgiven your "ten thousand talent" sins. Have you forgiven others their "hundred-penny" sins against you? Is all bitterness washed out of your soul by His blood? You surely won't want hard feelings lodged in your heart for eternity! Now is the time to be "at one," to be pure from all sin against God and fellowman.

For us and our children. "The things that are revealed belong to us and to our children." Deuteronomy 29:29. Some think that religion is for old people and dropouts, but Daniel was neither feeble nor a failure. He was brilliant, highly successful, and, when his story began, still a youth.

The stories in the book of Daniel hold the attention of young people, and its heroes inspire youth to stand true in temptation. When you think of the wise who shine like the stars forever, don't leave out children! God wants young as well as old in His kingdom. "Let the children come to me, and do not hinder them," says Jesus, "for to such belongs the kingdom of heaven." Matthew 19:14.

Little children who love their Redeemer are jewels, precious jewels; His loved ones and His own.

> Like the stars of the morning,
> His bright crown adorning,
> They shall shine in their beauty,
> Bright gems for His crown.[2]

So you want to share? Perhaps you have no children of your own. But you do know other children in your larger family or neighborhood. There are also, very probably, older members in your family—parents, in-laws, spouse. And you have a friend, and there are other people you would like to know better. You would like to share with them; by God's grace you would like to **"lead many to righteousness."**

One of the most valuable things you could do would be to set up a study group right now either in your own home or in the home of a friend. Prepare a list of several names—somewhere between five and ten people. Ask God to guide you and to prepare their minds. Then invite them to join you at a convenient time.

Make sure everyone has a Bible. Begin and end every study hour with prayer, and let the study hour be about sixty minutes. Turn back to page one of this volume and, using it as a guide, go through Daniel from start to finish, slowly enough so that everyone in the group can understand.

Let each one discover for himself how much and in what ways God cares. He will bless you! And may we all, very soon, see our **"Prince"** at His coming and **"shine"** with the saints **"like the stars, forever."**

Further Interesting Reading

In Arthur S. Maxwell, *The Bible Story,* vol. 6:
  "Daniel Sees Our Day," beginning on p. 71.

In *Bible Readings for the Home:*
  "The Home of the Saved," beginning on p. 545.

References

1. McNeill, *Rise of the West,* pp. 444, 452, 453.
2. W. O. Cushing, "Jewels," in *Christ in Song,* rev. ed., comp. F. E. Belden (Washington, D.C.: F. E. Belden, 1908), no. 852.

Acknowledgments

For sharing their expertise in the preparation of this volume, special credit is due Julia Neuffer, research editor for the Review and Herald Publishing Association; and William H. Shea, associate professor of Old Testament at Andrews University. Raoul F. Dederen, professor of Historical Theology; Kenneth A. Strand, professor of Church History; and other Andrews University scholars made helpful contributions at specific points. Earlene Papendick performed efficiently the vital clerical functions.

Selected Bibliography

Ancient Authors

Ammianus Marcellinus. *History*. Text and translation in Loeb Classical Library.

Barnabas. *Epistle*. Translated in Ante-Nicene Fathers, vol. 1.

Didascalia Apostolorum. Translated, with introduction and notes, by R. Hugh Connolly. Oxford: The Clarendon Press, 1929.

Eusebius. *Church History*. Translation in Nicene and Post-Nicene Fathers, 2d series, vol. 1.

Herodotus. *The Persian Wars*. Text and translation in Loeb Classical Library.

Hippolytus. *Commentary on Daniel*. Translation in Ante-Nicene Fathers, vol. 5.

_____. *The Refutation of All Heresies*. Translation in Ante-Nicene Fathers, vol. 5.

Josephus. *Against Apion*. Text and translation in Loeb Classical Library.

_____. *The Jewish War*. Text and translation in Loeb Classical Library.

Justin. *Dialogue with the Jew Trypho*. Translation in Ante-Nicene Fathers, vol. 1.

_____. *First Apology*. Translation in Ante-Nicene Fathers, vol. 1.

_____. *Second Apology*. Translation in Ante-Nicene Fathers, vol. 1.

Livy. *History of Rome*. Text and translation in Loeb Classical Library.

The Passion of the Holy Martyrs Perpetua and Felicitas. Translation in Ante-Nicene Fathers, vol. 3.

Polybius. *The Histories*. Text and translation in Loeb Classical Library.

Pontius the Deacon. *The Life and Passion of Cyprian, Bishop and Martyr*. Translation in Ante-Nicene Fathers, vol. 5.

Procopius. *History of the Wars*. Text and translation in Loeb Classical Library.

Socrates Scholasticus. *Church History*. Translation in Nicene and Post-Nicene Fathers. 2d series, vol. 2.

Tertullian. *On Prayer*. Translation in Ante-Nicene Fathers, vol. 3.

Victorinus. *On the Creation of the World*. Translation in Ante-Nicene Fathers, vol. 7.

Xenophon. *Anabasis*. Text and translation in Loeb Classical Library.

_____. *Cyropaedia*. Text and translation in Loeb Classical Library.

Encyclopedias

Encyclopaedia Judaica.

The Jewish Encyclopedia.

New Catholic Encyclopedia.

The Universal Jewish Encyclopedia.

The Zondervan Pictorial Encyclopedia of the Bible.

General

Ambrose. Letter 25. In *The Later Roman Empire, 284-602,* 2:983. By A. H. M. Jones. 2 vols. Norman, Okla.: University of Oklahoma Press, 1964.

Anderson, Roy Allan. *Unfolding Daniel's Prophecies.* Mountain View, Calif.: Pacific Press Publishing Association, 1975.

Andrews, John Nevins. *History of the Sabbath and First Day of the Week.* 2d ed. Battle Creek, Mich.: Steam Press of the Seventh-day Adventist Publishing Association, 1873.

Arlin, Marian. *The Science of Nutrition.* 2d ed. New York: Macmillan Publishing Co., Inc., 1977.

The Babylonian Talmud. Edited by Isidore Epstein. 35 vols. London: The Soncino Press Ltd., 1935-1952.

Bainton, Roland. *Here I Stand, a Life of Martin Luther.* New York: Abingdon-Cokesbury Press, 1950.

_____. *The Reformation of the Sixteenth Century.* Boston: The Beacon Press, 1952.

Bettenson, Henry, ed. *Documents of the Christian Church.* 2d ed. London: Oxford University Press, 1963.

Bevan, Edwyn. *The House of Ptolemy: A History of Egypt Under the Ptolemaic Dynasty.* Chicago: Argonaut, 1968.

Bevan, Edwyn Robert. *The House of Seleucus.* 2 vols. London: Edward Arnold, 1902.

Bible Readings for the Home. Rev. ed. Mountain View, Calif.: Pacific Press Publishing Association, 1963, 1967.

The Book of the Popes (Liber Pontificalis). Translated by Louise Ropes Loomis. Edited by James T. Shotwell, et al. Records of Civilization, Sources and Studies, no. 3. New York: Columbia University Press, 1916.

Boutflower, Charles. *In and Around the Book of Daniel.* London: Society for Promoting Christian Knowledge, 1923.

Bury, J. B. *A History of Greece to the Death of Alexander the Great.* The Modern Library. New York: Random House, n.d.

_____. *History of the Later Roman Empire from the Death of Theodosius I to the Death of Justinian.* 2 vols. New York: Dover Publications, Inc., 1958.

Caird, G. R. "Chronology of the N.T., The." *The Interpreter's Dictionary of the Bible.* Edited by George Arthur Buttrick. 4 vols. New York: Abingdon Press, 1962.

Cannon, William Ragsdale, *History of Christianity in the Middle Ages: From the Fall of Rome to the Fall of Constantinople.* New York: Abingdon Press, 1960.

Cary, M. *A History of the Greek World from 323 to 146 B.C.* 2d rev. ed. London: Methuen & Co., Ltd., 1951.

Clemence, G. M. to Francis D. Nichol. January 24, 1956. In *Seventh-day Adventist Bible Commentary,* 5:262. Edited by Francis D. Nichol. 7 vols. Washington, D.C.: Review and Herald Publishing Association, 1953-1957.

Collins, John J. *The Apocalyptic Vision of the Book of Daniel.* Edited by Frank Moore Cross, Jr. Harvard Semitic Monographs, no. 16. Missoula, Mont.: Scholars Press for Harvard Semitic Museum, 1977.

Contenau, Georges. *Everyday Life in Babylon and Assyria.* Translated by K. R. and A. R. Maxwell-Hyslop from the French, *La Vie quotidienne à Babylone et en Assyrie.* London: Edward Arnold (Publishers) Ltd., 1954.

Dobson, James. *What Wives Wish Their Husbands Knew About Women.* Wheaton, Ill.: Tyndale House Publishers, 1975.

_____. "What Wives Wish Their Husbands Knew About Women." *These Times,* December 1978, pp. 11-15.

Dougherty, Raymond Philip. *Nabonidus and Belshazzar: A Study of the Closing Events of the Neo-Babylonian Empire.*

Yale Oriental Series: Researches, vol. 15. New Haven, Conn.: Yale University Press, 1929.

Dubberstein, Waldo H. and Richard A. Parker. *Babylonian Chronology 626 B.C.-A.D. 45*. Studies in Ancient Oriental Civilization, no. 24. Chicago: The University of Chicago Press, 1942.

Easton, Stewart C. *The Heritage of the Ancient World from the Earliest Times to the Fall of Rome*. New York: Rinehart & Co., 1955-1960.

————. *The Western Heritage from the Earliest Times to the Present*. New York: Holt, Rinehart, and Winston, 1961.

Eck, John. *Enchiridion of Commonplaces of John Eck Against Luther and Other Enemies of the Church*. Translated by F. L. Battles. Grand Rapids, Mich.: Calvin Theological Seminary, 1978.

Emmerson, W. L. *The Bible Speaks*. Abridged, with added notes by Francis A. Soper. Mountain View, Calif.: Pacific Press Publishing Association, 1949, 1967.

Ferraris, Lucius. *Prompta Bibliotheca*. 8 vols. Venice: Caspa Storti, 1772.

Finegan, Jack. *Light from the Ancient Past: The Archeological Background of Judaism and Christianity*. Princeton: Princeton University Press, 1959.

Foxe, John. *Book of Martyrs*. New York: Charles K. Moore, 1842.

Frend, W. H. C. *Martyrdom and Persecution in the Early Church: A Study of a Conflict from the Maccabees to Donatus*. New York: New York University Press, 1967.

Froom, LeRoy Edwin. *The Prophetic Faith of Our Fathers*. 4 vols. Washington, D.C.: Review and Herald Publishing Association, 1946-1954.

Gauquelin, Michel. *The Cosmic Clocks: From Astronomy to a Modern Science*. n.p., 1967.

Grant, Michael. *The Twelve Caesars*. London: Weidenfeld and Nicholson, 1975.

Grayson, A. K. *Babylonian Historical Literary Texts*. Toronto Semitic Texts and Studies, no. 3. Toronto: University of Toronto Press, 1975.

Hales, William. *A New Analysis of Chronology and Geography, History, and Prophecy*. 2d ed., rev. 4 vols. London: C. J. G. & F. Rivington, 1930.

Handlin, Oscar. *A Pictorial History of Immigration*. New York: Crown Publishers, 1972.

Hasel, Gerhard. "Daniel Survives the Critics' Den." *Ministry*, January 1979, pp. 9-11.

————. "Sabbatarian Anabaptists of the Sixteenth Century." Two parts, *Andrews University Seminary Studies* 5 (July 1967):101-121, and 6 (January 1968):19-28.

Haskell, Stephen N. *The Story of Daniel the Prophet*. Battle Creek, Mich.: Review and Herald Publishing Co., 1901.

Hangel, Martin. *Crucifixion in the Ancient World and the Folly of the Message of the Cross*. Philadelphia: Fortress Press, 1977.

Herndon, Booton. *The Unlikeliest Hero*. Mountain View, Calif.: Pacific Press Publishing Association, 1967.

Heylyn, Peter. *History of the Sabbath*. London: n.p., 1636.

Hilprecht, H.V., ed. *The Babylonian Expedition of the University of Pennsylvania*. Philadelphia: Dept. of Archaeology, University of Pennsylvania, 1906. Series A: Cuneiform Texts, vol. 20, part 1, by H.V. Hilprecht.

Hodgkin, Thomas. *Italy and Her Invaders*. 2d ed. 8 vols. in 9. Oxford: The Clarendon Press, 1885-1899.

Horn, Siegfried H. "The Babylonian Chronicle and the Ancient Calendar of the Kingdom of Judah." *Andrews University Seminary Studies* 5 (1967): 12-27.

————. "New Light on Nebuchadnezzar's Madness." *Ministry*. April 1978, pp. 39, 40.

How to Hear Mass. Edited by Richard Morris. Original Series, no. 117. London: Early English Text Society, 1871.

The Interpreter's Dictionary of the Bible. Edited by George Arthur Buttrick. 4 vols. New York: Abingdon Press, 1962.

Jones, A. M. H. *The Later Roman Empire, 284-602: A Social Economic and Ad-*

ministrative Survey. 2 vols. Norman, Okla.: University of Oklahoma Press, 1964.

Keil, C. F. and F. Delitzsch. Biblical Commentary on the Old Testament. 27 vols. Grand Rapids, Mich.: Wm. B. Eerdmans Publishing Co., 1959. Vol. 25: Biblical Commentary on the Book of Daniel, by C. F. Keil, trans. M. G. Easton.

Latourette, Kenneth Scott. A History of Christianity. New York: Harper & Bros., 1953.

Lay Folks Catechism. Edited, with introduction, notes, and glossary, by Thomas Frederick Simmons and Henry Edward Nolloth. Original Series, no. 118. London: Early English Text Society, 1901.

Luther, Martin. Luther's Works, American Edition. Edited by Jaroslav Pelikan and Helmut T. Lehman. 55 vols. St. Louis, Mo.: Concordia Publishing House, 1955-.

_____. Sämmtliche Schriften. Edited by John George Walch. 23 vols. in 25. St. Louis, Mo.: Concordia Publishing House, 1881-1910.

McCracken, George E. and Allen Cabaniss, eds. Early Medieval Theology. Edited by John Baillie, John T. McNeill, and Henry P. Van Dusen. The Library of Christian Classics, vol. 9. Philadelphia: The Westminster Press, 1957.

McNally, Robert E. S.J. "The Reformation: A Catholic Reappraisal." In Luther, Erasmus and the Reformation: A Catholic-Protestant Reappraisal, pp. 26-47. Edited by John C. Olin, James D. Smart, and Robert E. McNally, S.J. New York: Fordham University Press, 1969.

McKenzie, John L., S.J. The Roman Catholic Church. Edited by E. O. James. History of Religion Series. New York: Holt, Rinehart and Winston, 1959.

McNeal, Edgar Holmes and Oliver J. Thatcher, eds. A Source Book for Mediaeval History. New York: Charles Scribner's Sons, 1905.

McNeill, John T., and Helena M. Gamer. Medieval Handbooks of Penance: A Translation of the Principal libri poenitentiales and Selections from Related Documents. Austin P. Evans, et al., eds. Records of Civilization, Sources and Studies, no. 29. New York: Columbia University Press, 1938.

McNeill, William H. The Rise of the West: A History of the Human Community. Chicago: The University of Chicago Press, 1963.

Mansi, G. D. Sacrorum Conciliorum Nova et Amplissima Collectio. Reprint of the 1901 ed. 53 vols. in 59. Graz, Austria: Akademische Druck- und Verlagsanstalt, 1960-1961.

Maxwell, A. Graham. Can God Be Trusted? Nashville, Tenn.: Southern Publishing Association, 1977.

Maxwell, Arthur S. The Bible Story. 10 vols. Mountain View, Calif.: Pacific Press Publishing Association, 1953-1957.

_____. Great Prophecies for Our Time. Mountain View, Calif.: Pacific Press Publishing Association, 1943.

_____. Your Bible and You: Priceless Treasures in the Holy Scriptures. Washington, D.C.: Review and Herald Publishing Association, 1959.

Mitchell, T. C. and R. Joyce. "The Musical Instruments in Nebuchadnezzar's Orchestra." In Notes on Some Problems in the Book of Daniel, pp. 19-27. By D. J. Wiseman, T. C. Mitchell, R. Joyce, W. J. Martin, K. A. Kitchen. London: The Tyndale Press, 1965.

Neugebauer, Otto., ed. Astronomical Cuneiform Texts. 3 vols. Princeton, N.J.: Institute for Advanced Study, c. 1955.

_____. The Exact Sciences in Antiquity. 2d ed. New York: Dover Publications, 1969.

_____ to Francis D. Nichol. January 19, 1956. In Seventh-day Adventist Bible Commentary, 5:263, 264. Edited by Francis D. Nichol. 7 vols. Washington, D.C.: Review and Herald Publishing Association, 1953-1957.

315

A New Catechism. New York: Herder and Herder, 1967.

Newman, Albert Henry. A Manual of Church History. 2 vols., revised and enlarged. Philadelphia: The American Baptist Publication Society, 1933.

Newton, Sir Isaac. Observations Upon the Prophecies of Daniel, and the Apocalypse of St. John, In Two Parts. London: n.p., 1733.

The North England Homily Collection. Edited by Gordon Hall Gerould. Published privately, 1902.

Odom, R. L. "The Sabbath in the Great Schism of A.D. 1054." Andrews University Seminary Studies 1 (1963):74-80.

Oman, Charles. The Dark Ages, 476-918. 4th ed. London: Rivingtons, 1901.

Oppenheim, A. L. Ancient Mesopotamia: Portrait of a Dead Civilization. Chicago: University of Chicago Press, 1964.

Oxford Dictionary of the Christian Church. Edited by F. L. Cross. London: Oxford University Press, 1957.

Owst, G. R. Preaching in Medieval England. Cambridge: Cambridge University Press, 1926.

Parker, Richard A. and Waldo H. Dubberstein. Babylonian Chronology 626 B.C.-A.D. 45. "Studies in Ancient Oriental Civilization," no. 24. Chicago: The University of Chicago Press, 1942.

Petersen, William J., ed. Run Your Life by the Stars? Wheaton, Ill.: Victor Books, 1972.

————. "Astrology: Fad, Fact, or Fraud?" These Times, September 1, 1978, pp. 22-25.

Poole, William, et al., composer. In Rodeheaver's Gospel Solos and Duets Number 3. Chicago: The Rodeheaver Hall-Mack Co., 1938.

Porteous, Norman W. Daniel, a Commentary. Edited by G. Ernest Wright, et al. The Old Testament Library. Philadelphia: The Westminster Press, 1965.

Previté-Orton, C. W. The Shorter Cambridge Medieval History. 2 vols. Cambridge: The University Press, 1953.

Price, George McCready. The Greatest of the Prophets: A New Commentary on the Book of Daniel. Mountain View, Calif.: Pacific Press Publishing Association, 1955.

————. The Time of the End. Nashville, Tenn.: Southern Publishing Association, 1967.

Pritchard, James B. Ancient Near Eastern Texts Relating to the Old Testament. 2d ed. Princeton, N. J.: Princeton University Press, 1955.

Rand McNally Atlas of World History. Edited by R. R. Palmer. Chicago: Rand McNally & Co., 1957.

Rock, Daniel. The Church of Our Fathers. New edition in 4 vols. Edited by G. W. Hart and W. H. Frere. London: John Murray, 1905.

Sadler, D. H. to Francis D. Nichol. January 24, 1956. In Seventh-day Adventist Bible Commentary, 5:263. Edited by Francis D. Nichol. 7 vols. Washington D.C.: Review and Herald Publishing Association, 1953-1957.

Sava, Anthony F. "The Wounds of Christ." The Catholic Biblical Quarterly 16 (1954):438-443.

Schwantes, S. J. " 'Ereb Bōqer of Dan 8:14 Re-examined." Andrews University Seminary Studies 16 (1978):375-385.

Seventh-day Adventist Bible Commentary. Edited by Francis D. Nichol. 7 vols. Washington, D.C.: Review and Herald Publishing Association, 1953-1957.

Shea, William H. "Daniel in Babylon." Research paper, Andrews University, 1978.

————. "Darius the Mede and Daniel His Governor." Research paper, Andrews University, 1978.

————. "An Unrecognized Vassal King of Babylon in the Early Achaemenid Period." 4 parts. Andrews University Seminary Studies 9, 10 (January 1971 to July 1972).

Shryock, Harold and Hubert O. Swartout. You and Your Health. 3 vols. Mountain View, Calif.: Pacific Press Publishing Association, 1970.

Skeat, Walter W., ed. The Vision of William Concerning Piers the Plowman in Three Parallel Texts Together with

Richard the Redeless. 2 vols. Oxford: Clarendon Press, 1886.

Smith, Sidney. *Babylonian Historical Texts Relating to the Capture and Downfall of Babylon.* London: Methuen & Co., Ltd., 1924.

Smith, Uriah. *The Prophecies of Daniel and the Revelation.* 1944 ed. Mountain View, Calif.: Pacific Press Publishing Association, 1946.

_____. *Thoughts, Critical and Practical, on the Book of Daniel.* 2d ed. Battle Creek, Mich.: Seventh-day Adventist Publishing Association, 1881.

Soedel, Werner and Vernard Foley. "Ancient Catapults." *Scientific American,* March 1979, pp. 150-160.

Spalding, Arthur Whitefield. *Origin and History of Seventh-day Adventists.* 4 vols. Washington, D.C.: Review and Herald Publishing Association, 1961-1962.

Spicer, W. A. *Our Day in the Light of Prophecy.* Mountain View, Calif.: Pacific Press Publishing Association, 1917.

Strand, Kenneth A. *Brief Introduction to the Ancient Near East: A Panorama of the Old Testament World.* Ann Arbor: Braun-Brumfield, Inc., 1969

_____, ed. *The Sabbath in Scripture and History.* Washington, D.C.: Review and Herald Publishing Association, forthcoming.

Swain, Joseph Ward. *The Ancient World.* 2 vols. New York: Harper & Row, 1950.

Talbot, H. Fox. "Translation of Some Assyrian Inscriptions." *Journal of the Royal Asiatic Society* 18 (1861):195.

ten Boom, Corrie, with John and Elizabeth Sherril. *The Hiding Place.* Washington Depot, Conn.: Chosen Books, 1971.

Thiele, Edwin Richard. *The Mysterious Numbers of the Hebrew Kings: A Reconstruction of the Chronology of the Kingdoms of Israel and Judah.* Rev. ed. Chicago: The University of Chicago Press, 1965.

_____. *Outline Studies in Daniel.* Angwin, Calif.: Pacific Union College, n.d.

This We Believe, By This We Live: Revised Edition of the Baltimore Catechism, No. 3. n.p.: Confraternity of Christian Doctrine, 1957.

Thompson, James Westfall and Edgar Nathaniel Johnson. *An Introduction to Medieval Europe, 300-1500.* New York: W. W. Norton & Co., Inc., Publishers, 1937.

Thompson, W. R. "Chronology of the New Testament." *The Zondervan Pictorial Encyclopedia of the Bible.* Edited by Merrill C. Tenney. 5 vols. Grand Rapids, Mich.: Zondervan Publishing House, 1975.

Trever, Albert A. *History of Ancient Civilization.* Vol. 1: *The Ancient Near East and Greece.* New York: Harcourt, Brace and Company, 1936.

Waggoner, E. J. *Prophetic Lights: Some of the Prominent Prophecies of the Old and New Testaments, Interpreted by the Bible and History.* Oakland, Calif.: Pacific Press Publishing Co., 1888.

Walvoord, John F. *Daniel: The Key to Prophetic Revelation, a Commentary.* Chicago: Moody Press, 1971.

Weiner, Bernard, et al. *Discovering Psychology.* Chicago: Science Research Associates, Inc., 1977.

The Westminster Dictionary of the Bible. Edited by John D. Davis and Henry Snyder Gehman. Rev. ed. Philadelphia: The Westminster Press, 1944.

White, Ellen G. *Prophets and Kings.* Mountain View, Calif.: Pacific Press Publishing Association, 1917, 1943.

_____. *The Triumph of God's Love.* Mountain View, Calif.: Pacific Press Publishing Association, 1911.

Whitla, William, ed. *Sir Isaac Newton's Daniel and the Apocalypse.* London: John Murray, 1922.

Wilson, Robert Dick. *Studies in the Book of Daniel: A Discussion of the Historical Questions.* New York: G. P. Putnam's Sons, The Knickerbocker Press, 1917.

Wiseman, Donald John, *Chronicles of Chaldean Kings (626-556 B.C.) in the British Museum.* London: The Trustees of the British Museum, 1956.

317

Wiseman, Donald John, T. C. Mitchell, R. Joyce, W. J. Martin, K. A. Kitchen. *Notes on Some Problems in the Book of Daniel*. London: The Tyndale Press, 1965.

Wood, Leon. *A Commentary on Daniel*. Grand Rapids, Mich.: Zondervan Publishing House, 1973.

Woolsey, Raymond H. *The Power and the Glory: God's Hand in your Future*. Washington, D.C.: Review and Herald Publishing Association, 1978.

Wright, Charles H. H. *Daniel and His Prophecies*. London: William and Norgate, 1906.

Yamauchi, E. *Greece and Babylon*. Grand Rapids, Mich.: Baker Book House, 1967.

Young, Edward J. *The Prophecy of Daniel: A Commentary*. Grand Rapids, Mich.: Wm. B. Eerdmans Publishing Co., 1949.

Topical Index

319

Scriptural Index

GOD CARES

1 Corinthians 3:16, 17, p. 88; **4:9,** pp. 72, 119; **5:7,** p. 167; **6:2, 3,** p. 242; **6:19, 20,** pp. 88, 165; **8:7,** p. 17; **10:4,** p. 42; **10:14-22,** p. 17; **10:22,** p. 269; **10:21,** p. 173; **11:20,** p. 173; **15:20,** p. 257.

2 Corinthians 3:18, p. 246; **5:10,** p. 117; **5:17,** p. 216; **5:19,** p. 184; **5:21,** p. 227; **6:2,** p. 88; **11:24-26,** p. 102; **ch. 12,** p. 126; **13:5,** p. 249.

Galatians 3:15-18, p. 228; **3:26-29,** p. 236; **3:28, 29,** p. 242; **4:4,** p. 205; **4:24,** p. 214; **4:26,** p. 214; **5:22,** p. 220; **6:1,** p. 133.

Ephesians 2:4, p. 115; **2:5,** p. 178; **2:8, 9,** p. 240; **2:12-14,** p. 236; **2:21, 22,** p. 165; **4:15,** p. 178; **5:20,** p. 103; **5:23,** pp. 173, 178; **6:4,** p. 44; **6:12,** p. 269; **6:12-18,** p. 274.

Philippians 4:3, p. 119; **4:4-7,** p. 103.

1 Thessalonians 4:16, p. 273; **4:17,** p. 241; **5:8,** p. 108.

2 Thessalonians 2:7, p. 121; **2:7, 8,** p. 123; **2:10,** p. 95.

1 Timothy 2:1, 2, p. 66; **2:1-4,** p. 274; **2:5,** pp. 116, 117, 178, 221; **2:6,** p. 215; **5:1,** p. 101; **6:16,** p. 166.

2 Timothy 2:18, p. 126; **3:12,** p. 126.

Titus 1:2, 3, p. 205; **1:11,** p. 126.

Hebrews, pp. 214, 241; **ch 1,** p. 170; **1:2,** p. 117; **1:9,** p. 220; **1:14,** pp. 72, 274; **2:17, 18,** p. 117; **ch. 3,** p. 170; **3:1,** p. 163; **3:14,** p. 245; **4:14-16,** p. 172; **5:9,** p. 214; **6:18,** p. 228; **6:19,** p. 241; **7:11-16,** p. 170; **7:19,** p. 170; **7:21-25,** p. 164; **7:22,** p. 170; **7:23, 24,** p. 170; **7:24,** p. 170; **7:25,** pp. 116, 244, 307; **8:1, 2,** pp. 163, 240; **8:2,** p. 241; **8:5,** p. 186; **8:6,** p. 170; **8:10, 11,** p. 228; **8:10-12,** pp. 170, 178; **8:12,** p. 162; **9:3,** p. 241; **9:8,** p. 241; **9:11,** p. 170; **9:11-26,** p. 214; **9:12,** pp. 169, 170; **9:12, 24, 25,** p. 241; **9:15,** p. 221; **9:15-17,** p. 228; **9:22,** pp. 169, 228; **9:22, 23,** p. 186; **9:25-28,** p. 170; **9:26,** p. 214; **ch. 10,** p. 243; **10:4,** p. 170; **10:4-9,** p. 220; **10:5,** p. 170; **10:7,** p. 229; **10:8,** p. 221; **10:11,** p. 221; **10:19,** p. 241; **13:8,** p. 277; **13:11,** p. 241; **13:12, 13,** p. 169; **13:13,** p. 169.

James 2:10-12, p. 142; **2:25,** p. 169; **3:8,** p. 96; **5:16,** p. 200.

1 Peter 1:19, p. 167; **2:9,** pp. 178, 235; **2:24,** p. 168; **3:7,** p. 118; **5:17,** p. 5; **5:8,** pp. 95, 274.

2 Peter 1:20, p. 279; **2:4,** p. 269.

1 John 1:7, p. 120; **1:9,** pp. 120, 173, 244, 245; **1:29,** p. 167; **2:1,** p. 116; **2:18,** p. 123; **2:22,** p. 122; **3:4,** p. 120; **4:3,** p. 123; **4:8,** pp. v, 115.

2 John 7, p. 122.

Jude 9, p. 272; **24,** p. 266.

Revelation 1, p. 100; **1:1,** p. v; **1:7,** p. 301; **1:13-16,** p. 268; **1:17,** p. 268; **1:18,** p. v; **1:19,** p. v; **2:10,** p. 299; **2:20-22,** p. 126; **ch. 3, 4,** p. v; **3:4,** p. 126; **3:10,** p. 299; **3:20, 21,** p. 165; **3:21,** p. 236; **5:11,** p. 119; **6:10,** p. 187; **7:14,** p. 308; **ch. 10,** pp. 302, 303; **ch. 10-14,** p. 303; **10:14,** p. 303; **ch. 11,** p. 270; **11:9,** p. 23; **11:17,** p. 187; **11:18,** p. 188; **ch. 12,** pp. 21, 69, 119, 124, 270;

Because you have enjoyed GOD CARES, I, you will want to read its sequel, GOD CARES, II, Dr. Maxwell's presentation on the book of Revelation.

You may get your copy of GOD CARES, II, from the same source you received Volume I, or by writing the publisher:

Pacific Press Publishing Association
Box 7000
Boise, ID 83707